EXPERT RESUMES FOR MANAGERS AND EXECUTIVES

THIRD EDITION

Wendy S. Enelow and Louise M. Kursmark

To Renew Books
Phone (925) 969-3100

jist *Works*
America's Career Publisher®

Expert Resumes for Managers and Executives, Third Edition

© 2012 by Wendy S. Enelow and Louise M. Kursmark

Published by JIST Works, an imprint of JIST Publishing
875 Montreal Way
St. Paul, MN 55102
E-mail: info@jist.com

Visit our website at **www.jist.com** for information on JIST, free job search tips, tables of contents, sample pages, and ordering instructions for our many products!

Development Editor: Heather Stith
Page Layout: Toi Davis
Cover Designers: Amy Peppler Adams, Aleata Halbig
Proofreaders: Laura Bowman, Jeanne Clark
Indexer: Kelly D. Henthorne

Printed in the United States of America
16 15 14 13 12   9 8 7 6 5 4 3 2

Library of Congress Cataloging-in-Publication data is on file with the Library of Congress.

ISBN 978-1-59357-885-5

TABLE OF CONTENTS

ABOUT THIS BOOK

Consider this important data from the U.S. Department of Labor's Bureau of Labor Statistics:

- Total employment is projected to increase by 15.3 million positions (10.1 percent) in the decade ending in 2018.

- The percentage of growth in business, management, and financial occupations is projected to increase 10.6 percent over that same 10-year period.

- Service-producing industries, as opposed to goods-producing industries, will add 14.6 million new jobs, representing 96 percent of the increase in total employment.

- The median annual wages of chief executives in 2009 (latest available data) was $167,280, as compared to median annual wages of all workers at only $43,460.

As management and executive opportunities increase in the U.S. economy, your challenge is to become a savvy career manager, realizing that career management is a lifelong process in which you must be actively engaged and not just a task to be undertaken when a job search or career move is imminent.

A vital component of your career management plan is your resume, which must instantly position you as a well-qualified and highly competitive candidate. The easiest way to accomplish that objective is by developing a powerful, performance-based resume. Of course, you have to include the essential details, but a resume is much more than just your job history and academic credentials. It is a concise yet comprehensive marketing communication that prominently showcases your career highlights and unique skills and qualifications.

In this book, we'll teach you how to create a resume that will get you noticed in the crowd of candidates. And we'll demonstrate how to prepare resumes for electronic distribution, in addition to the traditional printed resume. Read everything thoroughly, carefully review the scores of resume samples, and you'll then have the tools you need to write, format, design, and distribute your own winning resume.

By using *Expert Resumes for Managers and Executives* as your professional guide, you will succeed in developing a powerful and effective resume that opens doors, gets interviews, and helps you land your next great career opportunity!

INTRODUCTION

Job search and career management have become increasingly more complex and more competitive with each passing year. In no employment sector is that more true than in the management and executive ranks. According to the U.S. Bureau of Labor Statistics (BLS), keen competition will continue to be the norm for top executive positions because of the prestige and high pay that attract a substantial number of qualified applicants.

"Managers and executives" is a huge occupational group, encompassing virtually every industry worldwide. On the one hand, the size of this group is great because it means that many senior-level positions are available. The vast number of positions also means a lot of transition occurs as executives (1) move from one position to another, (2) start their own businesses or consulting ventures, and (3) retire.

On the other hand, the competition for these positions is fierce, particularly for individuals who are new to the management and executive ranks of the workforce. Getting that first management opportunity or that long-awaited promotion to COO can be tough. Over the past few years, it's been just as tough for those already in the management and executive ranks, but there is a more promising outlook for the market now.

According to the BLS, things will improve slowly over the coming years, with growth projected at 10.6 percent in the business, management, and financial sector. Yet forecasts for management and executive opportunities solely are projected to remain relatively flat as we move through 2012 and several years beyond.

The difficulty of the market isn't news to any of you who've been actively engaged in a job search over the past few years. It's tough—there's no doubt about it. However, you can do many things to make yourself visible and attractive in the market and position yourself ahead of the competition. Step 1 in that process is to write a powerful resume that is rich in content, achievements, and visual appeal.

That document—your resume—will be at the forefront of your job search and career management efforts forever, so you must be certain that it's the best it can be. Read on to learn how to do that.

The What, How, Which, and Where of Resume Writing

Before you ever begin writing your resume, you must answer four critical questions:

- **What type of position are you pursuing?** Your current career goals dictate the entire resume writing, formatting, and designing process—what you write, where you write it, how you write it, and why you write it. If you're looking for a position where you will have responsibilities similar to what you do now as a senior director of supply chain management, for example, you'll write your resume with one specific strategy and format. However, if you're now interested in a COO position or VP of operations assignment, your resume will be focused in an entirely different direction and will showcase different skills, qualifications, projects, and achievements.

- **How are you going to "paint a picture" of your skills and qualifications to position yourself as an attractive candidate for your targeted jobs?** What information are you going to highlight about your experience that ties directly to your current objectives? What accomplishments, skills, and qualifications are you going to showcase in your resume to support your goals? How are you going to brand yourself to align with current market opportunities?

- **Which resume format are you going to use?** Is a chronological, functional, or hybrid resume format going to work best for you? Which format will give you the greatest flexibility to highlight the skills you want to bring to the forefront of your resume to support your current career goals?

- **Where are you going to look for a job?** Once you have decided what type of position you are interested in, how do you plan to identify and approach those companies and organizations?

When you can answer the what, how, which, and where, you'll be prepared to write your resume and launch your search campaign. Without a clearly defined objective, resume writing becomes much more difficult because your resume has no direction and provides no clear guidelines for decision making. Even if you do not have a precise objective, start out with at least a general sense for where you're headed. Otherwise, your task becomes more complicated and your results less effective.

Use Chapters 1 and 2 to guide you in developing the content for your resume and selecting the appropriate design and layout. Your resume should focus on your skills, achievements, and qualifications, demonstrating the value and benefit you bring to a prospective employer. The focus should be on the role you want to fill now, not necessarily what you have done in the past.

Chapter 3 will lead you through the preparation of multiple formats of your resume that you'll need for both online and offline job searches. The well-designed resume that you print and hand to someone is not the same document that you'll upload to an online resume database. We'll walk you through the various formats, explaining what you'll need, why and when you'll need it, and how to prepare each version.

Review the sample resumes in Chapters 4 through 13 to see what other people—people in similar situations to yours and who have faced similar challenges—have done. You'll find interesting formats, unique skills presentations, achievement-focused resumes, project-focused resumes, and much more. Most importantly, you'll see samples written by the top resume writers in the world. These are real resumes that got real interviews and generated real job offers. They're the "best of the best" from us to you.

Next, review Chapters 14 and 15 for best-in-class cover letter strategies and samples. As you'll read, your cover letter is an essential partner to your resume and your entire job search effort.

Finally, don't overlook the appendices. We've provided two highly useful resources for managing your career now and in the future. Appendix A is a resume worksheet that you can use to develop your resume and capture career information in the years ahead to make updating your resume faster and easier. In Appendix B, you'll find every resume writer's "secret weapon"—a list of powerful, distinctive, and descriptive verbs that you can use to add meaning, impact, and variety to your resume.

Once you've written a powerful and well-focused resume, you're then ready to approach the market. The following sections provide some useful advice to help you plan and manage a successful employment campaign.

Finding a Job

Today's jobs are everywhere—from start-up tech ventures to multinational telecommunications conglomerates; from home health care companies to environmental engineering firms; from corporate security services to global nonprofit organizations. Jobs might not be as plentiful as in years past, but they still are everywhere. You just have to be a bit more clever and diversified in your job search strategy to identify and take advantage of the opportunities.

Whenever possible, focus your search and your career in the industries adding the most jobs and opportunities—technology, telecommunications, professional services/consulting, health care, engineering, social services, and personal services. As you can see, the vast majority of hiring action is in the service industries as our economy moves further away from goods-producing industries such as agriculture and manufacturing. Do note, however, that much to the surprise of labor analysts, manufacturing experienced an unexpected rise in opportunities in 2010 that is expected to continue for at least several years and, hopefully, well into the future.

As with any other project, an action plan will keep you moving steadily toward your goal of finding a new position. We've outlined the major steps in the job-finding process in the following sections. Use these steps to create—and follow—your own detailed action plan that is specific to you and your management/executive career goals.

STEP 1: WRITE A POWERFUL RESUME

As companies have undergone massive changes, employment has become increasingly competitive. As a job seeker, you must know how to position yourself above the crowd of other candidates applying for similar opportunities. The best way to achieve that is with a powerful resume that clearly communicates your accomplishments, your unique brand, and the value you bring to a new employer. That is what this book will teach you—the art and science of resume writing.

Most important, you must always remember:

> Your resume is a marketing tool written to sell YOU!

If you're a CEO, COO, or CFO, *sell* the fact that you've increased revenues, reduced operating costs, and improved profit margins. If you're a human resources manager, *highlight* the reduction in staffing costs that you've delivered. If you're a manufacturing manager, *focus* on your department's increases in productivity and product reliability. If you're a finance executive, *showcase* the fact that you've cut operating costs by a certain percentage while contributing to an increase in bottom-line profits.

When writing your resume, create a picture of knowledge, action, and results. In essence, you're stating "This is who I am, this is what I know, this is how I've used it, and this is how well I've performed." Success sells, so be sure to highlight yours. If you don't, no one else will.

STEP 2: BECOME A SAVVY JOB SEEKER

To be an educated job seeker, you must know what you want in your career, where the hiring action is, what qualifications and credentials you might need to attain your desired career goals, and how best to market your qualifications. It is no longer enough to be a successful senior executive, technology manager, administrative director, or management consultant. Now you must be a strategic marketer, able to package and promote your experience to take advantage of the ever-changing wave of employment opportunity.

The employment market has changed dramatically from only a few years ago. No longer is stability the status quo. The norm is movement, onward and upward, in a fast-paced and intense employment market. And to stay on top of all the changes and opportunities, you must proactively control and manage your career.

STEP 3: LAUNCH A SUCCESSFUL SEARCH CAMPAIGN

The single most important thing to remember is that a **job search is marketing!** You have a product to sell—yourself—and the best way to sell it is to use all appropriate *marketing channels* just as you would for any other product.

Suppose you wanted to sell gadgets. What would you do? You'd market your gadgets using newspaper, magazine, and radio advertisements. You might develop a company website to build your e-business, and perhaps you'd hire a field sales representative to market to major retail chains. Each of these is a different *marketing channel* through which you're attempting to reach your audience.

The same is true for a job search. You must use every marketing channel that's right for you. Unfortunately, there is no single job search marketing formula. What's right for you depends on your specific career objectives—position, industry preferences, geographic restrictions, compensation, and more.

The following is a recommended job search marketing plan for managers and executives. These items are ordered from most effective to least effective and should serve as the foundation on which you build your own search campaign.

1. **Referrals.** There is nothing better than a personal referral to a company, either in general or for a specific position. Referrals can open doors that, in most instances, would never be accessible any other way. If you know anyone who could possibly refer you to a specific organization, contact that person immediately and ask for assistance.

2. **Networking.** Networking is the backbone of every successful job search and is even more important for the management candidate than for other job seekers. Although you might consider it an arduous task, it is essential that you network effectively with your professional colleagues and associates, past employers, past coworkers, suppliers, neighbors, friends, and others who might know of opportunities that are right for you. Fortunately, the surge in online social networks makes it easier than ever for you to connect with the right person who can help you gain access to your target companies. Another good networking strategy is to attend meetings of trade or professional associations in your area to make new contacts and expand your network. And particularly in today's nomadic job market—where you're likely to change jobs every few years—the best strategy is to keep your network "alive" even when you're not searching for a new position.

3. **Responses to online job postings.** One of the greatest advantages of the technology revolution is an employer's ability to post job announcements and a job seeker's ability to respond immediately via e-mail. In most (but not all) instances, these are bona fide opportunities, and it's well worth your while to spend time searching for and responding to appropriate postings. However, don't make the mistake of devoting *too* much time to searching the Internet. It can consume a huge amount of your time that you should spend on other job search efforts that will yield even better results.

   Generally speaking, the higher the level of position you are seeking, the less value online job postings will offer. Most very senior-level management and executive positions are filled through networking, referrals, recruiter searches, and other person-to-person contact.

   To expedite your online searches, here are some of the largest and most widely used online job-posting sites—presented alphabetically and not in order of effectiveness or value. We've expanded this list to include some of our favorite sites designed specifically for managers and executives. Note that some of these are fee-based sites.

   6figurejobs.com: www.6figurejobs.com

   American Jobs: www.americanjobs.com

   BlueSteps: www.bluesteps.com (fee-based)

   The Business Journals: www.bizjournals.com/bizjournals/jobs/

   CareerBuilder.com: http://executive.careerbuilder.com/

   Dice: www.dice.com

   EmploymentGuide.com: www.employmentguide.com

   ExecCrossing: www.execcrossing.com

   ExecSearches.com: www.execsearches.com

   ExecuNet: www.execunet.com (fee-based)

ExecutivesOnly: www.executivesonly.com (fee-based)

FlipDog: www.flipdog.com

HireDiversity.com: www.hirediversity.com

TheLadders: www.theladders.com (fee-based)

LinkedIn: www.linkedin.com

Monster: www.monster.com

NETSHARE, Inc.: www.netshare.com (fee-based)

Net-Temps: www.net-temps.com

RiteSite: www.ritesite.com (fee-based)

4. **Responses to newspaper, magazine, and periodical advertisements (print).** So much of job searching has transitioned to the Internet and e-mail that people now often overlook a great hiring resource—the "help-wanted ads." Do not forget about this tried-and-true marketing channel. If they've got the job and you have the qualifications, it's a perfect fit. We've seen it work for decades and continue to do so!

5. **Targeted e-mail campaigns (resumes and cover letters) to recruiters.** Recruiters have jobs and you want one. It's pretty straightforward. The only catch is to find the "right" recruiters who have the "right" jobs. Therefore, you must devote the time and effort to preparing a targeted list of recruiters. There are many resources on the Internet where you can access information about recruiters (for a fee) and then sort that information by industry and position specialization. This enables you to identify the recruiters who would be interested in a management candidate with your specific qualifications. What's more, because these campaigns are transmitted electronically, they are easy and inexpensive to produce.

   Remember this: When working with recruiters, it's important to realize that they *do not* work for you! Their clients are the hiring companies that pay their fees. Recruiters are not in business to "find a job" for you, but rather to fill a specific position with a qualified candidate, either you or someone else. To maximize your chances of finding a position through a recruiter or agency, don't rely on just one or two, but distribute your resume to many that meet your specific criteria.

6. **Targeted e-mail and print campaigns to employers.** Just as with campaigns to recruiters (see item 5 above), you must be extremely careful to select just the right employers that would be interested in a management or executive candidate with your qualifications. The closer you stick to "where you belong" in relation to your specific experience, the better your response rate will be. If you are targeting technology companies, transmit your letters and resumes via e-mail. For companies in all other industries, we believe that print campaigns (paper and envelopes mailed the old-fashioned way) are a more appropriate and effective presentation for all management and executive candidates. Instead of being "one of a million" e-mailed resumes, yours arrives in an envelope and is placed on someone's desk. It truly can be the difference between being noticed and being ignored.

7. **Online resume postings.** The Internet is swarming with reasonably priced (if not free) websites where you can post your resume. It's quick, easy, and the only *passive* thing you can do in your search. All of the other marketing channels require action on your part. With online resume postings, once you've posted, you're done. You then just wait (and hope!) for some response.

Opportunities in Management Consulting

The term *consultant* or *contractor* generally refers to an individual who moves from one organization to another, from project to project, where his or her particular expertise is most needed and most highly rewarded (and compensated). Although people have worked as management consultants for decades, it is more in vogue now than ever before. According to the U.S. Bureau of Labor Statistics, the demand for consultants is strong and growing at an unprecedented rate. The government's data project a 24 percent increase in the number of consulting opportunities in the decade ending in 2018.

Although the vast majority of people have (and want) full-time jobs, many people are flocking towards consulting because of the tremendous flexibility it offers. And what a great phenomenon for companies! They can now hire the talent they need, when they need it, and *only* when they need it. The popularity of consulting is also great news for managers and executives who want to use the skills and knowledge gained during their distinguished careers to help other companies be more successful—but not as permanent employees.

If you are seriously considering a consulting career, pay close attention to the following recommendations:

1. **Market yourself constantly.** Regardless of your area of consulting expertise, one of your most vital functions as an independent consultant will be to market yourself. Consider the talented financial executive who now wants to pursue a financial consulting career specializing in mergers and acquisitions. Her success as a consultant will be tied not only to her financial expertise, but just as significantly to her ability to proactively market her consulting practice, establish her clientele, and build a strong revenue stream. If you're not an astute marketer and not willing to invest the time and resources essential to marketing your consulting practice, consider joining an established consulting company where the firm itself will capture the clients and you'll be responsible for service delivery.

2. **Practice targeted networking.** As part of your ongoing efforts to market your consulting practice, you'll need to invest your time in targeted online and offline networking. In fact, initially, this might be where you devote an extraordinary amount of time rekindling past business relationships and building new ones. You must commit yourself to a structured networking and relationship-development program to establish yourself within the consulting marketplace.

3. **Manage your finances.** The income streams of consultants often vary widely from month to month. There will be good months when money will be flowing in; there will be slow months when money will only trickle in. Established consultants know that this variation is the norm and have learned to manage their money accordingly. This can be an extremely difficult lesson and might

require some practice, but learning to manage your financial resources is critical to your long-term consulting success.

4. **Live with the risk.** Learning to live with the risk and the volatility of a consulting career can also be an extreme challenge. Unpredictability is the status quo for most consultants and, as such, you must learn to live comfortably with that risk and not allow the stress associated with it to overtake your life and your mental health!

5. **Check the Internet.** Before you proceed any further in evaluating your potential opportunities in consulting, be sure to take advantage of the thousands of online resources devoted to consulting. If you do an extensive Internet search, you'll find websites where you can search for consulting opportunities, sites where you can post your resume for review by companies seeking consultants, hundreds of sites with articles about consulting, other sites that offer the many tools you'll need to manage your practice, and much more. Many of these resources are free; others have a small fee associated with them.

Consulting can offer wonderful opportunities for managers and executives. If you do have a particular expertise and can commit yourself to marketing and building your practice, consulting might be just the right solution for you at this point in your career. How great to be able to work on the projects that interest you and then move on to something else! Working as a consultant allows you—not a company—to control your own career destiny.

In Chapter 13 you will find a variety of resumes for managers and executives seeking to enter the consulting field or to continue their careers in consulting. Be sure to take advantage of these resources if you are considering consulting as your next career step.

Conclusion

Although management and executive opportunities remain relatively flat in terms of growth, opportunities still abound. It might take a bit more time than in years past to find the "right" positions, but they are out there. What's more, thanks to the Internet and online networking, it has never been easier to learn about and apply for jobs. Arm yourself with a powerful resume and cover letter, identify your most appropriate online and offline marketing channels, and launch your search today. The right opportunity is out there and waiting for you!

PART I

Resume Writing, Strategy, and Formats

CHAPTER 1

Resume Writing Strategies for Managers and Executives

If you're reading this book, chances are you've decided to make a career move. It might be because of any of the following reasons:

- You're ready to leave your current position and move up the ladder to a higher-paying and more responsible management or executive-level position.

- The industry in which you've been working has been hit hard by economic decline, so you've decided to pursue opportunities in other industries where the prospects for growth and stability are much stronger.

- You've decided on a career change and will be looking at opportunities both within and outside your current industry.

- You're unhappy with your current employer or senior management team and have decided to pursue opportunities elsewhere.

- You've been laid off, downsized, or otherwise left your position and you must find a new one.

- You've completed a contract assignment or interim position and are looking for a new contract, consulting, or permanent opportunity.

- You've decided to resign from your current position to pursue an executive-level entrepreneurial opportunity.

- You're relocating to a new area and need to find a new management opportunity.

- You're returning to the workforce after several years of unemployment or retirement and are ready for new senior-management opportunities.

- You've just earned your graduate degree and are ready to take a step upward in your career.

- You're simply ready for a change.

No matter the reason behind your move, a powerful resume is an essential component of your job search campaign. In fact, conducting a job search without a resume is virtually impossible. A resume is your calling card that briefly, yet powerfully, communicates the skills, qualifications, experience, and value you bring to a prospective employer. It is the document that opens doors and generates interviews. It is the first thing people learn about you when you forward it in response to an advertisement or job posting and the last thing they remember when they review your qualifications *after* an interview.

Your resume is a sales document, and you are the product! You must identify the *features (what you know* and *what you can do)* and *benefits (how you can help an employer)* of that product and then communicate them in a concise and hard-hitting written presentation. As you work your way through the resume process, remind yourself over and over that you are writing a marketing document designed to sell a new product—YOU—into a new management or executive-level position.

Your resume can have tremendous power and a phenomenal impact on your job search. So don't take it lightly. Rather, devote the time, energy, and resources that are essential to developing a resume that is well-written, visually attractive, and effective in communicating *who* you are and *how* you want to be perceived.

Resume Strategies

Following are the nine core strategies for writing effective and successful resumes.

RESUME STRATEGY #1: Write to the Job You Want

Now that you've decided to look for a new position, the first step is to identify your current career interests, goals, and objectives. *This task is critical* because it is the underlying foundation for *what* you include in your resume, *how* you include it, and *where* you include it. You cannot write an effective resume without knowing, at least to some degree, what type or types of positions you will be seeking. You need to go more in depth than simply saying, "I'm looking for an executive position." You must have specific objectives in order to create a document that powerfully positions you for such opportunities.

There are two concepts to consider here:

- *Who you are:* This concept relates to what you have done professionally and/or academically. Are you a CEO, COO, CIO, CKO, or CFO? Are you a director of manufacturing, a director of purchasing, or a director of training and development? Are you the general manager of a large sales organization or the managing director of a nine-country European customer support organization? Are you a business manager, program manager, or technology manager? Have you just returned to school to complete your MBA or another advanced degree?

- *How you want to be perceived:* This concept relates to your current career objectives. If you're a financial manager looking for a position as a CEO, don't focus solely on your financial skills. Put an equal emphasis on your success in general management, strategic planning, organizational leadership, joint ventures, team building, marketing, and business development. If you're a production manager seeking a promotion to the next tier of management, highlight your accomplishments in reducing operating costs, improving productivity, stream-lining operations, eliminating product defects, and contributing profits to the bottom line.

The strategy, then, is to connect these two concepts by using the *Who you are* information that ties directly to the *How you want to be perceived* message to determine what information to include in your resume. By following this strategy, you're painting a picture that allows a prospective employer to see you as you want to be seen—as an individual with the qualifications for the type of position you are pursuing.

> **WARNING:** If you prepare a resume without first clearly identifying what your objectives are and how you want to be perceived, your resume will have no focus and no direction. Without the underlying knowledge of "This is what I want to be," you do not know what to highlight in your resume. In turn, the document becomes a historical overview of your career and not the sales document it is designed to be.

RESUME STRATEGY #2: Sell It to Me...Don't Tell It to Me

We've already established the fact that resume writing is sales. You are the product, and you must create a document that powerfully communicates the value of that product. One particularly effective strategy for accomplishing this is the "Sell It to Me...Don't Tell It to Me" strategy that affects virtually every word you write on your resume.

If you "tell it," you simply state facts. If you "sell it," you promote it, advertise it, and draw attention to it. Look at the difference in impact between these examples:

Tell It Strategy: Supervised customer service operations for two large sales locations.

Sell It Strategy: Full strategic planning, operating, and P&L responsibility for daily management of 2,000-employee customer-service operation supporting $25M+ in annual sales contracts for world's largest automotive brake manufacturer. Closed FY11 $250K under budget with 98% customer-satisfaction rating.

Tell It Strategy: Managed a large-scale reorganization of one of Kodak's manufacturing facilities.

Sell It Strategy: Spearheaded plantwide reorganization of Kodak's flagship manufacturing facility, impacting 1,000 employees and $450M in annual product throughput. Slashed operating costs 22%, reduced waste 18%, introduced lean manufacturing techniques, and added $14M+ to bottom-line profits.

Tell It Strategy: Supervised development of next-generation voice-recognition software for IBM.

Sell It Strategy: Led 8-person technology team in design, engineering, prototype development, and full-scale market launch of IBM's next-generation voice-recognition software (projected to deliver $20 million in first-year sales).

What's the difference between "telling it" and "selling it"? In a nutshell…

Telling It	Selling It
Describes features.	Describes benefits.
Tells what and how.	Sells why the "what" and "how" are important.
Details activities.	Includes results.
Focuses on what you did.	Details how what you did benefited your employer, department, team members, customers, and so on.

RESUME STRATEGY #3: Use Keywords

No matter what you read or who you talk to about job search, the concept of keywords is sure to come up. Keywords (or, as they were previously known, *buzz-words*) are words and phrases specific to a particular industry or profession. For example, keywords for management include *strategic planning, organizational design, organizational leadership, team building, revenue growth, profit improvement, cost reduction, P&L management, performance optimization, productivity and efficiency improvement, business planning, operating management,* and thousands more.

When you use these words and phrases—in your resume, in your cover letter, in your LinkedIn profile, or during an interview—you are communicating a specific message. For example, when you include the words *marketing management* in your resume, your reader will most likely assume that you have experience in strategic market planning, market positioning, new product launch, new business development, competitive analysis, multimedia marketing, promotions, and more. People will make inferences about your skills based on the use of just one or two individual words.

Here are a few other examples:

- When you use the words **corporate financial management,** people will assume you have experience with budgeting, tax, treasury, cash management, banking, investor reporting, financial analysis, financial reporting, and more.

- By referencing **technology leadership** in your resume, you convey that you most likely have experience in identifying technology needs, developing and commercializing new technologies, selecting and installing existing technologies, training technical personnel, managing technology projects and operations, and more.

- When you include **human resources leadership** as one of your areas of expertise, most people will assume you are experienced in recruitment, hiring, training and development, benefits, compensation, employee relations, employee supervision, performance evaluation, and more.

- When you mention **educational administration,** readers and listeners will infer that you have experience in curriculum planning and development, instructional materials design, technology-based learning, teacher selection and training, school board relations, and more.

Keywords are also an integral component of the resume-scanning process, whereby employers and recruiters electronically search resumes for specific terms to find candidates with the skills, qualifications, and credentials for their particular hiring needs. In today's modern age of e-based job search, keyword-based electronic scanning has replaced the more traditional method of initial resume reviews done by real-live people in tens of thousands of companies worldwide. Therefore, to some degree, the *only* thing that matters is that you have included the "right" keywords to match the company's or the recruiter's needs. In organizations where keywords drive the initial screening process, you are simply passed over without them.

Keyword scanning continues to increase in popularity because of its ease and efficiency, and electronic hiring systems are most often the preferred method for applying for specific positions and making initial contact with a company or recruiter. As such, you *must* be technologically savvy not only in your business life but in your job search efforts as well by staying current with the latest trends in technology-based recruitment and applicant tracking/management.

Once your resume passes the keyword scan, it will then be read by human eyes, so it's not enough just to throw together a list of keywords and leave it at that. It's not even necessary to include a separate "keyword summary" on your resume. A better strategy is to incorporate keywords naturally into the text within the appropriate sections of your resume.

Keep in mind, too, that keywords are arbitrary; there is no defined set of keywords for a CEO, sales director, telecommunications manager, hotel manager, or vice president of engineering. Employers searching to fill these positions develop a list of terms and core competencies that reflect the specifics they desire in a qualified candidate. These might be a combination of professional qualifications, skills, education, length of experience, alma mater, and other easily defined criteria, along with "soft skills" such as leadership, problem solving, and communication.

NOTE: Because of the complex and arbitrary nature of keyword selection, we cannot overemphasize how vital it is to be certain that all of the keywords that represent your experience and knowledge are included in your resume!

How can you be sure that you are including all the keywords and the right keywords? Just by describing your work experience, achievements, educational credentials, technical qualifications, and the like, you will naturally include most of the terms that are important in your field. To cross-check what you've written, review online or print job postings for positions that are of interest to you. Look at the precise terms used in the postings and be sure you include them in your resume (as appropriate to your skills and qualifications).

RESUME STRATEGY #4: Use the "Big" and Save the "Little"

When deciding what you want to include in your resume, try to focus on the "big" things—revenue and profit growth, new initiatives and ventures, special projects, cost savings, productivity and efficiency improvements, new products, technology implementations, sales successes, new market launches, and more. Give a good broad-based picture of what you were responsible for and how well you did it. Here's an example:

> Senior Finance and Operating Executive with full management responsibility for corporate financial affairs, daily business operations, administration, and all HR/employee-benefit programs. Concurrent responsibility for identifying and negotiating acquisitions to further accelerate growth and global expansion. Recruit, train, and lead a staff of 120 through 12 management reports.
>
> - Delivered strong and sustainable financial gains:
>
>   300% increase in revenues and 400% increase in bottom-line profits.
>
> $160,000 reduction in staffing and employee costs.
>
> $1 million collected in outstanding receivables.
>
> $95,000 savings in vendor and lease costs.

Then save the "little" stuff—the details—for the interview. With this strategy, you will accomplish two things: You'll keep your resume readable and of a reasonable length (while still selling your achievements), and you'll have new and interesting information to share during the interview, rather than merely repeating what is on your resume. Using the preceding example, when discussing this experience during an interview you could elaborate on your specific achievements—namely, how you increased revenues and profits so dramatically, how you were able to reduce personnel costs while still managing all operations, what you did to collect the $1 million outstanding debt, and more.

RESUME STRATEGY #5: Make Your Resume "Interviewable"

One of your greatest challenges is to make your resume a useful interview tool. After it's been determined that you meet the primary qualifications for a position (you've passed the keyword scanning test or initial review) and you are contacted for a telephone or in-person interview, your resume becomes all-important in leading and prompting your interviewer during your conversation.

Your job, then, is to make sure the resume leads the reader where you want to go and presents just the *right* information to stimulate a productive discussion. To improve the "interviewability" of your resume, consider these tactics:

- Make good use of Resume Strategy #4 (Use the "Big" and Save the "Little") to invite further discussion about your experiences.

- Be sure your greatest selling points are featured prominently, not buried within the resume.

- Conversely, don't devote lots of space and attention to areas of your background that are irrelevant or about which you feel less than positive; you'll only invite questions about things you don't want to discuss.

- Make sure your resume is highly readable—this means plenty of white space, an adequate font size, and a logical flow from start to finish.

RESUME STRATEGY #6: Eliminate Confusion with Structure and Context

Keep in mind that hiring authorities will read your resume quickly. You might agonize over every word and spend hours working on content and design, but the average reader will skim through your masterpiece and expect to pick up important facts in just a few seconds. Make it as easy as possible for readers to grasp the essential facts:

- Be consistent; for example, put job titles, company names, and dates in the same place for each position.

- Make information easy to find by clearly defining different sections of your resume with large, highly visible headings.

- Define the context in which you worked (for example, what the company does, what your specific organization/department does, and any notable challenges you overcame or opportunities you took advantage of) before you start describing your activities and accomplishments.

RESUME STRATEGY #7: Use Function to Demonstrate Achievement

A resume that focuses only on your job functions can be dry and uninteresting and says little about your unique activities and contributions. Consider the following example:

> Responsible for all operations at the Marriott Hotel in downtown Washington, DC.

Now consider using that same function to demonstrate achievement and see what happens to the tone and energy of the sentence. It comes alive and clearly communicates that you deliver results.

> Profitably manage a 235-room luxury Marriott property that generates over $150M in annual revenues. Revitalized property from loss position to double-digit profitability within two years through complete redesign of all sales, catering, front desk, and security operations. Currently ranked #3 for customer service out of 560 Marriott properties nationwide.

If you translate your functions into achievements, you'll create a more powerful resume presentation.

RESUME STRATEGY #8: Remain in the Realm of Reality

We've already established that resume writing is sales. And, as any good salesperson does, you may feel somewhat inclined to stretch the truth, just a bit. However, be forewarned that you must stay within the realm of reality. Do not push your skills and qualifications outside the bounds of what is truthful. You never want to be in a position where you have to defend something that you've written on your resume. If that's the case, you'll lose the opportunity before you ever get started.

RESUME STRATEGY #9: Be Confident

You are unique. There is only one individual with the specific combination of employment experience, qualifications, achievements, education, and technical skills that you have. In turn, this positions you as a unique commodity within the competitive job search market. To succeed, you must prepare a resume that is written to sell *you* and highlight *your* qualifications and *your* success. If you can accomplish this, you will have won the job search game by generating interest, interviews, and offers.

There Are No Resume Writing Rules

One of the greatest challenges in resume writing is that there are no rules to the game. However, there are certain expectations about information that you will include: principally, your employment history and your educational qualifications. Beyond that, what you include is entirely up to you. What's more, you have tremendous flexibility in determining how to include the information you have selected. In Chapter 2, you'll find a complete listing of each possible category you might include in your resume, the type of information that should be included in each, preferred formats for presentation, and sample text you can edit and use.

Although there are no rules for resume writing, there are a few standards to live by as you write your resume. The following sections discuss these standards in detail.

CONTENT STANDARDS

Content is, of course, the text that goes into your resume. Content standards cover the writing style you should use, items you should be sure to include, items you should avoid including, and the order and format in which you should list your qualifications.

Writing Style

Always write in the first person, dropping the word "I" from the front of each sentence. This style gives your resume a more assertive and more professional tone than the passive third-person voice, as shown in the following examples.

First Person:

> Manage 12-person team responsible for the global market launch of new OTC pharmaceuticals for Bayer's Consumer Division.

Third Person:

> Mr. Glenwood manages a 12-person team responsible for the global market launch of new OTC pharmaceuticals for Bayer's Consumer Division.

By using the first-person voice, you are assuming ownership of that statement. You did such-and-such. When you use the third-person voice, someone else did it.

Phrases to Avoid

Avoid using phrases such as "responsible for" or "duties included." These words create a passive tone and style. Instead, use active verbs to describe what you did.

Compare these two ways of conveying the same information:

> Duties included scheduling, job assignment, and management of more than 200 production workers, engineers, and maintenance support staff for a $52 million poultry-production facility.

or

> Directed scheduling, job assignment, and daily operations for more than 200 production workers, engineers, and maintenance support staff at a $52 million poultry-production facility.

Resume Style

The traditional *chronological* resume lists work experience in reverse-chronological order (starting with your current or most recent position). The *functional* style de-emphasizes the "where" and "when" of your career and instead groups similar experiences, talents, and qualifications regardless of when they occurred.

Today, however, most resumes follow neither a strictly chronological nor a strictly functional style. Rather, they are an effective mixture of the two styles, usually known as a *combination* or *hybrid* style.

Like the chronological style, the hybrid style includes specifics about where you worked, when you worked there, and what your job titles were. Like a functional resume, a hybrid resume emphasizes your most relevant qualifications—perhaps within chronological job descriptions, in an expanded summary section, in several "career highlights" bullet points at the top of your resume, in project summaries, or in many other ways. Most of the examples in this book are hybrids and show a wide diversity of organizational structures that you can use as inspiration when structuring your own resume.

Resume Formats

Resumes, principally career summaries and job descriptions, are most often written in a paragraph format, a bulleted format, or a combination of both. Following are three job descriptions, all similar in content, yet presented in each of the three different writing formats. The advantages and disadvantages of each format are also addressed.

Paragraph Format

Division Manager   2009 to 2012

National Medical Research Center, Lewiston, Maine

Created and led strategic planning, finance, accounting, administration, contracting, and partnerships for the start-up of a new entrepreneurial division launching new ventures in emerging health-care markets. Developed business plans and directed operating budgets for 8 distinct profit centers worldwide.

Identified opportunity; then structured, negotiated, and closed joint venture with Central Health, the largest nonprofit hospital system in the region. Created Limited Liability Corporation (LLC) to manage and market community-based health-care programs. Appointed to Board of Directors.

Created a portfolio of financial models, indices, and analyses to monitor/evaluate performance of all new ventures, new products, and new service-delivery programs. Collaborated with business partners to create a new respiratory-care company. Won 21 contracts with projections for an additional 12 by end of third year ($2+ million in revenue). Established program to facilitate new business-development opportunities in research, case management, and clinical services. Delivered $4 million in first-year revenue. Negotiated joint venture with medical technology company that included a valuable insider equity position prior to IPO.

Advantages

Requires the least amount of space on the page. Brief, succinct, and to the point.

Disadvantages

Achievements get lost in the text of the third paragraph. They are not visually distinctive, nor do they stand alone to draw attention to them.

Bulleted Format

Division Manager   2009 to 2012

National Medical Research Center, Lewiston, Maine

- Created and led strategic planning, finance, accounting, administration, contracting, and partnerships for the start-up of a new entrepreneurial division launching new ventures in emerging health-care markets. Developed business plans and directed operating budgets for 8 distinct profit centers worldwide.

- Identified opportunity; then structured, negotiated, and closed joint venture with Central Health, the largest nonprofit hospital system in the region. Created Limited Liability Corporation (LLC) to manage and market community-based health-care programs. Appointed to Board of Directors.

- Created a portfolio of financial models, indices, and analyses to monitor/evaluate performance of all new ventures, new products, and new service-delivery programs.

- Collaborated with business partners to create a new respiratory-care company. Won 21 contracts with projections for an additional 12 by end of third year ($2+ million in revenue).

- Established program to facilitate new business-development opportunities in research, case management, and clinical services. Delivered $4 million in first-year revenue.

- Negotiated joint venture with medical-technology company that included a valuable insider equity position prior to IPO.

Advantages

Quick and easy to peruse.

Disadvantages

Responsibilities and achievements are lumped together with everything of equal value. In turn, the achievements get lost farther down the list and are not immediately recognizable.

Combination Format

Division Manager   2009 to 2012

National Medical Research Center, Lewiston, Maine

Created and led strategic planning, finance, accounting, administration, contracting, and partnerships for the start-up of a new entrepreneurial division launching new ventures in emerging health-care markets.

(continued)

(continued)

Developed business plans and directed operating budgets for 8 distinct profit centers worldwide.

- Identified opportunity; then structured, negotiated, and closed joint venture with Central Health, the largest nonprofit hospital system in the region. Created Limited Liability Corporation (LLC) to manage and market community-based health-care programs. Appointed to Board of Directors.

- Created a portfolio of financial models, indices, and analyses to monitor/evaluate performance of all new ventures, new products, and new service-delivery programs.

- Collaborated with business partners to create a new respiratory-care company. Won 21 contracts with projections for an additional 12 by end of third year ($2+ million in revenue).

- Established program to facilitate new business-development opportunities in research, case management, and clinical services. Delivered $4 million in first-year revenue.

- Negotiated joint venture with medical-technology company that included a valuable insider equity position prior to IPO.

Advantages

Our recommended format. Clearly presents overall responsibilities in the introductory paragraph and then accentuates each achievement as a separate bullet.

Disadvantages

If you don't have clearly identifiable accomplishments, this format is not effective. It also might draw unwanted attention to positions where your accomplishments were less notable.

E-mail Address and URL

Be sure to include your e-mail address prominently at the top of your resume. E-mail is the preferred method of communication in a job search.

We advise against using your employer's e-mail address on your resume. Not only does this present a negative impression to future employers, it will become useless once you make your next career move. And because your resume might exist in cyberspace long after you've completed your job search, you don't want to direct interested parties to an obsolete e-mail address. Instead, obtain a private, professional e-mail address that will be yours permanently. A free e-mail address from a provider such as Yahoo! Mail, Hotmail, or Gmail is perfectly acceptable to use on your resume.

In addition to your e-mail address, if you have a URL (website) where you have posted your Web resume, be sure to also display that prominently at the top of your resume. For more information on Web resumes, see Chapter 3.

PRESENTATION STANDARDS

Presentation refers to the way your resume looks. It has to do with the fonts you use, the paper you print it on, any graphics you might include, and how many pages your resume should be.

Font

Use a font that is clean, conservative, and easy to read. Stay away from anything that is too fancy, glitzy, curly, and the like. Here are a few recommended fonts:

Tahoma	Times New Roman
Arial	Bookman
Krone	Book Antiqua
Soutane	Garamond
CG Omega	Century Schoolbook
Century Gothic	**Lucida Sans**
Gill Sans	Verdana

Although Times New Roman is extremely popular, it is our least preferred font simply because it is overused. More than 90 percent of the resumes we see use Times New Roman. Your goal is to create a competitively distinctive document. To achieve that, we recommend an alternative font.

The content, format, and length of your resume should dictate your choice of resume font. Some fonts look better than others at smaller or larger sizes; some have "bolder" boldface type; some require more white space to make them readable. After you write your resume, experiment with a few different fonts to see which one best enhances your document.

Type Size

Readability is everything! If the type size is too small, your resume will be difficult to read and difficult to skim for essential information. A too-large type size, particularly for senior-level professionals, can also give a negative impression by conveying a juvenile or unprofessional image.

As a general rule, select type from 10 to 12 points in size. However, there's no hard-and-fast rule, and a lot depends on the font you choose. Take a look at the following examples.

Very readable in 9-point Verdana:

> Won the 2011 "Manager of the Year" award at Ford's Indianapolis plant. Honored for innovative contributions to cost reduction, product development, and profit growth.

Difficult to read in too-small 9-point Gill Sans MT:

> Won the 2011 "Manager of the Year" award at Ford's Indianapolis plant. Honored for innovative contributions to cost reduction, product development, and profit growth.

Concise and readable in 12-point Garamond:

> Senior Training & Development Manager specializing in the design, development, and presentation of multimedia leadership training programs for all senior managers and executives.

A bit overwhelming in too-large 12-point Bookman Old Style:

> Senior Training & Development Manager specializing in the design, development, and presentation of multimedia leadership training programs for all senior managers and executives.

Type Enhancements

Bold, *italics,* <u>underlining</u>, and CAPITALIZATION are ideal for highlighting certain words, phrases, achievements, projects, numbers, and other information you want to draw special attention to. However, do not overuse these enhancements. If your resume becomes too cluttered, nothing stands out.

> **NOTE:** Resumes intended for electronic distribution have specific restrictions on font, type size, and type enhancements. We discuss these details in Chapter 3.

Page Length

Our recommendation to the "average" job seeker is to keep his or her resume to one or two pages. The same is true for many managers and executives. Keep it short and succinct, giving just enough to entice your readers. However, for others, it can be difficult to include all the relevant information in just two pages. In situations like this, your management career might warrant a longer resume, and that can be okay!

Let the amount of quality information you have to share be the determining factor in the length of your resume. Do not feel as though it *must* remain on two pages, although that would be the preference whenever possible. What it *must* do is attract prospective employers.

Here are a few situations when a longer resume may be in order:

- You have an extensive list of technical qualifications that are relevant to the position for which you are applying.

- You have extensive educational training and numerous credentials/ certifications, all of which are important to include.

- You have an extensive list of special projects, task forces, and committees to include that are important to your current career objectives.

- You have an extensive list of professional honors, awards, and commendations.

- You have an extensive list of media appearances and publications.

This type of information is extremely valuable in validating your credibility and distinguishing you from the competition. It must be included, even if just the highlights. You might consider including such information on a separate page as an addendum to your resume.

If you create a resume that's longer than two pages, make it more reader-friendly by carefully segmenting the information. For instance, begin with your career summary and your work experience. This will most likely take one to two pages. Then follow with education, any professional or industry credentials, honors and awards, technology and equipment skills, publications, public speaking engagements, professional affiliations, civic affiliations, volunteer experience, foreign-language skills, and other relevant information you want to include. Put each into a separate category so that your resume is easy to peruse and your reader can quickly see the highlights. You'll read more about each of these sections of your resume in Chapter 2.

Paper Color

Be conservative. White, ivory, and light gray are ideal. Other "flashier" colors are inappropriate for individuals in the management and executive tiers.

Graphics

For entry-level or midlevel management positions, an attractive, relevant graphic can add impact to your resume. When you look through the sample resumes in Chapters 4 through 13, you'll see a few excellent examples of the effective use of graphics to enhance the visual presentation of a resume. Just be sure not to get carried away; be tasteful and relatively conservative.

For those of you at the senior management or executive level, we do not recommend graphics on your resume. Clean, crisp, and conservative is our motto for an expertly professional resume at this level. An exception to this recommendation is if you can include a powerful graph or table to illustrate your management successes. Recent graphics of this nature that we've used in executive resumes include a graph that called attention to a dramatic rise in stock price, a chart that illustrated steady growth in number of new customers and volume of repeat business, and a table that presented exceptional revenue and profit growth in a strong visual format.

White Space

Readability is everything! If people have to struggle to read your resume, they won't make the effort. Therefore, be sure to leave plenty of white space. It makes a difference.

ACCURACY AND PERFECTION

The final step, and one of the most critical in resume writing, is the proofreading stage. Your resume must be well written; visually pleasing; and free of any errors, typographical mistakes, misspellings, and the like. We recommend that you carefully proofread your resume a minimum of three times, and then have two or three other people also proofread it. Consider your resume an example of the quality of work you will produce on a company's behalf. Is your work product going to have errors and inconsistencies? If your resume does, it communicates to a prospective employer that you are careless, and this message is the "kiss of death" in a job search.

Take the time to make sure that your resume is perfect in all the details that make a difference to those who read it.

CHAPTER 2

Writing Your Resume

For many managers and executives, resume writing is *not* at the top of the list of fun and exciting activities. How can it compare to negotiating a joint venture, solving a major production problem, reducing corporate debt, or launching a new product? In your perception, we're sure that it cannot.

However, resume writing can be an enjoyable and rewarding task. Once your resume is complete, you can look at it proudly, reminding yourself of all that you have achieved. It is a snapshot of your career and your success. When it's complete, we guarantee you'll look back with tremendous self-satisfaction as you launch and successfully manage your job search.

Resume writing is typically the first step in finding a new position or advancing your career and can be the most daunting of all job search tasks. If writing is not one of your primary job functions, it might have been years since you sat down and wrote anything other than notes to yourself. Even if you write on a regular basis, resume writing is unique. A resume has its own style and a number of peculiarities, as any specialty document does.

Therefore, to make the writing process easier, more finite, and more efficient, we've consolidated it into five discrete sections:

- **Contact Information.** This identification provides your resume's customers (hiring managers) with an easy way to respond.

- **Career Summary.** Think of your Career Summary as the corporate strategy of your resume. It is the big-picture view of everything that allows your organization to work—whether your organization is an entire company or just one department. It is the backbone of your corporate experience and the foundation of your resume.

- **Professional Experience.** The Professional Experience section is much like the operations that are the foundation of your organization. These specifics support your achievement of the corporate strategy. Your professional experience demonstrates how you put all your capabilities to work.

- **Education and Certifications.** Think of this section as your organization's credentials, the third-party validation of your qualifications, knowledge, and expertise.

- **The "Extras"** (Publications, Public Speaking, Honors and Awards, Technology Qualifications, Training, Professional Affiliations, Civic Affiliations, Foreign Languages, Personal Information, and so on). This section of your resume includes your *product or service features,* the extra stuff that helps distinguish you from others with similar qualifications.

Step-by-Step: Writing the Perfect Resume

In the preceding section, we outlined the five core resume sections. Now we'll detail the particulars of each section—what to include, where to place it, and how to present it.

CONTACT INFORMATION

Let's briefly address the top section of your resume: your name and contact information.

Name

You would think writing your name would be the easiest part of writing your resume! But there are several factors you should consider:

- Although most people choose to use their full, formal name at the top of a resume, it has become increasingly more acceptable to use the name by which you prefer to be called.

- Bear in mind that it's to your advantage to have readers feel comfortable calling you for an interview. Their comfort level might decrease if your name is gender-neutral, difficult to pronounce, or unusual; they don't know whether they're calling a man or a woman or how to ask for you. Here are a few ways you can make it easier for them:

> Lynn T. Cowles (Mr.)
>
> (Ms.) Michael Murray
>
> Tzirina (Irene) Kahn
>
> Ndege "Nick" Vernon

Address

In general, you should include your home address on your resume. If you use a post-office box for mail, include both your mailing address and your physical residence address. If you upload your resume to an online site, however, we recommend removing the address, leaving just your e-mail address and phone number as contact information.

Telephone Number(s)

We recommend that you include just one phone number on your resume—the number where you can be reached most readily and where callers can leave a voice mail message for a speedy return call. For many people, this number is your cell phone number; for others, it will be your home number.

In certain cases, you will want to include more than one number on your resume. If cell coverage is spotty or you are often unable to take calls on your cell phone, include your home as well as your cell number. Be sure to have a brief, professional-sounding voice mail greeting for all phone numbers that appear on your resume, and regularly monitor your messages.

E-mail Address

Always include your e-mail address on your resume. E-mail is now often the pre-ferred method of communication in a job search, particularly in the early stages of each contact. Do not use your employer's e-mail address, even if you access personal e-mail through your work computer. Instead, obtain a free, accessible-anywhere address from a provider such as Yahoo!, Hotmail, or Gmail.

As you look through the samples in Chapters 4 through 13, you'll see how resume writers have arranged the many bits of contact information at the top of a resume. You can use these as models for presenting your own information. The point is to make it as easy as possible for employers to contact you.

Now, let's get into the nitty-gritty of the core content sections of your resume.

CAREER SUMMARY

The Career Summary is the introductory section at the top of your resume that summarizes and highlights your knowledge and expertise.

You might be thinking, "But shouldn't my resume start with an Objective?" Although many job seekers still use Objective statements, we believe that a Career Summary is a much more powerful introduction. The problem with Objective statements is that they are either too specific (limiting you to an "engineering management position") or too vague (doesn't everyone want a challenging opportunity with a progressive organization offering the opportunity for growth and advancement?). In addition, they can be read as self-serving because they describe what *you* want instead of suggesting what you have to offer an employer.

In contrast, an effective Career Summary allows you to position yourself as you want to be perceived and to immediately paint a picture of yourself in relation to your career goal. It is critical that this section focus on the specific skills, qualifications, and achievements of your career that are related to your current job target. Your summary is not a historical overview of your career. Rather, it is a concise, well-written, and sharp presentation of information designed to *sell* you into your next position.

This section can have various titles, such as the following:

Career Summary	Management Profile
Career Achievements	Professional Profile
Career Highlights	Professional Qualifications
Career Synopsis	Professional Summary
Executive Profile	Profile
Expertise	Summary
Highlights of Experience	Summary of Achievements
Industry Summary	Summary of Qualifications

Or, as you will see in the first format example (headline format), your summary does not have to have any title at all.

Here are five sample Career Summaries. Consider using one of these as the template for developing your Career Summary, or use them as the foundation to create your own presentation. You will also find some type of Career Summary in just about every resume included in this book.

Headline Format

MANUFACTURING MANAGER / PRODUCTION MANAGER

Production Planning / Logistics / Multisite Operations

MBA—Executive Management

MS—Manufacturing Systems & Technology

Paragraph Format

═══════════ CAREER SUMMARY ═══════════

INSURANCE INDUSTRY MANAGER with an 18-year professional career highlighted by rapid advancement and consistent achievement in market, premium, and profit growth. Outstanding qualifications in building and managing relationships with sales producers and field management teams. Deep expertise in underwriting and policy rating. PC literate with word-processing and spreadsheet applications, email, and the Internet.

Core Competencies Format

SENIOR EXECUTIVE PROFILE

Start-Up, Turnaround & High-Growth Organizations

✓ Twenty-year management career with consistent and measurable achievements in

- Revenue & Profit Growth
- Operating Cost Reductions
- Market & Customer Expansion
- Productivity & Efficiency Improvement

✓ Successful in overcoming market, technological, financial and competitive challenges to drive growth, profitability and performance improvement. Expertise includes

- Strategic Planning & Leadership
- Finance, Budgeting & Cost Management
- Marketing, Sales & New Business
- Contracts, Outsourcing & Partnerships
- New Product & New Service Launch
- Technology Optimization
- Training, Development & Team Building
- Investor & Board Relations

✓ Guest Speaker, 2012 "Leadership Innovations" Conference

✓ Winner, 2011 McKinsey Award for Leadership Excellence

Bulleted List Format

PROFESSIONAL QUALIFICATIONS

▶ **Mergers, Acquisitions, Joint Ventures, Partnerships & IPOs.** Extensive qualifications structuring, negotiating, and transacting multiparty alliances to launch new ventures, expand market penetration, leverage business and financial resources, and improve bottom-line profitability.

▶ **Strategic Planning & Business Development.** Led high-level strategic planning for start-ups, turnarounds, high-growth companies, and Fortune 1000 corporations. Equally strong experience in marketing, sales, and public relations to drive business development and expansion initiatives.

▶ **Accounting, Financial Reporting & Financial Planning.** Hands-on responsibility for managing broad-based accounting, billing, budgeting, collections, financial analysis, financial reporting, and corporate administrative affairs.

▶ **Credit, Lending & Financial Transactions.** Managed commercial financing, leasing, and credit transactions in the capital equipment, telecommunications, and computer industries. Extensive qualifications in financial review, risk assessment, and ROI/ROA/ROE performance analysis.

Category Format

PROFESSIONAL CAREER HIGHLIGHTS

EXPERIENCE	12 years as a Maintenance Director & Manager for Dow Corning and its subsidiaries
EDUCATION	Graduate Certificate in Facilities Maintenance & Engineering—University of Washington BS—Operations Management—University of Oregon
PUBLICATIONS	"Improving Workforce Productivity Through Maintenance Systems Design & Optimization," *American Manufacturing Association*, 2012 "Redesigning Maintenance Processes To Enhance Productivity," *National Facilities Maintenance Association*, 2010
AWARDS	Employee of the Year, Dow Corning, 2012 Employee of the Year, Bell Laboratories, 2007

PROFESSIONAL EXPERIENCE

Your Professional Experience is the meat of your resume—the "operations," as we discussed before. It's what gives your resume substance, meaning, and depth. It is also the section that will take you the longest to write. If you've had the same position for 10 years, how can you consolidate all you have done into one short section? If, on the opposite end of the spectrum, you have had your current position for only 11 months, how can you make it seem substantial and noteworthy? And, for all of you whose experience is in between, what do you include, how, where, and why?

These questions are not easy to answer. In fact, the most truthful response to each question is, "it depends." It depends on you, your experience, your achievements and successes, and your current career objectives.

Here are seven samples of Professional Experience sections. Review how each individual's unique background is organized and emphasized. Consider your own background when using one of these as the template or foundation for developing your Professional Experience section.

Achievement Format

Emphasizes each position, the overall scope of responsibility, and the resulting achievements.

PROFESSIONAL EXPERIENCE

Human Resources Manager (2009 to Present)
ARNOLD & SMITH DISTRIBUTION CO., INC., Moneta, VA

Recruited by principals and given complete responsibility for defining organizational culture, developing strategic HR plans, and positioning HR as a proactive partner to operations and business units nationwide. Scope of responsibility impacts 1,500 employees in 25 operating locations and 2 NYC-based administrative office complexes. Supervise a 3-person management team and 22 other HR employees.

Achievements

- Created best-in-class HR organizations, systems, processes, and practices as Arnold & Smith has experienced dramatic growth and expansion over the past 2 years. Fully integrated 150 Prestige employees, 90 US General Life Insurance employees, and others as the company has accelerated growth through acquisition.

- Introduced a focused yet flexible corporate culture to facilitate seamless integration of acquired business units, product lines, and personnel.

- Led recruitment and selection for key positions throughout the organization, including the entire legal, finance, administrative, and accounting organizations.

- Designed and implemented benefit programs, a performance-based appraisal and incentive compensation system, a system of staffing models, and a complete HR infrastructure.

- Contributed $750K in salary cost reductions through redesign of internal staffing patterns and management tiers.

Challenge, Action, and Results (CAR) Format

Emphasizes the challenge of each position, the action you took, and the results you delivered.

■ Professional Experience ■

WIP Systems International, Bulverde, Texas   2007 to Present

VICE PRESIDENT OF OPERATIONS (2009 to Present)
PLANT MANAGER (2007 to 2009)

Challenge: Plan and direct the turnaround and return to profitability of $42M technology systems manufacturer plagued with cost overrides, poor productivity, dissatisfied customers, and multimillion-dollar annual losses.

Actions: Rebuilt the entire management team, introduced advanced technologies and systems to expedite production flow, retrained all operators and supervisors, and implemented team-based work culture.

Results: ■ Achieved/surpassed all turnaround objectives and returned the operation to profitability in first year. Delivered strong and sustainable gains:

- **70%** improvement in operating efficiency.
- **250%** reduction in cycle times.
- **75%** improvement in product quality ratings.
- **100%** on-time customer delivery.

■ Replaced obsolete equipment with state-of-the-art systems, redesigned and upgraded facility, introduced stringent standards to achieve OSHA compliance, and launched in-house day-care facility (with dramatic reduction in absenteeism).

■ Restored credibility with customer representing more than $30M a year in revenues. Resolved long-standing quality and delivery issues, implemented key account management strategy, and revitalized business relationship.

■ Partnered with HP, IBM, and Dell to integrate their technologies into WIP's software applications. Received more than $200K in technology resources at no charge to the company.

■ Quoted in the National Manufacturing Association's annual publication as one of 2010's ***"Leaders in Manufacturing."***

Functional Format

Emphasizes the functional areas of responsibility within the job and associated achievements.

PROFESSIONAL EXPERIENCE

Vice President   STAR FINANCIAL, INC., Dayton, Ohio   2007 to Present

Recruited by former advisor to help manage Star Financial, a large private-equity investment firm operating as an incubator for emerging, undercapitalized, rapidly growing, and turnaround businesses requiring hands-on management and leadership. Challenged to identify strategic investment opportunities, develop innovative business models, conduct due diligence, structure transactions, and negotiate private placements.

> **New Venture Start-Up** — Founded and invested in AAA Distributors, Inc., a privately held business-to-consumer (B2C) direct-marketing company focused on continuity-based direct marketing using the Internet, direct mail, telemarketing, and television advertising. Created a portfolio of 8 consumer-based direct-marketing products, orchestrated the entire go-to-market strategy, developed best-in-class financial infrastructure and all financial systems, and launched new venture in 2008.

> **Organizational & Financial Infrastructure** — Created a unique business/finance model leveraging outsourcing to deliver operating expertise in product development, manufacturing, packaging, media placement, inbound/outbound telemarketing, fulfillment, and customer service. Operated AAA with only 14 employees and a team of 12 core business partners/vendors. Controlled costs at less than 12% of revenue.

> **Financial Growth Through Strategic Marketing** — Rolled out national direct-marketing campaign using media to drive Internet and inbound telemarketing traffic. Generated $4.3M in sales in first 6 months and secured 70,000+ web-based/directed customers (majority were continuity-based).

> **Corporate Roll-Up** — Structured and negotiated sale of AAA Distributors to a large, international direct marketer to achieve economies of scale, improve operating efficiencies, and increase net profitability.

Career Track Format

Emphasizes fast-track promotion, overall scope of responsibility, and notable achievements.

RYNCON AMERICA, INC., Dallas, Texas — 2001 to Present

Vice President — Marketing (2010 to Present)
Vice President of Sales — New Products Division (2007 to 2010)
Sales Director (2005 to 2007)
National Accounts Manager (2003 to 2005)
Sales Associate (2001 to 2003)

Fast-track promotion through a series of increasingly responsible positions to current role as Vice President of Marketing Operations Worldwide. Credited with building a global marketing organization that led division to sixfold revenue growth in just 4 years. Recruited and developed a talented team of sales and marketing professionals who now serve as Ryncon's core marketing and sales management staff.

☑ Built division from $20M in annual revenues in 2002 to $120+M in 2010.

☑ Achieved #1 market position in North America and maintained position for 3 consecutive years.

☑ Surpassed all profit goals for 10 consecutive years, averaging 12%–15% annual profit growth.

☑ Conceived and implemented customer-focus strategy to drive long-term product development and service delivery. Currently maintain a 97+% customer-satisfaction rating.

☑ Outpaced competition as the first in the industry to enter the Northern Canadian, Puerto Rican, and Caribbean markets. Currently project new-market revenues of more than $20M by year 2.

Project Highlights Format

Places emphasis on the specific projects, their scope of responsibility, and their associated achievements.

MOLTEN METAL TECHNOLOGY *($650M metal products design & manufacturing company)*

PROJECT MANAGER: 2001 to Present

Travel to Molten facilities nationwide to orchestrate a series of special projects and assignments. Delivered all projects on time and within budget for 10 consecutive years. Recent projects include:

- **Recycling Facility Development & Construction** ($12.8M). Co-led fast-track design and construction team bringing project from concept to completion in just 16 months. **RESULT:** *Built an environmentally safe and regulation-compliant facility at 12% under projected cost.*

- **Capital Improvement Project** ($6.2M). Led $50+ million in capital improvements with individual project costs at $50,000 to $750,000. **RESULT:** *Upgraded facilities, production lines, technical competencies, product staging, and distribution areas for a better than 22% increase in productivity.*

- **SAP Implementation Project** ($1.8M). Led 12-person technology and support team in a massive SAP implementation project impacting virtually the entire facility and workforce. **RESULT:** *Created a totally integrated technology environment linking inventory, production planning, quality, cost accounting, and other core manufacturing and support functions.*

- **OSHA Compliance Project** ($500K). Led yearlong project to identify noncompliance issues and initiate appropriate remedial activity. **RESULT:** *Passed 2010 OSHA inspection with zero findings.*

- **Annual Shutdown & Maintenance Project** ($100K). Planned, scheduled, and directed annual plant shutdown and maintenance programs for 3 facilities, involving as many as 100 craftsmen. **RESULT:** *Restored all facilities to full operation within stringent time constraints.*

Skills-Based Format

Puts initial focus on specific skills rather than when and where they were used. Helpful in bringing less-current skill sets to the forefront and avoiding emphasis on employment gaps.

FOUNDER / GENERAL MANAGER — Law Offices of Earl W. Hadley   2000 to Present

Founded specialized legal practice providing corporate advisory services to CEOs, COOs, and other senior executives across a broad range of industries and on a broad range of business issues. Built new venture from start-up to 3 locations and 12 employees. Achieved and maintained profitability for 12 consecutive years. Excellent reputation for ethical performance and integrity.

Serve in the capacity of a **Senior Operating Executive/General Counsel** to client companies, providing hands-on leadership in:

– Strategic Planning & Vision	– Operations Management	– Human Resources
– Policies & Procedures	– Cost Control & Avoidance	– Technology
– Growth & Expansion	– Process Design & Analysis	– Capital Assets
– Market Analysis & Positioning	– Banking & Corporate Finance	– Executive Compensation
– Acquisitions & Valuations	– Asset/Stock Purchase Agreements	– A/R & Collections
– Letter of Credit & Intent	– Licensing & Leasing Agreements	– Bankruptcy/Turnaround

Clients range from start-up ventures to $200M corporations engaged in software development, high-tech manufacturing, industrial manufacturing, consumer products, heavy equipment, transportation, automotive and marine dealerships, services, and professional trades.

Firm responsibilities include: As **General Manager,** direct all daily and long-term business planning and management functions, staffing, technology systems, and all business process/infrastructure affairs. As **Marketing & Business Development Executive,** lead client development, networking, marketing, and client relationship management. As **Principal Attorney,** manage all legal affairs and client representation.

Experience Format

Briefly emphasizes specific highlights of each position. Best used in conjunction with a detailed Career Summary.

EXPERIENCE SUMMARY———————————————————————

Office Manager, WEST-QUEST TECHNOLOGIES, Lewisburg, ID — 2008 to Present

- ❑ Implemented cost savings that slashed $150,000 from annual operating costs.
- ❑ Selected and directed implementation of new PC network with Ethernet technology.
- ❑ Recruited, trained, and supervised 12 administrative and office-support personnel in two operating locations.

Office Manager, Century Technologies, Ames, IA — 2005 to 2008

- ❑ Independently managed all office, administrative, and clerical functions for a small technology start-up venture in the "train-the-trainer" market.
- ❑ Designed all internal recordkeeping, reporting, accounting, project-management, and client-management systems and processes.
- ❑ Selected office equipment and technology, negotiated leases, and coordinated installation.
- ❑ Represented owners at local business and Chamber of Commerce meetings/events.

Assistant Manager, Greenwalt Architectural Systems, Ames, IA — 2002 to 2005

- ❑ Worked with owners and architects to facilitate project completion by coordinating deadlines, deliverables, and client communications.
- ❑ Implemented PC-based project-tracking and accounting systems.
- ❑ Coordinated all purchasing and inventory-management functions for office supplies and design materials.

EDUCATION AND CERTIFICATIONS

Your Education section should include college, certifications, credentials, licenses, registrations, and continuing education. If any are particularly notable, be sure to highlight them prominently in your Education section or bring them to the top in your Career Summary (as demonstrated by the headline format in the previous section on writing career summaries).

The following five sample Education sections illustrate a variety of ways to organize and format this information.

Executive Education Format

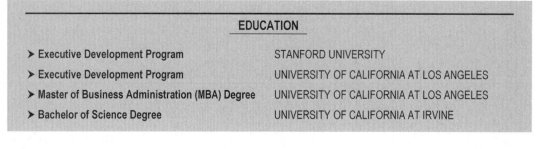

EDUCATION	
➤ Executive Development Program	STANFORD UNIVERSITY
➤ Executive Development Program	UNIVERSITY OF CALIFORNIA AT LOS ANGELES
➤ Master of Business Administration (MBA) Degree	UNIVERSITY OF CALIFORNIA AT LOS ANGELES
➤ Bachelor of Science Degree	UNIVERSITY OF CALIFORNIA AT IRVINE

Academic Credentials Format

EDUCATION: **M.S., Management Science,** University of Colorado, 2004
B.S., Industrial Engineering, University of Nevada, 1997

Highlights of Continuing Professional Education:

▸ Organizational Management & Leadership, Colorado Leadership Association, 2010

▸ Industrial Engineering Technology in Today's Modern Manufacturing Organization, Purdue University, 2009

▸ SAP Implementation & Optimization, American Society for Quality Control, 2007

▸ Conflict Resolution & Violence Management in the Workplace, Institute for Workplace Safety, 2003

Certifications Format

Technical Certifications and Degrees

Nurse Executive-Board Certified (NE-BC), Helen Keller School of Nursing & Health Care Administration, 2006

Bachelor of Science in Nursing (BSN), Missouri State University at Columbia, 2003

Certificate in Advanced Cardiac Life Support (ACLS), State of Missouri, 2003

Certificate in Basic Cardiac Life Support (BCLS), State of Tennessee, 2001

Nondegree Format

TRAINING & EDUCATION

UNIVERSITY OF TOLEDO, Toledo, Ohio

BS Candidate—Management & Administration (Senior class status)

UNIVERSITY OF MICHIGAN, Ann Arbor, Michigan

Dual Majors in Management & Human Resource Administration (2 years)

GRADUATE, 100+ hours of continuing professional education through the University of Illinois, University of Michigan, and University of Wisconsin.

No-College Format

PROFESSIONAL DEVELOPMENT

Management Training & Development	KELLOGG SCHOOL OF MANAGEMENT
Leadership Excellence	KELLOGG SCHOOL OF MANAGEMENT
Supervisory Training	CONNELLY COMMUNITY COLLEGE
Management Communications	PACE LEADERSHIP TRAINING

THE "EXTRAS"

The primary focus of your resume is on information (most likely, your professional experience and academic credentials) that is directly related to your career goals.

However, you also should include things that will distinguish you from other candidates and clearly demonstrate your value to a prospective employer. Often these "extras" get the interviews.

Following is a list of the other categories you might include in your resume, depending on your particular experience and your current career objectives. Review the information. If it's pertinent to you, use the samples for formatting your own data. Remember, however, that if something is truly impressive, you might want to include it in your Career Summary at the beginning of your resume in order to draw even more attention to it. Information included in the Career Summary section does not need to be repeated at the end of your resume.

Honors and Awards

If you have won honors and awards, you can either include them in a separate section on your resume or integrate them into the Education or Professional Experience section, whichever is most appropriate. If you choose to include them in a separate section, consider this format:

❖ Winner, 2011 **"Sales Leadership"** award from American Sales Association for outstanding contributions to sales revenues, new market penetration, and new business development.

❖ **"Corporate Sales Manager of the Year,"** ISP Systems, Inc., 2010

❖ **"Sales Manager of the Year,"** ISP Systems, 2007

❖ **"Sales Trainer of the Year,"** Delco Systems, 2005

❖ **Summa Cum Laude Graduate,** Yale University, 1997

Public Speaking

Experts are the ones who are invited to give public presentations at conferences, seminars, workshops, training programs, symposia, and other events. So if you have public-speaking experience, others must consider you an expert. Be sure to include this impressive information in your resume. Here's one way to present it:

• Keynote Speaker, **"Advancing Technology Innovation in the Workplace,"** 2010 National Association on Technology Excellence Conference, New York

• Panel Presenter, **"Emerging Multimedia Technologies & Applications,"** 2009 National Association of Information Technology Executives, Dallas

• Session Leader, **"Optimizing PC Technologies,"** 2007 Information Managers Association Annual Conference, Philadelphia

• Keynote Speaker, **"Technology for the Entrepreneur,"** 2006 Entrepreneurs World Conference, Chicago

Publications

If you're published, you must be an expert (or at least most people will think so). Just as with your public-speaking engagements, be sure to include your publications. They validate your knowledge, qualifications, and credibility. Publications can include books, articles, online website content, manuals, and other written documents.

Here's an example:

- Author, "Executive Compensation Systems," *Society of Human Resource Management Annual Conference Proceedings,* 2011

- Author, "International Hiring, Employment & Retention," *Society of Human Resource Management Journal,* 2010

- Author, "Expatriate Employment for U.S. Corporations," *IBM Corporation Employee Bulletin,* March 2009

- Coauthor, "Hiring for Long-Term Retention," *American Management Association Journal,* April 2008

Technology Skills and Qualifications

If you are a manager or executive in a field unrelated to technology, you might just include a brief statement in your career summary that communicates you are PC proficient, as in this example:

PC proficient with Microsoft Word, Access, Excel, and PowerPoint.

However, if you're employed in the technology industry or have unique technology qualifications, you'll want to include a separate section with this information (if it's relevant to your current career objectives). You'll also have to consider placement of this section in your resume. If the positions for which you are applying require strong technical skills, we would recommend you insert this section immediately after your Career Summary (or as a part thereof). If, on the other hand, your technical skills are a plus rather than a specific requirement, the preferred placement is after your Education section.

Here are two different samples of ways to format and present your technical qualifications:

TECHNOLOGY PROFILE	
Operating Systems:	Windows 7/XP, Novell NetWare, Linux
Protocols/Networks:	TCP/IP, NetBIOS, IPX/SPX
Hardware:	Hard drives, printers, scanners, USB flash drives, hubs
Software:	ARCserve, FileMaker Pro, Microsoft Office, Symantec pcAnywhere

TECHNOLOGY SKILLS SUMMARY		
ARCserve	Microsoft Exchange Server	SAP
DRP	Microsoft Office	Symantec pcAnywhere
FileMaker Pro	MRP	TCP/IP
IPX/SPX	Novell NetWare	Windows 7/XP

Teaching and Training Experience

Many managers and executives also teach or train at colleges, universities, technical schools, and other organizations in addition to training that they might offer "on the job." If you have this type of experience, you will want to include it on your resume. If someone hires you (paid or unpaid) to speak to an audience, it communicates a strong message about your skills, qualifications, knowledge, and expertise. Here's a format you might use to present that information:

- **Faculty,** Department of Finance & Economics, Morgan State University, 2009 to Present. Teach graduate-level studies in Economics, Economic Theory, Advanced Statistics, and Management Communications.

- **Adjunct Faculty,** Department of Economics, Coppin State University, 2008 to Present. Teach Microeconomics and Macroeconomics to third- and fourth-year students.

- **Guest Lecturer,** Department of Business & Economics, Purdue University, 2006 to Present. Provide semiannual, daylong lecture series on the integration of economic theory into the corporate workplace.

- **Lecturer,** Maryland State University, 2006 to 2008. Taught "Principles of Management" to first-year college students.

Committees and Task Forces

Many managers and executives serve on committees, task forces, and other special project teams either as part of, or in addition to, their full-time responsibilities. Again, this type of information further strengthens your credibility, qualifications, and perceived value to a prospective employer. Consider a format such as this:

- **Chairperson,** 2010–11 Corporate Planning & Reorganization Task Force
- **Member,** 2009–10 Corporate Committee on Global Market Expansion & Positioning
- **Member,** 2008–09 Study Team on "Redesigning Corporate Training Systems to Maximize Employee Productivity"
- **Chairperson,** 2005–07 Committee on "Safety & Regulatory Compliance in the Workplace"

Professional Affiliations

If you are a member of any educational, professional, or leadership associations, be sure to include that information on your resume. It communicates a message of professionalism, a desire to stay current with the industry, and a strong professional network. If you have held leadership positions within these organizations, be sure to include them. The following example shows a good way to present this information.

AMERICAN MANAGEMENT ASSOCIATION
Professional Member (2001 to Present)
Professional Development Committee Member (2007 to 2011)
Recruitment Committee Member (2005 to 2007)

AMERICAN HEALTH CARE ASSOCIATION
Associate Member (2006 to Present)
Professional Member (1997 to 2006)
Technology Task Force Member (2005 to 2007)

INTERNATIONAL HEALTH CARE SOCIETY
Professional Member (2008 to Present)
Training Committee Member (2008 to Present)

Civic Affiliations

Civic affiliations are fine to include if they

- Are with a notable organization,

- Demonstrate leadership experience, or

- Might be of interest to a prospective employer.

However, affiliations such as treasurer of your local condo association and singer with your church choir are not generally of value in marketing your qualifications. Here's an example of what to include:

Volunteer Chairperson, United Way of America—Detroit Chapter, 2007 to Present

President, Lambert Valley Conservation District, 2006 to Present

Treasurer, Habitat for Humanity—Detroit Chapter, 2005 to 2006

Personal Information

We do not recommend that you include such personal information as birth date, marital status, number of children, and related data. However, there might be instances when personal information is appropriate. If this information will give you a competitive advantage or answer unspoken questions about your background, then by all means include it. Here's an example:

☑ Born in Argentina. U.S. Permanent Residency Status since 1992.

☑ Fluent in English, Spanish, and Portuguese.

☑ Competitive triathlete. Top-5 finisher, 1998 Midwest Triathlon and 2004 Des Moines Triathlon.

Note in the preceding example that the job seeker is multilingual. Although this fact is listed under Personal Information in this example, such a critical selling point should also be mentioned in the Career Summary.

Consolidating the Extras

Sometimes you have so many extra categories at the end of your resume, each with only a handful of lines, that spacing becomes a problem. You certainly don't want to have to make your resume a page longer to accommodate five lines, nor do you want the "extras" to overwhelm the primary sections of your resume. Yet you believe the information is important and should be included. Or perhaps you have a few small bits of information that you think are important but don't merit an entire section. In these situations, consider consolidating the information using the following format. You'll save space; avoid overemphasizing individual items; and present a professional, distinguished appearance.

PROFESSIONAL PROFILE	
Education	BSEE, Florida State University
Technologies	MS Office Suite, SAP ERP, MRP, DRP, LAN, WAN
Affiliations	International Association of Electrical Inspectors American Electrical Association Florida Association of Electrical & Electronic Engineers
Public Speaking	Speaker, IEEE Conference, Dallas, 2009 Presenter, AEA National Convention, San Diego, 2007 Panelist, APICS National Conference, Miami, 2005
Languages	Fluent in English, Spanish, and German
Additional	Co-Chair, Education Committee, Tampa Technology Association Eagle Scout and Boy Scout Troop Leader Available for relocation worldwide

Writing Tips, Techniques, and Important Lessons

At this point, you've done a lot of reading, probably taken some notes, and highlighted samples that appeal to you. Now you're ready to plunge into writing your resume. To make this task as easy as possible, we've compiled some "insider" techniques that we've used in our professional resume-writing practices. We learned these techniques the hard way—through years of experience! We know they work; they will make the writing process easier, faster, and more enjoyable for you.

GET IT DOWN—THEN POLISH AND PERFECT IT

Don't be too concerned with making your resume "perfect" the first time around. It's far better to move fairly swiftly through the process, getting the basic information organized and on paper (or on-screen), instead of agonizing about the perfect phrase or ideal formatting. Once you've completed a draft, we think you'll be surprised at how close to "final" it is, and you'll be able to edit, tighten, and improve formatting fairly quickly.

WRITE YOUR RESUME FROM THE BOTTOM UP

We guarantee that the process of writing your resume will be much easier if you follow this "bottom-up" strategy:

- **Start with the easy things**—Education, Technology, Professional Affiliations, Public Speaking, Publications, and any other extras you want to include. These items require little thought and can be completed in just a few minutes.

- **Write short job descriptions for your older positions, the ones you held years ago.** Be very brief and focus on highlights such as rapid promotion; achievements; innovations; professional honors; or employment with well-respected, well-known companies.

Once you've completed this, look at how much you've written in a short period of time! Then move on to the next step:

- **Write the job descriptions for your most recent positions.** This part will take a bit longer than the other sections you have written. Remember to focus on the overall scope of your responsibility, major projects and initiatives, and significant achievements. Tell your reader what you did and how well you did it. You can use any of the formats recommended earlier in this chapter, or you can create something that is unique to you and your career.

Now, see how far along you are? Your resume is 90 percent complete with only one small section left to do:

- **Write your Career Summary.** Before you start writing, remember your objective for this section. The summary should not simply rehash your previous experience. Rather, it should highlight the skills and qualifications you have that are most closely related to your current career objective(s). The summary is intended to capture the reader's attention and "sell" your expertise.

That's it! You're done. Now, on to the next tip.

INCLUDE NOTABLE OR PROMINENT "EXTRA" STUFF IN YOUR CAREER SUMMARY

Remember the "extras" sections that are normally at the bottom of your resume? If this information is particularly significant or prominent—you won a notable award, spoke at an international conference, secured a patent for a new technology, or wrote an article for a respected industry publication—you might want to include it at the top of your resume in your Career Summary. Remember, you write the Career Summary section to distinguish yourself from the crowd of other qualified candidates. As such, if you've accomplished anything that clearly demonstrates your knowledge, expertise, and credibility, consider moving it to your Career Summary for added attention. Refer to the sample Career Summaries earlier in this chapter for examples.

USE RESUME SAMPLES TO GET IDEAS FOR CONTENT, FORMAT, AND ORGANIZATION

This book is just one of many resources where you can review the resumes of other managers and executives to help you in formulating your strategy, writing the text, and formatting your resume—these resources are published precisely for that reason. You don't have to struggle alone. Rather, use all the available resources at your disposal.

Be forewarned, however, that finding a resume that fits your life and career to a "T" is unlikely. It's more likely that you will use "some of this sample" and "some of that sample" to create a resume that is uniquely "you."

INCLUDE DATES IF YOU ARE YOUNGER THAN 50

Unless you are over age 50, we recommend that you date your work experience and education. Without dates, your resume becomes vague and difficult for the typical hiring manager or recruiter to interpret. What's more, it often communicates the message that you are trying to hide something. Maybe you haven't worked in two years, maybe you held each of your last three positions for only a few months, or maybe you never graduated from college. Being vague and creating a resume that is difficult to read will, inevitably, lead to uncertainty and a quick toss into the "not-interested" pile of candidates. By including the dates of your experience and your education, you create a clean and concise picture that one can easily follow to track your career progression.

Early Work Experience Dates

If you are over age 50, dating your early positions must be an individual decision. On the one hand, you do not want to age yourself out of consideration by including dates from the 1970s and early 1980s. On the other hand, those positions might be worth including for any one of a number of reasons. Further, if you omit those early dates, you might feel as though you are misrepresenting yourself (or lying) to a prospective employer.

To overcome those concerns while still including your early experience, create a separate category titled "Previous Professional Experience" in which you summarize your earliest employment. You can tailor this statement to emphasize just what is most important about that experience.

If you want to focus on the reputation of your past employers, include a statement such as this one:

- Previous experience includes mid- to senior-level management positions with IBM, Dell, and Xerox.

If you want to communicate the rapid progression of your career, consider this example:

- Promoted rapidly through a series of increasingly responsible operations management positions with Zyler Form Molding, Inc.

If you want to emphasize your early career achievements, include a statement such as this:

> • Earned six promotions in three years with Kodak based on out-standing performance in revenue growth, market development, and customer retention.

By including any one of the preceding paragraphs, under the heading "Previous Professional Experience," you are clearly communicating to your reader that your employment history dates further back than the dates you have indicated on your resume. In turn, you are being 100 percent aboveboard and not misrepresenting yourself or your career. What's more, you're focusing on the success, achievement, and prominence of your earliest assignments.

Education Section Dates

If you are over age 50, we generally do not recommend that you date your education or college degrees. Simply include the degree and the university with no date. Why exclude yourself from consideration by immediately presenting the fact that you earned your college degree in 1969, 1976, or 1982—possibly before the hiring manager was born? Remember, the goal of your resume is to share the highlights of your career and open doors for interviews. It is *not* to give your entire life story. As such, it is not mandatory to date your college degree.

However, if you use this strategy, be aware that the reader is likely to assume that there is *some* gap between when your education ended and your work experience started. Therefore, if you choose to begin your chronological work history with your first job out of college, omitting your graduation date could actually backfire, because the reader may assume you have experience that predates your first job. In this case, it's best either to include your graduation date or omit dates of earliest experience, using the summary strategy discussed above.

NEVER INCLUDE SALARY HISTORY OR SALARY REQUIREMENTS ON YOUR RESUME

Your resume is *not* the correct forum for a salary discussion. First of all, you should never provide salary information unless a company has requested that information and you choose to comply. (Studies show that employers will look at your resume anyway, so you might choose not to respond to this request, thereby avoiding pricing yourself out of the job or locking yourself into a lower salary than the job is worth.)

When contacting *recruiters,* however, we recommend that you do provide salary information, but only in your cover letter. With recruiters you want to "put all of your cards on the table" and help them make an appropriate placement by providing information about your current salary and salary objectives. For example, you could write, "Be advised that my current compensation is $170,000 annually and that I am interested in a position starting at a minimum of $200,000 per year." Or if you would prefer to be a little less specific, you might write, "My annual compensation over the past three years has averaged $150,000+."

Finally, in some instances you will not have the option for omitting salary information. A good example is an online application that requires you to submit your salary history and/or salary requirements along with your resume. In that case, be truthful and know that all candidates will be revealing similar information.

ALWAYS REMEMBER THAT YOU ARE SELLING

As we have discussed over and over throughout these first two chapters, resume writing is sales. Understand and appreciate the value you bring to a prospective employer, and then communicate that value by focusing on your achievements. Companies don't want to hire just anyone; they want to hire "the" someone who will make a difference. Show them that you are *that* candidate.

CHAPTER 3

Producing Your Resume for Online and Offline Distribution: Printed, Electronic, and Web Resumes

If you're like most job seekers (and professional resume writers), you will have worked long and hard to write a powerful resume that proudly showcases your career, your promotions, your achievements, and other highlights of your professional life. You've probably reviewed and edited your resume over and over, making certain that the wording is accurate and positions you precisely for your targeted career objectives.

Your next challenge is the design, layout, and presentation of your resume. It's not enough that your resume reads well; your resume also must have just the right look and feel for the right audience. As such, you must make a few choices and decisions about what your final resume presentation will look like.

In decades past, this would have been only a brief discussion during which we would have told you how important it was to use a "nice" font and to leave plenty of white space so that hiring managers and recruiters could easily peruse your resume. Resume production and distribution were easy. You typed (maybe even word processed!) your resume; printed it on white, ivory, or light gray paper; put it into an envelope; and mailed it. There were few decisions to be made. Even with the introduction of the fax machine, the process was largely the same.

Today's job search looks nothing like it did even a decade ago, because the Internet and e-mail have forever changed how job seekers distribute resumes and look for jobs! These technological tools now provide job seekers with a variety of methods to distribute their resumes.

How you produce your resume will depend entirely on how you will be using and distributing it. Answer these questions:

1. Will you be e-mailing your resume to colleagues and network contacts?

2. Will you be e-mailing your resume in response to specific employment opportunities?

3. Will you be posting your resume on various job boards?

4. Will you be pasting sections of your resume into online employment applications?

5. Will you be uploading your entire resume into a recruiter's database?

For most of you reading this book, the answer to those five questions is yes. Yes, you will be e-mailing, posting, pasting, and uploading as you manage a combination of both online and offline resume distribution efforts. As such, you will need at least two different versions of your resume: one for online use and one for offline use.

The Three Types of Resumes

In today's job search and employment world, there are three basic types of resumes:

- The printed resume (Word and PDF files)
- The electronic resume (text files)
- The Web resume

The following sections give details on how to prepare each type of resume and when you will most often use it.

You will need, at minimum, both a printed and an electronic resume. This is true for all managers and executives, whether you are a retail manager, marketing director, or vice president of information technology. In fact, if you work in IT or for a technology company, you should consider creating a Web resume in order to demonstrate your technical expertise and give yourself a competitive edge over others in the employment market.

Different employers have different preferences regarding resumes. Some prospective employers will request a printed copy of your resume, a copy that you might actually mail to them. More often, companies will ask you to e-mail your resume, at which point the recipient might print a copy and/or import it into the company database. Finally, other organizations will ask you to upload your resume (and, sometimes, cover letter) into their online applicant tracking and candidate management systems. Bottom line, today's job seeker needs both a printed resume and an electronic resume to manage a successful job search and career marketing campaign.

The Printed Resume

The printed resume is what we all know as the "traditional resume," the one that looks good on paper and might include graphic elements such as borders or shaded boxes. This is the version that you mail to a recruiter, take to an interview, use at networking events, and forward by mail and/or e-mail in response to a job posting. It's rare (and becoming more so with each passing year) that organizations would ask you to fax your resume to them. Faxing is, largely, a technology of the past when it comes to efficient job search and career management.

THE PURPOSE OF A PRINTED RESUME

When preparing a printed resume, your objective is to create a sharp, professional, and visually attractive presentation that will stand out from the crowd of other candidates' resumes without going "over the top." A distinctive typestyle such as Tahoma, Verdana, Calibri, Georgia, or Arial Narrow and a few bold lines or boxes can transform a resume from blah to brilliant! If you can make someone notice your resume, you'll instantly move your candidacy forward.

Always keep in mind that a few pieces of paper convey the first impression of you to a potential employer or recruiter, and that first impression goes a long way. Either it's sharp and distinctive, or it's lost in the crowd. Only you can make that difference, and you must. Never be fooled into thinking that just because you have the ultimate employment history and career path that the visual presentation of your resume does not matter. It is a key factor in elevating you above the crowd of other candidates, and that's an important step in the job search process.

E-MAIL ATTACHMENTS

Most likely, the vast majority of resumes you distribute will be through e-mail, so pay special attention to the following information.

E-mailing is so easy. Simply attach the Microsoft Word version of your resume to your e-mail message and you're set. Because the vast majority of businesses use Microsoft Word, this is the most acceptable format and will present the fewest difficulties in "translation" when attached. Be certain that you save and send your resume in the .doc format, not the .docx format that is standard with newer computer systems. You certainly don't want to send a resume that can't be opened or read by the recipient, and older systems cannot read .docx files.

If you do have a resume with a strong design component, graphics, charts, tables, or other visuals, you might prefer to attach a PDF (portable document format) version of your resume to ensure 100 percent integrity of the presentation. Even if you don't have the capability to create PDF files on your computer, you'll find it's quick, easy, and free to do so by using readily available online resources such as BCL Technologies' PDF Online at www.pdfonline.com.

By using a PDF file, you're certain that your resume appears exactly as you created it. The downside to PDF files is that they cannot be read into a company's resume-storage system unless they are printed and scanned in. In today's fast-paced world of job search and hiring, that step probably will not happen. Therefore, we recommend that you use Microsoft Word .doc files as your everyday standard and use the PDF format only when absolutely necessary.

Be sure you take the time to test your resume by e-mailing it, in .doc and/or PDF formats, to several friends or colleagues. Ask them to both view it and print it on their systems to be sure that everything at their end looks like it does at your end. You could bypass this step if you're sending a PDF file, but why would you? It's always a good strategy to test everything before you let it go "live"!

The Electronic Resume

An electronic resume is a plain-text version of your printed resume, stripped of all of the design, formatting, and other enhancements that you've used to make your resume sharp, attractive, and distinctive. All of the things that you would normally do to make your printed resume look attractive—bold print, italics, multiple columns, eye-catching font, and more—are stripped away to create a document that can be easily read and/or scanned.

UNDERSTANDING THE USES FOR AN ELECTRONIC RESUME

A plain-text resume makes professional resume writers cringe, but it does have several important uses that you will, most likely, encounter during your job search campaign:

- You can easily copy and paste the plain-text version into online job applications and resume databases, with no concern that formatting glitches will cause confusion. In today's technology-driven job search and employment landscape, this will be something you will do frequently when reaching out to both companies and recruiters. Don't make the mistake of copying and pasting your Word file into these applications! Often the formatting will be lost and/or presented incorrectly, and your information might not be accurately communicated.

- You can paste the plain-text version of your resume into the body of an e-mail message rather than sending your resume as an attachment. Some people are hesitant to open attachments from people they don't know, and you might encounter that situation. If so, the text file comes in handy and avoids any potential formatting problems.

- Although unattractive, the plain-text version is 100 percent scannable. It's rare anymore for a company or a recruiter to ask you to e-mail a scannable version of your resume. However, you never know when the situation may arise, and at least you'll be prepared.

CREATING A TEXT FILE

To create a plain-text version of your resume, follow these simple steps:

1. Open the Word file of your resume and create a new version using the Save As feature. Select Text Only, Plain Text, or ASCII in the Save As option box.

2. Close the new file.

3. Reopen the file, and you'll find that your resume has been automatically reformatted into the Courier font, all formatting has been removed, and the text is left-justified.

4. Review the resume carefully and fix any formatting "glitches"—of which there will probably be quite a few! Pay special attention to the following formatting recommendations:

   - Position your name, and nothing else, on the top line of the resume.

   - Replace odd characters that may have been inserted to take the place of "curly" quotes, dashes, accents, or other nonstandard symbols.

   - Feel free to use *common* abbreviations (for instance, *B.S.* or *BS* for Bachelor of Science degree). But when in doubt, spell it out.

   - Eliminate graphics, borders, and horizontal lines.

   - Avoid columns and tables, although a simple two-column listing can be read without difficulty.

   - Spell out symbols such as % and &.

   - If necessary, add extra blank lines to improve readability. Length doesn't really matter because people see the entire document and not a certain number of pages.

   - Consider adding horizontal dividers to break the resume into sections so that people can easily skim and review the document. You can use any standard typewriter symbols (such as *, -, (,), =, +, ^, or #).

To illustrate what you can expect when creating these versions of your own resume, the following figures show the same resume in a printed Word format and an electronic (text) format.

Sidney Lowenstein

24 Sharon Lane, Northford, CT 06472 • Home (203) 555-7039 • Cell (203) 555-9488 • s.lowenstein@mail.com

Operations Manager

Rapid Growth & Turnaround Operations • Multisite / Multistate Facilities

Innovative and energetic manager with proven ability to tackle diverse challenges and deliver strong operational gains. Proven talent for both strategic planning and results-oriented execution; experience includes plant construction, acquisition integration, and process improvement. Demonstrated ability to interact with diverse individuals, from the boardroom to the production floor, and to effectively manage relationships with Fortune 500 customers and multiple government agencies (DOT, EPA, county and city government) in relation to environmentally sensitive manufacturing practices.

A track record of leading operations and teams to consistent growth in revenue, profitability, and productivity.

Professional Experience

ELM CITY BARREL COMPANY, New Haven, CT   2010–Present

Operations Manager

Manage daily operations for $14 million manufacturer and distributor of reconditioned steel and plastic drums and IBC containers for industrial customers. Oversee 12 direct and 148 indirect reports in Manufacturing, Transportation, Environmental, and Maintenance; work collaboratively with Finance, Customer Service, and Administrative areas. Manage labor and union relations; report to President.

- Drove turnaround effort that led to $600 thousand reduction in operating loss in just 1 year.
- Increased production 30% and stabilized volume inconsistencies.
- Implemented safety procedures that reduced accidents by 60% and led to 7-year low in lost-time accidents.
- Spearheaded massive cleanup of company sites to improve appearance, environmental compliance, and relations with government and environmental agencies. Successfully passed all environmental audits.
- Increased customer base, acquiring new customers such as Sherwin Williams and BF Goodrich primarily through improved environmental compliance and production consistency.

ACME CONTAINER CORP., Hamden, CT   2002–2010

VP Operations, 2005–2010 • **Operations Manager,** 2002–2005

Directed all operating areas—Transportation, Environmental, Quality Control, Plant Operations, Procurement, Customer Relations, Union Relations, R&D—for $18 million, 5-plant, multistate drum manufacturer/distributor. Oversaw 5 operations managers supervising 120 employees.

- Grew business from $12.8 million to $18 million revenues and EBITDA from 1% to 12.3%.
- Drove the development of a new state-of-the-art facility built on existing site; managed on-time construction while maintaining full production.
- Reduced operating costs $520 thousand annually through manpower reductions, outsourcing of noncore functions, increased throughput, and reduced cost-per-unit.
- Designed and set up an innovative plastics cleaning line, one of the most efficient in the country. Reduced space required from 4,000 to 500 sq. ft. (an 87% reduction) and cut per-piece costs from industry-average $5.00 to $3.50 using an environmentally friendly process.
- Played a key role in the acquisition and integration of 2 companies.

PRIOR PROFESSIONAL EXPERIENCE

- **Operations Manager,** Worldwide Distribution Partners, New Haven, CT; progressed steadily from route driver through customer service and assistant management roles to operations leadership position.

Education

B.A. Psychology/Business Minor   Quinnipiac University, Hamden, CT

The printed Word version of an operations manager's resume.

```
SIDNEY LOWENSTEIN
24 Sharon Lane, Northford, CT 06472
Home (203) 555-7039 - Cell (203) 555-9488 - s.lowenstein@mail.com
==========================================
OPERATIONS MANAGER
Rapid Growth and Turnaround Operations * Multisite / Multistate Facilities

Innovative and energetic manager with proven ability to tackle diverse challenges and
deliver strong operational gains. Proven talent for both strategic planning and results-
oriented execution; experience includes plant construction, acquisition integration, and
process improvement. Demonstrated ability to interact with diverse individuals, from the
boardroom to the production floor, and to effectively manage relationships with Fortune
500 customers and multiple government agencies (DOT, EPA, county and city government) in
relation to environmentally sensitive manufacturing practices.

A track record of leading operations and teams to consistent growth in revenue,
profitability, and productivity.
==========================================
PROFESSIONAL EXPERIENCE
ELM CITY BARREL COMPANY, New Haven, CT, 2010-Present
Operations Manager
Manage daily operations for $14 million manufacturer and distributor of reconditioned
steel and plastic drums and IBC containers for industrial customers. Oversee 12 direct
and 148 indirect reports in Manufacturing, Transportation, Environmental, and
Maintenance; work collaboratively with Finance, Customer Service, and Administrative
areas. Manage labor and union relations; report to President.

* Drove turnaround effort that led to $600 thousand reduction in operating loss in just 1
year.
* Increased production 30% and stabilized volume inconsistencies.
* Implemented safety procedures that reduced accidents by 60% and led to 7-year low in
lost-time accidents.
* Spearheaded massive cleanup of company sites to improve appearance, environmental
compliance, and relations with government and environmental agencies. Successfully passed
all environmental audits.
* Increased customer base, acquiring new customers such as Sherwin Williams and BF
Goodrich primarily through improved environmental compliance and production consistency.

ACME CONTAINER CORP., Hamden, CT, 2002-2010
VP Operations, 2005-2010 - Operations Manager, 2002-2005
Directed all operating areas--Transportation, Environmental, Quality Control, Plant
Operations, Procurement, Customer Relations, Union Relations, R&D--for $18 million, 5-
plant, multistate drum manufacturer/distributor. Oversaw 5 operations managers
supervising 120 employees.

* Grew business from $12.8 million to $18 million revenues and EBITDA from 1% to 12.3%.
* Drove the development of a new state-of-the-art facility built on existing site;
managed on-time construction while maintaining full production.
* Reduced operating costs $520 thousand annually through manpower reductions, outsourcing
of noncore functions, increased throughput, and reduced cost-per-unit.
* Designed and set up an innovative plastics cleaning line, one of the most efficient in
the country. Reduced space required from 4,000 to 500 sq. ft. (87% reduction) and cut
per-piece costs from industry-average $5.00 to $3.50 using an environmentally friendly
process.
* Played a key role in the acquisition and integration of 2 companies.

PRIOR PROFESSIONAL EXPERIENCE
* Operations Manager, Worldwide Distribution Partners, New Haven, CT; progressed steadily
from route driver through customer service and assistant management roles to operations
leadership position.
==========================================
EDUCATION
B.A. Psychology/Business Minor - Quinnipiac University, Hamden, CT
```

The electronic version of an operations manager's resume.

The Web Resume

The newest evolution in resumes combines the visually pleasing quality of the printed resume with the technological ease of the electronic resume and the amazing capabilities of the Web. Instead of seeing only the information you can include on your Word or plain-text resume, the full-fledged Web resume is richer and deeper. It can be interactive and visually exciting as well.

The Reasons for a Web Resume

Why should you develop a Web resume? Nowadays, employers routinely search the Web for information about candidates at every stage of the selection process, from early identification of prospective employees to reference and character checks before hire.

Thus, it makes sense for you to know what employers will find when they search for you online. Of course, what will crop up is any public or published information about you—things as mundane as when you placed in the top 10 in a road race or as potentially damaging as an arrest or criminal conviction. Regardless of what's online now, you can add to the weight of positive information by creating a Web resume that reinforces all of the messages you've conveyed in your print resume.

From simplest to most complex, your Web resume can be any of the following:

- A profile on various social and business networking sites, such as Facebook or LinkedIn

- A complete portfolio posted through an online service such as VisualCV

- A full-blown personal website that you create and manage

If you are in a technology profession, a Web resume can be a valuable tool where you can often demonstrate your technical expertise. For example, if you're an expert in HTML programming, you don't just have to write about it; you can show it on your Web resume.

For all of these options, you can begin with your existing resume and add appropriate material to expand, reinforce, and complement your resume. Consider adding lists of all of your achievements, career highlights, project highlights, consulting engagements, publications, public speaking engagements, education, professional credentials, management skills, and more. Your portfolio might include a slide presentation that you developed or charts indicating the improvement in areas that you managed. A video of you in action at a conference, in the field, or in the boardroom would also be a great addition.

A Web resume or portfolio will not only showcase your skills, it will raise your online profile so that when potential employers search for you, they'll find information of value. At the very least, we strongly recommend that you create a professional profile on LinkedIn (www.linkedin.com), which is the most widely used professional networking site, and explore and use LinkedIn's extensive capabilities to build your online visibility and expand your network.

Finally, if you use Facebook or other sites for social networking, never include anything that could be damaging to your professional reputation. You might think these sites protect your privacy, but you can't be 100 percent certain, so don't risk your career success by sharing inappropriate content online.

THE NEW VIDEO BIO PHENOMENON

One of the newest technology additions to the portfolio of tech tools for job search and career management is the video biography. These bios allow you, the job seeker, to present yourself "live" to prospective employers and recruiters. Bios are growing in popularity because they can be helpful to companies in evaluating prime candidates. They can give you a competitive edge if your video bio shows that you are articulate and attractive.

Video bios are sometimes mistakenly labeled "video resumes." In fact, they are quite different. You certainly don't want to record yourself reading or reciting your resume—that would not make for an interesting video! The video bio instead allows you to showcase yourself in a different way by briefly sharing interesting information and demonstrating your communication skills. Intended as an adjunct to your resume, never as a replacement, the video bio can be effective in today's visually and technologically oriented culture.

The use of video bios is somewhat controversial because of the potential for bias and discrimination based on ethnicity, race, size, age, and other personal characteristics. You'll have to make a decision for yourself as to whether a video bio would be a positive addition to your portfolio of career and job search communications. You can read much more about video bios at videoBIO (www.videobio.com), one of the leaders in this emerging technology as it relates to personal marketing and branding for job search.

The Three Resume Types Compared

This chart quickly compares the similarities and differences between the three types of resumes we've discussed in this chapter.

	Printed Resumes (Word and PDF Files)	Electronic Resumes (Text Files)	Web Resumes
TYPESTYLE/ FONT	Sharp, conservative, and distinctive (see our recommendations in Chapter 1).	Courier.	Sharp, conservative, and distinctive. Attractive on-screen and when printed from an online document.
TYPE ENHANCEMENTS	**Bold,** *italics,* and underlining for emphasis.	CAPITALIZATION is the only enhancement available to you.	**Bold,** *italics,* underlining, and color available for emphasis.

(continued)

(continued)

	Printed Resumes (Word and PDF Files)	**Electronic Resumes (Text Files)**	**Web Resumes**
TYPE SIZE	10-, 11-, or 12-point preferred. Larger type sizes (14, 18, 20, 22, and even larger, depending on typestyle) will effectively enhance your name and section headings.	12-point.	Use type sizes that are readable on-screen and off.
TEXT FORMAT	Use centering and indenting to optimize the visual presentation.	Type all information flush left.	Use centering and indenting to optimize the visual presentation.
PREFERRED LENGTH	One to two pages; three if essential.	Length is immaterial; almost definitely, converting your resume to text will make it longer.	Length is immaterial; just be sure your site is well organized so viewers can quickly find the material of greatest interest to them.
PAPER COLOR	White, ivory, light gray, light blue, or other conservative background.	Not applicable for e-mailed documents. White for documents printed for scanning.	Paper is not used, but do select your background carefully to maximize readability.
WHITE SPACE	Use appropriately for best readability.	Use white space to break up dense text sections.	Use appropriately for best readability both on-screen and when printed.

Resume Checklist

Before you sit down to write your resume, carefully review the following checklist to be certain that you've addressed everything. Each item is a critical step in writing, formatting, and designing a powerful resume, the foundation of every successful job search campaign. Every item is applicable to just about any active job seeker:

❑ Clearly define who you are and how you want to be perceived (for example, business consultant, regional manager, executive administrator, CEO). The perception you want to create will align directly with your current career objectives, which may or may not be aligned with your past experience.

❑ Document your key skills, qualifications, competencies, and knowledge. You can create a Word file for this, write it on a piece of paper, or use the resume questionnaire in Appendix A.

❑ Document your career achievements, project highlights, contributions, honors and awards, and other notable accomplishments. As above, you can create a Word file for this, write it on a piece of paper, or use the resume questionnaire in Appendix A.

❑ Identify one or more specific job targets and positions that you will pursue. With these in hand, you're much better prepared to write your resume because you know where you're headed and what you want to showcase about your career.

❑ Identify one or more industries and companies that you will target. Just as with identifying target positions, once you've outlined this, you're much better prepared to write your resume because you know where you're headed and what to highlight about your career, responsibilities, achievements, and more.

❑ Research and compile a list of keywords and keyword phrases for the industries and professions that you are targeting, and then be certain to incorporate as many of them as you can in your resume (and cover letter).

❑ Collect several job postings or announcements that are similar to jobs you'll be applying for. Review carefully to be certain you understand the core qualifications as well as the "extras" so that you can highlight both in your resume.

❑ Determine which resume format will work best for you and your career—chronological, functional, or combination, often referred to as a hybrid resume, as discussed in Chapter 1.

❑ Get a personal e-mail address if you don't already have one. Using your employer's e-mail address on your resume is never appropriate. You can easily get a Gmail, Hotmail, or other free e-mail address.

❑ Write your resume using the strategies, guidelines, suggestions, and samples you'll find throughout this book.

❑ Select an attractive font (typestyle) that's appropriate for the industries and professions that you're targeting.

❑ Review resume samples for up-to-date ideas on resume styles, formats, fonts, organization, and content. You might like part of one resume and part of another. Great! Do not feel limited or believe that you have to format and structure your resume in exactly the same style as one of the sample formats.

❑ Determine which final versions of your resume you will need: printable (Word or PDF), electronic (plain-text format), and/or Web. This decision will depend entirely on how you plan to execute your search campaign.

❑ Ask several colleagues and/or friends to review and proofread your resume. Start by e-mailing a copy to them so you can see what they see. Ask for a critique of the content, formatting, presentation, and any other ideas they would like to share with you.

❑ Proofread. Proofread. Proofread. Then have one or two other people proofread. It's amazing how easy it is to overlook small grammar, punctuation, or format errors. Don't let a misspelled word stand in the way of getting an interview!

PART II

Sample Resumes for Managers and Executives

CHAPTER 4

Resumes for Managers and Executives in Retail, Customer Service, Sales, and Marketing

- Retail Manager
- Sales Manager
- Sales, Marketing, and Service Executive
- Customer Service Manager
- Sales Executive
- Global Sales and Marketing Executive
- Senior Sales Manager
- Director/Vice President of Sales
- Marketing Director
- Business Development Executive
- Marketing Manager
- Senior Marketing Executive
- Senior Sales and Marketing Executive

DEBORAH CORMIER

3 Cousins Crescent ➤ Aurora, Ontario ➤ L4G 9B7 ➤ 905-841-3998

RETAIL MANAGER

PROFILE

Client-driven, quality-focused, and safety-conscious with more than 20 years of progressive experience in retail operations and a **track record of top performance in a variety of challenging assignments.** Possess thorough understanding of store operations, based on actual hands-on experience, and ability to easily adapt to new and different environments. Strengths include:

- Operations Management
- High-Expectation Client Relations
- Staff Training, Scheduling, & Development
- Cash Management & Expense Control
- Advertising & Selling Techniques
- Product Receipt

- Inventory Control
- Till Set-Up & Reconciliation
- P&L Management
- Purchasing Management
- Merchandising Techniques & Colour Coordination

Well-developed interpersonal skills, easily able to establish and maintain favourable rapport with clients and staff from all cultures and organizational backgrounds. **Earlier professional experience includes 3 years as a Sales Associate at a local bed-and-bath boutique; assumed increasing responsibility for window treatments designed to boost customer traffic.** High level of personal and professional integrity; passionate about achieving organizational success.

PROFESSIONAL EXPERIENCE
MEGA-MART   1991–2011

2009–2011: Assistant Produce/Garden Manager — Aurora location
Promoted to oversee operations of a busy and established suburban store based on demonstrated ability to lead teams, boost employee morale, and foster client loyalty. Attractively set up merchandise in an effort to entice customers to buy product. Ensured neatness and orderliness throughout department. Revised prices and updated signage on a weekly basis to correspond with printed flyers and distribution material. Authorized to modify prices to generate additional revenues and discourage product shrinkage.

Selected Achievements:
- Created additional sales demand through effective set-up of in-store sampling demonstrations.
- Chosen to assume Produce Manager's duties in his absence. Strove to ensure smooth store operations.
- Consistently picked by Manager to brighten up store environment using seasonal themes and in-store promotional pieces.
- Assisted in apprehending two repeat offenders and dramatically reduced customer theft by introducing stringent loss-prevention measures.

1991–2009: Fast-track promotions in earlier career at Mega-Mart St. Catherines store during its start-up phase, with accountability for Cash, Produce, Health & Beauty Aids, Dairy, Bakery, Deli, Stock, and Courtesy Desk.

EDUCATION

Seneca College, Newnham Campus, Toronto
Colour Theory and Its Application Toward Effective Merchandising Techniques

Strategy: Highlight contributions and management-level activities for this grocery-store manager who wanted to change industries.

James Allen Borgen

1453 Little Fork Bridge
Tulsa, Oklahoma 74104   jamesborg@dotmail.com   918-884-3542 Residence
918-453-3484 Cellular

Sales Management Profile

Top-producing sales professional who is driven, motivated, and self-disciplined. Relationship-builder with successful track record in developing and retaining accounts in a highly competitive marketplace.

- Effective at mentoring/coaching colleagues to build customers for life.
- Profit-driven and focused on value-added consultative selling.
- Skilled at assessing customer needs and providing win-win-win solutions.
- Cognizant of key competition, market trends, and industry changes.
- Valued by customers for consistent follow-through and caring demeanor.

Professional Sales Experience

ENGINEERED SOLUTIONS, Tulsa, Oklahoma   **2005–Present**
Tulsa-based market leader in satellite-communication systems.

Sales Consultant. Recruited by Engineered Solutions' General Manager to aggressively pursue new business throughout the state of Oklahoma. Key functions:

Sales:

- Number-one-ranked, high-performance sales professional for four consecutive years in eight branches of the organization.
- Substantially increased sales volume of existing accounts.
- Effective in reading buy-signals; possess strong closing abilities.
- Recognized as the sole sales consultant out of company's 18 consultants to achieve sales goals during most recent fiscal year.

Growth/Profitability:

- Increased sales throughout four consecutive years, consistently exceeding sales goals as outlined below, while maintaining profit margins:

2010 — 165%	2008 — 122%
2009 — 135%	2007 — 115%

- Prospected and developed an entirely new market for the organization, with majority of accounts newly recruited through personal sales efforts.
- Successfully maintained profit margin despite strong competition.

Account/Customer Retention:

- Excel at identifying prospects and maintaining established accounts by consistent follow-through.
- Differentiate between suspects and prospects through strong consulting and interpretive skills.
- Played an integral role in developing large communications systems for major accounts. Initiated extensive infrastructure changes, working with subcontractors and city, county, and state officials.

Education

BSBA: Marketing Major with Economics Minor   University of Tulsa, Tulsa, Oklahoma, 2005

Strategy: Focus on strong results for this talented, aggressive sales professional.

SOFIA MAGARELLI

210 Sycamore Drive		(M) 805-398-5527
Simi Valley, CA 93065	sofia.magarelli@yahoo.com	(H) 805-398-2396

SALES, MARKETING & SERVICE EXECUTIVE
TURNAROUNDS | FINANCIAL & OPERATIONAL RESTRUCTURING

A highly skilled business development executive and technologist in the telecommunications industry who achieves exceptional revenue growth in both emerging and mature markets through unique ability to forecast industry trends. Proven track record of capturing opportunities, cultivating partnerships, and launching start-up ventures into competitive positions. A persuasive negotiator and engaging speaker who brings high-value visibility to an organization and builds strong partnerships. Recognized expert in telecommunications interviewed by major media including CBS (http://tinyurl.com/Magarelli-Interview).

PROFESSIONAL EXPERIENCE

TIME WARNER COMMUNICATIONS, California   2003–Present
Managed Services Company for medium and large business customers in California.

Vice President of Sales
Recruited by the executive VP and managing partner to implement a new business model that would generate fixed and reliable revenue sources for a start-up organization with no sales force, limited capital and products, and no channels of distribution. Over 3 intense days, collaborated with the CEO to develop a strategy and business plan.

Increased annual revenue to more than $34M.

◆

Established relationship policies to achieve 99% customer retention.

◆

Generated $120K revenue per month within 2 years.

➢ Given full P&L responsibility to create a 270-person organization for direct and indirect channel sales. Developed a stellar reputation and a customer base of 5,500 by focusing on branding and service quality.
➢ Increased revenue by more than 55% month-over-month to exceed $120K in new monthly revenue in all channels for 24 consecutive months.
➢ Responded to changing FCC regulations that directly impacted sales by repositioning the business strategy to include managed technical services such as VOIP, high-speed lines, VPNs, integrated products, web design, web hosting, CRM tools, and data backup and storage.
➢ Aligned operations with the corporate goal to expand nationwide by establishing the foundation to move forward; developed web-based marketing systems to expedite orders, increase product knowledge, and deliver online training tools to customers.

UNIFORM TELCOM, California (acquired CMM Network 2001)   2001–2003
Local Exchange Carrier providing voice and data services to customers in the Western U.S.

Executive Director of Sales
Strategic, tactical, and full P&L accountability for 150-person organization with direct and channel sales goals. Managed the entire sales organization, delivering $100K of new revenue per month.

Increased sales revenue 100% in every channel month over month for 3 quarters.

➢ Revitalized unprofitable indirect sales program, increasing sales staff 10-fold to 100 and doubling sales revenue.
➢ Increased revenue from existing customer base by creating new products and services, including collocation services, VPNs, integrated products, web design, web hosting, and other IT-related services.
➢ Launched marketing campaigns to attract customers and increase channel distribution by introducing new promotions focused on Latin America.

CMM NETWORK, California   2000–2001
High-speed Internet Service Provider located in the U.S.

National Senior Director, Sales & Business Development (30-person organization)
Developed and implemented successful plans to open and expand markets in tier 1 and tier 2 cities by providing IP, VOIP, VPN, storage services, and converged solution services. Directed all business activities in 15 states and 18

Strategy: Emphasize impressive achievements in attention-getting short statements on the left while including rich detail in the bullet points on the right.

SOFIA MAGARELLI

(M) 805-398-5527 | sofia.magarelli@yahoo.com | (H) 805-398-2396

markets, including budgets, negotiations, building and utility agreements, network deployment and design, and reports to the board of directors.

Raised capital to secure $65 million in 2nd round funding for start-up company. ◆ **Reduced capital expenditures by 20% per project.**	➢ Generated annual sales in 6 different tier 1 markets from zero to more than $2.5M per year in less than 12 months. Pre-sold more than $240K in monthly business by establishing indirect channel segments. ➢ Launched customer-driven marketing and promotional programs to expand market penetration and increase key account base by introducing new products and controls. ➢ Developed and successfully negotiated more than 500 building agreements for 300M square feet of commercial office property to secure access to central business districts in top U.S. cities.

COGENT COMMUNICATIONS, California   1998–2000
Competitive Local Exchange Carrier providing voice and data services to customers in the Western U.S.

Director of Sales & Real Estate (30-person organization)
Re-positioned a chaotic start-up into a revenue-generation model for new markets by creating a "facilities-based carrier" for U.S. niche market. Successfully shifted decision making to incorporate solid, fact-based opportunities that led to substantial ROI within a short time frame.

Built annual sales from zero to more than $25M in less than 24 months. ◆ **Exceeded Wall Street expectations.** ◆ **Received executive buy-in for 5-year financial business-case model.**	➢ Refocused sales strategy to add 3 new markets and expand existing markets, adding more than $5M in yearly recurring revenue. ➢ Established agent and reseller agreements with VARs, integrators, storage companies, ISPs, and indirect channel segments for high-demand services: VOIP, collocation, VPN, and IP services. ➢ Built and trained a motivated sales team to establish new business through market research, networking leads, cold calls, promotional mailings, and direct presentations to local and remote decision makers. ➢ Executed a strategic alliance with the largest building owner (40M square feet of office space) in San Francisco, enabling company to provide services to a desirable high-end customer base.

SBC COMMUNICATIONS, California   1995–1998

Area Marketing Manager (P&L for $20M budget) 1997–1998
Directed kiosk program operations, managing 8 retail account managers responsible for 300 sales representatives.

Determined profitability of distribution/expansion of service areas.	➢ Launched business and marketing plans to restructure hectic environment while reducing kiosk setup costs and setup time by 25%. ➢ Developed a POS system that completely changed operational functions; captured real-time sales information for impulse buy analysis, reduced purchase cycle time by more than 80%, eliminated time sheets, and increased inventory scanning control; reduced monthly expenses by more than 35%.

Contract Manager (managed 12-member team) 1995–1997
P&L and management responsibility for lease arrangements with all major telecommunication suppliers.

High-profit negotiator and decision-maker for annual $200M in telecom contracts.	➢ Restructed vendor qualifications in Service Level Agreements (SLAs) to clearly define responsibilities and expectations; a substantial aid in high-dollar negotiations. ➢ Drove completion of critical interim solution during enterprise-wide upgrade of backbone network. Negotiated contracts for largest leasing capacity project, saving $23M annually.

EDUCATION

MBA, Concentration in **International Business**, University of California, Berkeley CA
Bachelor of Science in Marketing, California State University, San Francisco, CA

LORENZO FERRER

5889 Mount Horeb Lane ▪ Santa Ana, CA 92704
714-545-2491 ▪ ferrer@gmail.com

SENIOR-LEVEL CUSTOMER SERVICE MANAGER
Personal Accounts / Customer Service / Inside Sales / Call Center Operations

Driving excellence in customer service ...
fostering "above and beyond" mindset to maximize customer loyalty.

Performance-driven customer service manager with stellar record of success leading teams and managing service operations, delivering exceptional results while meeting the time-sensitive needs of the medical and pharmaceutical markets. Respected, hands-on manager who leads by example; a skilled coach and mentor who leverages strong communication skills to articulate and gain buy-in to achieve shared goals. Valued company resource; a take-charge leader with a passion for service excellence and the clear ability to foster customer-centric business environments.

Core Competencies

- Managing sales and service operations, providing vision and leadership to drive service excellence while creating and implementing tactical plans to meet short-term and long-term goals.
- Building high-caliber teams, cultivating empowering work environments by rewarding top-notch performance.
- Leveraging collaborative style to deliver best-in-class service, proactively working with internal groups to address issues, remove roadblocks, and resolve customer problems.
- Promoting best practices across service teams to move beyond basic customer satisfaction to achieve priceless customer loyalty.

PROFESSIONAL EXPERIENCE

MCGUFF COMPANY, INC.   2008 to 2011
Inside Sales Manager (2009 to 2011)
Customer Service Manager (2008 to 2009)
Most recently, directed 5-member inside sales team charged with driving revenue growth of specialty products. Previously, led 12-member customer service team in supporting $100 million in distributor and OEM sales through 55 sales reps.

Drove dramatic improvements in both sales and service by establishing challenging goals and metrics
and then empowering teams to meet them.

Customer Service Management

- **Established performance metrics where none existed before, substantially improving customer service operation on all levels. Among successes:**
  - Surpassed all customer service metrics, achieving better than 3.6% ABD rate, 99% accuracy, and 90% customer satisfaction level.
  - Closed 3-year complaint backlog, addressing and resolving customer issues to rebuild customer satisfaction.
  - Implemented effective staff management and development practices, empowering staff to improve performance and morale. Testament to success, achieved zero voluntary turnover during tenure.
  - Earned praise of senior-level management for producing clear results, building department to the *"...best it has ever been since its inception."*
- **Frequently tapped to drive/assist with key strategic initiatives:**
  - Reporting to Supply Chain Director, worked on developing new reporting tool, an improved communication process designed to accelerate resolution of product back-order concerns.
  - Directed Customer Service Performance Survey used to drive supply chain service enhancements.
  - Selected to serve on Division Integration and Relocations teams; played key role in integration of both products and technology to ensure smooth transition following corporate merger.

Continued

Strategy: Create a strong Career Summary that includes a headline, branding statement, and core competencies, followed by a Professional Experience section that provides extensive evidence of this executive's abilities.

Lorenzo Ferrer	ferrer@gmail.com	Page 2

MCGUFF COMPANY, INC. Continued

Sales Support Management

- **Turned around performance of inside sales group by establishing and communicating goals and expectations while fostering a customer-focused, team-based work environment that recognized and rewarded top-level performance. Among successes:**
  - Achieved 84% increase in revenue in first year of tenure, increasing order volume by 59% and value of orders by 10% through effective upselling, product bundling, and promotional strategies.
  - Achieved 51% sales growth of new line of human ID products.
  - Created revenue opportunity scorecard that ultimately improved sales performance through better tracking of prospects, quotes, and samples.
- **Implemented plans and strategies to expedite delivery of orders and build customer loyalty:**
  - Expertly fielded escalated customer issues to afford quick, satisfactory resolution while modeling best practices to raise overall performance of sales team.
  - Stepped in to resolve service and delivery issues, engaging partners to resolve issues and remove roadblocks that endangered customer satisfaction. Initiated protocols to maximize service and ensure the highest levels of customer satisfaction and loyalty.
  - Collaborated with IT group to launch new data entry tool that reduced order processing time while increasing customer satisfaction.

ALLIED MEDICAL SUPPLY 1993 to 2008

Customer Service Manager (2002 to 2008)
Customer Service Supervisor (1997 to 2002)
Inside Sales Supervisor (1993 to 1997)

As customer service manager, reported directly to senior-level executives in overseeing all aspects of combined personal account/call center/customer service department in Fortune 500 company. Managed day-to-day operation of 36-member service group charged with supporting $175 million alternative care business.

As management's go-to resource for implementation of strategic programs, led a broad range of initiatives to ensure reliable delivery of best-in-class customer service.

- Initiated and implemented new sales support concept – the creation of a team exclusively dedicated to the needs of 75 field sales reps – that was deemed highly successful and adopted for use across company.
- Spearheaded launch of new ACD phone system that facilitated customer inquiries. Researched and implemented best-fit solution that met both immediate and future needs.
- Tapped to serve on Corporate Integration team, played key role in alignment of customers, products, and procedures across all newly acquired companies.
- Earned commendation for dedication and success in devising relay system that enabled receipt of calls for supplies in wake of 9/11 disaster and ensuing communication breakdown.

EDUCATION

UNIVERSITY OF SAN DIEGO
Master of Business Administration; Concentration in Marketing and Management
Bachelor of Science; Biology

Completed numerous high-level courses in leadership, management, customer service, and sales.

GEOFF LEWIS

1502 Woodcliff Lane ▪ Charlotte, NC 28277

Mobile: (704) 483-9991   glusa2002@aol.com   Home: (704) 347-2020

CAREER PROFILE

Dynamic, top-performing **Sports-Industry Sales Executive** with more than 15 years of experience in contracts procurement, project management, training, sports marketing, program development/ implementation, and public/media relations. Expertise includes:

- Contract Negotiation
- Account Development & Retention
- Logistics Management
- Relationship Management
- Staff Motivation & Mentoring
- Strategic Planning & Marketing
- Community Relations

PROFESSIONAL EXPERIENCE

FEDERAL WRESTLING ALLIANCE/INTERNATIONAL WRESTLING ALLIANCE   2008–Present
Charlotte, NC
Vice President

Direct contracts administration for this international wrestling sports-entertainment organization. Scope of responsibility is diverse and includes coordinating material and equipment transportation/logistics, handling travel arrangements, recruiting, developing new talent, and procuring contracts with wrestlers. Serve as liaison between the Federal Wrestling Alliance/International Wrestling Alliance and the Pentagon to ensure contract compliance. Negotiate contract renewals. Travel worldwide. Conceive, plan, develop, and publicize all story lines, special events, promotions, advertising, and public-relations campaigns to ensure optimum TV viewership.

- Negotiated, transacted, and procured a $1M federal contract providing professional wrestling sports entertainment to U.S. military troops and their dependents in Europe, Asia, the Balkans, the Caribbean, the Pacific Rim, Central America, and the United States. Won contract, displacing 30+ other major independent competitors. Conceived the initial procurement strategy.

- Grew company to the third-largest wrestling organization in the U.S.

- Developed concept and wrote format for BET-TV to provide syndication for the first minority-formatted pro-wrestling venue.

UNIVERSAL ENTERTAINMENT — Charlotte, NC   2006–2008
Chairman of Secondary Effects Study

Recruited to oversee research project, Universal Secondary Effects Study, to determine correlation between crime rates and property values in 20 local venues surrounding gentlemen's clubs.

- Organized and authored empirical study and hired all Ph.D. experts (criminologists, social psychologists, anthropologists, and urban planners) to ensure validity and authenticity of data. Worked and collaborated with Dr. David Wopak, University of Oregon; Dr. Keith Brooks, Chairman, Criminology Department, University of North Carolina at Chapel Hill; and Dr. Deborah Harrison, University of Virginia. Oversaw all aspects of study; made recommendations and implementations to ensure scientific accuracy.

page 1

Strategy: Reflect strong sales, negotiation, and professional mentoring skills and downplay the less "respectable" elements of his career as he sought to transition within the sports industry.

GEOFF LEWIS   glusa2002@aol.com   page 2

UNIVERSAL ENTERTAINMENT — continued

- Pioneered the development and implementation of the industry's *first* GED program for entertainers ("Operation Education"), providing the impetus for entertainers to achieve GED diplomas, while fostering self-esteem and lifetime learning skills. Taught weekly class (25 participants) and administered exams. Operation Education is certified by the State of North Carolina. Also coordinated open educational seminars (e.g., financial planning, health insurance, drug counseling, domestic violence) for entertainers.

- Orchestrated a series of aggressive marketing initiatives for the CrazyHorse Showclub that increased sales by 37% in one month. Realized growth through redesign of guest-services programs (conducting extensive interviews with entertainers and staff to identify improvement areas and empower employees), developing new marketing materials, creating theme-focused events, and building corporate relationships.

NORTHSIDE PHOTOGRAPHERS INTERNATIONAL — Nyack, NY   1998–2006
President/Owner

Founded company providing photography services to the U.S. military worldwide. Directed all operations, including sales, marketing, customer service, purchasing, and human resources. Managed 35 employees.

- Grew business to $4.25M in annual sales. Developed strategies to improve services to the military.

GANDY SPORTS MANAGEMENT — New York, NY   1994–1998
Vice President

Negotiated contracts between NFL teams and individual players, serving as players' representative. Also secured major product endorsements and negotiated endorsement contracts. Solicited, scouted, and recruited top college players. Booked speaking engagements and public-relations appearances for players. Provided financial-management counseling and educational assistance to NFL players and developed pre-season training programs.

- Represented professional NFL players, including Curtis Martin (New England Patriots and New York Jets) and Ricky Watters (Philadelphia Eagles). Reported directly to Bruce Gandy, former N.Y. Giant and Dallas Cowboy and currently CBS sports commentator.

ST. MARY'S REGIONAL HIGH SCHOOL — Montvale, NJ   1990–1994
Physical Education & Health Sciences Teacher/Coach

Instructed classes and served as head wrestling coach and assistant varsity football coach for this parochial high school recognized for academic and athletic excellence. Assisted students with applications process and acceptance into sports programs at Yale, Harvard, and the U.S. Military Academy at West Point.

- Led wrestling and football teams to 2 state wrestling and 4 state football championships. Football team was ranked 8th nationally in 1994.

EDUCATION

M.A., Sports Fitness and Management, 1998
B.S., Physical Education/Health/Sports Management, 1990
- State University of New York (SUNY), College at Brockport

Carole R. Weiss

65 Marblewood Road, Avon Lake, OH 44012
(h) 440.687.2349; (m) 440.791.2255
carole.weiss@verizon.net

GLOBAL SALES AND MARKETING EXECUTIVE
Start-Ups | High-Growth | Revitalizations | Turnarounds

ENGINEERING RADICAL, RATIONAL CHANGE

Consummate change agent who established or revamped 6 sales organizations using scientific strategies to create high-performing, modern sales and marketing engines.

Dynamic leader whose efficient, people-centered enterprises attract former colleagues, direct and indirect reports, and even higher-ups who are willing to switch roles to join in new organizational opportunities.

PROFESSIONAL EXPERIENCE

GENERAL ELECTRIC ENTERPRISE COMMUNICATIONS   East Cleveland, OH   January 2009–Present
A $3.5B joint venture of GE and an equity capital firm, ranking #2 globally in its offerings of Unified Communications, VoIP, and Business Telephony Solutions.

Senior Vice President, Global Inside Sales

MISSION ACCOMPLISHED: Restructured a franchise-model, multinational organization beset with grossly outdated technology, infrastructure, and operations to launch a highly integrated Global Inside Sales division.

Financial Results:
- Won $95M in North American order intake in first year, hitting 103% of goal.
- Achieved $49.4M annual margin in North America.
- Produced $47M in non–North American orders in only 1½ quarters, while still in ramp-up mode.
- Generated $84M in new pipeline in North America.

Sales Team, Operations, and IT Development:
- Recruited and trained 88 sellers in first year, easily on track to reach headcount of 212 in 2012.
- Developed plans and systems for global e-commerce, lead handling and Lead Management Automation (LMA), global maintenance contract reporting, Business Intelligence (BI), and propensity modeling.
- Collaborated closely with Global Marketing leadership on campaign management, promotions, EMM/MRM planning, pipeline cadence management, and web presence.
- Drove 9% boost in order intake on Moves, Adds, and Changes team in just 1 quarter by improving and integrating CRM, data hygiene, data augmentation, and BI. Crafted similar increases on other teams.

ERNST & YOUNG   Cleveland, OH   May 2001–December 2008
A $21.3B "Big Four" auditor and "Big Five" consulting firm.

Managing Director, Global Sales and Field Marketing

MISSION ACCOMPLISHED: After unanimous appointment by the approval board as Managing Director, designed and built every element of the first professional Inside Sales group ever launched in a Big Five consulting firm. Integrated it with the North American Business Development group and consulting practices.

Financial Results:
- Captured more than $1B in incremental pipeline and closed more than $100M in bookings annually.
- Increased sales velocity by about $75M annually by cofacilitating prospecting training workshops.
- Slashed the cost of acquiring incremental revenue through Inside Sales to 7/10 of a penny per dollar.
- Grew returns on incremental pipeline to 33 times marketing investment.

Strategy: Include a strong "Mission Accomplished" statement for every job, repeatedly reinforcing the message that this candidate is a top performer.

Operations Development:
- ♦ Strategized and implemented a programmatic approach to pipeline development, including processes to manage revenue generation programs, revenue tracking, forecasting, campaigns, and other operations.
- ♦ Introduced ROMI and pipeline measurement to the field marketing organization and enforced the sales/field marketing interlock.
- ♦ Drove automation and process through CRM, LMA, and MRM systems to create better efficiency, productivity, accountability, and ROMI.
- ♦ Forged a bridge between marketing, business development, and the practices by linking marketing efforts with the specific requirements of the target market.

EGON ZEHNDER INTERNATIONAL, INC.	Boston, MA	July 2000–May 2001
HIRED.COM	Boston, MA	April 2000–July 2000

The #2 provider of recruitment software and services for recent college graduates, Hired.com was acquired by Egon Zehnder, the world's third-largest executive recruitment company. Egon Zehnder then reengineered Hired.com, enabling it to close Hired's sales operations in May 2001.

Vice President of Inside Sales

MISSION ACCOMPLISHED: Helped Hired.com become acquired by a major industry player by building an Inside Sales organization from the ground up to attack the SMB market, where the company had no presence.
- ♦ Successfully launched the organization 2 months early and 60% under budget.

COMPAQ	Boston, MA	June 1998–April 2000
DIGITAL CORPORATION	Maynard, MA	July 1997–June 1998
DIGITAL CORPORATION	London, England	November 1994–July 1997

Digital, a worldwide leader in computer systems, software, and peripherals, was acquired by Compaq in June 1998.

National Sales Manager, Digital Direct USA   January 1999–April 2000

MISSION ACCOMPLISHED: Transformed an inbound supplies and accessories group into an outbound client solutions and networking sales organization.
- ♦ Achieved 127% of goal in first year, bringing in $20M.

U.S. Service Sales Manager   July 1997–January 1999

MISSION ACCOMPLISHED: Spearheaded a new service sales venture to maximize incremental service revenue growth, nearly doubling Digital's point-of-sale service contract revenues in first 12 months.
- ♦ Hit 124% of goal in first year.
- ♦ Increased service contract capture rate from 28% to 55% in 1 year.

EMEA Proprietary Business Unit Manager   November 1994–July 1997

MISSION ACCOMPLISHED: Architected a pan-EMEA organization and propelled it to $75M annualized, making it Digital's most successful European sales division.
- ♦ Simultaneously ran a separate, proprietary business unit and delivered $55M on a $40M budget, achieving 138% of revenue target while yielding 66% gross margin.

EARLY CAREER HISTORY

DIGITAL CORPORATION, Maynard, MA—Promoted from Field Support Specialist, District Service Manager, Account Executive, and Telesales Group Leader

SPERRY CORPORATION, Sperry Univac Division, New York, NY—Field Engineer in Charge

EDUCATION

Bachelor of Science, Organizational Management, Farmingdale State College, SUNY, Farmingdale, NY

Neal Lawrence

411 W. Fulton Pkwy.
Chicago, IL 60614
773-771-1440 ▪ neallaw@yahoo.com

SENIOR SALES MANAGEMENT
Expertise in telecommunications on both regional and national levels

PROFILE

Consummate **sales executive** recognized for ability to build, guide, and sustain successful sales teams. Time and again, present proven accomplishments within the highly competitive telecommunications and wireless industries. At ease interfacing with, establishing, and maintaining excellent relationships with the world's largest organizations, including AT&T, Verizon, and BellSouth, among others. Thoroughly familiar with wireless communications, manufacturing, and distribution processes.

Areas of Expertise

- Territory/Account Development and Management
- Product Launch
- Marketing Collateral
- Trade Show Presentations
- Build-to-Suit, Co-location, and Sale/Lease-Back Agreements

- Contract Negotiations
- Public Relations
- Staff Supervision
- Team Building, Coaching, and Mentoring
- Needs Assessment
- Customer Service

CAREER HIGHLIGHTS

CALVIN INSTRUMENT COMPANY — Raleigh, NC
(Among the largest manufacturers of steel infrastructure products in the U.S., selling to the telecommunications industry.)
MIDWEST REGIONAL MANAGER, 2008 – present
Direct customer service, sales, purchasing, and distribution for $25 million, 10-state region, which encompasses Illinois, Indiana, Ohio, Minnesota, Wisconsin, Kansas, Arkansas, Michigan, Missouri, and Iowa. Supervise and train staff of five customer service representatives and work closely with three engineers to promote, sell, and service product line throughout region. Oversee key account relationships with SBC, BellSouth, Verizon, and Qwest, among others.

Select Accomplishments:
- Secured $10 million account to provide hardware and rack-and-stack services to SBC. Closed deal as a result of relationship building and meeting stringent conditions sought by SBC, through several quality audits.
- The Midwest region **ranked 2nd** out of five nationwide in revenue for both 2009 and 2010.

UNI GROUP — Boston, MA
(Largest non-RBOC owner of wireless towers in the U.S., employing 3,000 nationwide. Acquired by Towers, Inc., in 2007.)
NATIONAL SALES MANAGER, 2007 – 2008
Key player in developing relationships with national wireless carriers such as AT&T, Sprint, Ameritech, and Nextel in an effort to obtain Build-to-Suit, Co-location and Sale/Lease-Back contracts on a national level. Personally conducted assessment interviews with prospective clients to identify needs and formulate appropriate solutions.

Page One

Strategy: Position this accomplished sales executive as an expert within the highly competitive telecommunications industry.

Neal Lawrence

Résumé ▪ neallaw@yahoo.com ▪ Page Two

CAREER HIGHLIGHTS

UNI GROUP *(continued...)*
Select Accomplishments:

- Attained multimillion-dollar contract with AT&T, which involved placement of 300 antennas by AT&T at 300 of Tower's sites. Contract terms specified rent of $1,200 to $3,000 monthly at each of the 300 sites for a period of 15 years. Contract was largest in UNI Group's history and instrumental in piquing Tower's interest in UNI Group.
- Developed marketing collateral and coordinated UNI Group's participation at the two largest wireless conventions.

BESTCO — Jacksonville, FL
(PCS company providing wireless services in the Southeast and Midwest U.S. Presently wholly owned subsidiary of Verizon.)
CORPORATE ACCOUNT MANAGER, 2005 – 2007
Targeted and sold high-revenue corporate customers in vertical markets comprising law firms, hospitals, financial institutions, and communications companies. Networked extensively throughout the business community at industry trade shows. Supervised five account coordinators that provided ongoing service to new and existing accounts.
Select Accomplishments:

- Played key role in the largest wireless commercial launch in the history of the industry, covering 11 national markets, including the state of Florida.
- Ranked in **top 10%** of all corporate account executives for 2006.

MOBILTEL (*A TeleSouth Company*) — Tampa, FL
(National provider of wireless data and paging services.)
MAJOR ACCOUNT EXECUTIVE, 2004 – 2005
SALES REPRESENTATIVE, 2003 – 2004
SALES ASSOCIATE, 2002 – 2003
Progressed rapidly in recognition of outstanding performance in sales and account management. Initially provided retail customer service and ultimately advanced to oversight of all major accounts within the state of Florida. Served as corporate liaison for training sales representatives on sales techniques, new technologies, and product launches.
Select Accomplishments:

- Placed within top **10% of 125** major account executives nationwide in 2000.
- **1st** among Jacksonville sales representatives in 2003.

EDUCATION

PROFESSIONAL DEVELOPMENT
- **STRATEGIC SELLING**
- **EAGLE SALES SYSTEM**
- Product Training on **CDMA** and **WIRELESS TECHNOLOGY**

GEORGIA SOUTHERN UNIVERSITY — Statesboro, GA
BA, MARKETING, 2002

RIVERSIDE MILITARY ACADEMY — Gainesville, GA
ACADEMIC DIPLOMA, 1998

Robert Geldof

rgeldof@gmail.com / 212-555-1212
65 Central Park West, Apt. 2PH, New York, NY 10024

Senior Executive: Software / Technology

B2B Marketing & Sales ▪ Strategic Business Development ▪ Enterprise SaaS Market ▪ Fortune 500

Growth catalyst for technology sales across multinational and multidivisional organizations: 20-year reputation for opening doors to new business opportunities in areas never before penetrated. Meticulously devised processes, structures, and checkpoints to drive market strategies and sales of complex products. Champion of revenue growth, backed by proven sales methodology that identifies, qualifies, and delivers.

Unique Value

- **Business Leader:** Executive with proven success in understanding markets, creating detailed business strategies, and precisely executing plans that effectively align with corporate goals.
- **Sales Driver:** Proven individual contributor, team member, and divisional leader talented in initiating, managing, and revitalizing consultative sales relationships with client accounts.
- **Team Mentor & Strategist:** Natural leader with strong team-building skills that inspire and empower individual members to perform beyond their own expectations.
- **Relationship Builder:** Expert in building relationships across organizations and with strategic partners to leverage internal capabilities with external opportunities for long-term sustainable growth.

Milestones

- **Created $10M life sciences business** of a $25M entrepreneurial enterprise software firm.
- **Led $300M division** of a billion-dollar UK-based company to successfully revive sales of a mature product in the consumer products marketplace.
- **Added $3.5M new revenue** to a $20M company in spite of fierce competition and the economic downturn.
- Spearheaded strategy that **propelled startup sales from $500K to $6M.**

Experience and Accomplishments

SOLUTIONS PROVIDER, INC. New York, NY, 2005–Present
Privately owned international software, hosting, and systems development solutions provider to online content publishers. Key products: Baseline digital publishing platform and Access enterprise platform. Solutions acquired Access (formerly BetaLime) from Visionwide Software in 2008. Annual sales: ~$20M.

Confronted steep challenges of growing competition, frequent administration change, and an economic crisis through 2 acquisitions in 3 years. Remained loyal to the brand and achieved exceptional results with each transition. Built new relationships that opened doors to new business opportunities. Grew revenue in spite of 2009's economic downturn. Taught and coached sales force to adapt to enterprise-level sales strategies with top-tier executives.

Director of U.S. Sales, 2008–Present

Accepted opportunity to stay with Solutions Provider following its acquisition of Visionwide's BetaLime enterprise operations. Vigorously energized sales of a brand that had lost much of its prominence in marketplace. Took on growing competition and the reality of a declining economy to become a key contributor to company results.

- During the financial decline of 2009 and without any formal marketing programs, new product development, or lead-generation services, identified target organizations in niche market to deliver $3.5M in sales.
- Through intensive, concentrated personal efforts, singlehandedly shored up existing client base during the administration transition and negotiated contracts with new clients totaling $4.8M.
- Salvaged lost relationship with disgruntled client and revived multimillion-dollar negotiations begun 3 years earlier to close one of the company's largest, still-expanding enterprise product contracts.

Major Account Manager—eCommerce & Entitlements Management, 2005–2008

Recruited to Visionwide Software, a $200M software solutions provider to the online publishing community. Drove sales of desktop, software license, and digital publisher enterprise solutions, onboarded new clients, and initiated strategic partnerships as the company grew through acquisitions.

- Carved local-level strategic partnership with Microsoft that quickly expanded nationally. Leveraged partnership to build new business through joint sales efforts and "best practices" seminars aimed at customers and the local user community.
- Negotiated and closed company's first U.S. digital publisher's deal of nearly $2M with Global Media and inked $millions additional contracts with Genzyme, Bose, EMC, Hasbro, Boston Legal, Polar Scientific, and more.

Page 1 of 2

Strategy: Emphasize "unique value" in the Summary along with impressive sales highlights from a 28-year career in technology sales.

Robert Geldof   rgeldof@gmail.com / 212-555-1212

SOFTWARE MANUFACTURER   New York, NY, 2002–2005
$45M entrepreneurial enterprise software manufacturer and distributor of web-enabled industrial label printing application for barcodes, sold on "as used" basis.

VP of Sales & Business Development—Life Sciences Group

Conceived, developed, and executed aggressive growth strategy for life sciences division. Created new business model, operational structure, and multi-channel marketing and distribution strategy to capitalize on highly regulated space of pharmaceutical/medical device and aerospace/defense industries. Trained, coached, and supervised pre-sales, sales, support, and implementation services team to generate $10M in sales. Direct reports: 7.

- Created channel partner program that drove 40% total sales.
- Grew bottom-line profitability 20% over 2 years.
- Inked first enterprise contract, valued at $1.7M, with Boston Legal.
- Added Stryker and CR Bar for additional $4M.

RFID, INC.   New York, NY, 2000–2002
Second-stage VC-funded RFID software and hardware manufacturer providing real-time locations data from tagged objects to the healthcare, manufacturing, and distribution markets. Estimated annual sales: $50M.

Director of Sales

Trained, coached, and guided Senior Account Managers in C-suite selling skills, a strategic change that elevated sales 8%. Developed and implemented new sales pipeline tracking process that improved accuracy 50% and reduced costs $800K. Direct reports: 3.

- Personally delivered contract sales of $2M.
- Cemented $15M opportunity with leading international shipping enterprise.
- Created $500K partnership with Philips Medical Systems.

PROVIDER SUPPORT, INC.   New York, NY, 1996–1999
$20M privately held startup software and services provider to wide spectrum of industries and government.

VP of Sales, Business Development & Marketing

Led, trained, and mentored regional account management team in developing customer-focused, cross-functional sales approach with professional services and support to increase average sale 20%.

- Singlehandedly sold $2.1M automobile tracing solution to U.S. Customs.
- Instrumental in igniting overall revenue from $500K to $6M.

TABLETOP TECHNOLOGY GROUP, INC.   New York, NY, 1995–1996
$200M industrial software and hardware integrator and reseller.

Northeast Regional Sales Manager

In one year, catapulted sales revenue from $900K to $12M. Direct reports: 9.

METALINK USA   Plattsburgh, NY, 1984–1993
$1B London-based consumer goods company, specializing in food and beverage.

National Divisional Sales Manager

Led $300M division to reenergize sales and market share of a mature product in a highly competitive market. Refocused sales strategy based on detailed analysis of internal operations and market dynamics.

- Key role in melding operations into newly formed organization following $5.76B acquisition of Baking Company.

Education / Community / Professional Affiliation

MBA, NEW YORK UNIVERSITY
BA in Marketing, STATE UNIVERSITY OF NEW YORK AT ALBANY

Board of Directors, Neighborhood Resource Center, New York, NY, since 2008

Member, National Technology Sales & Marketing Association, since 2000

ALISON K. DAILEY

212 132nd North, Seattle, WA 98133   (206) 523-8989   akdaily@hotmail.com

MARKETING PROFESSIONAL

Driving strategic growth and product visibility in global, competitive markets.

Seventeen years of experience in marketing, public relations, and international product management. Demonstrated success record in:

- Leading business units and motivated teams.
- Guiding complex global product launches and strategic Internet technology initiatives.
- Initiating growing accounts and channel/partner relationships.
- Branding, managing, and positioning product lines.
- Creating effective multichannel marketing campaigns.
- Providing pertinent research, content, white papers, and award-winning presentations.
- Incorporating emerging technology to achieve strategic goals. Expertise includes:

— Content management	— Personal computing operating systems
— GUI creation, testing, CRM	— Extensive list of software tools
— Deploying online services to ISPs/ASPs	— Network security/Internet file management

Industries: software, information technology, television broadcasting, and new media.

SAMPLE ACCOMPLISHMENTS

Led Executive Team and 30-person subsidiary though startup and public offering.

Increased direct-to-customer online sales by 300% as Marketing Director for ComputerConnect, Inc.

Secured profile of ComputerConnect CEO in the *Wall Street Journal*.

Demo God award winner, DemoMobile, 2010.

Managed corporate-identity project and successful IPO prospectus with Hornall Anderson.

PROFESSIONAL HISTORY

ComputerConnect, Inc. (formerly SCSI Software, Inc.), Redmond, WA   **2008–2011**

DIRECTOR OF BUSINESS DEVELOPMENT, Unit: RapidSync Technologies, Inc., Redmond, WA, 2010–2011
Named chief executive for new technology-licensing division, reporting to CEO. Charged with establishing business unit, developing business plan, overseeing transfer of intellectual property, creating software development kits, and securing potential licensees. Presented to potential investors. Led marketing, branding, sales, and legal research. Wrote white papers, technical data sheets, and application notes.

➤ **Managed Audio Labs partnership.** Forged licensing agreement, contract, and revenue plan.

MARKETING DIRECTOR, ComputerConnect, Inc., Redmond, WA, 2008–2010
Reported to CEO and managed a 12-person team with 3 director-level reports. Drove sales up 300%. Directed public relations, product marketing, marketing research, product branding, marketing communications, tradeshows and events, company websites, advertising, direct marketing, sales team support, and business development.

Spearheaded special projects; prepared company business plan. Managed press coverage, investor relations, and strategic/tactical industry analysts contacts. Initiated the development and delivery of all sales tools for the direct customer sales teams, the corporate sales teams, and the OEM sales team.

➤ **Created highly effective retail point-of-sale, direct mail, and national radio campaigns.**

➤ **Launched technology initiative,** Internet File Management, attracting Oracle/major storage clients.

➤ **Reorganized product development process** to incorporate customer feedback.

Page 1 of 2

Strategy: Eliminate the "job-hopper" image reflected in the candidate's prior resume by deleting some short-term jobs and using an umbrella heading to show continuity when the company name had changed. Stress significant achievements and expertise.

Alison K. Dailey	akdaily@hotmail.com	**Page 2 of 2**

StorageSecurity Technologies, Kirkland, WA   **2007–2008**

MARKETING MANAGER

Reported to Vice President of Marketing. Hired, supervised, and evaluated a 5-person team. Charged with developing partnership programs and directing customer communications, website sales, tradeshows and events, advertising, corporate identity, and sales-support programs. Supplemented rapid-growth phase with effective communication strategies, supporting successful IPO.

➢ **Delivered over $1,000,000 in sales per month** by creating a new website program.
➢ **Ran vendor-selection process for branding/IPO project,** selecting Hornall Anderson.
➢ **Produced cutting-edge event during N+I,** placing top management before key analysts and press.

MediaItalia-Presse, Milan, Italy   **2005–2007**

MANAGER, SALES AND MARKETING, North America, New York, NY, 2005–2007

Directed North American marketing communications including online/print promotions, direct mail, and VIP visits. Coordinated programs with Asian and European marketing directors. Researched North and South American information markets. Led and initiated strategic media product-development initiatives. Managed relationships/international contracts with information partners and major news organizations.

➢ **Led strategic initiative for "IntraSport" online real-time World Cup sports coverage.**
  — URL reached 94% of Spanish households.
  — Initiative enabled MIP to sign Spain's top 5 publications and Internet/portal companies worldwide.
  — Garnered record revenues from sales of MIP's World Cup coverage to Spanish media firms.

Associated Press/NewsLink, New York, NY   **2003–2005**

GENERAL MANAGER, MARKETING, Associated Press, Media Unit, New York, NY

Led marketing, public relations, and research initiatives for company's Internet-based platform, NewsLink. Developed comprehensive profiles of publishing customers and competitors. Conducted extensive marketing research to strategically position products.

➢ **Authorized interactive database tools for measuring/monitoring new marketing initiatives.**
➢ **Positioned 2 industry-leading product lines** including corporate identity, new brochures, sales kits, tradeshow messages, booth design, and direct-response marketing via an interactive website.
➢ **Developed strategic marketing relationships with international news information providers** including Agence France-Presse, Knight-Ridder/Tribune, Reuters, and UPI.

Dell Computer, Los Angeles, CA   **1996–2003**

MARKETING MANAGER, FEDERAL DIVISION, Washington DC, 2002–2003

➢ **Managed Dell's relationship with White House.**
➢ **Created direct-response programs, realizing 5%–8% response rates.**
➢ **Spearheaded development of cutting-edge multimedia Executive Briefing Center.**
➢ **Acted as Personal Consultant to Office of the Secretary of the Interior,** presenting first-ever interactive presentation to the United States Senate.

Other positions:
Regional Marketing Representative, Macromedia, Eastern Territory, New York, NY, 2001–2002
Assistant Interactive News Producer, NBC News, New York, NY, 1999–2001
Marketing Research Manager/Product Evangelist, GUIGuide, Inc., Washington DC, 1996–1999

EDUCATION/PUBLICATIONS

B.S., Information Marketing, with honors. Georgetown University, Washington, DC, 1996
Coauthor: *Strategic Positioning for On-Demand New Media Technologies.*

EDWARD GUERCI

85 Redwood Drive ◆ Los Altos, CA 94022 ◆ 650-344-8268 ◆ eguerci@gmail.com

SENIOR-LEVEL EXECUTIVE—BUSINESS DEVELOPMENT

**Business Development / Sales / Client Servicing / Client Relationship Management
Organizational Leadership / Team Building / Revenue Growth / Profit Maximization**

*Providing leadership and vision to drive business success ...
cultivating collegial work environments to promote performance excellence.*

Forward-thinking business executive with stellar record of success in leading business development initiatives and executing plans to explode sales and profitability. Respected, visionary leader; a recognized **"business-builder"** who is quick to see and capitalize on short-term opportunities while maintaining focus on sustaining long-term success. Incisive, process-oriented business manager who is highly effective in taking on new challenges and delivering immediate results for companies large and small.

Core Competencies

➤ Directing organizations, providing vision and leadership to drive dramatic revenue growth.

➤ Building and leading sales and business development teams, identifying and attracting best-in-class talent to execute plans and drive business goals.

➤ Developing well-conceived sales and marketing strategies, effectively penetrating target markets by building value propositions that resonate with specific audiences.

➤ Leveraging well-established networks to cultivate executive-level relationships, building partnerships to advance business goals.

➤ Managing client relationships, providing high-level support to protect and expand revenues.

PROFESSIONAL EXPERIENCE

NORTHSTAR SYSTEMS INTERNATIONAL, San Francisco, CA   2006 to present
Managing Director, Business Development/Client Management
Hired to develop/execute go-to-market strategy to penetrate major industry verticals and build dominant market share across West Coast client base. Mobilized sales team and managed client relationships to meet business goals.

*Built diverse pipeline of business while establishing organizational infrastructures ...
driving phenomenal revenue growth.*

▪ As key member of senior management team, brought vision and leadership to organization, expertly executing strategies that **more than tripled revenue over 3-year period**. At the same time, **exploded book of business**, adding diversity of clients to establish sound market base.

▪ Built high-performance sales team, attracting and retaining top talent to drive business goals. Built team around performance-based model designed to create funnel of opportunities to sustain growth.

▪ Developed new sales and marketing program, defining product to appeal to target market while developing value propositions to bring company up market.

▪ Established and managed key alliance/partner opportunities, exploring M&A, BOT (build, operate, transfer), and captive business models as strategies for adding revenue-generating resources.

Page 1

Strategy: Highlight the big-picture achievement of each job in an attention-getting format before detailing all of the smaller accomplishments and activities that produced the overall result.

Edward Guerci   eguerci@gmail.com   Page 2

INVECTIS CORPORATION, New York, NY   2002 to 2006
Executive Vice President, Business Development
Defining new position, introduced enterprise approach to package and sell investment service products. Developed and executed synergy sales techniques across 3 business lines as means to drive growth. Oversaw $550 million in business—52% of overall company revenue—through team of 30 worldwide managers.

Developed innovative sales strategies to drive dramatic year-over-year growth ...implemented holistic approach—aggregate packaging of products from disparate businesses—to open new business opportunities.

- Hired into new position to drive sales, implemented sales and marketing strategies that **generated in excess of $75 million in new revenue for 5 straight years, growing business from $500 million to $900 million** during tenure.

- Developed value propositions to accurately target markets, introducing refinements to increase precision and elevate customer base. Centralized sales organization, incorporating best practices across multiple business lines to unify and strengthen sales operations.

- Expertly managed consulting agreements and multiple alliance programs to maximize return. Developed business plan for top-line growth that included outsourcing, liftout, and acquisition activities.

GLOBAL BANK, New York, NY   1993 to 2002
Senior Vice President, Investor Services (1996 to 2002)
Vice President, Global Investor Services (1993 to 1996)
Oversaw worldwide 70-member team in managing $1.8 billion business, directing strategy development, product/technology investments, product development, client management, and business development. As senior manager, also participated in key merger, acquisition, and joint venture activities.

*Led global business development efforts for $1.8 million business ...
driving new revenue generation through target markets across North America, Europe, and Asia Pacific.*

- Led team that **generated in excess of $100 million in new annual revenue** through strategic market targeting practices.

- Leveraged company's strong global infrastructure to deliver comprehensive product/servicing packages to both institutional clients and their retail client base.

- Defined and instituted best practices for sales across all regions, increasing closing rates to 70%–80% to exceed annual sales targets year over year.

- Innovated marketing and communications, identifying linkages/opportunities to expediently meet information needs of all constituencies (media, clients, prospects, employees). Delivered results through a variety of traditional and non-traditional vehicles (print advertisements, intranet, Internet, video, etc.).

NEW YORK LIFE, New York, NY   1982 to 1993
Director of Banking/Assistant Treasurer; Manager, Cash Management Operations; Manager, Securities Lending Operations; Manager, Securities Accounting Division; Assistant Financial Analyst
Took on increasingly challenging roles in the accounting, treasury, and cash management departments.

EDUCATION

B.S., Business Finance and Administration, Fordham University, 1982

MICHAEL ENRIGHT

121 Wildflower Road, #2 ▪ Denver, CO 80205 ▪ 303-458-9077 ▪ michael.enright@gmail.com

BIOTECH MARKETING MANAGEMENT

Driving expansive, profitable growth in cutting-edge biotechnology markets by launching, building, and growing product lines via innovative strategies.

➢ **Goal-driven strategist** with impressive history of career steps in marketing communications and research at global, strategic, and development levels.

➢ **Well-rounded consummate manager** with solid academic background plus broad-based experience in scientific research, nursing, entrepreneurship, and marketing.

➢ **Fair-minded and congenial leader** who combines integrity and ingenuity with passion for learning to achieve desired results.

Areas of expertise include:
▪ Integrated Marketing Strategies
▪ Strategic Promotional Campaigns
▪ New Product Development
▪ Product Commercialization
▪ Portfolio Management
▪ Team Building & Leadership
▪ Brand Management
▪ Sales Targets & Forecasts

PROFESSIONAL EXPERIENCE

BIOSCIENCE CORPORATION, Denver, CO   2006 – 2011
Provider of progressive technologies, tools, and services for bioscience research and biopharmaceutical manufacturing.

Product Manager (2008 – 2011)

Promoted to support global sales team by providing solid lead generation and new product education. Personally interfaced with customers in academia, biopharma, and government with strong emphasis on innovative solutions and end user satisfaction. Charged with managing product portfolio and driving marketing initiatives for new product launches. Oversaw performance of +7-member R&D teams.

Became strategic partner by blending biotech background with marketing expertise to champion all sales team's needs.

- Grew revenues for portfolio 42% in first year by formulating strategic marketing plan for successful launch of new device.
- Restored double-digit sales growth to stagnant product and reduced complaints from 30% to 10% by discovering quick and easy fix to QC problems.
- Stabilized performance of product line and broke weakening freefall by promoting and highlighting product at conferences.
- Helped directors define their communications needs for integrated marketing plans by devising Creative Marketing Brief.
- Reversed sales drop on $3.2M marketing communications campaign for newly released product.

Marketing Manager (2006 – 2008)

Defined and clarified customer needs and industry trends by designing, conducting, and analyzing market research studies for all business units. Oversaw agencies/consultants, conducting primary market research studies, focus groups, and surveys. Developed new products, working jointly with R&D scientists, engineers, and academic researchers.

Helped determine which products had merit and supported profitable business cases.

- Contributed to 22% sales growth for product line by supporting market research and plan development.
- Helped boost revenues 24% for stem-cell products by bolstering marketing plan development.
- Devised method for prioritizing Market Research Projects that was adopted by directors company-wide.
- Created more robust evaluations that led to better correlations and conclusions by introducing SPSS as statistical tool for market research analyses.

Continued

Strategy: Build an easy-to-skim resume through the use of short paragraphs, concise bullet points, lists, and a bold key achievement statement for every position.

303-458-9077   MICHAEL ENRIGHT – Page 2   michael.enright@gmail.com

SMITH GOODWIN, Los Angeles, CA   2004 – 2006
Marketing research firm, pioneering industry's most innovative research methodologies and techniques to assess and track advertising and brand performance.
Market Research Executive

Spearheaded primary and secondary market research activities in advertising effectiveness, marketing evaluation, media assessment, and brand equity/performance. In charge of developing questionnaires, conducting interviews and focus groups, and analyzing data. Teamed with media planners to ensure proper data capture and ad agencies to evaluate marketing campaigns.

Advanced clients' brands/services by equipping them with a better understanding of consumer demand via full qualitative and quantitative research studies.

- Condensed overwhelming 20- to 50-slide presentations into 1 easily readable and digestible slide that was well received by clients.
- Provided sound recommendations for marketing campaigns for key clients.

UNIVERSITY OF MARYLAND, College Park, MD   2003 – 2005
Marketing Research Associate

Hired to gain better insight into consumer attitudes toward genetic technologies used in food and medicine production. Recruited all participants for focus groups and facilitated group activities. Developed regression model by scrutinizing data and pinpointing key drivers.

- Designed and conducted market research studies that accurately appraised consumers' perception of food and medicine developed through genetic technologies.
- Advanced understanding of marketing impact on mindset of consumers and adoption of biotechnology.

MARYLAND INSTITUTE OF TECHNOLOGY, College Park, MD   2002 – 2003
Marketing Research Associate

Played a role in better understanding underlying traits of Parkinson's disease. Helped explain tremors associated with the disease and dyskinesias by studying interaction between dopamine and RGS9.

ADDITIONAL EXPERIENCE

ARTISAN'S BREAD BAKERY, Silver Spring, MD   1997 – 2002
Owner / Manager

Started-up business offering finest natural and organic European breads and pastries. Successfully developed and marketed handcrafted product line of unique artistic breads prepared in traditional European style.

- Built profitable business in just 1 year by identifying need and capitalizing on niche market.
- Designated as "Emerging Enterprise of the Year" by Chamber of Commerce.

Early Career: **Nursing Assistant** with Johns Hopkins Hospital, Baltimore, MD (1994 – 1997)

PROFESSIONAL DEVELOPMENT

MBA Degree, Science & Technology Marketing (2005)
BS Degree, Cellular, Molecular & Microbial Biology
UNIVERSITY OF MARYLAND, College Park, MA (1997)

Nursing Diploma – JOHNS HOPKINS UNIVERSITY SCHOOL OF NURSING, Baltimore, MD (1994)

ROBERT S. MARTINO

198 Parkway Avenue
Chesapeake, VA 23322

(757) 626-1974
rsmartino45@earthlink.net

SENIOR EXECUTIVE — PRODUCT MARKETING AND MANAGEMENT

Record of defining, delivering, and marketing timely, profitable leading-edge products

High-powered senior product manager with 10 years of increasingly responsible experience driving product strategy and execution. Technology-product expertise includes networking and telecom hardware / software, enterprise-class software, brand-awareness products, and web-delivered products / services. Team builder / leader / motivator who emphasizes goal achievement.

Candidate differentiators include: a sophisticated understanding of marketing and finance that enables successful product-strategy development with a focus on profitability; ability to anticipate market trends and initiate timely product development.

HIGHLIGHTS

- Grew revenues by 250% through new- and existing-product development.
- Launched six major software product releases generating $30 million in annual revenues.
- Created a consumer-service product line that added 35% to bottom-line profits.
- Orchestrated the integration of product lines from four acquisitions, creating a unified product strategy.

PROFESSIONAL EXPERIENCE

AGILE ENTERPRISES, INC., Washington, DC   2007 to 2011
Develops and markets enterprise-software solutions to retailers, e-tailers, and publishers worldwide.

Provided strategic product and operational leadership. Defined product roadmap. Managed product-line P&L. Positioned products to customers, analysts, and sales force. Managed full product lifecycle from requirements definition through first customer ship. Directed a team of eight software engineers.

Vice President, Product Marketing and Management (2009 to 2011)

- Redesigned processes and accomplished turnaround of an underperforming function.
- Transitioned company from a focus on selling services to an out-of-the-box deployment model with higher profit margins.
- Launched six major software products generating $30 million in annual revenues.
- Built and institutionalized product-management and product-marketing functions.

Director, Product Marketing and Management (2007 to 2009)

- Drove the development of five major software releases, nine new products / services, and seven product enhancements within a $300 million business unit.
- Assessed market demand and developed service offerings for six industries.
- Added $2 million in annual revenues by identifying and delivering product enhancements with a profit margin of 80%.
- Integrated products, services, and business and financial infrastructure for four acquisitions representing a combined revenue stream of $50 million.

Strategy: Use a tagline to pinpoint the key value of this candidate and a Highlights section to emphasize four impressive achievements.

ROBERT S. MARTINO   PAGE 2

VIDEOSOLVE CORPORATION, Alexandria, VA   2006 to 2007
Markets and manufactures voice, video, and data-communications software and equipment.

Group Product-Line Manager
Defined market and product requirements for audio-conferencing software and hardware solutions; managed product programs, facilitated new business development, and led cross-functional project teams.

- Created requirements and roadmap for entry into IP-based products.

- Defined market and product requirements for Internet-based and client-server–based conference-scheduling applications.

- Recruited and managed beta customers.

- Product champion to customers, sales force, and partners.

TECHPHONE, INC., Alexandria, VA   2005 to 2006
A venture-backed startup that markets and manufactures a small-office PBX sold directly through an on-premise call center and commerce-enabled website.

Director, Product Marketing
Comprehensive and pivotal role that included defining the business plan for services and accessory products and developing content and e-commerce requirements for the corporate website. Managed $1.8M budget.

- Created value-added consumer-service products contributing more than 35% to the bottom line.

- Created an accessory product line. Selected products / vendors and negotiated OEM relationships, deliverables, and service agreements.

- Led e-commerce website project. Wrote RFQs, selected partners / vendors, and evaluated and selected commerce-related applications.

- Built and led a call-center applications team.

VIDEOTECH, INC., Washington, DC   2000 to 2005
Manufactures network equipment and software for use on circuit-switched and IP networks.

Director, Services Product Marketing
Accountable for services business development, technical-product definition, sales, customer and reseller contracts, corporate technical publications, and website.

- Increased revenues more than 250% during tenure by identifying demand-generation opportunities and driving programs for new and existing products.

- Consistently achieved ambitious sales goals in a highly competitive market.

- Defined, positioned, branded, marketed, and sold technical service products and programs accounting for $6+ million in annual sales.

EDUCATION

ROCHESTER INSTITUTE OF TECHNOLOGY, Rochester, NY   2000
Bachelor of Technology in Computer Science

KEVIN JOSEPH MCNEIL

500 Hero Avenue, Lake Forest, CA 92630 ▪ Home: 949.555.5555 ▪ Cell: 714.555.5555 ▪ kjmn@hotmail.com

SENIOR SALES & MARKETING EXECUTIVE

Strategic Sales & Marketing / Competitive Market Positioning / New Product Launch
Team Leadership / Advertising Production / Graphic Design & Layout

Twenty-year career as a member of several high-profile publishing-industry management teams. Goal-oriented individual successful in sales and marketing through expertise in business development and strategic business planning capabilities. Excellent presentation, negotiation, closing, and follow-through skills with a strong ability to build an industry presence. MBA degree.

CAREER HIGHLIGHTS

WEST COAST ADVERTISING SALES MANAGER – *Smith & Associates, Inc.*, San Francisco, CA (2008–Present)

Key member of sales management team for publishing-industry rep firm in charge of West Coast clients. Vital part of sales team that increases client and revenue base year on year for national publishers. Direct West Coast advertising sales and marketing of trade show and publishing representation for various high-growth magazines.

- Directed market launch of five new publications in three years, delivering revenue growth as follows:

Publication	Advertising Increase	Monthly Revenue Increase
Washington Times	20 pages	$ 180,000
The Nation	22 pages	$ 75,000
Foreign Policy	9 pages	$ 55,000
American Prospect	4 pages	$ 16,000
Jet	4 pages	$ 7,000

- Expanded monthly revenue stream for *Washington Times* magazine to over $270,000 from $90,000 (5 pages to 25 pages) through active participation in sales and business development that included banner-ad sales and email newsletter-sponsorship sales.

WEST COAST ADVERTISING MANAGER – *The Progressive Magazine Co., Inc.*, Los Angeles, CA (2001–2007)
Established West Coast office and oversaw all advertising-sales efforts for the launch of national publication serving as a voice of national and international social justice.

- Increased annual advertising-sales volume through strong prospecting, account retention, and sales skills.
- Assisted in advertising design and layout, offering suggestions and preparing client advertisements.
- Conceived marketing strategy for an extraordinarily effective four-color advertising package and rate card.
- Generated new accounts through participation in trade shows and professional golf tournaments.

REGIONAL SALES MANAGER – *Weekly World News,* Chicago, IL (1991–2000)
Oversaw regional sales team and managed facets of design, layout, and production for *Weekly World News* magazine.

- Led team responsible for increasing nationwide sales by 40%–80% year over year.
- Achieved recognition as a leading agency manager for worldwide magazine.
- Spearheaded campaign that resulted in 350% increase in subscriptions nationwide.
- Obtained incisive articles and in-depth political analyses from the most skilled and seasoned news professionals.
- Instrumental in spearheading the redesign of *Weekly World News* and placing it first in its field.

EDUCATION, PROFESSIONAL DEVELOPMENT & SPECIAL SKILLS

CALIFORNIA STATE UNIVERSITY – **MBA**, International Business (1994); **BS**, Business Management (1988)

PROFESSIONAL EDUCATION – Completed more than 900 hours of sales and business development courses. Participated in multiple graphic design and editorial layout conferences.

TECHNOLOGY – Proficient with GoldMine, Adobe InDesign, Microsoft Office, and others on both Mac and Windows platforms.

SPECIAL INTERESTS – Skilled in visual arts, including photography and design.

Strategy: Use a "front-and-center" chart for a compelling visual presentation of strong sales results.

CHAPTER 5

Resumes for Managers and Executives in Social Services, Associations and Nonprofits, Government and Military, and Law

- Administrative Director
- Director/Program Administrator/Development Coordinator
- Association Executive
- Senior Executive
- Senior Executive/Vice President/Director
- Senior-Level Manager/Administrator
- Law Enforcement Lieutenant
- Law Enforcement Commander
- Airport Manager
- Prosecutor
- Trial Lawyer
- Executive Director

KEITH A. GARDNER, LCSW

2551 Barton Avenue, Rotterdam, New York 12306 • 518-355-5600 • kagdirect@mindspring.com

ADMINISTRATIVE DIRECTOR

BUSINESS DEVELOPMENT — STAFF DEVELOPMENT — TRAINING/COACHING/MENTORING

RESIDENTIAL TREATMENT • HOSPITAL • FOSTER CARE • WILDERNESS PROGRAMS
Early Intervention and Group Treatment for Adolescent Sex Offenders

DYNAMIC, GOAL-ORIENTED LICENSED CLINICAL SOCIAL WORKER combining broad-spectrum life experiences with 18 years of extensive hands-on experience directing and working in all facets of 24/7 residential treatment. Solid track record of launching successful programs to enhance development and rehabilitation of youth. Strong interpersonal skills and innate ability to relate to diverse personalities with emphasis on team leadership and development. Demonstrated leadership skill to drive ground-breaking concepts to revolutionize change initiatives that affect social work industry-wide while expanding operational revenues. Will relocate and travel.

- ❑ **STRATEGIC AND CREATIVE THINKER** with solid background of delivering decisive, action-driven administrative leadership. Demonstrated insight and proficiency in developing and streamlining early-intervention programs.

- ❑ **RESULTS-ORIENTED**, with proven capacity to accelerate growth and deliver substantial profits. Catalyst for success with powerful capacity to build and create from concept.

- ❑ **PERFORMANCE-DRIVEN TEAM LEADER** with excellent interpersonal skills, optimally utilizing all channels of communication to develop team momentum, enthusiasm, and pride. Promote group harmony.

CORE LEADERSHIP QUALIFICATIONS

- Strategic Business Planning & Development
- Change Management
- New Business Development
- Project Management
- Problem Identification/Resolution
- Case Management/Support Services
- New Venture & Program Start-Up/Launch
- General Operating Management
- Process Reengineering
- Tactical Planning/Leadership
- Strategic Marketing & Sales
- Cross-Functional Team Leadership

"DRIVING CHANGE TO IMPROVE LIVES"

SELECTED ACCOMPLISHMENTS

- ❑ **SARATOGA RANCH:** Conceived, developed, and launched from ground up an early-intervention, work-ethics program for state-custody adolescent males age 13–17. Delivered innovative strategies and concepts to enhance the lives of more than 500 youth that **resulted in only 10% recidivism** after three years.

- ❑ **MAPLE GROVE BOYS RANCH:** Developed concept and format of program for 18-bed facility housing state-custody adolescent male sex offenders age 13–18. **First program of its kind in New York State.**

- ❑ **JUVENILES NETWORK ON OFFENDING SEXUALLY (JNOOS):** Cofounder and charter member. Developed and created initial standards and protocols. New York State, State University of New York at Albany, and the Commission on Criminal and Juvenile Justice endorse organization, with membership of about 100.

- ❑ **APPLE RIDGE RANCH SCHOOL:** Spearheaded development from conception to successful launch of accredited school delivering curriculum to 25 students and resulting in **dramatic increase in individual test scores.** Wrote proposals to receive funding of $240,000 annually through Youth in Custody grants.

- ❑ **BUILD A BETTER YOU RANCH:** Cofounder of 12-bed program for teenage girls age 12–17.

Page 1

Strategy: Highlight specific, significant programs in the Selected Accomplishments section, which follows a comprehensive summary outlining key qualifications. Emphasize successful outcomes throughout the resume.

KEITH A. GARDNER, LCSW

kagdirect@mindspring.com

Page 2

PROFESSIONAL CAREER HISTORY

Highland Ridge Youth Services, Schenectady, NY   1994–present
Private agency providing foster care and support services for adolescents in state custody.

CLINICAL DIRECTOR (2005–present)
MEDICAID ENHANCEMENT SERVICES COORDINATOR (2006–present, concurrent with above)

Manage and oversee residential care for three group homes providing sex-offender-specific program, residential group home care, clinical services, proctors, and tracking. Coordinate intake screenings, clinical treatment, and all oversight for seven licensed clinicians. Scope of responsibility includes quality assurance and Medicaid enhancement as well as training and staff development.

- ❏ Introduced Saratoga Ranch, which **increased revenues by 40%** ($700,000 annual budget) based on fixed contract as well as **consistent 90% occupancy rate.**
- ❏ Delivered **100% Quality Assurance rating,** with no sanctions.
- ❏ Oversee and direct Apple Ridge Ranch, 15-bed facility for non-sex-offending males and self-contained accredited school.
- ❏ Administer and manage Build A Better You Ranch, 12-bed group home for teenaged girls, as well as Maple Grove Aftercare Program.

CLINICIAN (2001–2005)
Facilitated sex-offender-specific program for clients in custody of Division of Youth Corrections and Division of Child and Family Services.

PROGRAM COORDINATOR — Maple Grove Boys Ranch (1996–2001)
Assisted in the development and launch of program for 18-bed inpatient treatment program for adolescent male sex offenders. Directed and oversaw all aspects of operation including supervision and coordination of staff. Provided clinical oversight for residents in program.

SUPERVISED RESTITUTION COORDINATOR (1994–1995)
Coordinated daily progress notes, monthly and court reports, summaries, intakes, and screening of adolescent youth for program.

EDUCATION & PROFESSIONAL DEVELOPMENT

Licensed Clinical Social Worker (LCSW), 2003
Master of Social Work Program, 2001
Bachelor of Science — Sociology, Criminology Certificate, 1997
STATE UNIVERSITY OF NEW YORK, ALBANY, NEW YORK

Primary Children's Child Protection Team, 2000
TREATMENT OF SEXUALLY REACTIVE CHILDREN AND VICTIMS OF SEXUAL ABUSE

Certificate: Treatment of Juvenile Sex Offender, 1998
SYMPOSIUM SPONSORED BY STATE UNIVERSITY OF NEW YORK
STATE UNIVERSITY OF NEW YORK / COMMISSION ON CRIMINAL AND JUVENILE JUSTICE

Certified Addictions Counselor, 1997
O'HENRY HOUSE ADOLESCENT UNIT — INTERNSHIP

PROFESSIONAL AFFILIATIONS

National Affiliation of Social Workers (NASW), 2008–present
Private Psychology Network, Member 1994–2012
Juveniles Network On Offending Sexually (JNOOS), Charter Member 2000–present

Diana M. Drexel

21 Towbridge Court, Lawrenceville, NJ 08648
(609) 883-5555 Home ▪ dmdrexel5555@hotmail.com

Director / Program Administrator / Development Coordinator
Not-for-Profit Service Agencies ▪ Professional & Trade Associations

Committed, experienced nonprofit administrator of federally funded human-services program, with additional leadership experience in diverse nonprofit activities. Successful in revenue raising and volunteer recruitment and retention, as well as corporate development, community outreach, and media relations. Expertise in:

✓ Special Events Management	✓ Volunteer Recruitment & Training	✓ Grant Writing
✓ Marketing Communications	✓ Financial / Budgetary Management	✓ Fundraising
✓ Educational Programming	✓ Public / Private Partnerships	✓ Public Relations

Effective organizational skills, proactive team involvement, and independent decision-making have yielded dramatic results for development and program expansion. Proven talent for writing, interpersonal relations, and communications. Computer literate: Word, Excel, Outlook, Internet.

PROFESSIONAL EXPERIENCE

Seniors in Service to America (SSA), Princeton, NJ   2007–present
United Way of Central New Jersey program serving seniors age 55 and older in member-driven organization. Provides volunteer opportunities for work or mentoring in nonprofit agencies throughout Mercer County, as well as member development, education, and services.

Director
Recruited to oversee revitalization of established federal program. Collaborate with Advisory Council in strategic planning, policy development, and mission planning. Administer 3 key programs concurrently, including daily operations, public and media relations, and marketing. Budget allocation ($200K) kept on target.

- **Organizational Leadership.** Direct and supervise 800-member volunteer activities at 80 local agencies, as well as the Breast Screening Awareness Program and Food Direct Program (providing homeless shelters with food). Serve as liaison with United Way senior management, agency directors, site managers, corporate sponsors, community groups, and government officials.

- **Volunteer Recruitment.** Acquired 175 new volunteers through persuasive public speaking at targeted community / senior centers and corporations. Kept member-retention figures stable in challenging times.

- **Member Services and Training.** Promote realistic expectations for volunteer services, ensuring proper volunteer training at site agencies, as well as staff development and training for site managers. Expanded member communications (including quarterly newsletter) and updated marketing collaterals.

- **Program Expansion.** Grew Breast Screening Awareness program from 3 to 8 sites, recruiting 12 new leaders. Quadrupled grant awards for Food Direct Program and secured high-profile community ties.

- **Grant-Writing and Fundraising.** Wrote successful grant proposal for renewed federal and United Way funding. Won state funding for Breast Screening Awareness Program by showing program's viability.

- **Sponsorship Procurement.** Gained corporate sponsorship from CommunityOne (Princeton nursing home) for the Food Direct Program, contributing to increased revenues and improved community visibility.

- **Event Planning.** Spearheaded and directed all aspects of annual Recognition Brunch for 800+ participants including volunteers, public officials, sponsors, and site managers. Doubled revenues from previous year.

Continued

Strategy: Interrupt reverse-chronological work history with a category for Volunteer Activities because they are more directly related to the candidate's present career focus than are her previous jobs.

Diana M. Drexel

(609) 883-5555 Home ▪ dmdrexel5555@hotmail.com　　　　　　　　　　　　Page 2

VOLUNTEER / NONPROFIT EXPERIENCE

Community Ties, Inc., Princeton, NJ　　　　　　　　　　　　　　　　2005–2010
Steering Committee / Publicity Chairperson

- Created and implemented a comprehensive public-relations and advertising program for the annual Gourmet Tour Dinner fundraising event, benefiting local hunger-relief programs. Increased revenues year-over-year at this event attended by 600 people. Grew revenues by 50% in 5 years to $90,000 in 2010.

South Brunswick High School, South Brunswick, NJ　　　　　　　　　　2001
- Won highest level of corporate giving from local and national companies (such as Kraft Foods), including $17K in contributions and $21K in gifts-in-kind, as Chairperson of one-day post-prom event for 750 seniors. Directed and integrated activities of 8 committees providing food, entertainment, and prizes.

Rotary Club of Central New Jersey, Trenton, NJ　　　　　　　　　　　2000
- Pioneered concept of restaurant and gourmet gift shop for annual Community House Tour event, which raised $25K in revenues within 3 weeks of operation for this nonprofit fundraiser.

- Coordinated year-long project management, supervised staff of 10, and assisted in planning successful advertising campaign, including increasing advertising from corporate sponsors in program book.

OTHER RELATED EXPERIENCE

Account Consultant, Psychometric Consulting, Inc., Woodbridge, NJ　　　2006
- Advised and consulted with Fortune 500 and other companies on psychological assessment results for this international human-resources consulting firm. Analyzed test results and wrote 5–8 in-depth individual reports daily, clearly and concisely communicating complex psychological constructs and impact of results.

Freelance Writer and Consultant　　　　　　　　　　　　　　　　1995–2006
- Wrote general-interest and investigative feature articles published in local newspapers and national trade publications including *The Princeton Packet, The Trenton Times, Holistic Living* magazine, *ACT/Advertising Communications Times,* KYW News Radio, AARP's *Modern Maturity* magazine, and *Philadelphia NOW.*

Instructor—Journalism Department, **Rutgers State University,** New Brunswick, NJ　　1992–1995
- Taught introductory journalism courses (including Introduction to Mass Media) to undergraduate students.

Feature Writer & Investigative Staff Reporter, *The Trenton Times,* Trenton, NJ　　1991–1993
- Published revealing feature article on teenage drug abuse that proved instrumental in the award of a $100K federal grant for a methadone maintenance clinic, enabling the clinic to remain in operation.

EDUCATION & TRAINING

Bachelor of Science—Communications, Rutgers State University, New Brunswick, NJ

Ongoing Professional Development:
Grant Writing Skills Seminar, Rutgers University, New Brunswick, NJ (2010)
Leadership and Team Excellence Workshop, United Way of America, Washington, DC (2009)
Community Service in Action Training Conference (2008)

AFFILIATIONS

Association of Fundraising Professionals (AFP) ▪ Communications and Marketing Association (CAMA)

JON ROSENBERG

105 Remsen Road ◆ Yonkers, NY 10710 ◆ 914-963-8228 ◆ jrosenberg@gmail.com

ASSOCIATION EXECUTIVE

**Team Leadership / Strategic Planning / Program Development / Performance Maximization / Staff Development
Strategic Communications / Relationship Building / Program Outreach / Public Relations**

*High-energy leader who leverages an inquisitive, out-of-the-box nature to identify solutions ...
and a passion for excellence to drive success.*

Forward-thinking leader with a proven record of success in developing and executing strategic plans to drive organization goals while cultivating an environment of excellence. Performance-driven executive focused on maximizing program effectiveness to increase engagement of members. Respected, influential leader; a persuasive communicator who is effective in engaging others to gain support and funding for programs. A consummate relationship-builder with an extensive network of well-placed connections and a polished public presence. Critical thinker who asks the tough questions to consistently deliver results that exceed expectations.

Core Competencies

- **Providing vision and leadership to organizations,** developing and executing plans to advance strategic goals.
- **Building teams,** attracting strong talent and providing tools and support to deliver best-in-class performance.
- **Serving as public ambassador,** leveraging stellar relationship-building and presentation skills to raise organizational profile.
- **Promoting strategic initiatives,** capably demonstrating value to gain buy-in and support of key stakeholders.
- **Revitalizing organizations and programs,** capitalizing on entrepreneurial spirit to drive growth and improvement.

PROFESSIONAL EXPERIENCE

AMERICAN INSTITUTE OF CHEMICAL ENGINEERS, New York, NY   2005 to present
Executive Director
Oversee day-to-day operations of 40,000-member professional organization, leading 32 staff and managing $3 million budget. Direct program initiatives and oversee marketing, communications, finance, and technology teams. Set strategic direction of organization. Cultivate and maintain relationships across all departments.

Leveraged keen entrepreneurial mindset to refine operations ...
implemented organizational and program initiatives to maximize return on investment.

Leadership & Performance Excellence

- Recruited to bring entrepreneurial approach to association and its programs. Launched staff reorganization to gain synergy, unifying programs under a single senior program manager to improve department communications and achieve more-efficient utilization of resources.
- Secured 3 new full-time staff positions to help advance goals, highlighting strategic plan, association priorities, and potential return on investment in well-received presentation that was successful in gaining approval and funding.
- Launched comprehensive review of all 74 existing programs, engaging staff to define and implement appropriate performance criteria. As a result, shed underperforming programs, making way for more-effective, better-targeted programs. Identified good programs that could be better and implemented changes to improve benefit to members.
- Developed relationships with industry and academia representatives to provide greater collaboration on programs.

(Continued)

Strategy: Emphasize relevant association leadership on page 1 and appropriately feature impressive business success on page 2. Communicate both hard facts and soft skills throughout the resume.

Jon Rosenberg	914-963-8228 ◆ jrosenberg@gmail.com	Page 2

AMERICAN INSTITUTE OF CHEMICAL ENGINEERS   Continued

Program Successes

- Led overhaul of cumbersome, difficult-to-use online application for members, delivering user-friendly engagement website that featured expanded, role-based directory and complete suite of online management tools. Led cross-department team in gap analysis, benchmarking, and product design activities to build top-notch tool.
  - ➢ Generated 35,000+ unique visitors and nearly 2,000 new program registrations in first 6 weeks after site launch.
- In face of economic crisis, gained funding for and launched new website to meet impending member career needs.
  - ➢ Generated 19,479 unique visits (42,400 total) with 275,000 page views in 16 months.
  - ➢ Attracted 18,000 members to private LinkedIn group and 1,400 registrations with free career search tool.
  - ➢ Sparked creation and delivery of a series of career resource seminars across the country.
- Launched new AICHE-branded credit card that, in only 3 months, earned ranking among the top 5 association-affinity cards in the nation. Effectively marketing benefits of card, program is projected to be the association's largest revenue-generator within 1 year.

CRESTLINE, Lewiston, ME   1990 to 2005
CEO
Oversaw operations of newly purchased promotional products company, growing to $15 million before selling the firm in 2005.

Rapidly turned around performance of floundering company, driving dramatic sales improvement.
Once righted, re-invented company to meet ongoing market challenges.

- Taking over struggling business, reversed losing performance, achieving 30% to 40% growth in each of the first 6 years. Totally retooled company, rebuilding it to a market-driven, customer-centric organization. Refreshed product line based on customer preferences to dramatically increase sales and satisfaction.
- Seeing sales slump in late '90s and early '00s, launched major rebranding effort, re-engineering company to thrive in tough market. Testament to incredible success, averaged 82% increase in sales in each of the last 5 years of operation, despite having more than 100 competitors.
- Built and managed high-performance sales team, recruiting and attracting seasoned, talented reps from across the industry by persuasively communicating vision and opportunity.
- Garnered industry's most prestigious "Supplier Star Award" and recognition as "Supplier Entrepreneur of the Year."
- Gained acquisition attention from world-class company based on standout growth, products, quality, service, and reputation. Participated in negotiations and successful sale of company to well-known suitor.

EDUCATION

UNIVERSITY OF CONNECTICUT, Storrs, CT
Bachelor of Arts Degree, History

Cassandra Dixson

925-734-1743 | cassdixson@msn.com
160 Remington Avenue, Walnut Creek, CA 94567

SENIOR EXECUTIVE – MEDIA INDUSTRY

**Passionate about making a difference—challenging assumptions, uncovering insights,
and building strategic and sustainable programs with long-lasting impact.**

Award-winning media expert with a 16-year record of creative innovation, leadership, and results in the national arena. Catalyst for purpose-driven initiatives that align organizational mission with industry trends. Idea generator whose strong management skills motivate teams, execute complex strategies, and drive concepts to successful reality. Sensitive to cultural differences and the global landscape. Fluent in French and Spanish.

Career Milestones

- **Association Leadership:** Accepted opportunity to fulfill role of the President & CEO of a 6500-member national association during transition to a new administration.
- **Partnerships:** Built strong relationships with the Board of Directors and Executive Committee to navigate the organization through a challenging period of operational upheaval and industry change.
- **Advocacy:** Launched benchmark studies of the status of women in the cable industry to advance pay equity, upward mobility, and resources for work/life support to perpetuate the organization's vision and brand.
- **Event-Planning & Sponsorship:** Led production of fund-raising galas attended by more than 1000. Directed everything from theme creation and stage design to awards program and entertainment planning.

**Strategic Vision & Planning | Financial Austerity | Research Design & Execution
Social Change & Advocacy | Consensus & Influence Building | Concept Development | Diversity Initiatives**

CAREER TRACK

WOMEN IN NATIONAL COMMUNICATIONS (WINC), Los Angeles, CA
National association advocating upward mobility of women in the media industry. 6500 members. 25 chapters.

Senior Vice President—Strategic Initiatives | 2007–Present
Interim President & Chief Executive Officer | 2009
Vice President—Strategic Initiatives | 2005–2007
Director—Issues & Advocacy | 2000–2004
Manager—Association Outreach | 1998–2000
Program Researcher | 1996–1998

Overview: High-profile, progressive leader during 14 years of organizational growth and transformation. Repeatedly challenged with complex issues and repeatedly deliver—executing mission and brand to decisively impact the advancement of women in the cable and telecommunications industry. Orchestrate the planning, launch, and ongoing operation of far-reaching events and initiatives.

Scope of Responsibility: Collaborate with CEO, Board of Directors, and department heads to effectively plan and manage the organization's strategic roadmap, programming, and advocacy programs.

- Tapped for role of **Interim President and CEO** to lead the organization's transition to a new administration (2009). Partnered with the Board to facilitate operations and manage governance and played key role in on-boarding the new administrator.

- **Led Executive Team** in responding to a request for information from an industry review committee, providing detailed financial, programming, and staffing information that accurately reflected the organization's vision and brand.

- **Conceived and developed the WINC Leadership Conference,** the preeminent event for educating women in the industry. The 2011 conference attracted 800 attendees and focused on "the business of leadership."

Continued

Strategy: Stack all the job titles from a 5-year stint with a national association to be able to highlight key achievements that spanned the entire tenure.

Cassandra Dixson
925-734-1743 | cassdixson@msn.com

- **Established the Research Department** to generate benchmark surveys, white papers, and resource guides for women in the cable industry. Notable initiatives include:
  - **Salary Equity, Advancement Opportunities, and Lifestyle Resources for Women:**
    - Built the initiative that became WINC's advocacy platform. In addition to the original benchmark study that produced a list of the best companies for women in media, the program has expanded to newsletters, follow-up reports, human resources tools, and webinars.
    - Generated an advertorial on the initiative in *Media Magazine* that attracted the attention of Congresswoman Beth Weinstein (CA), who sponsored the *WINC on the Hill* event, a panel discussion on the annual results.
  - **Additional initiatives include:**
    - **Diversity Through Investment**—white paper compilation of results of best practices benchmark survey.
    - **Case for Diversity**—tools arising out of best practices initiative research.
    - **Promoting Your Workplace**—resource providing contacts and information on industry best practices.
    - **Salary Parity Analyses**—based on groups of employees according to area of expertise.
- **Planned and coordinated fund-raisers,** including annual gala that generated $800,000 in donations.
- **Oversaw the awards program** to recognize corporate leaders in the industry.
- **Relocated corporate office from Chicago to DC area:**
  - Tapped by Board to head relocation effort, complicated by massive layoffs and low morale.
  - Worked hand-in-hand with personnel to communicate plans and provide individual counseling.
  - Met all project goals and trained the new staff in the new location.

Earlier Experience
- World Bank—Telecommunications & Informatics Division, Washington, DC
- International Telecom Satellite Organization, Washington, DC

AWARDS & HONORS

Executive Development
- Elizabeth Feinstein Leadership Institute Fellow, 2006

Media Arts Magazine Awards
- Top Women in Media, 2010, 2009, 2007, 2006
- Most Powerful Women, 2009
- Women on the Move, 2008

EDUCATION & AFFILIATIONS

Master of Arts (MA), CALIFORNIA STATE UNIVERSITY, Los Angeles, CA, 1993

Bachelor of Science (BS) in Communications, PURDUE UNIVERSITY, West Lafayette, IN, 1991

Memberships
- Communications Industry Human Resources Association
- National Association of Ethical Practices in Media
- Diane Foster Foundation for Minority Interests—Award Selection Committee
- Rosalind Mendoza Foundation—Intern Selection Committee

Page 2

MARRIAN AYERS-COMPTON

macompnfp@gmail.com | 585.555.8712
12 Gloveshead Hill | Pittsford, NY 14534

SENIOR EXECUTIVE | VP | DIRECTOR — NONPROFIT ORGANIZATIONS

Drive Global Organizational Growth & Change — Cultural, Educational, Social Service, Government, Foundation

Resourceful leader who inspires, innovates, and executes exceptional achievements in global nonprofit organizations. Committed to growing sustainable communities that effectively address societal issues.

- **Leadership** — Provide vision and direction to achieve mission goals; lead strategic and tactical planning including goal setting, measurement, and results reporting.
- **Business Development / Marketing / Membership** — Infuse enthusiasm and engage in cross-organizational and cross-cultural team development. Build and strengthen strategic alliances.
- **Volunteer Management / Talent Development** — Inspire, lead, and mentor staff; establish performance standards through ongoing guidance and evaluation.
- **Fundraising / Public Relations / Partnerships** — Serve as a public face of the organization and galvanize staff, board members, partners, volunteers, and funders to support the mission.
- **Fiscal Management** — Administer fiscal controls; develop budgets; manage organizational finances.

Excel in building consensus, uniting stakeholders to achieve corporate goals. Understand dynamics of working with diverse cultures to establish and maintain a worldwide presence. Loyal, hard working, entrepreneurial.

EXECUTIVE PERFORMANCE

INTELLIGENCE AND NATIONAL SECURITY ALLIANCE (INSA), Annapolis Junction, MD   2008 to 2011
Organization of professionals in the intelligence field, primarily focused on National Security to help members stay abreast of intelligence and national security community issues

EXECUTIVE DIRECTOR, MEMBERSHIP

Engaged to create a new executive role and drive strategic direction and relationship management to attract, retain, and grow membership of respected 86,000-member organization in 140 countries. Guided association affairs and managed $10M budget.

- Credited with retaining and growing membership during the most challenging business climate in 70 years. Set strategy around improved communication, segmented marketing, greater chapter / channel cooperation, and volunteer development. Retention improved from 75% to 79% — the highest rate in 5 years.
- Spearheaded pioneering IT services — rated as the "best new benefit" by the membership and the second most valuable of all benefits.
- Orchestrated a multiyear strategy that exceeded revenue goals by $300K, chartered 7 new chapters, and coached the turnaround of 4 existing chapters worldwide.

PRODUCT DEVELOPMENT AND MANAGEMENT ASSOCIATION (PDMA), Albany, NY   2005 to 2008
Nonprofit professional society that organizes and publishes information about the development of new products

DIRECTOR, ORGANIZATION RELATIONS | MEMBER MARKETS

Aligned vision, strategy, and operational insight to recruit, maintain, and enhance PDMA's relationships with its 135,000 members, 1,200 chapters, and 300 corporate, government, nonprofit, and association partners worldwide. Governed $33M budget and 25 staff engaged in account management, advocacy, and service operations in New York, Washington DC, London, Brussels, Singapore, Beijing, and Hong Kong.

Director, Organization Relations • 2006 to 2008

- Championed global market development strategies and vital account management structure to cultivate organizational partnerships and enhance customer satisfaction — triggered 400% ROI.
- Realigned corporate engagement model that expanded organizational visibility 300% while costing 50% less, increased corporate participation 100%, and grew membership from 50,000 to 135,000.
- Authored business / operational plans in India, China, Korea, Japan, and Australia / New Zealand that expanded membership and certification holders 491%.

Strategy: For each position, clearly identify the primary challenge or reason for being hired, followed by strong results that communicate "mission accomplished."

Product Development and Management Association (continued)

Director, Member Markets • 2005 to 2006

- Expanded the Leadership Institute to serve more than 6,000 member and chapter leaders worldwide through a blended learning program in cooperation with Harvard Business School.
- Crafted 3-year plan that strengthened member retention from 69% to 80%.
- Conceived and implemented innovative global advocacy program that improved organizational visibility and lead generation by 300% at half the cost of prior efforts.

PROTECH INDUSTRY ASSOCIATION, Ann Arbor, MI   2000 to 2005

Nonprofit trade association advancing global interests of information technology (IT) professionals and companies

DIRECTOR, EDUCATIONAL FOUNDATION • 2002 to 2005

Tapped to establish and grow a nonprofit market segment for certification and build the ProTech Educational Foundation to provide the IT industry with a well-trained, diverse workforce.

- Raised more than $14M in individual, corporate, foundation, and government funding.
- Developed innovative programs including the National IT Apprenticeship System with the U.S. Department of Labor and the award-winning Building Community grant program with industry, government, foundations, and educational institutions worldwide.

DIRECTOR, STRATEGIC INITIATIVES • 2000 to 2001

Instituted the nonprofit market segment and the Educational Foundation to create award-winning programs that built a qualified and diverse workforce. Originated strategies that returned $20M on $500K investment.

- Raised more than $14M in individual, corporate, foundation, and government funding.
- Advised U.S., EMEA, and Asia-Pacific government agencies on international information and communications technology industry issues, skill standards, and programs.
- Spearheaded groundbreaking online skills management system.

THE RESOURCE FOUNDATION, New York, NY   1999 to 2000

CHIEF OPERATING OFFICER — Initiated and spearheaded corporate vision, strategy, and policies to conduct $10M endowment campaign and achieve agency accreditation. Chief Executive of $40M human service organization with staff of 800 (50% unionized), responsible for oversight of program, financial, administrative, legal, and strategic planning activities agency-wide.

- Managed $4.5M of joint ventures in education and training, affordable housing, and healthcare.

NEW YORK ARCHITECTURE FOUNDATION, New York, NY   1996 to 1999

EXECUTIVE DIRECTOR | CHIEF EXECUTIVE OFFICER — Transformed a failing community-based organization into one of New York's leading cultural institutions.

- Increased revenues +300%, earned income 229%, contributed income 84%, and endowment 161%. Erased $127K operating deficit in 2 years. Enlarged volunteer corps 300% and membership 200%.
- Established the "Architecture Bay Tour" as one of New York's leading tourist attractions.

MUSEUM OF NATURAL HISTORY, Detroit, MI   1992 to 1996

PLANNING OFFICER — Pioneered integrated approach to strategy, budget, operational and personnel planning, and forecasting that established the baseline for the museum's growth strategy. Member of senior management team responsible for $25M operating budget and $40M capital program. Internal consultant to the President.

- Launched museum's first marketing plan that increased visibility and grew admissions revenue 21%.

EDUCATION | PROFESSIONAL ASSOCIATIONS

MBA — UNIVERSITY OF MICHIGAN, School of Management, Ann Arbor, MI
BLA — UNIVERSITY OF MARYLAND, College Park, MD

American Association of Grant Professionals (AAGP) | Society for Nonprofit Organizations | Non Profit Organizations' Financial Administrators' Network (NPO-FAN) | Volunteer Management Association | Alliance for Nonprofit Management

Walter E. Cook, Jr.

4218 Springfield Drive
Knoxville, TN 37075

waltcook@comcast.net

Home (865) 826-3908
Office (865) 736-8300

SENIOR-LEVEL MANAGER / ADMINISTRATOR

Veterans Affairs / Disability Claims / VA Health-Care Eligibility / VA Law

- More than 20 years of successful performance in the diverse and complex arena of Veterans Affairs, including 15 years of management experience as a National Service Officer for Disabled American Veterans.

- Sound leadership and business-management abilities complemented by professional, hands-on, administrative style that inspires a goal-oriented work environment and ultimately enhances the quality of care for veterans.

- Consistently achieve budget and grant-funding goals. Ten-year history of successfully preparing annual grant proposals for DAV Colorado Trust and DAV Charitable Trust.

- Solid business insight, with the ability to ascertain and analyze needs, forecast goals, streamline operations, and implement new program concepts. Proven skill at reorganization and successful turnaround of nonproductive, inefficient operations.

- Strong strategic vision coupled with overall business sense and attention to detail.

- Extensive knowledge of anatomy, medical terminology, and physiology; VA claims processing (from initial application, to rating decision, through appellate process); VA Nursing Program; Aid to States for Care of Veterans in State Homes; and VA Benefit Delivery Network (BDN).

- Accredited to practice before US Department of Veterans Affairs. Have testified before US Congress and state legislatures of Maryland and Montana.

Professional Experience

DISABLED AMERICAN VETERANS — US Department of Veterans Affairs   1987–Present

Supervisor, National Service Officer, 1997–Present, Knoxville, TN & Fort Hamilton, MT
Associate National Service Officer, 1987–1997, Washington, DC

Operations Management
- Oversee and direct all daily operations, functions, and decisions of state nonprofit veterans' organization that represents veterans in dealing with VA health-care eligibility and processing disability claims.
- Ensure effective representation of DAV clients through application of laws and regulations administered by US Department of Veterans Affairs.

Budget Development / Grant Writing
- Develop budgets and write grant proposals to ensure sufficient funding for Field Service Office program. Secure funding from DAV Colorado Trust and DAV Charitable Trust.
- Create budgets for six field offices, including salary, training, travel, and supplies.

Human Resources Management
- Supervise four National Service Officers, six Field Service Officers, and two secretaries, as well as volunteer support staff throughout the state.
- Created state program to define and develop job descriptions, employment policies, and employee manuals for state field offices.
- Have trained and supervised professional, accredited Service Officers to practice before US Department of Veterans Affairs.

Continued

Strategy: Emphasize veterans background plus general administrative skills for this federal government administrator seeking to transition into a management role for the VA at the state level.

Walter E. Cook, Jr.   waltcook@comcast.net   Page 2

Professional Experience (continued)

Persuasive Communication
- Develop and nurture effective dialogue and cooperation between DAV state office and directors of each VA Medical Center and Regional Office Center in Tennessee.
- Extensive interaction with elected officials at federal, state, and local levels; nonprofit veterans' organizations; volunteer agencies; and oversight committees.

Educational Background

MANAGEMENT AND LEADERSHIP PROGRAM — 2005 — University of Colorado at Denver

DAV STRUCTURED AND CONTINUING TRAINING PROGRAM, PHASES I, II, & III

BACHELOR OF SCIENCE — University of Baltimore

Military Service

US Army Military Police, 1978–1981

Presentations / Public Speaking

- **Instructor, DAV Training Academy,** University of Colorado at Denver, October 2009

  Led two-week course on proper application of Parts III and IV of 38 Code of Federal Regulations. Developed detailed lesson plan and created practical models to clearly demonstrate specific rating concepts. Also developed comprehensive final examination to fully evaluate each trainee's knowledge and understanding of principles of rating disabilities.

- **Keynote speaker** before delegates of state DAV conventions; federal, state, and local conferences; and panels with leading veterans' organizations regarding veteran-related issues. Spoke to Johns Hopkins School of Law to argue legal defense of post-traumatic stress.

- **Conducted seminars** on readjustment problems of returning war veterans. **Made numerous presentations** to mental health professionals and medical schools, up to 2,000 audience members.

- **Testified** before Maryland State Assembly, Montana State Assembly, and Veterans Affairs Subcommittee in Washington, DC. **Submitted written briefs** before US Department of Veterans Affairs supporting specific arguments.

Professional Affiliations

Disabled American Veterans' Guild of Attorneys-in-Fact
Life Member, Knoxville Chapter, Disabled American Veterans

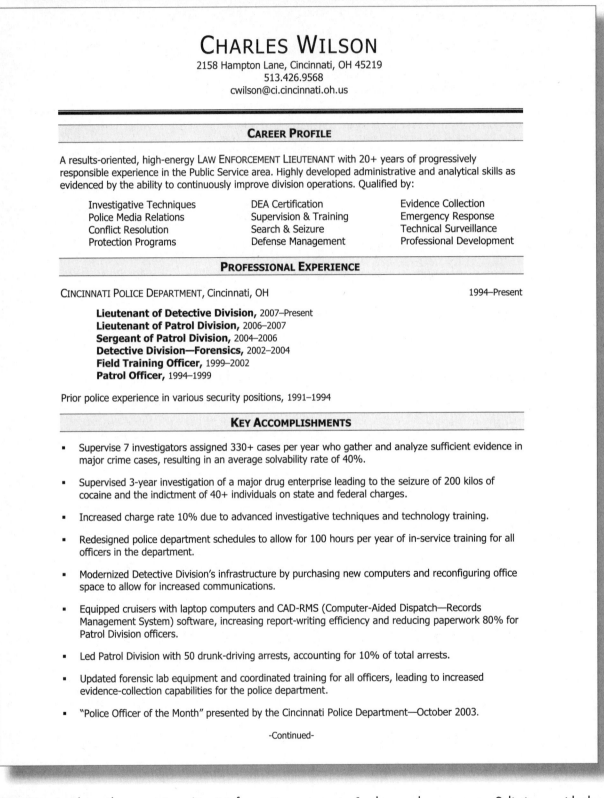

CHARLES WILSON

2158 Hampton Lane, Cincinnati, OH 45219
513.426.9568
cwilson@ci.cincinnati.oh.us

CAREER PROFILE

A results-oriented, high-energy LAW ENFORCEMENT LIEUTENANT with 20+ years of progressively responsible experience in the Public Service area. Highly developed administrative and analytical skills as evidenced by the ability to continuously improve division operations. Qualified by:

Investigative Techniques	DEA Certification	Evidence Collection
Police Media Relations	Supervision & Training	Emergency Response
Conflict Resolution	Search & Seizure	Technical Surveillance
Protection Programs	Defense Management	Professional Development

PROFESSIONAL EXPERIENCE

CINCINNATI POLICE DEPARTMENT, Cincinnati, OH   1994–Present

Lieutenant of Detective Division, 2007–Present
Lieutenant of Patrol Division, 2006–2007
Sergeant of Patrol Division, 2004–2006
Detective Division—Forensics, 2002–2004
Field Training Officer, 1999–2002
Patrol Officer, 1994–1999

Prior police experience in various security positions, 1991–1994

KEY ACCOMPLISHMENTS

- Supervise 7 investigators assigned 330+ cases per year who gather and analyze sufficient evidence in major crime cases, resulting in an average solvability rate of 40%.

- Supervised 3-year investigation of a major drug enterprise leading to the seizure of 200 kilos of cocaine and the indictment of 40+ individuals on state and federal charges.

- Increased charge rate 10% due to advanced investigative techniques and technology training.

- Redesigned police department schedules to allow for 100 hours per year of in-service training for all officers in the department.

- Modernized Detective Division's infrastructure by purchasing new computers and reconfiguring office space to allow for increased communications.

- Equipped cruisers with laptop computers and CAD-RMS (Computer-Aided Dispatch—Records Management System) software, increasing report-writing efficiency and reducing paperwork 80% for Patrol Division officers.

- Led Patrol Division with 50 drunk-driving arrests, accounting for 10% of total arrests.

- Updated forensic lab equipment and coordinated training for all officers, leading to increased evidence-collection capabilities for the police department.

- "Police Officer of the Month" presented by the Cincinnati Police Department—October 2003.

-Continued-

Strategy: Place the most important information on page 1; then enhance page-2 listings with the logos of highly sought-after accomplishments in law enforcement.

CHARLES WILSON

2158 Hampton Lane, Cincinnati, OH 45219
513.426.9568
cwilson@ci.cincinnati.oh.us

Page 2

EDUCATION

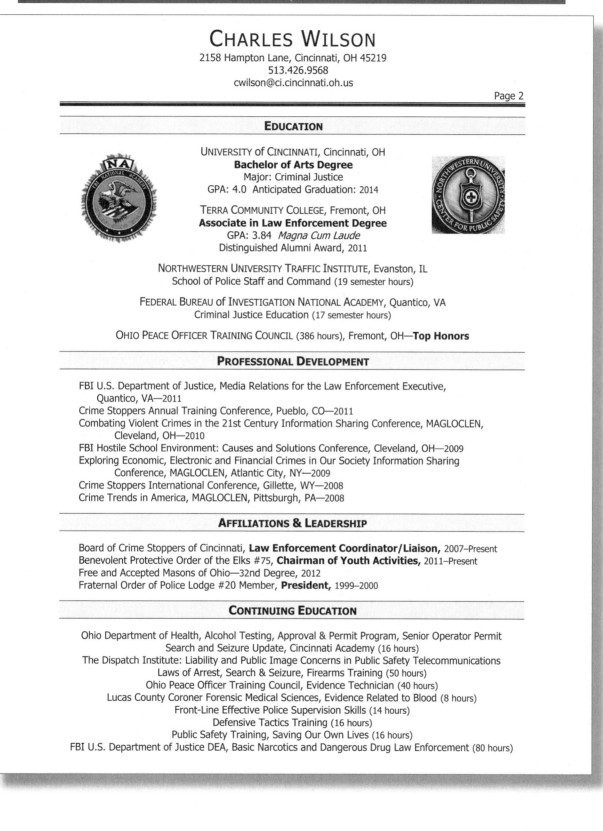

UNIVERSITY of CINCINNATI, Cincinnati, OH
Bachelor of Arts Degree
Major: Criminal Justice
GPA: 4.0 Anticipated Graduation: 2014

TERRA COMMUNITY COLLEGE, Fremont, OH
Associate in Law Enforcement Degree
GPA: 3.84 *Magna Cum Laude*
Distinguished Alumni Award, 2011

NORTHWESTERN UNIVERSITY TRAFFIC INSTITUTE, Evanston, IL
School of Police Staff and Command (19 semester hours)

FEDERAL BUREAU of INVESTIGATION NATIONAL ACADEMY, Quantico, VA
Criminal Justice Education (17 semester hours)

OHIO PEACE OFFICER TRAINING COUNCIL (386 hours), Fremont, OH—**Top Honors**

PROFESSIONAL DEVELOPMENT

FBI U.S. Department of Justice, Media Relations for the Law Enforcement Executive,
    Quantico, VA—2011
Crime Stoppers Annual Training Conference, Pueblo, CO—2011
Combating Violent Crimes in the 21st Century Information Sharing Conference, MAGLOCLEN,
    Cleveland, OH—2010
FBI Hostile School Environment: Causes and Solutions Conference, Cleveland, OH—2009
Exploring Economic, Electronic and Financial Crimes in Our Society Information Sharing
    Conference, MAGLOCLEN, Atlantic City, NY—2009
Crime Stoppers International Conference, Gillette, WY—2008
Crime Trends in America, MAGLOCLEN, Pittsburgh, PA—2008

AFFILIATIONS & LEADERSHIP

Board of Crime Stoppers of Cincinnati, **Law Enforcement Coordinator/Liaison,** 2007–Present
Benevolent Protective Order of the Elks #75, **Chairman of Youth Activities,** 2011–Present
Free and Accepted Masons of Ohio—32nd Degree, 2012
Fraternal Order of Police Lodge #20 Member, **President,** 1999–2000

CONTINUING EDUCATION

Ohio Department of Health, Alcohol Testing, Approval & Permit Program, Senior Operator Permit
Search and Seizure Update, Cincinnati Academy (16 hours)
The Dispatch Institute: Liability and Public Image Concerns in Public Safety Telecommunications
Laws of Arrest, Search & Seizure, Firearms Training (50 hours)
Ohio Peace Officer Training Council, Evidence Technician (40 hours)
Lucas County Coroner Forensic Medical Sciences, Evidence Related to Blood (8 hours)
Front-Line Effective Police Supervision Skills (14 hours)
Defensive Tactics Training (16 hours)
Public Safety Training, Saving Our Own Lives (16 hours)
FBI U.S. Department of Justice DEA, Basic Narcotics and Dangerous Drug Law Enforcement (80 hours)

Melinda P. Morales

1827 Davenport Dr.
319-555-4876   Iowa City, IA 52245   mpm222@network.net

LAW ENFORCEMENT COMMAND

~ Administrator ~ Supervisor ~ Detective ~ Certified Police Officer ~

Accomplished leader, trainer, and mentor with more than 20 years of experience in the local law enforcement community in increasingly responsible positions. Excellent rapport with area police and fire departments as well as state and federal agencies. Progressive thinker, knowledgeable about modern police operations and tactics. Expert in accident investigation and reconstruction, death investigations, and computer forensics. Recipient of multiple departmental citations for professional excellence.

CAREER CHRONOLOGY

OFFICE OF JOHNSON COUNTY SHERIFF—Iowa City, Iowa   1987–Present
Lieutenant—Detective Bureau (2004–Present)
Manage people, programs, and special assignments across the department.

Law Enforcement
- Respond to and coordinate crime scenes. Collect, secure, process, and analyze evidence. Interview witnesses and interrogate suspects. Conduct initial investigations. Obtain and execute warrants.
- Manage complex investigations of felonies and misdemeanors including homicides, narcotics, fraud, property crimes, cybercrime, kidnapping, public corruption, crimes against children, and pornography, among others. Generate reports. Share information with other jurisdictions and agencies.
- Oversaw investigations of multi-county serial bank robber, home invasion, and commercial breaking and entering cases leading to arrest and conviction of suspects.
- Collaborate with prosecuting attorney's office to prepare cases for prosecution and court testimony.

Administration
- Provide training to deputies on alcohol enforcement procedures, department's new 800 mghz radio system, and computer operations.
- Assist command staff with developing policies and procedures.
- Respond to union grievances. Participate in contract negotiations with union.
- Conduct internal investigations resulting in exoneration, discipline, or criminal prosecution.
- Coordinate investigations in Liberty Township as part of agreement to provide contractual services.

Special Assignments
- Crimes Against the Elderly Task Force (2007–Present) — Investigate backlog of cases.
- Medical Examiner Investigator (2001–Present) — Conduct death investigations for medical examiners' offices in Johnson and Cedar counties; to date have completed more than 500 cases.
- Communities Against Drunk Driving [CADD] (2004–2006) — Appointed to multi-jurisdictional team to investigate serious and fatal traffic accidents in which alcohol may have been involved.

Detective/Precinct Commander—Oxford Township (2002–2004)
Selected to lead precinct station under contractual agreement between the county and the township. Managed police service for 18,000 residents averaging 8,200 calls per year with a $2.2 million budget.
- Directed, scheduled, trained, and supported 11 deputies. Responded to emergency calls as needed.
- Reported to township board. Prepared and analyzed budget.
- Represented the township to the public and the media on law enforcement and public safety matters.
- Consulted with Oxford Area Schools superintendent regarding safety issues impacting the district. Planned and implemented critical incidence and other safety training for teachers.
- Coordinated 12-member reserve officer program.

Strategy: Emphasize local connections and length and breadth of service to position this candidate for promotion to Police Chief.

Melinda P. Morales   mpm222@network.net   319-555-4876

OFFICE OF JOHNSON COUNTY SHERIFF (continued)
Sergeant/Supervisor—Court Security (1999–2002)
Supervised 24 police officers transporting prisoners to and from court appearances and other correctional facilities across the state.
- Oversaw court operations during year-long reconstruction of the county Court House.
- Played significant role in overhauling court security procedures following 9/11, modifying changes already in progress. Collaborated with elected officials, judges, court staff, attorneys, and sheriff's department administration to develop protocols that protected the building while continuing to allow public access to court services.
- Narcotics (1999–2000) — Worked as undercover officer assigned to the sheriff's drug team.

Sergeant/Supervisor—Corrections Division (1997–1999)
Managed daily operations for jail housing approximately 435 inmates. Supervised 28+ deputies and civilian personnel. Scheduled staff, processed payroll, and monitored overtime.
- Ensured safety of deputies and inmates. Monitored compliance with work rules, regulations, statutes, and mandates for incarcerated persons.
- Initiated new policy to streamline procurement of biological specimens required for criminal investigations, resulting in cost savings.

Road Patrol Deputy/Accident Investigator (1992–1997)
Corrections Deputy (1989–1992)
Marine Patrol Deputy/Diver (1987–1989)

RELATED PROFESSIONAL EXPERIENCE

Kirkwoood Community College—Cedar Rapids, Iowa (2008–2010)	**Guest Lecturer**
Cedar Rapids Regional Police Academy—Cedar Rapids, Iowa (1997–1999)	**Instructor**
Liberty Township Police Department—Hills, Iowa (1993–1994)	**Patrolman**
Washington County Sheriff Department—Washington, Iowa (Seasonal 1990)	**Marine Patrol Deputy**

EDUCATION

IOWA LAW ENFORCEMENT ACADEMY—Des Moines, Iowa
Certified Law Enforcement Officer   1991
- Self-sponsored and self-funded

KIRKWOOD COMMUNITY COLLEGE—Cedar Rapids, Iowa
Associate in Applied Science—Criminal Justice   1989
- Additional business and management courses

SELECTED PROFESSIONAL DEVELOPMENT
(complete list available on request)
- ❖ NIMS ICS-300, -700, -800 (2007) — Federal Emergency Management Agency
- ❖ Crash Data Retrieval (2007) — Iowa State Patrol
- ❖ Forensic Computer (2006) — International Association of Computer Investigative Specialists
- ❖ Forensic Investigations (2005) — Digital Intelligence
- ❖ 800 mghz Radio Train the Trainer (2005) — Iowa State Patrol
- ❖ Medicolegal Death Investigation (2003 & 2004) — Drake University & Johnson County
- ❖ Accident Reconstructionist (1995) — Iowa State Department of Civil & Environmental Engineering
- ❖ Supervision and Management (ongoing) — Multiple providers
- ❖ Medical First Responder (Current) — Iowa Department of Public Health

Page 2 of 2

James C. Nickerson   JCNickerson@aol.com | 360-555-5555

AIRPORT MANAGER

Versatile professional with rich and deep knowledge of federal and state safety and environmental regulations.

- Created strategy to bring airport into compliance with government mandates.
- Remedied runway deficiencies: Discovered dangerous electrical problem and coordinated its repair.

Profit-minded manager with expertise in developing financial processes that drive gains in income, reduce operating costs, and improve bottom-line profitability.

- Improved annual revenue streams more than $17K by improving management of rental properties.
- Cut costs: Developed preventive measures to reduce maintenance expenses and preserve health of existing airport infrastructure.
- Ended each fiscal year on or under budget.

Quick-thinking leader with solid track record of smooth handling of emergency situations.

- Demonstrated leadership during on-airport emergency of crashed aircraft.
- Mitigated risk of additional damage or injury caused by airport incident.

Professional Experience

AIRPORT MANAGER   2004 to Present
Grove Field Airport (1W1), Port of Camas-Washougal, Washougal, Washington

Recruited to assume leadership of one of the poorest-performing general aviation airports in Washington State. Challenged to improve revenue streams, cut costs, and bring airport into compliance with government mandates. Executed command control in airport emergencies and breaches of airport security.

- Streamlined rent collection process: Introduced automated payment for hangar and FBO rents.
- Increased revenue by $19K/year by improving procedures to evict tenants for nonpayment of rent.
- Rewrote existing hangar rental contracts to strengthen tenant lease obligations.
- Developed capital improvement plan:
    - Identified and assessed deficiencies with runway and taxi separation, runway length and width, and runway object-free areas (ROFA).
    - Instrumental in developing FAA-approved Airport Layout Plan to expand runway and ROFA.
- Assumed role of Incident Commander coordinating rescue effort of victims of on-site airport crash.
- Promptly issued emergency NOTAM at 2:40 AM and coordinated with local authorities after GA aircraft landed gear-up on runway, forcing closure of the airport.

■ Continued ■

Strategy: Combine strong financial results with other important characteristics of an airport manager: crisis management, safety, and overall leadership.

James C. Nickerson
JCNickerson@aol.com | 360-555-5555

AIRPORT MANAGER   2000 to 2004
Anacortes Airport (74A), Port of Anacortes, Anacortes, Washington

Hand-selected to improve bottom-line performance of 120-acre airport in northwest Washington. Reduced hangar vacancy rate and increased rental income. Maintained airport facilities in compliance with FAA standards. Built cooperative working relationships with staff to raise productivity and lower employee turnover.

- Streamlined financial reporting:
  - Hired CPA to restructure and modernize accounting operations.
  - Discovered $13K in previously forgotten bank account.
- Lowered hangar vacancy rate to 0% and brought in additional $800/month in new rent by persistently contacting and following up with prospective tenants on hangar waiting list.
- Performed comparative market analysis of tie downs and hangar rentals; then raised rates to market levels, generating over $17K new income.
- Avoided costly repairs: Proactively discovered hidden problem in runway lighting system and ordered emergency repair.
- Minimized employee turnover by improving hiring process and revamping compensation and benefits.

COMMERCIAL PROPERTY MANAGER   1995 to 2000
Evergreen Capital Investments, Inc., Everett, Washington

Hired by a major privately owned multifamily housing firm in western Washington to supervise 8 buildings comprising 120 residential and retail units, plus 146 mini-storage units. Oversaw tenant selection, lease management, insurance, budgeting, and maintenance.

- Reduced 25% vacancy rate to 5% in 4 months by spearheading innovative marketing campaign.
- Finished first fiscal year 6% under budget through tenant evictions and aggressive rent collection.
- Recovered missing $36K after confronting ex-employee with evidence of accounting irregularities.
- Cleared up 2-year record-maintenance backlog by hiring temporary data entry clerk.

PROPERTY MANAGER   1991 to 1995
Coast Real Estate Services, Inc., Everett, Washington

Turned occupancy rate of a 9-building distressed student housing project from 40% to 95% in 3 months.

Education | Training | Affiliations

Bachelor of Science in Business, 1990, University of Washington, Seattle, WA

Property Maintenance and Risk Management, 1991, Institute of Real Estate Management, Chicago, IL
Marketing and Leasing, 1991, Institute of Real Estate Management, Chicago, IL
Commercial Pilot Training, 1994, Out of the Blue Aviation, Inc., Arlington, WA
Airport Certified Employee—Operations, 2001, American Association of Airport Executives, Alexandria, VA

American Association of Airport Executives | National Business Aviation Association

■ Page 2 ■

PETER H. DESMOND, ESQ.

123 Garden Street
Hackensack, New Jersey 07602
(201) 321-9376 (Days) / (201) 209-6204 (Evenings)
desmondph@netscape.net

Admitted to the Bar — State of New Jersey

SUMMARY

Accomplished felony prosecutor with 12-year track record that encompasses successfully trying rapes, robberies, armed assaults, and firearms crimes in New Jersey Superior Court, County Court, and municipal courts.

- **Demonstrated capacity to cooperate effectively with a broad array of law-enforcement agencies and prosecuting attorneys at federal, state, and local levels.**
- **Extensive experience researching, analyzing, and interpreting case law relating to both criminal and civil issues.**
- **Direct experience prosecuting firearm felonies as part of "Project Exile" task force.**
- **Highly organized, with excellent time-management skills and ability to balance demands of heavy caseload.**

LEGAL EXPERIENCE

BERGEN COUNTY DISTRICT ATTORNEY'S OFFICE; Hackensack, New Jersey (2000–Present)
Assistant District Attorney
Twelve years of experience prosecuting a broad range of misdemeanor and felony cases at various levels and in various courts within the jurisdiction.

Major Felony Bureau   **June 2010–Present**
Accountable for prosecuting violent felonies, including assaults with firearms and weapons, robberies, rapes, and burglaries.

- Confer with police investigators to review case evidence.
- Appear in court and before Grand Juries to seek arraignments and indictments.
- Interview witnesses and prepare them for trial.
- Meet with defendants and defense counsel to negotiate plea agreements.
- Develop cases for trial and handle all aspects of trying cases in court, as appropriate.

Gun Interdiction Unit / Project Exile   **June 2008–June 2010**
Served as member of this cross-jurisdictional task force charged with curtailing illegal firearms trafficking and illegal use of firearms in commission of other felonies.

- Collaborated with FBI, US Attorney, BATF, and state/local police agencies to further program goals.
- Conferred with representatives of other agencies to assess appropriate venue for prosecuting cases.
- Developed and managed confidential informants in conjunction with other agencies.
- Attended regular meetings to maintain rapport and enhance cooperation between agencies.

City Court — Non-Violent Felonies & Property Crimes   **Feb. 2007–June 2008**
Felony DWI / Fatal Traffic Accident Bureau   **Dec. 2005–Feb. 2007**
City Court — Misdemeanors   **Sept. 2003–Dec. 2005**

Municipal Courts   **Jan. 2000–Sept. 2003**
In addition to criminal prosecutions, participated in Drug Diversion Court over an eight-month period. This program offered alternatives to incarceration for non-violent drug offenders with no significant criminal records.

Page One

Strategy: Highlight cross-jurisdictional experience for this individual seeking a position with the Department of Justice, where interagency cooperation is highly valued.

Peter H. Desmond, Esq.   desmondph@netscape.net   **Résumé — Page Two**

LEGAL EXPERIENCE (continued)

LEGAL ASSISTANCE OF NORTHERN NEW JERSEY; Hackensack, New Jersey
Legal Aid Attorney   **May–Dec. 1999**
Assisted economically disadvantaged clients with landlord/tenant issues and other routine legal matters.

US DISTRICT COURT — NORTHERN DISTRICT OF NEW JERSEY; Hackensack, New Jersey
Judicial Intern to Hon. Warren G. Nestor   **Sept. 1998–May 1999**
Researched legal issues and drafted Memoranda Decisions and Orders for habeas corpus petitions, civil rights actions, and Social Security actions. Discussed case decisions and rulings on motions with judge to gain further understanding of trial law and procedures.

STATE OF NEW JERSEY DEPARTMENT OF TAXATION & FINANCE; Trenton, New Jersey
Law Clerk — Litigation Division   **May 1996–Aug. 1998**
Researched laws pertaining to real property transfer and corporate transfer taxes. Analyzed statutory and regulatory issues and prepared memoranda based on interpretations. Developed case strategies and drafted briefs and motions.

US ATTORNEY'S OFFICE — DISTRICT OF COLUMBIA, SUPERIOR COURT DIVISION; Washington, DC
Undergraduate Legal Internship   **Sept. 1994–Dec. 1994**
Reviewed evidence, interviewed witnesses, and conducted legal research in support of attorneys preparing misdemeanor cases for trial.

EDUCATION

Juris Doctor   **June 1998**
College of Law, Syracuse University; Syracuse, New York

Bachelor of Science, Criminal Justice   **May 1995**
Syracuse University; Syracuse, New York
Graduate With Honors / GPA: 3.68
Published article on Entrapment Defense in undergraduate law review.

PROFESSIONAL DEVELOPMENT

Trial Advocacy II, National Advocacy Center; Columbia, South Carolina   **Aug. 2006**
Intensive week-long program focusing on DNA, Trace, Firearm, and Psychiatric Evidence; Forensic Pathology; and Examination of Expert Witnesses. Program culminated with practical experience conducting direct and cross-examinations of experts and delivering closing arguments.

Angela Ferguson, Esq.

142 Concord Avenue
Hollywood, FL 33021
954.585.7445 • AngieFerg2@aol.com

PROFESSIONAL PROFILE

- Effective *Trial Lawyer* routinely handling caseload of 100+ cases.
- Resolve legal matters quickly and effectively yet persistently pursue the most effective and appropriate course of action.
- Strengths include witness interviewing and preparation, case theory development, presentation of facts, and persuasive argument abilities.

BAR MEMBERSHIPS

Florida Bar, admitted March 2008.

Georgia Bar, admitted July 2008.

LEGAL EXPERIENCE

Florida County District Attorney's Office (Miami, FL) **Trial Division** **ASSISTANT DISTRICT ATTORNEY**	09/07 to **Present**

Individually handle all phases of criminal prosecutions from pre-trial practice through trial, post-trial motions, and sentencing. Responsibilities include extensive legal research, drafting pleadings, motions, discovery, witness interviewing and preparation, drafting pre-sentencing memoranda, and routinely and effectively negotiating plea bargains with opposing counsel.

Extensive courtroom experience includes arraignments, calendar appearances, hearings, arguing motions to suppress evidence and motions in limine, conducting voir dire, and all other aspects of trial and arguing post-trial motions. Consistently establish credibility and trust with juries through a combination of effective presentation of facts and persuasive argument skills.

Manage rotating caseload of 100+ felony and misdemeanor cases, involving:

- **Felonies:** domestic violence assault, stalking, burglary, robbery, grand larceny, A-1 drug possession and sale, and identity theft.

- **Misdemeanors:** assault, petit larceny, trademark counterfeiting, and aggravated harassment.

Selected achievements and accomplishments

- Within 2 years, successfully tried and won convictions in 2 bench and 5 jury trials.
- Convicted defendant for Criminal Sale of a Controlled Substance On or Near School Grounds. **Result:** Despite minimal evidence (one rock of crack cocaine), successfully argued that defendant receive 4 ½-to-9-year prison sentence.

United States District Court, D.F.L. (Tallahassee, FL) **Federal Judicial Clerkship** **STUDENT INTERN for Honorable Ken Stern**	8/06 to 5/07

Conducted extensive research and writing. Prepared federal habeas corpus opinions and orders. Obtained exposure to court procedures through attendance at trials, arraignments, and hearings.

Selected achievements and accomplishments

- Drafted extensive opinion denying habeas corpus relief to defendant convicted of aggravated sexual assault, sexual assault, and endangering the welfare of a child, based on defendant's erroneous claim of, *inter alia*, a violation of his Sixth Amendment rights.

Continued

Strategy: Redesign resume for an experienced attorney seeking to transition from a role as prosecutor to a general litigation position with a law firm. Emphasize transferable skills as well as education and experience.

Angela Ferguson, Esq.   Page 2

LEGAL EXPERIENCE (continued)

United States Attorney's Office (Boston, MA)   5/06 to 8/06
Criminal Division, Narcotics Unit
SUMMER INTERN

Conducted research and writing. Observed judicial process and courtroom procedure including pleas, verdicts, summations, and sentencings. Met with cooperating informants, interviewed witnesses, and prepared warrants.

Family Court of Boston (Boston, MA)   5/05 to 8/05
SUMMER LAW CLERK for Honorable Judith Steiner

Managed juvenile delinquent and dependency case files. Conducted legal research and wrote opinions and appeals.

EDUCATION

JD, University of Florida, Gainesville, FL   2007
Dean's Honor List, Fall 2006 and Spring 2007

Awards
- C.A.L.I. Award for Excellence in Advanced Trial Advocacy
- Victor A. Jaczun Award for Excellence in Trial Advocacy

National / Regional Trial Team Competitor and Champion
- National Champion, NACDL Student Trial Competition (2007)
- National Champion, ATLA Student Trial Competition (2006)
- Eastern-Regional Champion, ATLA Student Trial Competition (2006)
- Finalist, NACDL Student Trial Competition (2006)
- Best Advocate (Semifinal Round), NACDL Student Trial Competition (2006)
- Semifinalist, National ATLA Student Trial Competition (2007)

Achieved Distinguished Class Performance in the following courses:
Civil Procedure I; Contracts II; Evidence; Criminal Procedure I; and Advanced Trial Advocacy

BA ENGLISH, Florida State University, Tallahassee, FL   2002
Dean's List, Spring 1999 and Spring 2001.

PROFESSIONAL DEVELOPMENT

Regularly participate in CLE seminars. To date, have completed 53+ hours of continuing education courses spanning areas including Criminal, Family, Real Estate, Landlord/Tenant, Small Business, Civil, Administrative, Professional Responsibility and Wills/Trusts.

PROFESSIONAL ASSOCIATIONS
- American Bar Association
- Florida State Bar Association
- Association of Trial Lawyers of America
- National Black Prosecutors Association

COMPUTER SKILLS

Proficient in Westlaw, Lexis-Nexis, Microsoft Office Suite, Internet, and e-mail applications.

BUFFY A. CARLTON

1037 Grand Vista Drive • Irving, TX 75039
Home: (972) 831-2435 • Cell: (972) 820-4243 • E-mail: buffycarlton@mailbox.com

EXECUTIVE DIRECTOR

Senior nonprofit and educational development specialist with a unique education-industry background, having served effectively in senior management, supervisory, and foundation-administration positions. Demonstrated history of success in creating and implementing comprehensive nonprofit funding programs. Adept at developing multimillion-dollar partnerships with corporations and in securing foundation grants.

PROFESSIONAL EXPERIENCE

EDUCATION INNOVATIONS, Dallas, TX   2009–Present
Executive Director for Strategic Alliances

Develop partnerships with nonprofit and for-profit organizations that deliver technology-based instruction for this Internet-based, customized network of online learning communities.

Key Achievements
- Developed a three-year, $2 million financial-literacy program for students through corporate sponsorship.
- Secured a three-year, $1.5 million online homework-assistance program with Mega Corporation.
- Fostered successful partnerships with national newspapers, the Smithsonian Institution, major book publishers, and the U.S. Department of Education.

TEXAS ART GROUP, Dallas, TX   2007–2009
Executive Director

Developed and directed a philanthropic donation program and created innovative national sales events for this internationally renowned, culturally diverse group of more than 100 U.S. and European artists and craftspeople.

Key Achievements
- Collaborated with nonprofit organizations on revenue-producing promotional events at national venues.
- Penetrated new markets through creative approaches in reaching non-traditional markets for art sales.
- Coordinated special gallery events, including a four-day international art sale extravaganza.

NATIONAL ORGANIZATION OF SCHOOL PRINCIPALS (NOSP), Washington, DC   1997–2007
Associate Executive Director

Managed a $15 million annual budget and supervised a staff of 40, among five departments, for this 46,000-member school leadership organization that provides professional development programs to assist students and administrators in the U.S. and abroad.

Key Achievements
- Generated more than $14 million in corporate contributions within six years.
- Reengineered the $3.3 million travel budget, reducing annual costs by $150,000.
- Launched an NOSP foundation that generated more than $110,000 within six months.
- Recruited corporate partners and jointly designed programs with international organizations.

DISTRICT OF COLUMBIA PUBLIC SCHOOLS, Washington, DC   1978–1997
Principal, Presidential High School (1993–1997)

Promoted through increasingly responsible positions with one of the largest high-school districts in the U.S., serving more than 35,000 students. (Prior positions include the following: Assistant Principal, Guidance Counselor, Vocational Design/Development Specialist, and Teacher.)

EDUCATION

M.Ed., Administration • **B.S., Vocational Education,** Georgetown University, Washington, DC

Strategy: Develop a one-page "calling-card" resume for a highly experienced executive targeting a specific nonprofit educational organization.

CHAPTER 6

Resumes for Managers and Executives in Human Resources, Organizational Development, and Education

- Senior Human Resources Executive

- Human Resources Manager

- Program Director

- Vice President, Human Resources

- Senior Education Executive

- Secondary Education Administrator

- Elementary Principal/Administrator

Daniel da Silva

9 Albert Embankment • London SE1 7HF • UK
daniel.dasilva@postmaster.co.uk • mobile +44 20 555 5555 • home +44 20 555 5678

SENIOR HUMAN RESOURCES EXECUTIVE / STRATEGIC BUSINESS PARTNER

*Delivering transformational HR leadership to drive success of international growth initiatives
in FMCG and Pharma / Consumer Health industries*

Proactive and business-minded HR leader with a dynamic 15-year career steering organisations through complex transitions and building an empowered and talented workforce in cross-cultural environments within highly competitive consumer products and pharmaceutical / healthcare industries.

Proven expertise in defining organisational structure and human capital requirements to align HR functions with business goals, providing the catalyst to optimise performance, enhance productivity, and drive revenue and profit growth. Articulate communicator and highly skilled negotiator. Fluent in English and Portuguese (native); intermediate Spanish.

CORE COMPETENCIES

• Talent Management	• Strategic Planning / Business Analysis	• Business Partnering
• Succession Planning	• Executive Committee Membership	• Organisation Design
• Staffing & Recruitment	• Due Diligence / Divestiture	• Corporate Restructuring
• Compensation & Benefits	• Human Capital Requirements Planning	• HR Risk Assessment

PROFESSIONAL EXPERIENCE & ACCOMPLISHMENTS

PHARM-GLOBAL CONSUMER HEALTH, London, UK   2006–Present
(Privately held subsidiary of Pharm-Global Worldwide, Pharm-Global Consumer Health is a world leader in the research, development, manufacture, and marketing of pharmaceutical self-medication brands.)

Head of Organisational Performance (London; 2009–Present)
Head of Human Resources, Europe (London; 2007–2009) Directed team of 8–10.
Head of HR Processes, Europe (Lisbon; 2006–2007) Directed team of 6–9.

Rapidly promoted through a series of increasingly strategic HR business partner roles to drive regional and global change initiatives during period of complex organisational restructuring. Consistently successful in HR director-level and specialist roles with significant contributions in the areas of strategic workforce planning, headcount reduction, talent management, business partnering, and organisational development.

Key player in meeting bottom-line profit objectives in challenged economic market. As Member of Senior Leadership Executive Committee for Pharm-Global Consumer Health worldwide, collaborated with senior leadership in designing HR solutions to support business objectives in the areas of brand planning, marketing, finance, strategic planning, and business plan development.

Notable Achievements:

➢ **Business Partnering & Organisational Design:** Developed and executed HR headcount reduction strategy for market business operating plan that was instrumental in 12-month turnaround of Pharm-Global Consumer Heathcare business in the UK, following 8-year decline. Reduced headcount 10% year-over-year, resulting in 15% profit improvement in a shrinking market.

➢ **HR Infrastructure Development / Staffing & Recruitment:** Transformed HR infrastructure at London headquarters office of 900 with 11 entities. Redesigned staffing and recruitment function, re-negotiated agency fees, and shifted recruitment focus to internal and web-based systems. Reduced time-to-hire by 10% and cut agency expenses 50%, achieving overall cost savings of 80%.

➢ **Talent Management:** Implemented succession planning and internal recruitment measures for Lisbon organisation of 120 to secure top talent pipeline during the largest reorganisation in company history. Achieved target performance metrics of 70 / 30 within 18 months.

Continued

Strategy: Use the functional format (described on page 26) to emphasize diverse areas of activity and accomplishment during progressively challenging HR leadership roles.

Daniel da Silva – Page Two
daniel.dasilva@postmaster.co.uk • mobile +44 20 555 5555 • home +44 20 555 5678

PHARM-GLOBAL CONSUMER HEALTH, *continued*

➢ **Workforce Design and Realignment:** Conducted due diligence and workforce realignment following business unit divestiture. Saved £1 million, met headcount objectives, and ensured attainment of P&L target.

➢ **Employee Relations / Vendor Management:** Transformed inefficient, audit-critical HR function in London into reliable, structured, and risk-averse organisation within 12 months. Delivered cost improvement of £1 million p.a. through cost-effective vendor management and reduction of legal cases by 70%.

➢ **Organisational Performance Assessment:** Implemented strategies and HR programs that improved communication engagement results by 6 basis points on average across all HR categories, outperforming results of previously administrated substandard Pricewaterhouse Coopers global survey.

➢ **HR / Business Integration:** Spearheaded cross-functional HR / business planning process throughout Euro Zone market, using functional dialogue methodology to ensure HR / business alignment for workforce planning, competency development, and budget planning. Introduced process to all Pharm-Global European HR leaders.

➢ **Retention and Risk Assessment:** Designed and implemented workforce planning and retention strategy using risk-value matrix. Improved employee retention through 25% reduction of voluntary turnover at corporate HQ.

IBERIAN CONSUMER PRODUCTS (ICP), Global Corporate Headquarters, Lisbon, Portugal   2000–2006
(Global consumer products company and world leader in the household health and personal care sectors)

Compensation & Benefits Director—Top 400 Executives (2002-2006)
Special Project Manager (2002)
Human Resources Manager, Western Europe (2000–2002)

Excelled in strategic HR leadership roles and was selected for special project with global scope.

Notable Achievements:

➢ **Compensation & Benefits / Business Partnering:** Developed variable bonus plan for top 400 executives, laying groundwork for 200% increase in new product development project pipeline that delivered significant incremental net revenue and gross margin improvement.

➢ **Compensation & Benefits / Vendor Management:** Replaced global tax provider and managed transition within 6-month project cycle, delivering immediate 3.6mGBP impact, 10% cost savings, and significant improvement in service delivery.

FRANCISCA PRODUCTS, Lisbon, Portugal
(Manufacturer of adhesive products)

Human Resources Manager

➢ Generalist role with an operational focus. Managed staffing and recruitment, employee relations (commercial, supply, labour), and HR administration / payroll (PAISY).

EDUCATION & PROFESSIONAL DEVELOPMENT

University of Coimbra, Portugal

➢ Baccalaureate 1994; Post-Graduate Specialisation in Organisational Development, 1995

Numerous corporate-sponsored training and leadership development programs in management development, coaching and mentoring, change management, 360° feedback, global project management, and negotiations.

Matthew D. Thomas

109 West Lindenview Drive
Bloomington, Indiana 41331

388-650-0483
mdthoma@comcast.net

Human Resources Management · Strategic Planning · Organizational Design

Professional career reflects more than 20 years of experience in administrative leadership, human resources management, resource utilization, and organizational development in highly competitive and diligently structured institutions. Leadership abilities have been utilized in re-organization of programs, services, and resources for leading academic institution. Entrepreneurial skills were developed in the start-up of retail specialty operation from concept to implementation.

Selected Accomplishments

- Established strategic business plan from concept to implementation to start two retail specialty shops that grew in size, market share, and customer base, with revenues in excess of $350K per year.

- Held supervisory responsibility for all aspects of student life, capital facilities, program management, and event planning, to position Franklin as one of the top 7 American Higher Education "best buys."

- Took strategic steps to enhance interaction between professional staff, board members, and students to create a world-class environment for success and leadership development.

- Held multi-functional management responsibilities, including vendor/distributor contracts for supplies, lease negotiations, purchasing, payroll, marketing, promotions, training and development, policy development, and fund utilization.

- Served as key facilitator between student groups and administration in event planning, leadership development, public relations, pre-construction facility design, and administration of services.

- Supervised campus-life event-planning projects and established student-life policies for university campus with 300 diverse organizations and an enrollment in excess of 33,000.

- Developed and demonstrated excellent oral/written communication skills in extensive interface with public relations and news media from New York City, Kansas City, St. Louis, Denver, Louisville, Indianapolis, and Detroit.

Career History

Owner/President	Pictures Incorporated	2007–present
Director of Student Affairs	Franklin University	1998–2006
Human Resources Associate	Michigan State University	1991–1997
Administrator of Leadership Programs	Purdue University	1985–1991

Academic Credentials

MA Student Personnel Services in Higher Education, Michigan State University
BS Business Administration—Human Resource Management focus, Purdue University

---

Strategy: Use a functional resume to focus attention on relevant achievements within academic HR/student services rather than a recent entrepreneurial venture.

KAREN L. HOLLMANN

822 SW Dosch Road
Portland, OR 97239

(503) 224-5201 Residence   k_hollmann@hotmail.com   (503) 235-1198 Business

Workforce Development Program Director

PROFESSIONAL SUMMARY

Creative, visionary human-services manager with more than 20 years of experience in the employment and training field in both public and private sectors. Over 10 years of experience directing regional workforce-development programs and managing a continuous-improvement organization. Strong skills in facilitating team building and an open work environment. Sound ability to successfully work with the ebb and flow of funding sources, including innovating fee-for-service programs. Excellent skills in assessing organizational challenges and creating solutions. Strategic thinker, passionate, true leader.

Personnel Management: Led staff of workforce-development professionals to consistently exceed goals for participant numbers and expense control on all contracts.

Fiscal Management: By leveraging $750,000+ in extra funding, staff was able to serve twice as many needy clients as in the previous year.

Organizational Development: Facilitated innovation and change in multiple companies, both as director and as consultant.

PROFESSIONAL EXPERIENCE

PORTLAND COMMUNITY COLLEGE, Portland, OR   1998–Present
Director, Employment Programs (2000–Present)
Manager of Operations and Programs (1998–2000)

Oversee the planning and operation of various federal, state, and private employment, training, and management contracts averaging over $5 million annually. Manage three local offices in two counties. Coordinate and direct all administrative and program activities for staff of 40+. Establish and manage program plans, goals, budgets, contracts, and performance standards. Act as national strategic partner for Profiles International, an employment assessment system. Fiscal Agent and One-Stop Operator to regional Workforce Investment Board.

- Leveraged more than $750,000 in extra funding beyond allocated job-training contracts for the region in 2010, nearly four times the leveraged funding of the previous year.
- Empowered staff to innovate several fee-for-service programs, including a coffee cart run by program participants, fiber-optics training to assist clients from the fishing industry change careers, and private contract-management and employment seminars. Fee-for-service programs accounted for nearly $70K in company revenues in 2010.
- Sought out to serve at the national, state, and local levels on One-Stop program initiatives, helping to influence legislation and program regulations.
- Consistently receive outstanding financial and program audits, including Department of Labor, State of Oregon, The Oregon Consortium, and independent audits.
- Worked closely with local elected officials, private-sector members, and workforce partners to operate the Region #2 Workforce Investment Board, implement the state-approved five-year workforce plan for the region, and enforce a Memo of Understanding among partners.
- Active in One-Stop System development in partnership with regional, state, and employer partners, resulting in delivery of seamless, high-quality services.

Continued

Strategy: Use a professional summary to highlight strong skills in managing people and dollars and in organizational development; enhance these facts with strong personal descriptors. Create an optional third page that includes an extensive list of distinguishing activities and affiliations.

KAREN L. HOLLMANN   k_hollmann@hotmail.com   Page Two

Professional Experience, Continued

MT. HOOD COMMUNITY COLLEGE, Gresham, OR   2009–Present
Instructor

Instructor for cohort-based community-college 39-credit credential in Workforce Development. Developed curriculum; designed and marketed Career Development Specialist certificate program.

♦ Developed curriculum/program from the ground up in three-month period for one of the few Workforce Development programs in the U.S.

J.E.C. CONSULTING, Portland, OR   1996–2000
Co-Owner/Consultant

Provided contracted services to businesses for on-site assessment of employee needs and system/procedural challenges. Designed and implemented programs and trainings for staff development and system reorganization/organizational development.

EMPLOYMENT, TRAINING, AND BUSINESS SERVICES, Marylhurst, OR   1994–1998
Trainer/Account Representative/Competency Specialist

Trained youth in employment and job-search techniques. Developed training activity competencies. Completed participant enrollments and program modifications and terminations as required. Collaborated with colleagues to develop employability plans for program enrollees. Wrote curriculum, competency systems, and assessment tools. Facilitated agency-wide retreats and training sessions for 100+ employees.

STATE OF OREGON EMPLOYMENT DEPARTMENT, Oregon City, OR   1993–1994
Job Service Representative/Liaison

Contacted employers within the community and solicited job orders. Matched job orders with qualified job seekers. Instructed job seekers in job-search techniques through workshops and one-to-one counseling sessions. Acted as liaison between Employment Department and Employment, Training, and Business Services.

EDUCATION

Ed.M. in Organizational Development, Portland State University, Portland, OR, 2009

B.A. in Speech Communications, University of Oregon, Eugene, OR

Additional Professional Development Coursework:

Profiles Executive Advanced Training Certification, Dallas, TX, 2009

PROFESSIONAL AWARDS

National Advancement of the Workforce Profession Customer Service Award, 2010
Oregon Governor's Workforce Award, 2008
Job Corps Community Supporter of the Year Award, 2007
Certificate of Leadership, Oregon Career Network, 2005–2007
Commitment in Action Award for Passion, Innovation, and Energy, Oregon Employment and Training Association, 2004

Continued

KAREN L. HOLLMANN   k_hollmann@hotmail.com   Page Three

HIGHLIGHTS OF PRESENTATIONS

"Profiles—Job Match Assessments," OETA The Rendezvous 2001, Bend, OR, 2009
"Overcoming Barriers to Employability," NAWDP Annual Conference, Reno, NV, 2008
"Fee for Service," Washington State Workforce Development Providers' Conference, Seattle, WA, 2006
"The Instructions Are Inside the Box," NAWDP Annual Conference, Miami Beach, FL, 2006
"Beyond JTPA: Becoming a Community Service Provider," National Association of Counties Workforce Development Conference, Tulsa County, OK, 2005
"Integration: What Does It Really Mean?" Georgia Workforce Development Conference, Atlanta, GA, 2004

PROFESSIONAL AFFILIATIONS

National Department of Labor Appointments

National Summit on the Future of the Workforce Development Profession, Washington, DC, 2010
Labor Force Measures Workgroup, 2006–2007
Performance Measures and Applications Technical Workgroup, 2006–2007
JTPA SPIR Revision Technical Workgroup, 2006–2007
Performance Standards Workgroup, 2005–2007
Workforce Development Performance Measures Initiative: Efficiency Workgroup, 2005–2007
Technical Assistance Group for Performance Standards, 1998–1999

Boards

Board Member, Region #2 Regional Workforce Investment Board, 2007–Present
Executive Board Officer, National Association of Workforce Development Professionals and Partnership Education Fund, 2003–2010
Board Member, Oregon Career Information System, 2007–2008
Chairperson, The Oregon Consortium Program Directors, 2005–2007
Board Member, Oregon Employment and Training Association, 1995–1998, 2008
Board Member, Rotary Club International, 2005

Working Committees

National Certification Team, Workforce Development Professional Certification, National Association of Workforce Development Professionals, 2007–Present
Co-Chair, Oregon Governor's State Workforce Investment Act Performance Accountability Task Force, 2007
Executive Officer, North Coast Workforce Quality Committee, 2002–2007
State Committee Member, Governor's Student Retention Initiative, Paroled and Incarcerated Youth, 1996–1997

Professional Association Memberships

National Association of Workforce Development Professionals, 2002–Present
Oregon Workforce Partnership, Oregon Directors of Workforce Development Programs, 2000–Present
Oregon Employment and Training Association, 1995–Present
Rotary Club International, 2001–2007; Paul Harris Fellow, 2007

◆ ◆ ◆

SUSAN B. ALMANN

589 Brighton View
Croton, NY 10520

(914) 271-5567

Sbalm345@aol.com

CAREER PROFILE

Strategic **Human Resources Executive** and proactive business partner to senior management to guide in the development of performance-driven, customer-driven, and market-driven organizations. Proven effectiveness in providing vision and counsel in steering organizations through periods of accelerated growth and economic downturn. Diverse background includes multinational organizations in the medical equipment and manufacturing industries.

Expertise in all generalist HR initiatives:

Recruitment & Employment Management … Leadership Training & Development … Benefits & Compensation Design … Reorganization & Culture Change … Merger & Acquisition Integration … Union & Non-Union Employee Relations … Succession Planning … Expatriate Programs … Long-Range Business Planning … HR Policies & Procedures.

PROFESSIONAL EXPERIENCE

<u>**MARCON MANUFACTURING COMPANY**</u>, Peekskill, NY
Vice President, Human Resources (2004–Present)

Challenge: Recruited to create HR infrastructure to support business growth at a $30 million global manufacturing company with underachieving sales, exceedingly high turnover, and lack of cohesive management processes among business entities in U.S. and Asia.

Action: Partnered with President and Board of Directors to reorganize company, reduce overhead expenses, rebuild sales, and institute solid management infrastructure.

Results:
- Established HR with staff of 5, including development of policies and procedures; renegotiated cost-effective benefit programs that saved $1.5 million annually.
- Reorganized operations and facilitated seamless integration within parent company of 150 employees from two recent acquisitions.
- Reduced sales-force turnover to nearly nonexistent and upgraded quality of candidates hired by implementing interview-skills training and management-development programs. Results led to measurable improvements in sales performance.
- Recruited all management personnel, developed HR policies, and fostered team culture at new Malaysian plant with 125 employees.
- Initiated business reorganization plan, resulting in consolidation of New York and Virginia operations for $6.5 million in cost reductions.

<u>**BINGHAMTON COMPANY**</u>, New York, NY
Director, Human Resources & Administration (2001–2004)

Challenge: Lead HR and Administration functions and staff that support 1,600 employees at $500 million medical equipment manufacturer. Contribute to company's turnaround efforts, business unit consolidations, and transition to focus on consumer products.

Action: Established cross-functional teams from each site and provided training in team building to coordinate product development efforts, implement new manufacturing processes, and speed products to market. Identified cost reduction opportunities; instrumental in reorganization initiatives that included closing union plant in Texas and building new plant in North Carolina.

Page 1

Strategy: Use the Challenge, Action, and Results format (see page 25) to emphasize extensive experience in key areas that impact an organization's business performance well beyond HR.

(914) 271-5567   **SUSAN B. ALMANN** • PAGE 2   Sbalm345@aol.com

Director, Human Resources & Administration, continued...

Results:
- Instituted worldwide cross-functional team culture that provided foundation for successful new product launches and recapture of company's leading edge despite intense market competition.
- Spearheaded flawless integration of two operations into single, cohesive European business unit, resulting in profitable turnaround.
- Restructured and positioned HR organization in the German business unit as customer-focused partner to support European sales and marketing units.
- Initiated major benefit cost reductions of $3 million in first year and $1 million annually while gaining employee acceptance through concerted education and communications efforts.

ARCADIA CORPORATION, New York, NY
Director, Human Resources (1997–2001)
Assistant Director, Human Resources (1995–1997)

Challenge: HR support to corporate office and field units of an $800 million organization with 150 global operations employing 4,500 people.

Action: Promoted to lead staff of 10 in all HR and labor relations activities. Established separate international recruitment function and designed staffing plan to accommodate rapid business growth. Negotiated cost-effective benefits contracts for union and non-union employees.

Results:
- Oversaw successful UAW, Teamsters, and labor contract negotiations.
- Established and staffed HR function for multimillion-dollar contract with U.S. government agency.
- Introduced incentive plans for field unit managers and an expatriate program that attracted both internal and external candidates for international assignments in the Middle East.
- Resolved HR issues associated with two business acquisitions while accomplishing a smooth transition and retention of all key personnel.
- Restructured HR function with no service disruption to the business while saving $1.5 million annually.

EDUCATION

M.B.A., Cornell University, New York, NY
B.A., Business Administration, Amherst College, Amherst, MA

AFFILIATIONS

Society for Human Resource Management
Human Resource Council of Albany

RESUME 30: BY ILONA VANDERWOUDE, ACRW, MRW, CCMC, CJST, CEIP, CPRW

ELENA VARGA

9 Olive Street
San Diego, CA 92104
C: 619.233.9985
E: e.varga@hotmail.com

SENIOR EDUCATION EXECUTIVE

Focus: Regional Vice President of Operations

**Combine natural talent for selecting, developing, and motivating staff
with business acumen and consistent record of generating sustainable bottom-line results:**

Within months of assuming current position, reduced costs and bad debt related to attrition; slashed student attrition; boosted revenues through new starts and increased student sign-up; promoted institution's brand; created new programs; reshaped, trained, and motivated organization; skyrocketed student net promoter score; and spearheaded housing program.

Additional experience includes living/working in Mexico, Latin America, and the Caribbean,
directing operations across multiple locations (also across the U.S.). Bilingual English/Spanish.

EXECUTIVE PERFORMANCE

Coleman University · San Diego, CA · 3/2010 to Present
$40 million educational institute providing technical education for the motorcycle and marine technical industries.
PRESIDENT
Achieved organic revenue growth through brand extension, introduction of new products and services, and field and campus rep efficiencies.

P&L responsibility for $40 million in gross revenues and $5 million net earnings. Oversee 120 employees and 7 directors. Charged with revenue and earnings growth, customer satisfaction, brand equity, student population growth, student graduation and placement rates, and federal and corporate compliance (CCI).

Achievements within 7 months of assuming position:

- **16% YOY and 12% QOQ Revenue Growth** – Increased tuition and salvaged inherited in-house admissions reps' initiative by adding up to 27 reps but also adding instructors and equipment to handle doubling of student load per instructor. Additional results: 25% increase in student satisfaction score.
  - **Reduced attrition 12%** from 6% to 5.28% by teaming up with career services department for marketing campaign "It Pays to Stay" and by hiring and training new Director of Education.
- **88% FY2010 Placement Rate** – On pace to be #1 in the organization for FY2011.
- **Awards for Q1-2011 for Best Bad Debt and for Best Cash Collection (Companywide)** – Slashed bad debt 25% (related to attrition) to 1.2% net sales by hiring loan specialist and designing student awareness campaign.
- **Restructured Education Department by Program Type** – Reassigned department heads and delivered greater management control, increased decision-making, and reduced overall department cost by 6.4%.
  - Appointed 1 educational coordinator per specialty and added accountability for budgets, student satisfaction, attrition, and instructor staffing.

National Technical Institute (NTI) · Denver, CO · 2008 to 2010
Educational provider with 10+ U.S. campuses offering technical education for students seeking careers as professional automotive, diesel, collision repair, motorcycle, and marine technicians. $300 million in revenues and 16,000+ students.
CAMPUS PRESIDENT
Unwavering organizational focus and commitment on profitability, cost leadership, and customer satisfaction.

P&L responsibility for $50 million organization; $5 million in EBIT, 8 direct reports, 120 total employees, 1600 students, and 280,000 sq ft state-of-the-art automotive, industrial, and diesel facility. Developed, retained, and recruited top operational talent and instructional team. In charge of retention, accreditation, operations, local and graduate employment, and key metrics relative to student and employee satisfaction, financial aid, and enroll-to-show conversion.

... Continued

Strategy: Use functional headings to call attention to diverse areas of accomplishment. Highlight strong financial results that are essential in the for-profit educational arena.

ELENA VARGA

Page 2 of 2
C: 619.233.9985
E: e.varga@hotmail.com

National Technical Institute (NTI) · continued

- **Starts & Placements** – Increased YOY starts by 123% from 2008 to 2009 and 67% from 2009 to 2010. Achieved top-5 ranking among 11 campuses in graduate placement with 80% placement rate.

- **Profitability** – Achieved campus profitability within 1.5 years in 3Q2010…first time in 5 years.

- **Employment Program** – Launched education and employment cooperative program with top employers in Denver metropolitan area. **Increased student retention to 97%, forged industry relationships, and increased graduate placement by 6% to 80%.**

Lennox Investment Ltd. · San Diego, CA · 2006 to 2008
Holding company focused on land and property development as well as small business acquisitions.

INTERIM OPERATING OFFICER

Hired as key member of executive team to turn organization around to profitability.

Held P&L responsibility for $10 million organization; developed strategic business plan and operating budget.

- **Return to Profitability** – Turned company around from flat earnings growth, soaring operating costs, and lack of goal-setting to achieve goal of 15% ROIC on existing and new acquisitions by providing clear direction for entire organization with regard to objectives and developing new business model focused on company's strengths.

AT&T Security · San Diego, CA · 2003 to 2005
Subsidiary of AT&T with $21+ billion in 2012 revenues.

GENERAL MANAGER, SOUTH CALIFORNIA & MEXICO

Recruited to combat flat revenue growth, deteriorating market share, poor sales rep productivity, installation backlog, high customer discontinuance rate, declining customer base, and low employee morale.

Managed P&L and annual budget for $35 million organization. Met budget, sales, and cost targets.

- **Revenue & Earnings Growth Increase** – Delivered $15 million increase in annual gross revenues (from $20 million to $35 million) – 26% increase in revenue per employee and 22% increase in sales rep productivity.

A.B. Massa Paper Corporation · Darien, CT · 1998 to 2003
Global leader in paper and packaging product manufacturing and distribution with $21.8+ billion in 2012 revenues.

COUNTRY MANAGER, JAMAICA AND THE CARIBBEAN BASIN
(Promoted from Business Development Manager within 3 months)

Challenged to turn around Jamaican territory facing declining customer demand, hostile union workforce, $2.1 million in internal fraud, large entrenched competitors, and excess manufacturing capacity.

Offered job based out of Miami but elected to move to Jamaica to maximize effectiveness of turnaround efforts.

- **Turnaround** – Took territory from $38 million to $60 million in gross revenues within 2 years, from highest-cost to lowest-cost manufacturer in the company and the only company division to achieve world-class manufacturing status. Transformed hostile workforce to fully engaged team.

Additional Experience: Calvin Klein, New York, NY – General Manager, Central America (1993 to 1996); Kraft Foods, Fair Lawn, NJ – Plant Manager (1990 to 1993)

EDUCATION

MBA in Finance – 1998, MIT GRADUATE PROGRAM, Cambridge, MA
MS in Applied Management & Industry – 1991, DEVRY UNIVERSITY, Sacramento, CA
BS in Industrial Engineering – 1988, CALIFORNIA COLLEGE, San Diego, CA

Pat Sanderson

psanderson@snet.net

Home 203-488-0956 • Mobile 203-309-8909
89 Benson Drive, North Branford, CT 06471

SECONDARY EDUCATION ADMINISTRATOR

Accomplished professional with a track record of improving educational and operational performance through vision, leadership, and team building. Experience spans urban and rural school districts and includes 6 years of administrative experience complemented by 7 years of classroom teaching and extensive athletic coaching experience.

Strengths include defining goals, creating and enforcing policies, and accomplishing objectives by empowering staff. Advanced skills in scheduling classes and managing/manipulating EMIS data. Consistent record of building community and family connections. Proven ability to effect change and drive continuous improvement.

PROFESSIONAL EXPERIENCE

MILLVILLE REGIONAL HIGH SCHOOL, Millville, CT   2005–Present
Principal, 2007–Present • **Assistant Principal,** 2005–2007

Led a performance turnaround of 550-student high school, recording substantial improvements in both measurable and intangible areas of evaluation: student attendance, test scores, state evaluations, morale, student participation, teacher engagement, and school population driven by the school's growing reputation for excellence.

Directly responsible for all personnel, curriculum, instruction, and daily operations of junior-senior high school (grades 7–12). Manage $220K budget for facilities and operations.

Challenges and Results

Lax discipline and substandard attendance (89%) were creating a poor educational environment and negatively affecting test scores. Recruited as Assistant Principal to improve these fundamentals.

- Set new discipline and attendance policies—and enforced them.
- Gained community support/culture shift through an intensive and ongoing communications campaign.
- Personally supervised after-school and Saturday detentions, becoming the visible face of the new culture.
- Encouraged attendance through meaningful incentives and recognition events.

   In one year, improved attendance to state standard (93%); increased to 95.5% (highest building attendance in Essex County) by 2008–2009 school year.

School had been designated as "academic emergency" by state evaluation board. Upon promotion to Principal, designed and led multiple, aggressive initiatives to improve academic performance.

- Developed performance data on every student in the building and used data to customize tutoring and support.
- Gained parental support through frequent personal communication.
- Implemented short-cycle assessments, aligning teaching and testing with mandated test standards.
- Reduced overcrowded classrooms through better scheduling and more proactive monitoring of student progress.
- Converted full-block schedule to semi-block, allowing greater freedom and flexibility for students.
- Empowered teachers, gained their support for changes, and percolated culture of performance excellence into every classroom in the building.

   Delivered immediate and sustainable improvements in meeting building report-card standards:

2005–2006	2006–2007	2007–2008	2008–2009	2009–2010
3 of 12 (**25%**)	7 of 12 (**58%**)	11 of 12 (**92%**)	11 of 12 (**92%**)	7 of 7 (**100%**)

   Improved proficiency test results—in 2010, 10th grade passed all 5 indicators with 85% and above; 9th grade passed all 5 indicators with 75% and above; 8th grade passed 4 of the 5 indicators with 75% and above.

   Graduation rate improved from 75% to 86%. AP program participation jumped 35%. Student population grew more than 12% as increasing numbers of students and parents chose Millville (open enrollment district).

Continued

Strategy: Emphasize impressive results in multiple areas of measurement—student performance, graduation rates, attendance, participation, and so forth—to position high school principal for the larger role of school superintendent.

Pat Sanderson   Home 203-488-0956 • Mobile 203-309-8909 • psanderson@snet.net

MILLVILLE REGIONAL HIGH SCHOOL   continued

In an era of shrinking resources, faced with managing facilities and operations on a tight budget.

- Created new system for supplies and materials—improved control and ensured equitable allocation.
- Focused attention on energy efficiency; eliminated substantial waste and saved $20K over prior year.

   Came in under budget every year.

Athletic program had been operated by "seat-of-the-pants" standards and lacked proper accountability. Requested by School Board to take on concurrent position as Athletic Director (2006–2007 school year).

- Created new athletic policy and ensured it was followed.
- Ensured all coaching staff were properly trained and certified.
- Developed new processes for communicating athletic news to parents and the community.

   Athletic participation increased by one-third.

EAST HAVEN CITY SCHOOLS, East Haven, CT   2001–2005
Site Base Manager, 2004–2005 • Administrative Internship, Hyde Middle School, 2004
Discipline Coordinator (7th and 8th Grades), Hyde Middle School, 2003–2004
Mathematics Instructor, Horace Mann Middle School, 2001–2003

NORTH BRANFORD SCHOOL DISTRICT, North Branford, CT   2000–2001
Elementary Teacher (4th Grade)

COGINCHAUG REGIONAL SCHOOL DISTRICT, Durham, CT   1996–2000
Mathematics and Computer Science Instructor

EDUCATION AND CERTIFICATION

UNIVERSITY OF CONNECTICUT, Storrs, CT: Master of Administrative Educational Leadership, 2010
SOUTHERN CONNECTICUT STATE UNIVERSITY, New Haven, CT: Bachelor of Science, Elementary Education

CERTIFICATIONS: Connecticut Superintendent Certificate • Connecticut Secondary Administrator Certificate

COMMITTEE PARTICIPATION

MILLVILLE REGIONAL HIGH SCHOOL: Site-Based Management Committee • Connecticut Special Education Review • Intervention Assistance Chair • Attendance Incentive Grant Committee Chair

EAST HAVEN CITY SCHOOLS: Discipline Committee Team • Nonviolent Crisis Intervention Team

NORTH BRANFORD SCHOOLS: Mentor Program • Mathematics Course of Study Revision Committee Chair

COACHING HISTORY

EAST HAVEN CITY SCHOOLS: Reserve Boys Basketball Coach • Reserve Boys Baseball Coach • Reserve Girls Softball Coach • Middle School Football Coach • Middle School Basketball Coach

EAST HAVEN CITY SCHOOLS: Varsity Boys Basketball Assistant Coach • Varsity Girls Volleyball Coach • Varsity Boys Basketball Coach—District Champions • Reserve Boys Basketball Coach

COGINCHAUG REGIONAL SCHOOL DISTRICT: Varsity Boys Basketball Assistant Coach • Reserve Boys Baseball Coach • Junior High Football Coach • Junior High Girls Basketball Coach

GORDON CHAPMAN
Email: GChapman@aol.com

1433 Meadowlark Lane	Cell: (608) 255-6710
Madison, Wisconsin 53405	Residence: (608) 873-2398

PROFILE

I believe that Gordon Chapman has the special qualities of understanding, compassion, discipline, and the exceptional work ethic that would make him an excellent elementary school principal.

An enthusiastic and dynamic education professional with 17 years of successful elementary-level teaching experience seeking a position as **Elementary Principal/Administrator.** Innovative and creative with a positive, can-do attitude and genuine compassion for others. Expertise working with Special Education populations/processes and a core belief that all children can have a successful educational experience. Excellent interpersonal, group presentation, and written communication skills. A well-respected and active community leader with documented, positive results from participation in school and civic projects. Demonstrated core competencies include:

- Strategic & Tactical Planning
- Visionary Leadership
- Continuous Process Improvement
- School/Community Relations
- Special Programs & Events Planning
- Textbook Review
- Instructional Resource Selection

- High Standards Curriculum, Instruction, & Administration
- Team-Based Culture
- Training & Development
- Crisis Planning & Emergency Preparedness
- Classroom Technology Initiatives

PROFESSIONAL EXPERIENCE

MADISON PUBLIC SCHOOL DISTRICT—Madison, Wisconsin   1993 to Present

Summer School Assistant Principal—Practicum (January 2010 to Present)

- Practicum administered under direction of John Fliss, Summer School Coordinator and Elementary Principal, Lincoln School.
- Pre-program accountabilities include timeline development, program scheduling, and staff selection.
- Accountabilities during program (7 weeks) include daily program monitoring, parent/staff communications, busing coordination, and behavior/discipline issues.

Third-Grade Classroom Teacher—Forest Elementary (2007 to Present)
Third-Grade Classroom Teacher—Linden Avenue Elementary (2001 to 2007)

He has the support of his fellow workers, which would be of extreme importance in the position for which he is applying. His experience ... and his many job descriptions give him the knowledge that would be very beneficial to the school community.

Shelly Hughes
Former Madison Schools Staff Member

- Serve as Principal-In-Charge (Forest) with full accountability for building supervision, parental communications, staff/classroom scheduling, and student behavior/discipline.
- Selected as Grade-Level Team Leader (Linden Avenue); served 2 years.
- Serve on District Science Committee accountable for new curriculum selection and adoption.
- Initiated and organized biannual Science Day (Forest & Linden Avenue), a hands-on, interactive learning activity involving students, volunteers, and staff. Coordinate annual Science Fair (Forest).
- Implementing Professional Learning Community Initiative (Forest) through team collaboration, shared decision making, and sound leadership.
- Implemented Student Council (Forest); teach problem-solving skills and assist students with service projects such as food/clothing drives and fundraisers.
- Serve on Planning Committee (Forest) charged with initiating programs to develop a distinct identity for school.
- Serve on Technology Committee (Forest & Linden Avenue) challenged to assess classroom hardware/software needs and determine staff training requirements.

Page 1 of 2

Strategy: Embed strong recommendations in the left column of the resume so that these powerful sales tools won't be overlooked.

Gordon Chapman	Cell: (608) 255-6710	Residence: (608) 873-2398	Page 2 of 2
RÉSUMÉ			

PROFESSIONAL EXPERIENCE (continued)

MADISON PUBLIC SCHOOL DISTRICT (continued)

Primary LD Teacher—Linden Avenue Elementary (1993 to 2001)
- Implemented mainstreaming with team teaching and other inclusionary efforts.

Assistant Varsity Football Coach—Madison High School (1995 to 2009)
- Led team to 11 consecutive Division II Playoff appearances; State Runner-Up in 2008.

CAREER ACHIEVEMENTS

- Received the Wisconsin Elementary and Middle School Teachers (WEMST) Distinguished Teacher Award for efforts to promote science education within the state.
- Received the Madison Education Foundation "A Class Act" Award in 2004 for excellence in the classroom.
- Awarded Madison Foundation Grant in 2002 for LEGOs in the Classroom initiative. Grant supplied simple machine kits to all district schools, currently used in third-grade classrooms. Designed and presented teacher in-service on classroom implementation.
- Recognized by the Madison School District's Board of Education with Certificates of Appreciation in 2001, 2002, 2004, and 2006 for excellence in teaching.

EDUCATION

MA in Educational Leadership—Marquette University, Milwaukee, Wisconsin, 2010
BA in Education—Appleton College, Appleton, Wisconsin, 1993

Professional Development
Professional Learning Community Training—Lincolnshire, Illinois, 2009

LICENSURE & CERTIFICATIONS

Certified Principal (PK–12), State of Wisconsin 51, 2010
Certified Elementary Teacher (K–8), State of Wisconsin 108, 1993
Certified Learning Disabilities (K–8), State of Wisconsin 811, 1993

PROFESSIONAL AFFILIATIONS

Director-at-Large for Wisconsin Elementary and Middle School Teachers (WEMST)
- Lead strategic planning efforts to promote science initiatives statewide.

Lead Teacher for Academy of Staff Development Initiative (ASDI)

Presenter at District In-Services, Workshops, and WEAC Conference

CIVIC ACTIVITIES

Co-Chair, Facilities Advisory Committee—Monona Public School District, 2006
- Assessed district facility requirements, prioritized needs, and presented Board of Education with options to address current and future expansion plans, community utilization of facilities, safety issues, and community growth projections.

CHAPTER 7

Resumes for Managers and Executives in Real Estate and Construction

- Site Development Executive

- Senior Real Estate Executive

- Facilities and Property Manager

- Chief Engineer

- Project Manager/Site Superintendent/ Field Superintendent

- Senior Transit Planner

- Construction Manager

- Commercial Construction Superintendent

Roy Paterson

425 Greenwood Way • Redwood City, CA 94062 • Tel: (415) 601-3392 • Email: roy.pat@gmail.com

Land and Site Development

Nationally Recognized Expert on Zoning and Entitlement

Appointed by Governor of California to the State Board of Architecture

Land Acquisition • Site Planning • Real Estate Development • Construction Management

Highly accomplished Site Development Executive with passionate interest and all-around expertise in all aspects of real estate, site development, and construction. Exceptional negotiation, conflict-resolution, and consensus-building skills. Legendary reputation for delivering "impossible" projects on time, as promised, and within budget.

- Citadel Investment Properties: Secured $102M for 1,480 hotel rooms, building, and land.
- Empire Realty Corp: Delivered $175.8M office development and $142M industrial park.
- Paterson & Smith LLC: Managed numerous projects—land planning, site design, plat packages—for more than 2,500 home sites, 160 stores, and 1.5M square feet of commercial development.

CAREER HIGHLIGHTS

Zoning and Entitlements

Frequently invited to testify as expert witness during legal proceedings that involve complex and precedent-setting cases. Member of California Metropolitan Council, Governor's Environmental Committee, and The Real Estate Round Table.

Land and Site Development

Land and Site Acquisition • Zoning • Site Feasibility Analyses • Master Planning • Due Diligence • Trade Area Market Analyses • Purchase Agreements • Pro Forma Financials • Letters of Intent • Lease Negotiations • Construction Management • Cash Flow Forecasting • Strategic Planning • P&L • Plat Packages

Extensive Portfolio of Projects

<u>Please see separate Project Portfolio for full details</u>. Completed more than 125 progressively complex and challenging projects during 25+ years in real estate. Deal sizes and land areas up to $213M and 12,000 acres for hotels, master-planned mixed use, golf resorts, office-and-industrial parks, shopping centers, and marinas.

Appointment by the Governor of California

Commissioned as a State Official to the California Board of Architecture—Legislative and Enforcement Committees for Engineering, Land Surveying, Landscape Architecture, and Geo-Science.

PROFESSIONAL EXPERIENCE

PATERSON & SMITH LLC, San Francisco, CA   2008–Present
Consulting firm focused on real-estate development in CA, FL, Dallas–Fort Worth, and Minneapolis.

Principal

Currently performing site selection of new development and renovating existing properties (multi-family housing, hotels, and industrial). Prepare financial pro-formas for projects and perform site and due-diligence investigations. Report on competitive rate analysis, tax basis, utility availability, zoning, and market feasibility.

- Delivered projects for 4 multifamily housing properties valued at $3.1M; several hotels with package value of $84M; 2 industrial sites with buildings valued at $6.9M; and several finished residential lots.
- Achieved several prestigious awards for design innovation and community enrichment: Excellence in Innovation, California Land Institute (2008); The Gold Award for Best New Community, National Association of Home Builders (2010); Developer's Award, 1000 Friends of California (2009).

CITADEL INVESTMENT PROPERTIES, San Francisco, CA   2007–2008
Privately held real-estate development firm. Develops, builds, and currently operates 25 hotels in 9 states.

Director of Development Services

Reported to CEO and tasked to take charge of hotel development. Collaborated closely with state agencies, lenders, and franchisors. Made presentations at public hearings and managed all aspects of development projects that included entitlements, legal, engineering, outside consultants, and financial feasibility. Established new procedures for project development and construction tracking and financial reporting.

- Arranged $102M for 1,480 hotel rooms (15 hotels), site and building zoning, and permit entitlements.
- Reorganized Land Acquisition, Development, and Construction Departments and moved each from the "silo" model to cross-functional project management.

Strategy: Use an expanded Summary section to showcase diverse areas of expertise within a lengthy career in real estate development. Notice the mention of a separate project portfolio.

Roy Paterson .... Tel: (415) 601-3392 ....Email: roy.pat@gmail.com.......................................Page 2

TOLL LUXURY PROPERTIES, Bonita Springs, FL   **2005–2006**
Private developer, owner, and operator of 5-star luxury golf, spa, and resort communities in southeast US.
Director of Development and Planning

Prepared in-depth parcel evaluations—via contract management of 16 outside consulting firms—for new land acquisition, financial analyses, due diligence, design, and land-use permitting. Secured *Developments of Residential Impact* (DRIs) for 3 golf-and-spa resort proposals in Florida and West Virginia.

- Completed $1.2B in cost and financial-feasibility analyses for 3 resort proposals. Directed theme design, sketches, and feasibility studies for new resort opportunities.
- During early planning stages of Pete Dye GC resort—total value $213M—quickly stopped project after discovering that surface collapse from an underlying coal mine would cripple building construction.

STANFORD REALTY CORP, Walnut Creek, CA   **2000–2004**
Leading REIT and general construction company. Total market capitalization more than $8B. Owns or manages industrial, office, and retail properties with more than 110M square feet in 13 cities.
Development Manager

Led development of new offices, industrial parks, individual buildings, shopping centers, colleges, and medical facilities. Reported to Corporate EVP Construction; managed 40+ external consulting firms; and directed land acquisition, PM, and contract management. Made public presentations and prepared master budgets.

- Secured government approvals for several projects, including Norman Pointe office park, 1.2M square feet; Crosstown North, 100-acre industrial park and buildings; and a 15-acre college facility ($22M).
- Completed more than $200M in office development and $142M in industrial development.
- Prepared preconstruction cost to complete proposals, bid assessment, bonding, and LOCs.
- Obtained Tax Increment Financing (TIF) for industrial projects, including a $1.5M TIF for General Motors Spare Parts (a 380,000-square-foot build-to-suit project in Hudson, WI).

SENIOR CELEBRATION DEVELOPMENTS, Phoenix, AZ   **1998–2000**
Privately held, national real-estate developer of tax-credit, rental, independent-living senior housing.
Vice President of Land Development

Directed consultants during site acquisition and building design. Initiated all land acquisition deals.

- Drove fast-track entitlements to satisfy IRS regulations. Completed 13 deals—valued at approximately $8M each—within 18 months. Prepared financial feasibility analyses for lenders and government agencies.
- Identified land parcels in 11 states. Led acquisition and tax-credit staff during preparation of cost and impact-fee analyses, pro-forma models, and financial underwriting.

———————————**ADDITIONAL SITE-DEVELOPMENT EXPERIENCE**———————————

SEASIDE LUXURY HOMES, San Luis Obispo, CA (1996–1998): Vice President of Land Development for national town-home and single-family home developer and builder. Prepared, presented, and completed 7 communities totaling 1,370 acres and 3,560 units. Led development teams for grading, utilities, and streets.

PATERSON LAND PLANNING CONSULTANTS INC, Redwood City, CA (1990–1996): Principal and Owner. Created a land-development and site-design firm, starting from scratch. Developed new business, built a list of "A" clients, and created innovative market partnerships.

- Planned more than 2,500 residential units and 1.5M-square-foot office, industrial, and retail development. Project-managed site-plan approvals for more than 160 convenience stores and cell towers.
- Recognized as land-use expert witness in Los Angeles and Santa Barbara County District Courts.

SANDER PROPERTIES, Los Angeles, CA (1985–1990): Director of Land Planning.

———————————**EDUCATION, CERTIFICATIONS, AND REGISTRATIONS**———————————

Bachelor of Landscape Architecture (with Thesis), University of California, Los Angeles, CA, 1985
Professional Degree, Equivalent to a Masters of Landscape Architecture
Landscape Architect, registrations in California (#45333) and Arizona (#14432)

STAN DUBEK, CFA

415-781-0904 291 Vallejo Street #701, San Francisco, CA 94510 sdubek@gmail.com

SENIOR REAL ESTATE EXECUTIVE

Broadly experienced leader with successful 20+-year career in the strategic management of real estate investments. Repeatedly spearheaded major initiatives launching new products (U.S. and international) and leading high-growth-potential investment programs. Delivered millions of dollars in profitable returns through effective leadership of property acquisitions and sales, portfolio management, and commercial and residential development activities. Expert in identifying, negotiating, structuring, closing, and managing complex investments. Chartered Financial Analyst. Stanford MBA.

Key Areas of Expertise

- Portfolio & Asset Management • Property Acquisitions & Sales • Single- & Multifamily Development
- Financial Analysis, Forecasting & Due Diligence • Staff & Team Development • Product Design & Marketing

EXPERIENCE & ACHIEVEMENTS

ENTERPRISE INVESTMENTS, San Francisco, CA 2008–Present
Institutional real estate capital source; subsidiary of one of the world's leading investment firms.

Senior Investment Officer

Recruited to run one of 4 deal teams in the Enterprise Real Estate Group.

- Closed investment in a 275-unit condo conversion in Phoenix; on track to achieve $16M in profits.
- Funded mezzanine loan to develop Aerial Towers, a 23-story condo development in Scottsdale with an expected sell-out of $104M on total cost of $86M.
- Executed letter of intent to fund Waterside Square, a Tampa condominium development forecast to generate gross sales proceeds of $86M on costs of $66M.

BRIGHT PROPERTIES, INC., Mill Valley, CA 2006–2008
Premier developer/owner of class-A multifamily communities, a NYSE-listed REIT with assets of $1.7B and offices in 6 cities.

Executive Vice President—Development

Recruited to lead real estate development organization and execute a strategic expansion program. Led planning, product design and implementation, investment structure and pricing, and underwriting. Managed 11 staff and $4M development P&L. Served on Asset Allocation and Operating Committees.

- Oversaw a $450M portfolio of 14 developments with 3,549 apartment homes.
- Strengthened the development team through judicious hiring of experienced executives.
- Restructured compensation system, tying pay to performance and achievement of strategic business goals.
- Established a new environmental protocol and due diligence process.
- Achieved year-over-year G&A cost savings of $100,000+.

TRU-FINANCE REAL ESTATE INVESTORS 1992–2006
One of the largest and most accomplished international real estate investment managers; $11.7B in assets under management.

Managing Director, Tru-Finance Real Estate Investors International, Miami, FL (2004–2006)

Selected to lead Tru-Finance's entry into Latin American real estate. Led market investigation, strategic planning, and launch of investment-management practice with a focus on Brazil. Spent 50% of time in Brazil, investigating market practices and identifying and nurturing strategic partnerships with South American institutions.

- Instrumental in forming the JV partnership that is the investment-management platform currently in use for Tru-Finance's successful Brazilian initiative.
- Chosen as delegate to the Frank Russell Company 20–20 Program, South America, October 2005.

Managing Director, Tru-Finance Residential Investment Advisors, Seattle, WA (1998–2004)

Identified market opportunity and spearheaded profitable entry into the for-sale residential investment market. Led newly formed company, a registered investment advisor, providing counsel to 4 limited partnerships funding lot-development and homebuilding projects across the U.S.; 34 staff, offices in Seattle and Charlotte.

- Generated $100M+ profits (15% after-fee IRR) on $385M capital—74 investments representing 12,400 single-family lots or homes. Oversaw solicitation, negotiation, structuring, and asset management.

Page 1

Strategy: Use a chronological format to showcase strong accomplishments, steady career progression, and deep expertise in the real estate investment industry.

415-781-0904   **STAN DUBEK, CFA** — Page 2   sdubek@gmail.com

TRU-FINANCE REAL ESTATE INVESTORS, continued

- Produced a cumulative 25.4% return for Tru-Finance as shareholder in the advisor.
- Solicited, analyzed, and closed $170M in working capital lines from Chase Morgan.
- Designed, marketed, and closed 4 residential programs ($288M capital commitment) to a number of domestic and international funds; investors included large and mid-sized corporate and public pension plans and involved the use of insurance company separate account contracts.
- Created and managed a comprehensive quarterly reporting system for all investors.

Vice President, Tru-Finance Realty Group, Seattle, WA (1996–1998)

Corporate staff position, managing large-scale investment projects and special assignments.

- Purchased 13 industrial warehouse properties in 8 states in a $95M sale-leaseback transaction, successfully executing complex transaction within a tight timeframe.
- Structured forward commitment acquisition of 300-unit multifamily community in Ohio.
- Determined carrying value for General Account impaired assets.
- Participated in formation of Tru-Finance Worldwide — a $2B, multi-investor, commercial real-estate fund. Chaired internal task force commissioned to determine viability of international expansion.

Director, Acquisitions & Sales, Tru-Finance Realty Group, Chicago, IL (1994–1996)

Challenged to reinvigorate and expand Midwestern commercial property investment program after an 8-year absence from the market. Headed commercial property acquisition and sales; recruited, trained, and managed investment staff; created and executed strategy to build portfolio and market presence.

- Acquired 7 major commercial properties ($107.8M total acquisition), including high-profile corporate HQ.
- Sold whole or partial interests in 5 major properties representing $245M in assets.

Investment Manager, Tru-Finance Realty Group, Seattle, WA (1992–1994)

- Performed primary due diligence and forecasting for 2 key initiatives: 1) IPO of REIT sponsored by Tru-Finance; 2) Tru-Finance Offshore Fund, a limited partnership marketing U.S. properties to European investors.

J.P. MORGAN REALTY GROUP, New York, NY   1989–1992

Vice President

- Participated in underwriting, due diligence, and financial structuring of a NYSE-listed, $136M master limited partnership, created to own Mall of Middle America in St. Louis.

PROFESSIONAL PROFILE

Education   **MBA,** Finance, Stanford University Graduate School of Business, Stanford, CA
                BS, Economics: UC Berkeley, Berkeley, CA

Credentials   Chartered Financial Analyst
                NASD Series 7, 24, 63, and 65
                Licensed Real Estate Broker — Washington and California

Affiliations   Association for Investment Management and Research
                Society of Security Analysts

Civic   San Francisco Civic Improvement Board, 2008–Present
                Seattle Chamber of Commerce, Board Member, 2001–2003

SARAH STONE

245 Lower Fountain Street   Spokane, Washington 99202
(509) 555-7653   sstone245@aol.com

FACILITIES AND PROPERTY MANAGER
Lease Management / Facility Planning / Purchasing

Professional Profile:

Creative facilities planner and manager with more than 20 years of experience planning, organizing, and coordinating facility expansion, renovation, relocation, and construction. Coordinate spatial planning with expertise in combining function and aesthetics in business, medical, and warehouse environments. Work with design consultants in developing schematic designs for new and existing facilities. Utilize superior organizational skills to ensure that the total facility, down to the smallest detail, meets user needs while upholding corporate standards.

Core Skills: Cost Savings … Space Planning … Vendor Sourcing / Selection … Contract Negotiation … JIT Purchasing / Delivery … Microsoft Office … Strategic Planning … Team Building … OSHA Compliance … Inventory Reduction … Interior Design … Staff Supervision … Ergonomics

Experience:

<u>Mount Mercy Healthcare</u>, Spokane, Washington   1988–Present
Senior Manager of Purchasing and Facility Support
Assist senior management with strategic facility planning for 13 corporate, warehouse, and medical facilities, totaling 480,000 square feet. Supervise nine-member staff. Procure capital equipment for all facilities. Coordinate ergonomics program for work stations and office space. Oversee the production of space-planning drawings, color presentation boards, and signage. Develop and maintain standards program for interior design elements, including color and finish, for furniture, upholstery fabrics, and floor coverings. Select and acquire accessories, artwork, wall coverings, carpeting, plants, and furnishings.

Conduct quarterly assessment of facilities for appropriateness of design, ensuring maintenance of corporate standards. Negotiate bids and purchase a diversity of commodities, including medical supplies, printed materials, and office supplies. Coordinate delivery and installation of equipment and furniture for all facilities. Administer and maintain space-planning guidelines. Maintain fixed asset register and prepare monthly depreciation reports. Serve on Supply Cost Reduction and Value Analysis Teams. Ensure compliance with OSHA regulations. Maintain facility management database.

Accomplishments:

➢ *Served on Corporate Facilities Team responsible for relocating 732 employees from two locations (62,000 square feet) to new corporate headquarters (145,000 square feet) in 2010.*
➢ *Implemented "Just in Time" purchasing and delivery program for medical, office, and computer supplies, resulting in $1 million savings in inventory costs.*
➢ *Negotiated new office supply contract, achieving $275,000 savings over four years.*
➢ *Managed renovation project for two medical centers and saved $125,000 by eliminating need for outsourcing of all construction work.*

Continued

Strategy: Highlight exceptional work experience; amplify Professional Profile section to compensate for lack of a degree; include strong Core Skills list that encompasses several diverse job targets.

Sarah Stone	sstone245@aol.com	**Page Two**

Accomplishments (continued):

➢ *Reduced leasing costs by relocating In-Home Services Department from leased office space to corporate office.*

➢ *Received peer-voted Employee Recognition Award for outstanding and dedicated service.*

➢ *Coordinated interior design of Archway Physical Therapy facility, winning Washington 2009 design award for healthcare construction.*

Education:

Washington State Real Estate Licensing Course	2000

Spokane University, Spokane, Washington	
Courses in Business Administration	1988–1993

Professional Development:
SkillPath's Conference on Women and Communication, 2009
National Association of Purchasing Management Seminar on Purchasing and the Law, 2008
Symposium on Healthcare Design, 2008
Seminars on Team Building, Corrective Actions, and How to Avoid Discrimination, 2005–2007

Affiliations:

International Facilities Management Association (IFMA)
National Administrative Services Purchasing Council (NASPURC)
Institute for Supply Management (ISM)

Daniel E. Guzman

9838 Bowling Green Avenue
Chicago Heights, Illinois 60690

deguzman@aol.com
(773) 779-9908

CHIEF ENGINEER

Facilities Planning / Construction Management / Building Operations

Highly motivated quality-engineering professional with more than 15 years of experience in project management, construction management, building systems, grounds maintenance, special-event coordination, and safety management. Exceptional organizational, problem-solving, team-building, leadership, budget-management, and negotiation skills. Effective interpersonal, communications, and conflict-management abilities. Computer literate.

Core Competencies:

◆ Maintenance Engineering	◆ Preventive Maintenance	◆ Safety Management
◆ Facilities Engineering	◆ HVAC/R Systems	◆ Training & Development
◆ Plant Operations	◆ Grounds Maintenance	◆ Supervision
◆ Operations & Maintenance	◆ Building Trades	◆ Purchasing Management
◆ Project Management & Planning	◆ OSHA Recording	◆ Relationship Management

PROFESSIONAL EXPERIENCE

WRIGHT COLLEGE, Chicago Heights, Illinois   1995 to Present
Chief Engineer
Spearhead maintenance-engineering day-to-day activities, including budget management, purchasing, salaries, contracts, and contracted work. Charged with facility maintenance for the City Colleges of Chicago. Schedule preventive maintenance of HVAC/R and fire-protection systems, including landscaping and housekeeping equipment. Utilize MS Windows, Word, and Excel for reporting/documentation processes.

Supervise 25 housekeeping and 8 engineering staff; implement and prioritize work orders, purchasing, and various contracts with trade-related companies to meet fluctuating and tight deadlines. Cultivate relationships with building owners and administrators; attend meetings to provide reports and technical assistance. Oversee construction-management affairs and all building trades during construction projects.

Key Accomplishments / Values Offered

❑ Delivered departmental efficiency through advanced engineering, technical support, and documentation procedures.

❑ Analyzed efficiency and energy savings potential, resulting in 30% reduction in utility-consumption costs.

❑ Noted for exercising good judgment in hiring work crews, technical competence, work ethic, staff training and development, and take-charge-teamwork attitude.

❑ Appointed as representative for the college on all capital improvement projects from project conception, specifications, and pre-bid to construction management.

❑ Outsourced vendors, negotiated contracts, coordinated competitive bidding, and monitored quality of services and products.

...Continued...

Strategy: Equally emphasize three areas of expertise: facilities planning, construction management, and building operations. Show relevant accomplishments and values.

Daniel E. Guzman	deguzman@aol.com	Page Two

Professional Experience, Continued

FINE ARTS CENTER MUSEUM, Decatur, Illinois   2009 to Present
  Construction Consultant
  Concurrently assist as consultant for new construction of $8.1 million museum addition. Advise on security concerns and administer contract work. Train building engineer and housekeeping staff. Develop work schedules for all shifts. Research equipment specifications and construction prints to establish infrastructure development.

Additional **5+ years prior experience** working at Peoples Energy Corporation.

LICENSES AND CERTIFICATIONS

License: City of Chicago Stationary Engineer
Certification: Universal Proper Refrigerant Practices

EDUCATION AND TRAINING

University of Illinois, Chicago, Illinois
Illinois Institute of Technology
Concentration: **Mechanical Engineering**

Technical: HVAC/R Technician, Coyne American Institute, Chicago Heights, Illinois
Pneumatic Controls, Building Engineers Institute, Chicago Heights, Illinois

Professional Development

OSHA Recording, Padget Thompson ....(02/10)
Industrial Electricity II, Performance Training Associates ....(04/09)
Building Electrical Systems I & II...(04/09)
Direct Digital Controls, Refrigeration Service Engineers Society ....(02/09)
Deregulation, ComEd .... (11/08)
Basic Supervision, American Management Association... (11/08)
LCN Door Closer Installation and Maintenance, Ingersol Rand Corp. .... (09/08)
BEST Door Hardware Maintenance, Best Access Systems .... (04/08)
Von Duprin Panic Hardware Installation and Maintenance....................................... (01/08)
Conflict Resolution, American Management Association .... (07/07)
Hydronic Systems Service and Maintenance, ITT Fluid Handling Div........................ (02/06)
CVHE/CVHF Chiller Operation, Chicago Trane University....................................... (01/06)
Direct Digital Controls, Andover Controls Corporation .... (07/04)
Proper Refrigerant Usage, Refrigeration Service Engineers Society .... (04/03)

PUBLICATIONS

Maintenance Technology, Building Systems Solutions, Buildings, The News-HVAC
Building Design and Construction, Refrigeration Service Engineers Society Journal, Engineered Systems

MEMBERSHIPS

Refrigeration Service Engineers Society, #0039324

TED A. HOFFMAN
Route 9, Box 2255
Martinsburg, WV 25411
304-555-7640 ▪ 304-555-0703 (cell)

Project Manager ▪ Site Superintendent ▪ Field Superintendent with comprehensive construction experience, from initial clearing and sediment/erosion control to final punch-out. Seasoned builder of commercial, industrial, and residential sites, including bridge, tunnel, and highway construction.

- Outstanding safety record; committed to quality improvement and environmental compliance.
- Motivated by mastering the challenges of complex projects or learning new skills; have earned numerous professional certifications.
- Effective crew leader; promote continuous learning and advancement through on-the-job training; demonstrate a natural teaching ability.
- Well organized; implement a system of thorough documentation through maintenance of daily activity logs.

Broad-based responsibilities in the following areas:

- materials purchasing management	- arbitration & conflict resolution
- vendor/supplier negotiations	- quality assurance & inspection
- contract negotiation & review	- heavy equipment troubleshooting & maintenance
- reading & scaling blueprints	
- coordinating subcontractors	

EMPLOYMENT HISTORY

Grading Superintendent, SW BUILDERS, Leesburg, VA   2008–Present
- Recruited based on professional reputation and expertise in the field.
- Currently involved in a 168-acre site development for a shopping mall in Dulles, VA. This $14M project is slated for completion in November 2011.

General Superintendent, EAST COAST DEVELOPMENT, Fredericksburg, VA   2006–2008
- Simultaneously managed four job sites in Maryland (Frederick, Gaithersburg, Silver Spring, and Lexington Park).
- Responsible for site equipment and movement; managing all personnel; coordinating with the project manager; and meeting one-on-one with city, county, and state inspectors.

Key Project: Completed, on-time and under budget, a $1M housing development (single-family and townhouses).

Field Superintendent, ARNOLD CORPORATION, Rockville, MD   2003–2006
- Effectively managed numerous simultaneous projects, including work for the Army Corps of Engineers.

Key Project: Built the Major League Stadium. Coordinated 109 pieces of machinery and a crew of 139 personnel. This $16.5M, two-year project was completed in 17 months.

Project Manager/Site Superintendent, REESE EXCAVATION, INC., Mt. Airy, MD   2000–2003
- Managed site development for four new schools and expansion of two existing businesses in Frederick County, MD.
- Demonstrated a proven track record in passing inspection on first as-built.

Key Projects: Damascus Middle School, $1.5M; Clarksburg Middle School, $1.3M; Urbana High School and football stadium, $1.3M; COMSTAT, $1M; Solarex, $1M.

Strategy: Match resume style with the individual: right to the point, shooting for immediate results with high impact. Citing size, value, and outcome for each position is an effective way to communicate his expertise and diverse experience.

TED A. HOFFMAN
304-555-7640
PAGE 2

EMPLOYMENT HISTORY (continued)

Site Superintendent, CITY CONSTRUCTION COMPANY, New York, NY   1998–2000
- Completed major site development for a 200-acre, $3M housing development off Martin Luther King Boulevard in Washington, DC.

Site Superintendent, LMS, INC., Frederick, MD   1992–1998
- Built a 7.5-mile stretch of major highway, coordinating with both state and county inspectors. This $14.6M project involved four bridges and three major Class A stream crossings.

Shift Superintendent, WESTERN HEIGHTS CORPORATION, Colorado Springs, CO   1989–1992
- Sunk two tunnels under the Anacostia River for the Washington Subway System. This two-year, $10M project presented the additional challenge of working under air pressure, 110 feet underground.

Five years of prior experience: BUFFALO COAL COMPANY, Bayard, WV
   Responsible for all above- and below-ground blasting.

PROFESSIONAL TRAINING AND CERTIFICATION

Mining Enforcement & Safety	U.S. Department of the Interior
Explosive Engineer	Allegheny Community College
Health & Safety Underground Mining	Garrett Community College
Diesel Mechanics Certification	Diesel Institute of America
Seismology	Vibra Tech
Medic First Aid	State of Virginia

Certificates of Competency from the State of Maryland:

Confined Space	**Traffic Control**
First Responder & First Aid	**Sediment & Erosion Control**

FORMAL EDUCATION

Frostburg State University, Reality Therapy & GPI
Certificate program designed to teach skills in personnel management, effective communication, crisis intervention, and anger management.

University of Maryland, Teaching/Environmental Engineering
Completed two years of Bachelor's degree program.

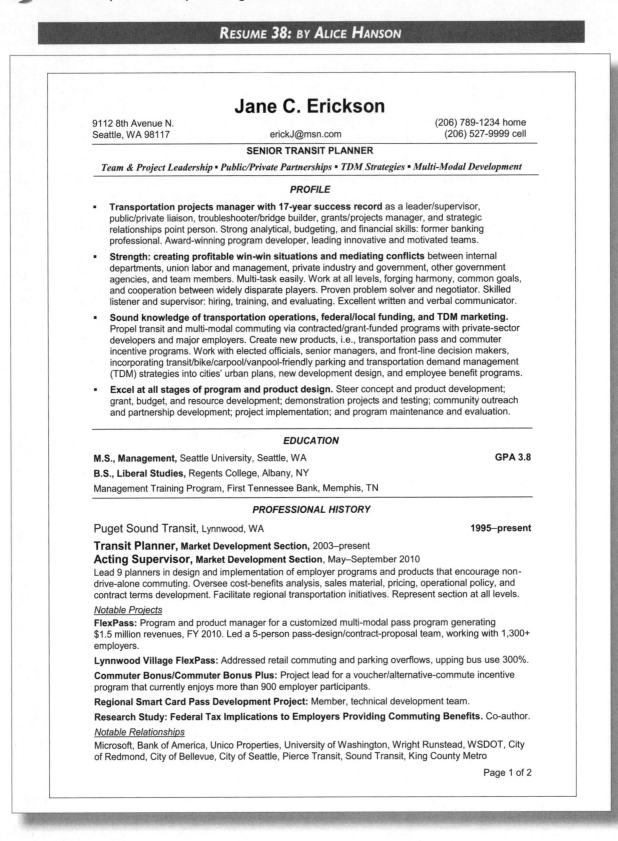

Jane C. Erickson

9112 8th Avenue N.
Seattle, WA 98117

erickJ@msn.com

(206) 789-1234 home
(206) 527-9999 cell

SENIOR TRANSIT PLANNER

Team & Project Leadership ▪ Public/Private Partnerships ▪ TDM Strategies ▪ Multi-Modal Development

---

PROFILE

- **Transportation projects manager with 17-year success record** as a leader/supervisor, public/private liaison, troubleshooter/bridge builder, grants/projects manager, and strategic relationships point person. Strong analytical, budgeting, and financial skills: former banking professional. Award-winning program developer, leading innovative and motivated teams.

- **Strength: creating profitable win-win situations and mediating conflicts** between internal departments, union labor and management, private industry and government, other government agencies, and team members. Multi-task easily. Work at all levels, forging harmony, common goals, and cooperation between widely disparate players. Proven problem solver and negotiator. Skilled listener and supervisor: hiring, training, and evaluating. Excellent written and verbal communicator.

- **Sound knowledge of transportation operations, federal/local funding, and TDM marketing.** Propel transit and multi-modal commuting via contracted/grant-funded programs with private-sector developers and major employers. Create new products, i.e., transportation pass and commuter incentive programs. Work with elected officials, senior managers, and front-line decision makers, incorporating transit/bike/carpool/vanpool-friendly parking and transportation demand management (TDM) strategies into cities' urban plans, new development design, and employee benefit programs.

- **Excel at all stages of program and product design.** Steer concept and product development; grant, budget, and resource development; demonstration projects and testing; community outreach and partnership development; project implementation; and program maintenance and evaluation.

EDUCATION

M.S., Management, Seattle University, Seattle, WA   **GPA 3.8**

B.S., Liberal Studies, Regents College, Albany, NY

Management Training Program, First Tennessee Bank, Memphis, TN

PROFESSIONAL HISTORY

Puget Sound Transit, Lynnwood, WA   **1995–present**

Transit Planner, Market Development Section, 2003–present
Acting Supervisor, Market Development Section, May–September 2010
Lead 9 planners in design and implementation of employer programs and products that encourage non-drive-alone commuting. Oversee cost-benefits analysis, sales material, pricing, operational policy, and contract terms development. Facilitate regional transportation initiatives. Represent section at all levels.

Notable Projects

FlexPass: Program and product manager for a customized multi-modal pass program generating $1.5 million revenues, FY 2010. Led a 5-person pass-design/contract-proposal team, working with 1,300+ employers.

Lynnwood Village FlexPass: Addressed retail commuting and parking overflows, upping bus use 300%.

Commuter Bonus/Commuter Bonus Plus: Project lead for a voucher/alternative-commute incentive program that currently enjoys more than 900 employer participants.

Regional Smart Card Pass Development Project: Member, technical development team.

Research Study: Federal Tax Implications to Employers Providing Commuting Benefits. Co-author.

Notable Relationships

Microsoft, Bank of America, Unico Properties, University of Washington, Wright Runstead, WSDOT, City of Redmond, City of Bellevue, City of Seattle, Pierce Transit, Sound Transit, King County Metro

Page 1 of 2

Strategy: Create a strong profile that encapsulates the candidate's extensive, broad experience within the transportation industry. Identify key projects and relationships under her current high-profile position.

JANE C. ERICKSON	erickJ@msn.com	Page 2 of 2

PROFESSIONAL HISTORY (continued)

Puget Sound Transit (continued)

Management Analyst, Transit Operations Division, 1995–2003

Monitored and maintained $98 million annual budget. Managed special projects. Researched, analyzed, and monitored special issues for division.

First Tennessee Bank, Memphis, TN   **1992–1995**
Marketing Services Representative

Supported corporate and division marketing and public relations projects for financial institution.

U.S. Department of Defense, Catania, Sicily (Italy)   **1990–1992**
Training Coordinator

Curriculum developer and presenter, delivering 40-hour educational programs to overseas military personnel. Studied Italian, developing fluency.

University of California, San Diego, CA   **1988–1990**
Career Needs Assessment Program Coordinator ▪ Office Manager

AWARDS & NOMINATIONS

2010
Special Recognition: Association for Commuter Transportation (ACT)
Awarded for co-chairing planning and implementation of 2010 International Conference

2008
Washington State Commuter Choice Governor's Award for Excellence — Team lead
Harvard University John F. Kennedy School of Government Innovations Award — Team member

2007
U.S. Environmental Protection Agency (EPA) and Renew America "Way to Go" Award
Awarded for Lynnwood Village FlexPass Project — Project Lead

2005
Washington State Wall of Fame, Nominee — Team member
Washington State Wall of Fame, Awarded individually for driving project success
Association for Commuter Transportation (ACT), Nominee, Joint Service Award — Team member

PROFESSIONAL ACTIVITIES

Boards, Conferences & Task Forces
Excellence in Commuting (employer recognition program) — Chairman of the Board — 2010
Women's Transportation Seminar (WTS) — Board member for 5 years — 2000–present
ACT International Conference, Spokesperson/Moderator Multiple Sessions — 2009
National Academy of Sciences Transportation Research Board (TRB) — Presenter — 2009
National Task Force, Federal Reauthorization (TEA-3) — 2006

Memberships
Transportation Research Board (TRB) — 2008–present
Association for Commuter Transportation (ACT) — 2007–present
Regional Representative, National Public Policy Committee — 2007–present
Washington State Rideshare Organization (WSRO) — 2006–present

RESUME 39: BY WANDA KISER, MBA, CPRW, ACRW, CPCC, CEIP

DAVID J. CASON

| 16777 E. Wildrose Drive | Phoenix, AZ 85268 | E-mail: djcason@hotmail.com | Mobile: (480) 987-2771 |

CONSTRUCTION MANAGER—Energy, Oil & Infrastructure

Proactive, performance-driven professional with 20+ years of progressive expertise in leadership and problem-solving for energy, oil, and infrastructure operations. Keen understanding of business priorities. Team player committed to managing operations and projects flawlessly while contributing to revenue-producing activities. Cross-functional communicator, easily interacting with high-profile staff, vendors, and customers. Well-respected industry leader known for achievements in both project construction management and business management.

Demonstrated Core Competencies

Project Management ▪ Strategic Planning ▪ Process Improvement
Start-Ups/Turnarounds ▪ Team Leadership/Motivation ▪ Management/Manufacturing ▪ Logistics
Outsourcing ▪ Vendor Relations ▪ Cost Reduction ▪ Scheduling
Ops Management ▪ Budgeting ▪ Financial Analysis

——PROFESSIONAL EXPERIENCE & ACHIEVEMENTS——

NORTHEAST CONLEY CORPORATION   2001–Present
Northeast Conley Corporation (NYSE:NCC) is a publicly owned engineering, procurement, construction, and maintenance services organization. The Fortune 500 company employs more than 41,000 employees and maintains offices in over 25 countries.

Area Construction Manager, CONLEY ARABIA, LTD., Jubail, Saudi Arabia (2006–Present)
Selected to work closely with project management based on previous history of project success, and fulfilled an integral role on a $15B Saudi Kayan Petrochemical Complex project for Saudi Arabia Basic Industries Corporation (SABIC)."Held full P&L responsibility for $400M utilities and offsite budget. Coached, mentored, and directed an action-oriented team of 16 field superintendents with 3,000 field labor workers. Identified and leveraged core competencies to drive productivity, quality, and revenue growth.

- Played a major role assuring review of contractors' technical submittals, including start-up plans and schedules, quality control program, change-order requests, and other technical requirements.

- Established quality standards for contractor performance and assured guidelines were adhered to by responsible contract workers.

- Assisted in preparation of Work Plan and recommended solutions to staffing and interface problems.

- Identified potential problem areas and suggested corrective measures to staff leadership, ensuring project timeliness while avoiding cost and schedule overruns. Significant project achievements included:
  - ✓ Received excellent client ratings from SABIC for successfully leading development of an offplot module fabrication yard constructed for assembly of 164 process piperack modules (15m x 30m x 12m high).
  - ✓ Managed heavy-rigging engineering, foundation design coordination, and sea-transportation-to-land heavy-haul-to-site for two major utility steam mechanical equipment packages.
  - ✓ Directed construction of first-of-its-size-ever, above-ground, 120-inch-diameter steel-pipe-parallel cooling water supply and return lines built on concrete sleeper-way under main piperacks.
  - ✓ Led mass excavation of piperack for foundation-pile cap work and subsequent rapid backfill, utilizing stabilized backfill sand and water flooding and achieving 90% density compaction.

Area Construction Manager, CONLEY MIDDLE EAST, LTD., Doha, Qatar (2001–2006)
Oversaw all trades and effectively managed daily on-site activities for RasGas Common offplots project. Scope of responsibilities included managing construction of Condensate I and II plant areas, new piping tank farms, horizontal and vertical pumps, metering, control room, and substations.

- Leveraged well-rounded project experience and management skills to effectively lead and direct construction of 44 temporary buildings and infrastructure.

- Engaged and professionally interacted with design professionals, consultants, and clients while successfully directing sub-contractors and other construction-related personnel in planning, coordinating, and safely executing work in accordance with contract documents, schedule, and budget.

Continued

Strategy: Mingle construction and engineering details with a sharp focus on business goals and overall performance. Note space-saving presentation of early career experience.

DAVID J. CASON   djcason@hotmail.com | (480) 987-2771   ***Page Two***

ARAMCO OIL COMPANY   1991–2000
A fully integrated international petroleum company with the world's largest oil reserves.

Project Engineer/Team Leader, Dhahran, Saudi Arabia
Brought on board to lead project management for Southern Area Plant's Project Department. Managed projects valued at $100M–$400M, aligning with corporate goals, organizational strategies, and core business competencies. Acted as business partner to senior management, evaluating trends in the marketplace and defining new corporate strategy for market positioning and revenue growth. Maintained strong and sustainable internal and external relationships for the express purpose of advancing business strategies and maximizing profitability.

- Directed and monitored analog-to-digital control conversion projects across plant facilities and new plant buildings. Oversaw workshop modernizations and upgrades for several process gas/oil separation plants (GOSPs) throughout the Eastern province.
- Served as team leader for a major upgrade involving East/West Main Transport Pipeline.

PRIOR PROFESSIONAL EXPERIENCE
- **Construction Manager:** Fluor Daniel Construction Division, Oswego, NY
  - Supervised $110M expansion project on behalf of the ALCAN Aluminum Plant, overseeing demolition removal of existing areas with PCB oil contamination.
  - Led new rolling mill and smelting project for AI Recycling, directing newly created thin-gauge aluminum designed for the soft drink can market, with a 2.0M sheet spool width for 15Twt rolls.

- **Owner/Managing Director:** Coastline Construction, Inc., Mission Viejo, CA
  - Launched a successful new construction company specializing in single-family residential subdivisions.
  - Hired by the hospitality industry as preferred building contractor for Travel Inns.
  - Completed several assignments as facilities contractor for military installations across Southern California.

- **Assistant Construction Manager:** Fluor Construction Arabia, Ltd., Saudi Arabia
  - Successfully managed $200K onplot storage tankage and utility systems, seawater intake, and outfall KEMEYA Polyethylene Plant built for Exxon Chemical.
  - Transported and established 11 process modules from Jubail Port.

- **Area Superintendent:** Fluor Construction S.A. PTY., Ltd., Secunda, South Africa
  - Directed all aspects of an 8-kilometer, main-interconnecting piperack construction project.
  - Served as offsite and interconnecting-piping-system-turnover coordinator for all testing and pre-commissioning work.
  - Selected as Area Construction Superintendent for turnkey construction of Sasol II Distillation Process Unit.

- **Cost Scheduling Manager:** Fluor Mining and Metals, San Mateo, CA
  - Established cost control systems and monitored costs and scheduling on contracts requiring validations for Copper Mining Process and Uranium Yellow Cake Mine Process Plants.

EDUCATION & CERTIFICATION

BS, Mechanical Engineering, CALIFORNIA POLYTECHNIC UNIVERSITY, San Luis Obispo, CA

California Licensed Engineer
Certified OSHA Construction Safety Professional
Project Management Institute (PMP) Certified

PROFESSIONAL AFFILIATIONS

Member, American Society of Mechanical Engineers (ASME)
Member, Project Management Institute (PMI)
Member, American Society of Safety Engineers (ASSE)

CHARLES "CHUCK" TIMPER

2335 Boulevard • Richmond, VA 23834 • Home: 804-504-6600 • Mobile: 804-504-0002 • timper@gmail.com

COMMERCIAL CONSTRUCTION SUPERINTENDENT

Site Management / Construction Supervision / Negotiation / Bidding / Contractor Relations

Accomplished Superintendent with more than 20 years of broad-spectrum experience in all phases of commercial construction, directing projects valued to $36 million. Skill includes concrete tilt-ups, steel erection, ceramic tile, and carpentry. Trade proficiency includes mechanical, electrical, and framing. Strong capacity to provide team leadership and training; supervised staff of up to 120 with 50 direct reports. Goal oriented and results driven with strong ability to combine cutting-edge technologies with expert problem identification and resolution. Outstanding communication skills with capacity to interface with inspectors, auditors, engineers, architects, and other team members associated with a project.

Core competencies include:

- Purchasing / Estimating
- Vendor Relations / Customer Service
- Project Planning & Management
- Building & Site Layout

- Logistics & Strategic Planning
- Team Building & Leadership
- Plan & Spec Reading
- Problem Identification & Resolution

> **HIGH PERFORMANCE LEADER** who goes above and beyond to exceed expectations.
> *"I give it everything I've got."* —Chuck Timper

SELECTED PROJECTS

• **Colonial Heights County Hospital**—$6 million addition/remodel	Colonial Heights, VA
• **Richmond Museum & Library**—$7.5 million	Richmond, VA
• **State of Virginia Youth Authority Prison/School**—$7 million	Chesterfield, VA
• **Colonial Heights Retirement Center**—$5 million	Colonial Heights, VA
• **United States Post Offices**—combined value over $36 million	VA, MD, NC & SC

Additional projects and details available upon request.

CAREER HISTORY

Oversaw, managed, and directed all aspects of commercial construction and development strategy, including supervision of all direct-hires and subcontractors to coordinate all facets of construction. Ensured streamlining of operations to produce cost savings; increased productivity and business capacity to generate profitability.

Bowers-Fontaine Company, Richmond, VA **PROJECT SUPERINTENDENT**	1995–1999 / 2001–2010
Arch Oakland, Richmond, VA (concurrent with above) **PROJECT SUPERINTENDENT**	2002–2003
T. Clark Jones, Baltimore, MD **PROJECT SUPERINTENDENT**	2000–2001
Otis & Goodman Construction, Scranton, PA **ASSISTANT SUPERINTENDENT**	1994–1995

EARLY HISTORY

Between 1986 and 1994, worked on a variety of projects encompassing remodeling, carpentry, steel buildings, and storage systems as both business owner and employed professional. These formative years constructed the backbone of my expertise and skill, which I utilize as a Superintendent today. Details of prior experience available upon request.

Strategy: Create a concise, one-page presentation that emphasizes skills and selected projects while listing the candidate's career history with minimal details.

CHAPTER 8

Resumes for Managers and Executives in Food and Beverage, Hotels, and Travel and Tourism

- Hospitality/Food Service Manager
- Food and Beverage/Hospitality/Restaurant Manager
- Hotel Director
- Hospitality Executive
- Senior Manager, Hospitality
- Travel and Tourism Executive
- Restaurant Manager

James E. Hansen

222 Baker Street • Danville, California 94526 • home (530) 333-4900 • cell (530) 779-9004

HOSPITALITY / FOOD SERVICE MANAGEMENT

Seeking to Leverage Strong Guest Relations, Service Management Skills, and Budget Management

FOOD AND BEVERAGE MANAGER offering 15+ years of combined experience in general management, sales, and marketing for full-service hospitality operations. Catalyst for change, transformation, and performance improvement. Respond rapidly and appropriately to changing circumstances. Consistently successful in increasing service standards, quality, and profitability. **Core competencies include:**

❑ Menu Planning/Pricing	❑ Service Enhancements	❑ Project Management
❑ Organizational Development	❑ Revenue Growth	❑ Marketing Strategies
❑ Public Relations Skills	❑ Inventory & Cost Control	❑ Revenue Projections
❑ Vendor Sourcing/Negotiations	❑ Turnaround Strategies	❑ Cross-Functional Team Training
❑ P&L Budget Accountability	❑ Food Sanitation Practices	❑ Staff Supervision/Motivation

—— Career Highlights ——

MANAGEMENT & ADMINISTRATION

- Proven track record in turnaround management through close attention to budget administration, organizational structure, and staff supervision and development.

- Combine leadership and management skills to maximize assets in both vendor relations and corporate growth—quickly resolve problems that hinder progress or create disputes.

- Exceed employer expectations with "above and beyond" focus on guest satisfaction and retention, strict attention to quality service, and consistent applications of extra effort.

- Highly skilled in managing budgets above $5 million.

SALES & MARKETING

- As Director of Sales, worked cooperatively with sales staff and set up appropriate distribution networks for product nationwide; expanded network reach to distributors and sales staff; rapidly expanded market penetration and grew revenue.

- Delivered presentations to groups for large-scale product promotion of Nicolini Winery.

- Gained exposure globally for company's marketed product.

—— Professional Experience ——

DOMINIC'S, Redding, California   2007–Present
General Manager (2011–Present)
General Manager, Yolo County Fairgrounds, Davis, California (2007–2011)
Establish operating and financial goals of the Dominic's mission statement set for food and beverage operations of several venues. Report directly to the Vice President. Supervise and evaluate 1,500+ staff. Review and assist in the development of menus and marketing plans with appropriate department heads.

- Structured and developed 3 different budgets for increased flexibility.

- Increased profit margins 7% through operational improvements and efficiencies.

- Grew sales revenues in Ventura, Yolo, and Sacramento Counties.

…Continued…

Strategy: Focus on food service management because of current career interests, but convey strong achievements from prior management career as well.

James E. Hansen	cell (530) 779-9004	**Page Two**

Professional Experience, Continued

MARINA RESORT, Sacramento, California   2003–2007

Director of Food and Beverage

Charged with budget management for nightclub/restaurant. Streamlined catering, concerts, and special events. Recruited, supervised, trained, and scheduled staff. Oversaw scheduling, inventory management, and menu development. Maintained daily and annual sales records.

CATERINA'S SPAGHETTI HOUSE, Davis, California   2002–2003

Bartender / Customer Service

Acted as Event and Entertainment Coordinator during holidays, weekends, and special events.

MARINA RESORT, Sacramento, California   1999–2002

Club Manager

Oversaw event planning and coordination.

WAREHOUSE CONCERT SERIES, Davis, California   1998–1999

Special Event Coordinator

Coordinated and supervised concert beer sales for the Fish Market and Petra's Restaurants at the Warehouse Concert during popular rock-band performances.

NICOLINI WINERY, Napa, California   1992–1998

Director of Sales and R & D

Brought on board as the driving force to spearhead rapid, profitable growth. Vigorously pursued strategic partnerships to build visibility and support product. Developed progressive marketing and negotiated exclusive contracts with 176 distributorships.

Professional Development

Seminars: General Management, Dale Carnegie—Leadership and Presentation Training

Computer Skills: PC skills, Internet, and proprietary applications

Marketing Development Expertise: New Client Development, Territory Management, Key Account Management, New Product Introduction, and Sales Presentations

Certification: California Food Certification

Military: United States Marine Corps, Honorable Discharge
Leadership Training, Noncommissioned Officers' School

BERTRAND KELLY

24620 Avenue Scott
Stephenson Ranch, California 91381

661-362-1824   kellyb@earthlink.net

FOOD & BEVERAGE / HOSPITALITY / RESTAURANT MANAGEMENT
Worldwide professional and personal commitment to exceed guest service expectations

---

Dedicated, multitasked, detail-oriented manager with a history of innovation and rapid professional advancement. Full knowledge of all facets of the industry based on an extremely integrated background involving hands-on experience at every level for exclusive hotels, restaurants, conference centers, resorts, and catering events.

Expert in identifying and capitalizing on market opportunity to build revenue, capture key accounts, and outperform competition. Excellent qualifications in marketing, budgeting, expense control, staffing, training, and quality management. Contributed to significant revenue gains and cost reductions. Seeking a new challenge. Available for relocation.

Multinational experience. Fully bilingual (English/Spanish) and multicultural: worldwide travel and work in South and Central America, Australia, Asia, and Europe.

Strengths:
- Leadership, team building, training, management, and motivation.
- Vendor sourcing and negotiations.
- Image development and positioning, public relations, and customer management.
- Strategic planning, decision making, and problem solving.
- Knowledge of OSHA regulations and health and food safety procedures (cross contamination).
- High computer literacy in PC and Microsoft programs and restaurant POS operating systems.

PROFESSIONAL EXPERIENCE

Restaurant Management

Multifaceted food theme experience: Mexican, South American, American Grille, French White Tablecloth Service, Caribbean, Jewish Delicatessen, and Contemporary California Cuisine.

Recruited to plan and direct the start-up of 4 high-volume, high-energy restaurant and bar operations within resort and urban locations. Managed all pre-opening activities (e.g., operations, purchasing, equipment, staff recruitment, training) and a high-profile marketing and business development effort. Executed F&B operations, VIP relations, contract negotiations, event planning/logistics, kitchen operations, and all customer service functions. Handled all menu development and costing. Initialized all equipment and verified calibration; secured funds and contracted for local advertising; acquired required health permits.

- Built 4 restaurants (Rio Bravo, Cowboy's, The New Place in Town, Hacienda del Fuego) from concept into 25–150-employee operations generating annual revenues from $1.4 million to $4.2 million.
- Developed extensive experience with fine wines, liqueurs, alcohol, and beers.
- Created policies, procedures, standards, and performance goals.
- Full P&L responsibility; designed budgeting, expense control, and month-end reporting methods; monitored in-restaurant controllable costs, including product-line variance, waste control, labor percentage, cash variance, customer service, food safety and quality, and cleanliness/sanitation.
- Trained both permanent and contract staff in quality-based service; wrote performance reviews and cross-trained staff to ensure efficient operation under all circumstances.
- Contracted vendors based on research to determine cost and quality of service and product.
- Consistently achieved projected profit-and-loss objectives through effective budget management.

continued

Strategy: Use a functional format to tie together the diverse activities and achievements of a career spent traveling from one resort to the next as both a ski instructor and food-and-beverage manager. Highlight restaurant experience because of goal to continue in this field.

661-362-1824 **BERTRAND KELLY** — Page 2 kellyb@earthlink.net

Management

Operations Manager leading Gunnison Ski & Golf Company's Ski and Snowboard Schools' $1.6 million division through tremendous growth. Held full P&L responsibility; all strategic and business planning functions, finance and budgeting, operating management, marketing, human resources, MIS, and administrative affairs.

Financial Achievements:
- Increased revenues from 50% to 70% of department's net.
- Launched an aggressive reengineering of existing operations to reduce costs, improve service, and accelerate profit gains. Reduced operating costs by more than 20%.
- Consistently exceeded budget in projected revenues and profit margins.

Operating Achievements:
- Developed dynamic organizational infrastructure responsive to constantly changing market and financial and customer demands.
- Created high-profile marketing, advertising, service, and employee-incentive programs critical to the company's sustained growth cycle.
- Spearheaded development, training, and implementation of a fully computerized system for all department products.

AWARDS / HONORS

Company Manager of the Year	Gunnison Ski & Golf Company	2008
12-time nominee for Employee of the Month	Gunnison Ski & Golf Company	2003–2009
Top 5 Revenue Producer (out of staff of 500)	Ski Schools of Aspen	2000–2003
Board of Directors — 2 terms	Professional Ski Instructors of America	1998–2003

EMPLOYMENT HISTORY

Restaurant/Food & Beverage Management

General Manager	Rio Bravo Cantina, Simi Valley, CA	2010–2012
Manager	Maria's Delicatessen, Sedona, AZ	2003
Manager	Kansas City Banquet, Kansas City, MO	2002
Assistant Manager	The Cantina, Kansas City, MO	2001
Floor Manager	Cowboy's Grille, Telluride, CO	2000–2001
Manager	The New Place in Town, Silverstar Hotel, Aspen, CO	1999
General Manager	The Mine Company Restaurant, Vale, CO	1998–1999
Assistant F&B Director	The Great Lakes Country Club, Aspen, CO	1996–1998
Captain Dining Room	Le Soleil French Restaurant, Reno, NV	1994
Bar Manager	Hacienda del Fuego, Reno, NV	1989–1990

National & International Group Sales and Management

Guest Relations Docent	Gunnison Historical Museum, Gunnison, CO	2010
Supervisor, Group Sales	Gunnison Ski & Golf Company, Gunnison, CO	2003–2009
Asst. Ski School Director	Sal Si Puede Ski Resort, Sal Si Puede, Chile	1992–1994
Senior Instructor	Falls Creek Ski Resort, Falls Creek, Australia	1990–1992

EDUCATION

Master of Arts, Psychology, San Diego State University, San Diego, CA
Bachelor of Arts, Psychology and Business Administration, University of Arizona, Tucson, AZ

Cliff Stanton

HOTEL DIRECTOR
OPERATIONS / ROOMS / FOOD AND BEVERAGE
CONTROLLER / SALES

REVERSING UNDERPERFORMING PROPERTIES AND OPERATIONS
TRANSFORMING ORDINARY PROPERTIES INTO EXTRAORDINARY PROPERTIES

STRENGTHS
- Improving guest relations and enhancing the overall guest experience.
- Controlling costs and tenaciously demanding quality service.
- Strengthening financial performance—reducing expenses, recovering write-offs, up-selling services.
- Reducing employee turnover by developing "team-spirited" organizations and employees.
- Gaining market position and market share in highly competitive locations.
- Mentoring/training employees for promotion to management.

CERTIFICATIONS AND TRAINING
- Blood-Borne Pathogens Certification (2008)
- POS Certification (Micros 8700)
- Property Automation Training Certification (2007)
- Hotel Management and REVPAR Training (2006)
- Management Certification (2006)
- Restaurant Management Training (2004)

TECHNICAL EXPERTISE AND KNOWLEDGE
- PMS (Micros 3500, Innsure, Innstar)
- UMS (accounting software)
- PBX System
- POS (Microns 8700, Aloha)
- Vincard Vision 3.1
- Harmony Database System

PROFESSIONAL HISTORY

General Manager, Imperial Hotel, Denver, CO   **2009–Present**
(A full-service hotel with 198 guest rooms, restaurant, lounge, pool, exercise room, and 6,800 sq. ft. of meeting rooms and banquet facilities.)

Recruited as Assistant General Manager and promoted to General Manager within 4 months. Challenged to turn around declining property—formulate new development plans and budgets, tackle staffing problems, and address customer-satisfaction issues.

- ✓ Actively engaged in marketing activities resulting in increased occupancy.
- ✓ Won multiple contracts with breakthrough accounts: airlines and major trucking company.
- ✓ Developed operational and remodeling budgets for changeover to an assisted living facility.
- ✓ Recognized by customers for outstanding customer service.

Rooms Division Manager/Controller, Sturbridge House Historic Inn, Sturbridge, MA   **2007–2009**
(An award-winning historic-register hotel dating back to the Revolutionary War, comprising 126 rooms, 3 restaurants, and 11 banquet rooms across 4 locations on 120 acres.)

Managed all aspects of the rooms division. Appointed by Area VP to replace outgoing controller. Requested to manage and assist major functions for the dining/banquet areas on holidays and special events.

- ✓ Simplified pricing structure resulting in $159K increase in revenue and significant improvements to ADR.
- ✓ Reduced renovation costs by $39K through contract negotiations and close supervision of work.
- ✓ Reduced guest complaints by 89% by training employees on proactive customer service and raising cleaning standards.
- ✓ Improved management/labor relations through wage compensation and incentive programs saving over $53K in annual labor expenses. Reduced employee turnover rate by 75%. Achieved highest Sturbridge Group employee-satisfaction ranking.
- ✓ Developed operating budgets for Sturbridge Group, 5 separate units with total sales of $10M.
- ✓ Recovered 76% ($430K) of over-120-days receivables from previously abandoned accounts.

P.O. Box 15342 • Denver, CO 80239 • Home (303) 555-5210 • Mobile (303) 555-1823 • cliffs@yahoo.com

Strategy: To meet the candidate's goal of a management position with a top hotel chain, emphasize his solid track record of turning around faltering properties.

Cliff Stanton
Page 2

Hotel General Manager, Quality Inn, Amarillo, TX   2006–2007

Recruited to turn around faltering 121-room hotel. Analyzed operations/business processes; recommended and implemented corrective actions to restore profitability, increase employee morale, and raise customer satisfaction.

- ✓ Transformed hotel into a lucrative $1M operation through innovative marketing/business strategies, enthusiastic guest relations, and improved operations.
- ✓ Increased revenue by $110K ($89K of controllable profit).
- ✓ Recognized as the first manager to maintain costs at optimal levels to show yearly profitability.
- ✓ Consistently ranked #1 of 15 in area for the most improved occupancy.
- ✓ Increased hotel's quality score from 52 to 90 (out of 100).

Food and Beverage Director, Lafitte Town House, New Orleans, LA   2003–2006

Managed all food and beverage operations of an upscale private club, generating over $1.5M annually. Directed human resources, marketing, purchasing, financial reporting, inventory control, regulatory compliance, and guest relations. Led a staff of 20+ in an 8,000-sq.-ft., 3-story building.

- ✓ Revitalized languishing food operation by introducing new menus and offering functions, meetings, and catering based on guest preferences and seasonal considerations.
- ✓ Increased revenues 167% over three years by increasing member base and check average.
- ✓ Reduced annual labor expenses by $50K by changing staffing mix, improving guest/staff ratio, and employing part-time help.

Banquet Manager, Holiday Inn, Lafayette, LA   2001–2003

Coordinated and directed all aspects of the banquet operations in a 3-star, 300-room hotel with over 7,500 sq. ft. of meeting and banquet facilities.

- ✓ Generated $1.2M in food and beverage sales.
- ✓ Trained largely inexperienced staff to implement the highest standards of customer service and productivity.
- ✓ Achieved 45% controllable profit through strategic marketing planning (up-selling most functions by 15%), creative labor engineering (less than 50% turnover), cost controls, and high service standards.
- ✓ Recognized for strong leadership and customer focus, earning a series of promotions to increasingly more responsible positions.

PROFESSIONAL AFFILIATIONS

Member, Colorado Hotel Association
Past Board Member, Worcester County Convention & Visitor Bureau (WCCVB)
Past Member, Sturbridge Economic Development Association (SEDA)

EDUCATION

Auburn University, Microbiology Major—completed 3½ years of Bachelor of Science Degree, 1999–2001
University of Southwestern Louisiana, Associate of Applied Science, Business Management, 1998

MILITARY SPECIAL HONORS

United States Army, Operation Sergeant/Squad Leader
- ✓ Chosen "Honor Graduate" out of the 250 enrolled in the Primary Leadership Development Course.
- ✓ Awarded 3 Army Achievement and 2 Good Conduct Medals for outstanding performance.

P.O. Box 15342 • Denver, CO 80239 • Home (303) 555-5210 • Mobile (303) 555-1823 • cliffs@yahoo.com

DARCY KNOWLTON

HOSPITALITY EXECUTIVE

*Driving RevPar and GSI improvements through strategic leadership,
culture transformation, and deep understanding of the luxury hotel experience.*

Eleven-year track record of leading luxury hotels/hotel groups to exceptional performance. Delivered the best guest-satisfaction scores in the entire *Everest Hotel Group;* led *Ritz-Carlton Atlanta* to GSI scores consistently above 8.5. Turned around faltering hotels and brought flagship properties to new heights.

Expertise includes strategic leadership, organizational development, P&L and operations management, sales and marketing, and leadership team development. Repeatedly create competitive advantage through staff training, development, and motivational programs that build teamwork and deeply instill a quality/service culture.

EXPERIENCE AND ACHIEVEMENTS

Ritz-Carlton Hotels   **2009–Present**

GENERAL MANAGER: RITZ-CARLTON ATLANTA

Built a cohesive leadership team and rapidly delivered measurable improvements in guest-service scores and financial performance. Hold full P&L accountability for 175-room hotel. Lead a 12-member management team and 400 employees with an emphasis on total quality, premier service, and the luxury hotel experience.

- Delivered strong and sustainable increases in GSI scores year-over-year:

	Jan	*Feb*	*Mar*	*Apr*	*May*	*Jun*	*Jul*
2010	8.41	8.60	8.68	8.62	8.52	8.68	8.62
2009	8.38	8.36	8.40	8.28	8.29	8.52	8.42

- Year to date, improved financial performance in all areas of measurement:
  - RevPar +$14.82 (second only to Four Seasons in our market)
  - ADR +$17.01
  - Revenue +$1.4M
- Restructured the management team to improve communication while creating a leaner operating structure. Developed communications skills and management strengths of individual team members.
- Performed market studies to justify $4M conversion to state-of-the-art spa; first-month revenues exceeded projections by 43%.

Everest Hotel Group   **2000–2009**

DIRECTOR OF HOTEL OPERATIONS: Miami, FL, 2008–2009

Selected as GM of the group's flagship property with concurrent role as area managing director for 6 additional properties in South Florida (combined rooms 1,000+). Rose to the challenge of implementing fiscal controls while continuing to deliver the best guest-satisfaction scores in the company.

- Turned around flagship South Beach Hotel, a boutique (250-room) property.
  - Restructured staff, implemented a creative job-sharing plan, and invested in low-cost/high-touch customer experiences.
  - Invigorated the sales team and developed long-term sales contracts for sustained, reliable revenue.
  - Managed conversion of low-use space to executive meeting rooms.
  - Achieved the #1 ranking for customer service among all hotels in the Everest Group; earned ranking for guest service on Condé Nast Traveler's 2003 Gold List.
- Set the bar for guest service and development at all 7 properties in the group.

2743 Pine Manor Drive, Atlanta, GA 30345   M: 404-579-7612 • H: 404-299-0787 • dknowlton@yahoo.com

Strategy: Lead off each position with a powerful achievement statement and further showcase strong accomplishments with an eye-catching table format.

DARCY KNOWLTON   M: 404-579-7612 • H: 404-299-0787 • dknowlton@yahoo.com

Everest Hotel Group, continued

VICE PRESIDENT, HUMAN RESOURCES AND ORGANIZATIONAL DEVELOPMENT, Miami, FL, 2007–2008

Transformed HR from a functional department to a "business partner" integral to organizational strength and financial success of group comprising 35 hotel and 34 restaurant properties in key U.S. markets. Executive team member accountable for strategic HR functions for 6,000-employee organization. Managed 4 HR Directors.

- Designed and launched innovative training/development program ("Everest Academy"), incorporating advanced communication tools and customer-service strategies into company culture.
    - Expanded program to more than 30 training topics and orientation programs serving 6,000 employees.
    - Delivered extensive communications training at the executive level.
- Initiated biannual employee opinion surveys and earned consistent rise in satisfaction scores (8%–10%).
- Served on task force that evaluated customer service. Implemented new metrics and performance measurements and added independent QA audit, with scores typically in the +90% range.
- Helped open 8 newly acquired hotels and restaurants. Led pre-opening training in Everest culture as well as organizational development and operations issues. All openings were successful.

CITY MANAGER, New York, NY, 2005–2007

Promoted to executive management accountability for portfolio of 5 New York City luxury hotels (4-star rating)—800 rooms, 400 employees, and combined budget of $30M.

- Provided leadership to hotel management teams in critical management areas: sales, marketing, guest relations, and staff development and motivation.

GENERAL MANAGER: EVEREST NEW YORK, New York, NY, 2002–2005

Led 139-room luxury hotel to strong revenue increases, managing P&L and all operations.

- Recorded 19% revenue growth (more than $1.03M) in first fiscal year.
- Architect for new leased-restaurant operation that delivered profits on space with a 3-year history of losses.
- Member of corporate development team for new hotel properties in East/South market.
- In 5-month "rescue" role as GM of Everest Baltimore (4/98–9/98), quickly reversed a 10% declining revenue trend to finish year in the black.

GENERAL MANAGER: EVEREST BOSTON, Boston, MA, 2000–2002

Reconstructed the management team and achieved top guest-service scores for 107-room boutique hotel. Played an active sales role for both the property and the company.

- Grew annual revenues 15% to $2.9M.
- Increased profitability by more than $360K.

Marriott Hotels, Inc.   **1998–2000**
Winegardner & Hammons, Inc.   **1995–1998**
Walt Disney Company, Anaheim, CA   **1992–1995**

EDUCATION

BS, 1992: Food, Hotel, and Tourism Management   **University of Miami, Miami, FL**

RESUME 45: BY GAYLE HOWARD, MRW, CERW, CPBS, JLRC, CWPP, CRS-IT

ANGUS O'SULLIVAN

Apartment 2, 5 Foelsche Street San Francisco, CA 94101
Email: angsul@yahoo.com

Residence: (918) 942-1211
Mobile: (918) 999-3178

SENIOR MANAGER – HOSPITALITY

General Management • Venue Management • Operations

Participative management professional; results focused, entrepreneurial, and practical. 12+ years of progressive leadership experiences have created a passion for surpassing financial and service objectives via a combination of world-class service delivery, lean operating methods, renewed marketing directions, and incentive-driven rewards for team achievement. Acknowledged for capacity to observe, calculate, and react swiftly to avert conflict and restore workplace harmony. Derive genuine pleasure from transforming high-potential staff into outstanding leaders demonstrating the creativity critical to financial and operational success. Flourish in turnaround situations, restoring profits and instituting the essential infrastructure crucial to sustained prosperity.

Professional strengths include:

- ✓ Profit Maximization
- ✓ Multimillion-Dollar Budgets
- ✓ Team Building & Motivation
- ✓ Staff Training & Development
- ✓ Retail Operations Management

- ✓ Profit & Loss Accountability
- ✓ Marketing & Promotions
- ✓ First-Class Customer Service
- ✓ Venue Management
- ✓ Stock & Inventory Control

- ✓ Supplier Negotiations
- ✓ Risk Management & Minimization
- ✓ Upgrade/Refurbishment Projects

Technology – Microsoft Word, Excel, Access, PowerPoint; Email; Internet; Visypay

EDUCATION

Bachelor of Science, Business Administration (Marketing)
University of Southern California

Bachelor of Engineering (Mining)
University of New South Wales, Australia

Hundreds of hours devoted to ongoing professional development throughout career including workshops, conferences, information sessions, and formal short courses. Includes Train Small Groups – Certificate IV (California Chamber of Commerce and Industry).

BENCHMARKS & MILESTONES

- ✓ **Relocated to Australia and revitalized hotel with worn reputation and steady financial losses into a dynamic, economically buoyant award winner,** recognized for excellence by the prestigious Australian Hospitality Association. Won Best Hotel for the Northern Territory 2009; awarded Best Northern Territory Bottle Shop two years consecutively and Best Bar Presentation 2007.

- ✓ **Transformed nightclub with steeply declining profits into a money-spinner** that quadrupled revenue returns to $45,000 in just 16 months. Executed plan to refocus entertainment offerings towards patrons with high disposable incomes; introduced daily "theme nights" featuring R&B music and styles from the '70s, '80s, and '90s, attracting older patrons with inherent capacity to spend.

- ✓ **Increased bottle-shop gross profits to 27%.** Overhauled pricing levels through minimal discounting on traditionally slow trade nights and vigorously promoted slow-moving stock. Renewed customer patronage prompted additional "on sales" that increased average bottle shop GP by 4%.

Angus O'Sullivan · Page 1 · Confidential

Strategy: Convey vibrant and current image through striking design and upbeat language while not losing "management" feel of the resume.

CAREER CHRONOLOGY

CROSSMODE GROUP OF COMPANIES   2007–Present

General Manager/Licensee, Hi-UP Hotel, Darwin, Australia

Report to: Director, Hotels Crossmode

Hi-UP Hotel, Darwin, boasts up to 100 staff in peak periods and revenues of $9.5 million per annum generated from 5 bars, a bottle shop, 40-room accommodations, and function rooms.

Handpicked to turn around hotel in Australia, combating declining profits and aggressive market competition. Established a 12-point strategic blueprint aimed at delivering across-the-board improvements in staff numbers, availability, entertainment, security, and departmental operations through intensive cost assessment and market analysis. With scant attention paid to marketing, the necessity of establishing an image as an innovator was critical, as was the need to revitalize grounds, revamp sluggish and costly processes, and instill a sense of pride and achievement throughout a largely dispirited staff.

Hotel complex has realized remarkable turnaround, becoming a venue of choice for the local customer base and generating $3 million in healthy and sustainable profits over 3 years.

Actions & Contributions:

✓ Consolidated entertainment decision-making by appointing an entertainment professional, savvy to local band pricing, and a seasoned negotiator on contract benefits.

✓ Improved tracking systems for staff rosters and payroll, monitoring labor costs and more effectively assessing the need for senior personnel.

✓ Reduced headcount and recovered funds earmarked for revenue generation by removing costly in-house accountant from the payroll.

✓ Tripled revenues and cut costs 90% by transforming the poorly attended 5-star restaurant into a conference room open to bookings for personal and corporate celebrations.

✓ Managed major refurbishment project—a combined hotel and motel upgrade, from concept through implementation without incident.

✓ Divided year into "wet" and "dry" segments that responded to the peaks and troughs of seasonal patronage and allowed a "floating" dollar emphasis to be placed in areas most needed.

✓ Transitioned focus from tourist operation to local trade base capitalizing on the 8 months of the year Darwin is outside tourism season. Completed extensive SWOT analysis providing the foundation to respond to patrons' requests for live entertainment, pub food, good atmosphere, and good service.

✓ Established in-house training program. Investing in a core group of high-performance team members, won outstanding loyalty and unparalleled staff retention.

✓ Established series of "signature" events attracting up to 7,000 people per night to maintain interest and momentum. Includes the Beer Festival (7,000 pax), Miss Swim Suit (4,000 pax), Wine Festival (4,000 pax), October Fest (6,000 pax), Greek night (1,000 pax), and R & B Night (2,000 pax).

✓ Defended noise complaint vigorously and successfully, winning case and establishing reputation as a responsible licensee with solid business practices and community affinity.

Results:

✓ Improved bottom line by over $3M in 3 years.

✓ Doubled 2009/2010 projections in budget.

✓ Transitioned hotel from breakeven to 17% ROI.

PRIOR EMPLOYMENT

HOLIDAY TODAY CHAIN, San Francisco, CA, **Food & Beverage Manager**   2003–2007

RFT CATERING, San Francisco, CA, **Restaurant Staff**   1998–2002

DENISE CHAN

denisechan@email.com

125 Morrison Avenue
San Francisco, California 94132

Residence: (415) 555-3344
Mobile: (408) 555-2222

TRAVEL & TOURISM INDUSTRY EXECUTIVE

Extensive Knowledge of Tour and Cruise Industry
Innovator in Packaging Cruise Programs and Tours

- Well-respected Industry Executive with 20+ years of professional and managerial experience leading tour companies from start-up through fast-track growth and market expansion.
- Consistently successful in identifying and capitalizing upon market opportunities to drive revenue growth and expand market penetration.
- Pioneer in strategic alliances and business partnerships to grow business.
- Strong leadership and team-building skills with a participatory management style.

Sales & Marketing / Key Account Management / P&L Management / Information Technology
Team Building / Public Relations & Promotions / Strategic Business Partnerships

PROFESSIONAL EXPERIENCE

President • 2003 to Present
INTERNATIONAL SPECIALTY TOURS, LTD., San Francisco, CA

Recruited by Chairman to spearhead growth of mass-market tour company with programs to Europe, Britain, and the Mediterranean. Charged with full responsibility for U.S. operations including P&L accountability, business and market planning, sales training and management, information technology, and administrative affairs. Negotiate and manage strategic partnerships with travel agencies, airlines, and cruise lines.

- Delivered consistent increases in sales performance, building revenues from $12 million to $32 million within 2 years. During the same period, reduced expenses by 15% and improved bottom line by more than $1 million.
- Evaluated market trends and implemented strategies to reposition company as a niche operator.
- Developed key strategic partnership with leading international cruise line.
- Secured sole representation for major airline vacation packages.
- Introduced improved computerized technologies including online connection to Apollo Leisure Shopper. Work on additional tour systems and electronic distribution methods.
- Improved brand recognition through focus on improved product and service.
- Awarded "Office of the Year" in 2007 and "Executive of the Year" in 2008.

Sr. Vice President Sales & Marketing • 2002 to 2003
WORLDTRAVELER TOURS, Tampa, FL

Charged with all sales and marketing functions for $150 million Caribbean tour operator. Hired, trained, and managed sales team. Developed and implemented marketing budget. Created sales/marketing strategies including development of collateral materials and seminar presentations.

- Repositioned regional company as a national competitor.
- Increased revenues by 30% within 1 year.
- Brought a "Sales and Reservations" approach to focus on top producers, which increased revenues and reduced selling cost.

(continued)

Strategy: Use bold and italic text to promote the candidate's expertise as an innovator as well as some key market strengths. Throughout, demonstrate bottom-line results contributed throughout her career.

DENISE CHAN   denisechan@email.com   Resume (Page 2)

PROFESSIONAL EXPERIENCE, continued

Vice President Sales and Marketing • 1993 to 2002
BARKELEY TOURS, INC., New York, NY

Recruited for newly formed company to package and market tours of Europe and Eastern Mediterranean with full autonomy for establishing marketing plans and building a competitive presence. Established initial marketing infrastructure and developed long-term strategic and short-term tactical marketing plans.

- Drove revenues from start-up to $120 million, positioning company as the mass-market leader to Europe.
- Obtained exclusive contracts with airlines, including vacation tour program to Europe with major airline.
- Created innovative, distinctive, and successful direct-mail, advertising, promotion, and business-development campaigns.
- Built national sales and marketing network, negotiating strategic partnerships and alliances.
- Awarded "Salesman of the Year," 2001, 1998, 1996, 1995.

EDUCATION

OXFORD POLYTECHNIC, Sheffield, UK
Degree in Hotel Management and Tourism

Management Training: Suisse Hotels and Restaurants, Switzerland; Hotel Geneve, Geneva, Switzerland.

Continuing Education / Professional Development: Stephen Covey seminar: *7 Habits of Highly Effective People;* Tom Peters *WOW Seminars;* Harvard Business School training.

Certified Travel Counselor Course, 1989

FOREIGN LANGUAGE SKILLS

Fluent in French; working knowledge of Spanish

PROFESSIONAL AFFILIATIONS

Member—USTOA (United States Tour Operators Association)
Member—ASTA (American Society of Travel Agents)
Member—New York Athletic Club
Member—Skål International

ADDITIONAL SKILLS

Accomplished and articulate public speaker, frequently selected to deliver presentations to industry gatherings of 250 to 1,500 people.

—Available for Domestic/International Travel and/or Relocation—

Alfonse Natley

2583 Juniper Dr. • Cicero, Illinois 60804

anat@network.com
708-555-4133

PROFESSIONAL PROFILE

Successful restaurant management professional with 20+ years of experience in fast-paced, high-volume national chains. A change agent, recognized for introducing stability and turning around lackluster locations. Entrepreneur at heart, consistently increasing sales while controlling operational costs to maximize profits. Management style engenders respect and builds cohesive, committed teams.

AREAS OF EXPERTISE

Building Teams	Reducing Shrinkage	Monitoring P&L
Controlling Food & Labor Costs	Developing Employees	Establishing Goals

CAREER HISTORY

BOB EVANS • 10 locations in 4 states (1994–2011)

General Manager

Managed and held bottom-line responsibility for operations, finance, and human resources for restaurants/retail shops with 200–240 employees generating $3.2 million–$7+ million in annual sales. Highlights:

Leadership

- Frequently tapped by corporate management to revitalize poor-performing stores. Provided direction and introduced stability. Increased profitability and reduced turnover by more than 100%.
- Assigned to orchestrate launch of 5 new locations. Hired staff, established corporate processes and procedures, and established tone of operations. Continued as GM for at least 1 year after each opening.

Operations

- Coordinated purchase and tracked inventory of grocery, perishable, and supply items from corporate distribution center and local vendors, ensuring local purchases met company's exacting standards.
- Initiated and implemented restaurant promotions; represented the restaurant in the community

Staffing

- Met challenge of operating store without full complement of staff due to unusual circumstance of negative unemployment rate in area; consistently outperformed fully staffed locations.
- Developed associate managers for promotion; at least 7 ultimately earned General Manager and/or District Manager positions.
- Recruited, hired, trained, and motivated retail managers, associate restaurant managers, servers, cooks, and support staff.

Performance Recognition

- ❖ General Manager of the Year
- ❖ 5 annual Team Builder awards
- ❖ Top 15% company-wide (600 locations) for Customer Loyalty
- ❖ Clean Sweep award for excellence in sanitation

Additional 10+ years of management experience with several national chain restaurants.

EDUCATION

Bachelor of Science in Business Administration • Northwestern University (Evanston, Illinois)
Associate in Business Administration • Triton College (River Grove, Illinois)

Company-provided training on management, conflict management, hiring, and sanitation topics.

Strategy: Create a concise one-page resume that showcases notable honors and awards in an eye-catching shaded box.

CHAPTER 9

Resumes for Managers and Executives in Health Care

- Legal Nurse Consultant/Nurse Paralegal

- Home-Care Executive and Legislative Advocate

- Public Health Administrator

- Chief Marketing Officer/President/Chief Operating Officer for Healthcare Services

- Chief Operating Officer/Vice President/Executive Director for Health and Fitness Organizations

- Diagnostic Technology Manager

- Navy Health-Care Administrator

Danielle Winker R.N.
15 Boynton Beach Court
Deerfield Beach, FL 33441
954.567.6196 daniellewinker@aol.com

LEGAL NURSE CONSULTANT / NURSE PARALEGAL
Registered Nurse / Case Management & Assessment / Chart Review

Accomplished nursing professional with 13+ years of clinical experience as Staff Nurse and Charge Nurse. Recent graduate of *Legal Nurse Consulting / Paralegal Studies program*. Studied all aspects of legal process with emphasis on tort law, legal research, litigation skills and support, and principles and concepts of legal nurse consulting. **Key strengths include:**

- Registered Nurse, States of New York and New Jersey; Certified Childbirth Educator; Certified Inpatient Obstetrics Nurse.
- BA in English. Superior writing skills and ability to draft concise, effective legal documents with meticulous attention to detail.
- Strong interpersonal skills with proven ability to establish rapport with difficult clients, patients, and other medical personnel.
- Highly organized, with demonstrated ability to set priorities and manage multiple projects.
- Results-driven. Work well under pressure and against deadlines.
- Experienced Office Manager with strengths in accounts payable and receivable, vendor negotiations, payroll, billing, insurance, and fee collection.

PROFESSIONAL TRAINING AND EDUCATION

DIPLOMA, LEGAL NURSE CONSULTING / PARALEGAL STUDIES
FAU College, Boca Raton, FL 2012 **(GPA: 4.0)**
Honors Graduate
Delta Epsilon Tau International Honor Society

Legal Coursework Included: *Principles and Concepts of Legal Nurse Consulting; Tort Law; Civil Litigation; Criminal Law Process; Contracts; Insurance Law; Wills/Trusts/Estate Planning; Interviewing and Investigation; Business Organizations; Legal Research Specialty; Legal Ethics; Litigation Assistantship Specialty; Administrative Law; and Risk Management.*

AAS NURSING, Grady Hospital School of Nursing, Atlanta, GA
Recipient, Mary Frances Betar Scholarship Award for Scholastic Excellence

BA ENGLISH LITERATURE, City College of Boca Raton, Boca Raton, FL

RELEVANT SKILLS AND EXPERIENCE

Legal Core Competencies
- Analyze and summarize medical records.
- Perform personal injury case analysis for plaintiffs and defendants.
- Assist attorneys in screening medical malpractice cases and determining "case worthiness."
- Prepare fact and expert witnesses for deposition and trial.
- Assist attorneys in preparation of various discovery requests, demand letters, and other correspondence.
- Assist in locating and evaluating qualified medical experts.

Page 1

Strategy: Show strong qualifications for the niche of Legal Nurse Consultant, combining legal and health-care expertise; place education up front because it is recent and required; show core skills and related achievements under three functional headings.

| Danielle Winker R.N. | daniellewinker@aol.com | Page 2 |

Obstetrical Nursing

- Implemented high quality of care for low- and high-risk patients (premature labor, multiple births, and critical-care situations) throughout entire labor and delivery process at large, tertiary-care centers.
- Proficient in fetal monitor strip interpretation.
- Monitored and assessed patients at risk for pre-term labor, wrote weekly reports for physicians, and provided post-partum summary of patients' care and outcome.
- Designed and delivered highly informative childbirth education classes for audiences of 8 to 10 couples for over 10 years. Frequently recognized and recommended by doctors as "preferred" childbirth educator.
- Assisted with "rape kit" evidence collection while on staff at large inner-city hospital.
- Specially chosen for 3-month rotation in Recovery Room at Mt. Sinai to care for critically ill patients.
- Coordinated all aspects of patient care for large infertility practice, requiring ability to synchronize multiple events to increase probability of successful outcome.

Leadership / Office Management / Administration

- As Staff Nurse for medical corporation, chosen to relocate to Miami to lead and establish new branch office. Responsible for space planning, ordering supplies and equipment, and organizing all office-management procedures.
- As Charge Nurse, assisted in establishing start-up labor and delivery unit. Designed and wrote policies and procedures manual, directed scheduling, managed staff, and coordinated patient care in delivery room.
- Managed all aspects of multi-physician GYN office, including bookkeeping, billing, accounts payable and receivable, and vendor negotiations.
- Implemented highly efficient accounting and payroll structure for OB/GYN office by creating filing system and organizing payables and receivables.
- Managed entire labor and delivery units in absence of supervisor.

WORK HISTORY

Treasurer, Medical Associates of Metropolitan Atlanta, Atlanta, GA (2007 to 2010)

Staff Nurse, Grady Medical Center, Atlanta, GA (1998 to 2002)

Staff Nurse, Tokos Medical Corporation, Boca Raton, FL (1996 to 1998)

Staff Nurse, Memorial Hospital, Hollywood, FL (1994 to 1996)

Charge Nurse, NW Regional Hospital, Miramar, FL (1993 to 1994)

Childbirth Educator, Boca Raton Community Hospital, Boca Raton, FL (1991 to 1993)

Assistant Office Manager, Kaufman, Bernard & Gross M.D., P.C., Deerfield Beach, FL (1991 to 1993)

Staff Nurse, Jackson Medical Center, Miami, FL (1990 to 1993)

PROFESSIONAL ASSOCIATIONS

- American Association of Legal Nurse Consultants (Member)
- International Association of Forensic Nurses (Member)
- Delta Epsilon Tau International Honor Society (Member)

COMPUTER SKILLS

PC proficient: Lexis-Nexis (familiar), Windows, MS Word, Internet, and e-mail applications.

NICKOLE ANDREWS PENN

113 N.E. 21st Street	nickole@yahoo.com	Home (503) 894-2646
Portland, Oregon 97201		Cell (503) 226-7315

HOME-CARE EXECUTIVE AND LEGISLATIVE ADVOCATE

▶ **Prominent home-care leader driving advancement of personal-care industry through federal, state, and local legislative activities.**

▶ **Top-flight administrator dedicated to promoting the highest standards of care in the industry.**

▶ **Recognized speaker/presenter at workshops throughout the United States.**

▶ **Business owner/entrepreneur in home-care industry.**

▶ **Published author, teacher, trainer.**

PROFESSIONAL ACHIEVEMENTS

HOMECARE   Portland, OR
Founder • VP, Human Resources • VP, Quality, Regulatory Affairs, Training   2008–2011

Co-founded company to provide quality home-care services for elderly and disabled. Grew from start-up to $45 million in three years by launching key initiatives associated with company's strategic goals: Set industry standard for quality, training, innovation, and professionalism; streamlined and standardized operating processes and procedures to improve quality, consistency, and overall client care; integrated new acquisitions into company; incorporated back-office functions into centralized delivery systems; developed team of customer-focused management and staff.

Staff Leadership & Training
- Led managers and inter-departmental teams new to home care.
- Structured and delivered new-hire orientation and ongoing training/customer-service programs for new managers, caregivers, and staff.

Operations & Financial Performance
- Managed annual budget of $2.25 million. Supervised department of seven with four direct reports: HR, Administration, Training, and Risk Management.
- Designed and successfully implemented company-standard policies, procedures, and processes.
- Fostered development of business rules, training materials, and integration process for home-care-specific software.
- Increased efficiency and reduced cost by $83,560 annually as result of recommended change in background-check vendor.
- Restructured Risk Management Department, reducing Workers' Comp Experience Modification Rating from 123 to 75 in two years for savings of $250,000 annually.

Technology Leadership
- Successfully completed software conversion of 18 locations in six months, with support staff of two, achieving company's strategic goal of centralizing back-office functions.
- Managed complex HR, operations, and systems integration with newly acquired companies.
- Provided functional home-care expertise to development team tasked with designing proprietary IVR (Interactive Voice Response) system.

Industry & Regulatory Leadership
- Advocated legislatively at national, state, and local levels for protection of state and federal home-care exemptions. Gained national reputation for driving opposition to Department of Labor's attempt to eliminate patient exemptions.
- Designed and executed company-wide customer-satisfaction survey used to develop quality improvement objectives and positive client outcomes.

continued

Strategy: Highlight accomplishments in teaching, training, legislative activities, and management within the industry to position this experienced individual for her target positions: training newcomers to the field or serving as an industry lobbyist.

Nickole Andrews Penn
nickole@yahoo.com

Home (503) 894-2646
Cell (503) 226-7315

PROFESSIONAL ACHIEVEMENTS, continued

HEALTH CARE FOR HANDICAPPED   Seattle, WA
Owner/Executive Director   2002–2008

Grew, from start-up, successful business providing in-home personal-care services to elderly and disabled. Directed all aspects of business start-up and growth including operations, strategic planning, business development, budgeting, hiring, and training. Established and implemented quality standards specific to home-care organizations.

- Tripled revenue in 18 months and grew from start-up to $6 million in six years.
- Leading advocate in home-care legislative concerns, attending national policy conferences and developing relationships with and lobbying local, state, and federal legislators.
- Launched use of satisfaction surveys and QI process in home-care industry.

SEATTLE UNION SCHOOL DISTRICT   Seattle, WA
Special Needs Teacher   1996–2002

- Engaged in many district-wide committees for development of programs, processes, and curriculum for special-needs children ages three to five.
- Significant contributor to grant-writing projects resulting in $3 million for Special Education programs.

NORTHWEST WASHINGTON BOARD OF COOPERATIVE EDUCATIONAL SERVICES   Seattle, WA
Special Needs Teacher   1993–1996
- Served as Program Specialist coordinating speech/language services for nine rural districts.
- Member of nine-district team selected to write and implement $90,000 grant proposal to develop innovative programs for special-needs students; served as consultant to district administrators/teaching professionals during implementation phase.
- Provided speech/language services to three school districts, preschool through twelfth grade. Instrumental in integrating speech/language services into the classroom.

PORTLAND SCHOOL DISTRICT   Portland, OR
Speech/Language Specialist   1991–1993

Created program for six mainstreamed, hearing-impaired students. Provided speech/language services to children in kindergarten through second grade.

OREGON DEPARTMENT OF HEALTH   Salem, OR
Consultant/Parent Trainer   1989–1991

Empowered parents of hearing-impaired infants by providing skills related to auditory training, communications, language development, and hearing-aid maintenance.

EDUCATION

M.A. Speech Pathology   1991
Arizona State University, Flagstaff, Arizona

B.S. Speech Pathology/Audiology   1984
Oklahoma State University, Stillwater, Oklahoma

David T. Evans, M.D., M.P.H.

5110 Creekbranch Drive
Chapel Hill, NC 27512
919-942-8888
davidevansmd@earthlink.net

HIGHLIGHTS OF QUALIFICATIONS

Public Health Administrator with directorial and clinical experience at the federal, state, and county government levels. Proven ability to identify problems and implement practical solutions. Develop innovative programs from a long-range perspective. Able to work effectively with people of various cultural backgrounds, ages, and socioeconomic statuses.

Core competencies include:

- Program management
- Data collection and analysis
- Budgetary management
- Public health education
- Community-based health-care interventions

- Grant writing
- Public health monitoring
- Legislative involvement in public health
- Staff training and supervision
- Media relations

PROFESSIONAL EXPERIENCE

Director of Preventive Medicine/Assistant Professor   2008–present
University of North Carolina, Chapel Hill, NC

- Led a faculty team in developing a community-based preventive-medicine program that was suitable for a rural population and cost only 30% of the projected curriculum expense.
- Created and tested the region's first community-health survey instrument in 20 years.
- Serve as a public health advocate before the governor and state legislature.
- Recruited by the governor to institute a hypertension-reduction program for a 4-county area where the prevalence of hypertension is 3 times greater than the national average.
- Obtain funding to address the special medical needs of the local population.

Associate Chief of Staff for Preventive Medicine   2005–2008
Veterans Administration Medical Center, Winston-Salem, NC

- Fostered the increased utilization of primary care clinics. This reduced the use of emergency rooms for primary care.
- Developed and implemented a preventive care program consisting of age-specific physical exams, screening tests, and medical services.
- Instituted a daycare program for homeless veterans that included treatment of mental illness.
- Hired, trained, and managed a medical staff of 230.
- Established policies that promoted high-quality patient care. Analyzed clinical problems such as violations of patients' rights or breaches in protocol.

continued

Strategy: Emphasize strong contributions within the public health field, using a traditional chronological format and a keyword-dense summary.

David T. Evans, M.D., M.P.H. davidevansmd@earthlink.net **Page 2**

Medical Director 1998–2004
Fayette County Department of Public Health, Lexington, KY

- Recommended and instituted a high-school health program that resulted in a 12% decrease in teenage pregnancy and STDs among inner-city adolescents.
- Obtained federal funding to launch a county health-care program for individuals who did not qualify for Medicaid, yet were unable to afford primary care. This program utilized local health departments and decreased emergency-room visits for primary care.
- Actively lobbied for 12 health-care bills that concerned indigents. Nine of the bills were passed.
- Participated on a team that proposed and implemented the purchase of public health clinics by the University of Kentucky College of Medicine. This pilot program provided effective medical care for many of the area's uninsured or underinsured residents.

Clinical Director 1996–1998
South Bend Federal Detention Center, South Bend, IN

- Established protocols that emphasized preventive care and decreased poly-pharmacy.
- Reduced clinical expenses 28% by bringing all services in-house except for surgery.
- Ensured that all medical staff members were licensed and certified. Implemented a CME program for staff.
- Trained and supervised a multidisciplinary staff of 20.

EDUCATION

Master of Public Health 2006
University of North Carolina, Greensboro, NC

Doctor of Medicine 1990
Temple University School of Medicine, Philadelphia, PA

RESUME 51: BY MARJORIE SUSSMAN, ACRW, MRW, CPRW

RACHEL PHILLIPS

617-778-5270 | rachel.phillips@gmail.com
1272 River Road, Watertown, MA 02472

SENIOR EXECUTIVE: CMO | PRESIDENT | COO
HEALTHCARE & FINANCIAL SERVICES — TRANSACTION & PAYMENT PROCESSING

Driving growth and profitability through fact-based, metric-driven strategy development and product deployment in the healthcare and financial services industries.

Sixteen-year record of success in high-profile, top-tier roles with industry-leading organizations, including Consumer Health Group and NASD. Full range of executive leadership skills steering complex initiatives from concept to completion through periods of transformation and change. Plan and execute business start-ups and rapid growth, restructuring and repositioning, and cost-cutting and rightsizing. **Managed $2B revenue and $750M expense P&L.**

MBA, New York University, Stern School of Business
Executive Leadership Program, Wharton School of Business

Strategic Planning & Tactical Execution | Board-Level Relationships | Operations Start-Up & Reorganization | P&L Oversight
Healthcare Analytics | Nimble & Responsive Work Style | Trend Forecasting | New Business Development
Client Relations & Key Account Management | Team Building & Leadership | Entrepreneurial Mindset

CAREER TRACK

TRAINER SEAFORD PARTNERS   Boston, MA | 2007–Present
Boutique consultancy focused on business strategy and product development for healthcare and financial services firms. Clients include Fiserv, Walgreens, Simeon, First Bank, Destiny Health Plan, TransUnion, Fell Payment Systems, and MasterCard.

▶ **Founding & Managing Partner**

Built company from the ground up to provide advisory services to major corporations on business strategy, market assessments, and tactical roadmaps. Perform due diligence for private equity and venture capital firms on emerging healthcare investments. Interact extensively with Boards of Directors, CEOs, and other top-tier executives.

- Ignited rapid growth: achieved profitability in first month and $2M–$3M annual revenue.
- Recruited 5 high-performing consultants qualified to deliver the firm's unique value proposition.
- Instituted "flat" hierarchy, empowering individual team members to assume project leadership in areas of expertise.
- Form strong, long-term client partnerships, earning trust and sharing vision so that engagements extend beyond original parameters.

Notable Engagements:

- Launched industry-leading ePayment, retail lockbox, wholesale lockbox, and merchant services healthcare products.
- Integrated healthcare credit card with plan-sponsored Health Spending Accounts.
- Completed business cases for global financial organization that opened up 2 new business verticals with projected 5-year revenues of $59M.
- Validated health-plan business closing through assessment of competitive capabilities and operational performance.
- Identified strategic partners for US-based card-processing platform to expand into Brazil, Russia, India, and China.
- Developed major financial institution's consumer-friendly prepaid card.

CONSUMER HEALTH GROUP (NYSE: CHG)   New York, NY & Boston, MA | 2002–2006

Overview: Held challenging leadership roles during 4 years of frequent organizational change (new administration, government inquiry, economic constraint, and business transformation). Consistently strengthened business model by adapting strategy to corporate vision. Repeatedly asked to take on complex issues and repeatedly delivered stellar results—pioneering nation's first healthcare-dedicated bank, orchestrating organizational rightsizing, and transforming declining operations to vibrant growth.

▶ **Chief of Staff—Duoprize Strategic Solutions (DSS)** | 2005–2006
One of 3 divisions under Duoprize umbrella, delivering all sales, customer installations, and account management services to 5000+ self-insured employers, including 180 Fortune 500 companies. 800 employees. $2B revenue.

Page 1 of 2

Strategy: Write tight, crisp accomplishment statements that allow the impressive results to shine through. Lead off with a strong summary and clear branding statement.

RACHEL PHILLIPS Page 2 of 2 617-778-5270 | rachel.phillips@gmail.com

CONSUMER HEALTH GROUP *(continued)*

Hand-picked for critical leadership role to create new business model that improved customer service, revamped customer acquisition strategy, and reorganized the division through rightsizing and belt-tightening. Successfully achieved goals while managing $780M expense and $2B revenue budget on behalf of the Division President:

- Reduced workforce 10%, reaping annual savings of $6.5M.
- Improved customer support efficiency ratio by 25%.
- Worked with senior leadership and gained organizational consensus to increase revenue by $69M.
- Instrumental in planning and implementing strategy that reduced operating expenses by $39M.

▶ **Chief Marketing Officer (CMO)—CHG Financial Services (Capital Bank)** | 2002–2005
Capital Bank is the top healthcare bank nationwide, focused on health savings and reimbursement accounts, flexible spending accounts, commuter expense reimbursement accounts, and electronic payments and statements.

Member, Executive Leadership Committee commissioned to plan and implement nation's first-ever healthcare-dedicated bank. Assembled and led 50-member cross-functional product, sales, and marketing team. Reported to Division CEO.

- Launched 3 product lines within first 2 years: healthcare accounts (HSA, HRA, CERA), card-based products (electronic ID, debit), and provider electronic payments and statements.
- Hit breakeven profitability by year 3.
- Soared to market-share leadership (health savings accounts) by year 4.
- Lead inventor, US Patent Application 20040172309 (method, system, storage medium for multiparty transactions).

NATIONAL ASSOCIATION OF SECURITIES DEALERS (NASD) New York, NY | 1999–2002

▶ **Technology Chief of Staff—American Stock Exchange** | 2000–2002

Recruited by CIO for leadership role in disassociation of NASDAQ and American Stock Exchange. Collaborated with NASD and NASDAQ to extract technology infrastructures previously consolidated with merger of Amex and NASD in 1998. Represented Amex to work with Credit Suisse First Boston (CSFB) for sale of the exchange. Reported to Chief Technology Officer (CTO).

- Led SWAT team for in-sourcing technology, including assumption of 300 employees and consultants, hardware, and telecommunications infrastructures, totaling $100M in annual budget.
- Led $15M cost-containment exercise on behalf of CTO.

▶ **Lead Technology Controller—NASDAQ & American Stock Exchange** | 1999–2000

Sought out by CFO to manage $300M expense budget. Instituted cost savings that included:

- $16M by shifting from purchasing to leasing mainframe hardware.
- $160M by formulating activity-based costing model for use in technology outsourcing to EDS, a deal that *Future Banker* ranked #11 of Top 25 deals in 1999.

Prior professional experience:

Senior Consulting Manager—RANKIN PARTNERS, NYC, 1997–1999 | Developed activity-based costing system for NASD.

Assistant Treasurer—Corporate Trust Group, THIRD TRUST, NYC, 1994–1997 | Designed and implemented risk evaluation tool and interest income forecast model.

EDUCATION

NEW YORK UNIVERSITY (NYU) / LEONARD STERN SCHOOL OF BUSINESS
- ▶ Executive MBA, Management. Class rank: #2 of 60, 2006
- ▶ Bachelor of Science, Finance & International Business, 1996

WHARTON SCHOOL OF BUSINESS
- ▶ President's Leadership Development Program, Consumer Health Group (6-month executive program), 2004

DAVID A. WILLIAMS

215 James Place
Ladera Ranch, CA 92694

(714) 336-8998
dwilliams@mailnet.net

COO / VICE PRESIDENT / EXECUTIVE DIRECTOR
Expertise in Multi-Facility Health and Fitness Organizations

PROFILE

Operations and Sales Executive with a track record of increasing sales and profits, turning around under-performing locations / regions, and leading expansion for multi-unit operations with up to $10 million in annual revenues (both profit-driven and non-profit). Consistently exceeded goals, sales plans, and turnaround objectives for each employer.

Expert in analyzing existing operations and implementing the necessary strategies and formal business practices to improve profit performance, grow membership sales, and increase retention rates. Proven financial and business acumen combined with practical experience and formal training in health and fitness. Strong educational foundation with MA and BBA degrees. Areas of strength include:

- **Multi-Unit Operations Management**
- **Budgeting / Expense Control**
- **Sales Management / Sales Training**
- **Marketing / Sales Promotions**
- **Business Development**
- **Fitness Program Development**
- **New Facility Design / Opening**
- **Staff Leadership / Motivation**

PROFESSIONAL EXPERIENCE

ORANGE COUNTY COMMUNITY HEALTH AND FITNESS ORGANIZATION — Tustin, CA   2009 to Present
(Non-profit organization offering sports, aquatics, and fitness programs for member families)

Vice President, Health and Fitness

Hired to orchestrate an aggressive turnaround for the region from a $1.2 million loss to sustainable net gains within 2 years. Hold full responsibility for the planning, staffing, and operating performance of 6 locations with 200+ employees, 18,000+ members, and $5.5 million in annual revenues.

Broad scope of accountability includes day-to-day operations, revenue performance, membership sales, staff training, program development / implementation, and customer service. Supervise 6 facility directors and 18 program managers. Develop and manage a $5.5 million program budget. Provide leadership to capital campaign and facility design phase for 2 new locations with a $20 million budget.

- **Turned region around from a $1.2 million loss to a projected positive net in 2 years.**
- **Grew new membership sales from 3,500 in 2008 to more than 7,000 in 2010.**
- **Increased revenue from personal training programs more than 100% within 1 year.**
- **Strengthened member-retention rate to 70% across all locations through improved customer-service training and procedures.**
- **Improved lead generation 15% by designing a prospect-management / tracking system.**

T.S. FITNESS / EMERALD GYM – locations in TX and SC   2004 to 2009
(Operator of fitness clubs in 2 states)

Chief Operating Officer

Senior operations manager with full responsibility for day-to-day facility operations, sales, accounting, human resources, and fitness programs for a newly established company with 3 facilities, 60–80 full- and part-time staff, and $2.5 million in annual sales.

continued

Strategy: Create an executive presentation to position the candidate as viable in an industry where few senior-level positions exist.

David A. Williams   **Page 2**   **(714) 336-8998**

T.S. FITNESS / EMERALD GYM *(continued)*

Established formal business practices and standardized sales and operations processes across all locations to support continued growth and expansion.

- **Grew profits more than 20% each year.**
- **Developed and implemented formal sales procedures that resulted in a 20%–30% increase in new memberships each year.**
- **Increased personal-fitness and group-fitness revenues more than 50% per year.**
- **Developed new business by establishing relationships / alliances with corporate and allied health providers.**

MEGA FITNESS / MEGA GYM — Houston, San Antonio, and Dallas, TX   2001 to 2004
(Operator of fitness clubs with $10 million in annual revenues)

Vice President, Sales and Operations

Led operations, sales, staff training, and fitness programs for 12 Mega Gyms with nearly 100,000 members and up to $10 million in combined annual sales. Provided leadership and direction for 250+ sales and fitness staff, 12 general managers, and 4 regional managers in a rapidly growing organization. Worked closely with general managers of each location, providing guidance in maximizing sales and increasing member-retention rate while reducing expenses.

- **Delivered double-digit sales growth each year.**
- **Maintained member retention rate at more than 70%.**
- **Established and launched a comprehensive fitness and nutrition program, which included more than 200 personal trainers.**
- **Contributed to design and pre-sale phases for 5 new facilities.**

FORT BEND GENERAL HOSPITAL — Needville, TX   1998 to 2001
(A 150-bed community hospital)

Director, Business Development

Directed business-development activities to revitalize an older hospital in an industrial suburb of Houston. Developed and coordinated promotions, community-relations activities, and special programs for physician recruitment.

- **Built a local Preferred Provider Organization (PPO) from scratch to more than 10,000 participants. Model was duplicated at other Houston-area hospitals.**

EDUCATION

SOUTHWEST TEXAS STATE UNIVERSITY — New Braunfels, TX
- **Master of Arts, Kinesiology,** GPA 4.0 (1999)
- **Bachelor of Business Administration,** Cum Laude (1997)

Available to travel and/or relocate

LAWRENCE A. MAKRIS

44 West Greene Street • Coral Springs, FL 32405 • Cell: (407) 555-4994 • Home: (407) 555-8889
lmakris@aol.com

QUALIFICATIONS PROFILE

Motivated and dedicated senior-level professional with extensive healthcare experience and proven track record of success in hands-on leadership, organizational management, acquisitions, and strategic planning. Accomplished in team development and empowerment, instilling sense of pride and autonomy in staff. Highly skilled in ROI analysis and capital-expenditure budget administration. Recognized for ability to identify key markets, customers, and vendors, leading to increased revenue.

PROFESSIONAL BACKGROUND

MEDICAL SOLUTIONS, INC., Miami, FL   2006–Present
President & Founder

Established 3 distinct entities of corporation—Medical Device Sales & Leasing, Diagnostic Testing, and Diagnostic Imagery—to meet diagnostic technology needs of healthcare facilities and communities.

Positioned company for long-term sustainable growth and profitability. Responsible for hiring staff, building effective teams, financial planning, budgeting, corporate acquisition, and operations management for 5 locations with a staff of 25. Created and led strategic initiatives. Developed and established policies and procedures. Oversaw P&L for all locations.

- In 5 years grew business from 1 to 6 locations with gross annual revenue of $2.4 million.

- Increased client base from zero to several thousand, including 250 facility-based clients.

- Developed and implemented strategic plans to target both facilities and patients, significantly increasing revenue and efficiency.

- Originated and implemented budget-analysis system to track operational expenses, marketing, billing, and inventory for each facility on a quarterly basis. Consistently met or exceeded goals.

- Established centralized computer networking system, enabling facilities to interface with each other, monitor inventory, and track client base.

- Managed private and third-party billing and collections in-house.

<u>MEDICAL DEVICE SALE & LEASING</u> (2008–Present)

- Provided per-diem leasing of diagnostic devices to rehabilitation facilities and hospitals.

- Successfully negotiated leases directly with manufacturers, sub-leasing to clients and avoiding need to maintain huge inventory of product.

- Expanded market into durable medical equipment (DME) company within 6 months, significantly increasing revenue through patient referral system.

- Acquired Southern Medical Equipment Company and all assets, establishing Medical Solutions, Inc., as competitive DME provider.

- Led company from zero revenue to $340,000 within the first year and $750,000 within 2 years.

- Managed and directed 6 sales representatives for entire region between Florida and Texas.

Continued

Strategy: Paint a picture of an accomplished industry leader with strong business achievements to help this individual transition from a self-owned business to a larger corporation.

LAWRENCE A. MAKRIS   lmakris@aol.com   **PAGE TWO**

DIAGNOSTIC TESTING (2007–Present)

- Initiated polysomnogram testing (sleep studies) to patients and provided patients with DME for treatment for conditions.

- Established in-house diagnostic center and eliminated single-vendor outsourcing systems previously utilized at VA Hospital in Tampa.

- Streamlined purchasing through alliance with Acme Buying Group.

- Established contracts with 6 facilities, providing technical and clinical component.

DIAGNOSTIC IMAGERY (2006–Present)

- Streamlined organization through addition of Diagnostic Imagery to list of services available to existing clients.

- Expanded market into Texas through alliance with Southwestern Medical Center in Dallas, which led to contracts with West Texas Rehabilitation Center and Timothy J. Harner Burn Centers.

EDUCATION

HARVARD UNIVERSITY, Cambridge, MA
Master of Business Administration, 2004

FLORIDA STATE UNIVERSITY, Tallahassee, FL
Bachelor of Business Administration with emphasis in Financial Analysis, 1998
Alpha Lambda Delta National Scholastic Honor Society, 1997
Outstanding College Students of America, 1996

PROFESSIONAL ASSOCIATIONS

National Association of Medical Equipment Suppliers
Miami Kiwanis

Vice President of Business Development, VP of Acquisitions, Corporate Officer

RAYMOND J. CASEY

1445 Tinker Court, Brandon, FL 33650
(813) 555-1212 • raycasey@aol.com

OBJECTIVE	**Healthcare Administration**
EXPERIENCE	U.S. Navy, 08/87–08/11

Regional Medical Administrator, Tampa, FL   **May 04–Aug 11**
Director of a 5-office, 30-member medical department.
- Coordinate routine and occupational health programs for more than 800 employees throughout the Southeast.
- Advise CEO on all organizational issues involving employee health and safety.
- Manage Workers' Compensation, Back-to-Work Program, and medical claims.
- Monitor the installation of new medical information systems software. Implement employee training.
- Schedule and coordinate medical support and supplies for more than 25 national and international operations.
- Authorize contracts and medical supplies and equipment purchases through vendors.
- Negotiate bids for building renovations. Saved more than $125K, acquiring 3 portable classrooms for free.
- Awarded Commendation medal for orchestrating large-scale medical exercise involving 150 personnel.

Administrative Director, Atlanta, GA   **May 00–May 04**
Directed 20 staff in administrative services for employee outpatient clinic providing health-care services to more than 100,000 members, averaging 20,000 visits annually.
- Assisted COO in developing, implementing, and monitoring strategic plans.
- Administered $2.4M budget—forecasting, planning, accounting, and purchasing.
- Negotiated fees and contracts with specialty physician group practices.
- Saved $150K annually and increased man-hours 20,000 through strategic analysis.
- Managed $5M warehouse inventory. Reduced inventory, saving $35K annually.

Safety Manager, New York, NY   **Dec 96–May 00**
Supervised 5 employees of a large industrial-maintenance facility employing over 300.
- Managed occupational health programs, medical records, and mishap reports.
- Monitored hearing, sight, respiratory, and asbestos medical-surveillance programs.
- Inspected machinery, equipment, and working conditions to ensure compliance with OSHA regulations.
- Disseminated information regarding toxic substances, hazards, carcinogens, and risk management.
- Awarded 2 Achievement medals for superior service. Named Employee of the Year.

EDUCATION & TRAINING	Bachelor of Science in Health Care Leadership National-Louis University, Wheaton, IL	2006
	Claims Management & Legal Issues in Risk Management	2007
	Medical Staff Planning	2005
	Total Quality Management/Team Facilitator Instructor	2004
	Health Resources Management	2004
	Government Contracting	2003
	Adult Education Instructor	2002
PROFESSIONAL MEMBERSHIPS	Associate, American College of Healthcare Executives Member, American Society for Healthcare Risk Management	

Strategy: Use a concise chronological format to detail 15 years of strong health-care administration experience gained during more than two decades in the U.S. Navy.

CHAPTER 10

Resumes for Managers and Executives in Science, Engineering, and Technology

- Project Manager
- Systems Administrator
- Information Manager
- Global Software Executive
- Senior Technology Manager
- CTO/CIO
- IT Executive
- Enterprise Architect
- Vice President of Engineering

TOM WESTERLY

8450 North Minnolta Dr., Apt. 7 • Carson City, NV 89703 • (P) 795-712-3232 • (E) TomW8742@gmail.com

IT PROJECT MANAGER

Government & Public Sector
Named "Technical Leader" of EAS software implementation

Profile: Forward-thinking visionary with technical acumen, involved in developing and managing complex multiplatform DB2 proprietary systems with EMC's web-based Entity Analytic Solutions for the state of Nevada's Welfare and Supportive Services Division. Deliver high-quality design and flawless execution of unique, robust, and secure programs built to last through years of changes, threats, security breaches, and upgrades. Translate intricate applications and processes across diverse enterprise platforms.

CORE STRENGTHS

- Reduce operating expenses
- Build complete business solutions
- Increase productivity
- Advance the use of technology methods
- Envision new products and services

- Resolve long-standing problems
- Improve database processes
- Expand client relationships
- Deliver market intelligence
- Execute complex database conversions

SELECTED PROJECT ACCOMPLISHMENTS

✓ **EAS Project**: Planned, implemented, and completed 4-year rollout of identity resolution system that eliminated 35,000 duplicate identities and significantly reduced the potential for redundant claims.
✓ **Access Nevada**: Developed technical foundation and built sophisticated interface applications, key features, and user-friendly concepts with team of 10 that exceeded state of Nevada's expectations.
✓ **DRA Deficit Reduction Act–EAS preliminary**: Led team of 16 to develop welfare cash-assistance programs that improved database performance.
✓ **State On-Line Query (SOLQ)**: Allowed caseworker access to real-time Social Security Administration client benefit information that eliminated a 3-day waiting period by working with Welfare analyst and SSA staff to deliver technical requirements within compliance standards.
✓ **Benefit Issuance Address Implementation**: Reduced address data-sharing and ownership issues nearly 100% through "behind the scenes" self-cleaning functions that performed corrections and read-only benefits.

PROFESSIONAL EXPERIENCE

EMC GLOBAL BUSINESS SERVICES, Carson City, NV
IT Project Manager and "Go-to Guy"   1995–Present

Joined Nevada's Welfare Distribution Division application data team and improved 1-million-person database. Took ownership of EAS project and, from the ground up, built new system that validated an individual's identity to determine eligibility for benefits. Became a subject matter expert in person search software, resolution, and identity cleanup.
- ***Drove multiple EAS technical tasks*** that included database mapping, EAS interface technical specifications, database triggers, XML Extract/Transform/Load (ETL) applications, data conversion strategy, software setting customization, resolution rule development, and testing.

Page 1 of 2

Strategy: Keep the focus on key projects and results rather than too much emphasis on specific technology. A technology summary on Page 2 ensures that the resume will be found in an automated keyword search.

TOM WESTERLY

TomW8742@gmail.com

- ***Mastered citizen information and mitigated fraud*** through multiple project life cycles that involved increased technical responsibility and knowledge. Supported all operations and help desk.

Measurable Benchmarks
- ***Advanced EAS database*** upload performance by 1000%, setting new record.
- ***Decreased manual hours from 90 to 15*** on new updated web-based system by managing initial load of EAS XML data extract and download strategy for data conversion from state of Nevada's legacy system that included 2.6 million records and addresses.
- ***Saved $8,000 in EAS DB2 costs per month*** by revising database triggers.
- ***Improved help desk ticket turnaround 97%*** by resolving public assistance problems within 5 days.
- ***Reduced processing time 38%*** (about 20 minutes per merge) by designing and implementing Java post-merge quality check automation that eliminated 5 manual merge steps.
- ***Diminished manual backlog 50%*** in months by building and administering automation system.

EDUCATION

Bachelor of Science—Information Systems Management   1995
University of Connecticut, Hartford, CT

TRAINING

EMC Rational Application Developer, Visual Age Generator   2006–present
- Extensive Self Study in Java, IDE, and C++ Languages

EMC Entity Analytic Solutions   2006
- Identity/Relationship Resolution for system administrators and operators;
- JSP development course

EMC eBusiness Professional College   1999
- Proficient in wide variety of web-building skills

EMC Global Services Institute   1996
- Solutions Development

TECHNICAL SKILLS

Hardware: Mainframes, PCs, Compatibles
Operating Systems: MVS, UNIX/AIX, Windows, MS-DOS
Computer Languages: Java, C++, C, Visual Basic, HTML, COBOL, JCL,
Development Tools: Rational Application Developer V6, Visual Age Generator, WebSphere, Visual Age for Java, SQL, WinSQL, SPUFI, QMF, Omegamaon, File-Aid, C++ BUilder4, iRise
Applications: DB2 Identity/Relationship Resolution (Entity/Analytic Solutions), File Manager/Fault Analyzer/Debug Tool/Application Monitor, TSO/ISPF, Abend-Aid, Hummingbird
Microsoft: Windows, Excel, Word

JOHN P. LOOMIS

1117 S Michigan Blvd, Dayton, OH 45390
937-505-9985 • jploomis@hotmail.com

SUCCESSES

Gained CNET "Best All Around Hosting Service" for company.

Key in gaining major commercial and celebrity clients including Hall and Oates, KIT Digital, and Matthew Lesko.

Personally closed major media website accounts.

Recruited to work for VA Linux.

Selected for prestigious SourceForge Project.

Specifically chosen by clients, including OneWorldHosting, to manage their projects.

Built personal accounts into employer's largest out of 5,000 total.

Successfully helped clients through infamous 2007 migration disaster.

Quickly became company's resident Linux expert.

Chosen for post–Level III escalations for special clients.

ADVANCED LINUX SYSTEMS ADMINISTRATOR

"Where escalations stop"

Talented Senior Systems Administrator with more than 10 years of progressive experience in all aspects of IT program/project design and management and systems design/management with particular expertise in Linux systems.

Expertise in webservers, email management, VPS, database management, and LAMP. Accomplished at debugging, scripting, e-commerce and routing, and security and anti-spam applications. **Advanced knowledge of particular applications combined with big-picture overview of systems functions; ability to effectively analyze systems to identify trouble spots.**

Effective Level III troubleshooter, combining technical skills with strong and strategic outlook. Proven program/project manager. Member of SourceForge project team developing open source alternatives to proprietary software. Excellent communicator with strong people management skills.

PROFESSIONAL EXPERIENCE

LOOMIS WEB HOSTING SERVICES, Dayton, OH   **2001–Present**

Webserver management/consulting firm offering webserver administration and website management services with as many as 30,000 domains under management, including commercial, not-for-profit, and academic websites.

Chief Consultant / Program Manager
Lead team of 12 technicians managing up to 30,000 domains, including manufacturing, ecommerce, advocacy, and private sites, to ensure client problem solving, expansion, and 24/7 uptime.

Final point for all escalations after levels I, II, and III have passed them on. Provide 24/7 monitoring/response for both hardware and software needs, including system monitoring, problem diagnosis, backups, account, permission maintenance, mailflow, traffic analysis, team response, and escalation management.

Direct all configuration, process automation for patches, file changes, software installation/removal, and other routine processes. Serve as lead project manager for new product development; evaluate client needs and expand accounts by upselling with newly developed applications.

• Developed innovative new Tritico mail handling system that successfully handles 7M emails/month with effective spam removal, archiving, and redundancy.

• Attracted and retained major media website clients, including *The American Conservative* magazine and Air America radio network. Maintained system integrity during dramatic traffic spikes.

• Gained major commercial and celebrity clients, including founders of Tom's of Maine and Petsmart, Hall and Oates, KIT Digital, and Matthew Lesko.

Continued

Strategy: Balance deep technical descriptions with left-column "successes" that present a quick snapshot of abilities and results.

JOHN P. LOOMIS • jploomis@hotmail.com   PAGE TWO

COMPETENCIES

Systems Administration
Systems Analysis
Project/Program Management
Webservers
Information Systems
Network Administration
VPS
LAMP
Testing
QA/QC
Business Analysis
Needs Analysis
IT Strategy
IT Security
Mail Archiving
Database Management
Technical Support
Technical Writing
Policy Development
Deployment/Migrations
Client Relations
Negotiations
Customer Service
Ecommerce
Programming

TECHNICAL SKILLS

FTP • MYSQL • POP • SMTP
HTTPD • Cloud-Based Systems
SpamAssassin • Cpanel Mail
WHM • OsCommerce
Miva Merchant • OpenWebmail
NewMail • SourceForge
Tritico • Perl • AWK • SED
Bash Windows • Mac • Linux

VIYU HOSTING, Dayton, OH   **1999–2002**
Pioneer of web hosting automation software offering solutions and infrastructure services to client companies. Staff of 400. Sold to VA Linux in 2000, now owned by Navsite.

System II Administrator
Specifically recruited by Viyu management. Administered more than 1,000 webservers serving clients that included hosting companies and small businesses. Provided support to clients. Member of team maintaining KnowledgeBase for clients and technical support staff.

Quickly mastered Linux to become staff DNS and Sendmail expert. One of just three administrators selected for large-client Client Relations Group, tasked with resolving escalated or special client needs. Own clients became Viyu's largest and fastest-growing clients.

- Key in gaining CNET "Best All Around Hosting Service" award for company.

- Chosen for analytic and client service abilities as one of few employees retained by company when it was sold to VA Linux.

- Chosen to represent company on SourceForge project to evaluate, accept, or refuse SourceForge project applications.

TECHEWEB SYSTEMS, Orlando, FL   **1997–1999**
IT staffing and services company, part of the international staffing and workforce services giant Allegis Group. TechSystems provides IT support and staffing for applications, network infrastructure, end-user support, and communications technology needs.

Desktop and Network Support Specialist
Consulting member of in-house team providing IT support to PNC Bank's Y2K preparation involving replacement and configuration of 5,000 workstations and related hardware at both PNC Tower and the Steel Tower in Pittsburgh.

Transferred to HighMark Blue Cross Blue Shield team providing Y2K remediation involving replacement and configuration of almost all of client's IT equipment.

WORLDNET DATA CORP., Redding, CA   **1993–1996**
Startup subsidiary of Transamerica Corporation providing real estate tax data to real estate industry; 300 employees.

Research Analyst, Assistant Network Administrator
Researched county records, plat maps, and other sources to create county-specific real estate information databases. Maintained office network during evening shift, including troubleshooting and repair.

EDUCATION AND PRESENTATIONS

Bachelor's Degree, Liberal Arts, St. John's College, Santa Fe, NM

Provided core staff training on Sendmail, Apache, and DNS.

RYAN SIMMONS, PMP

PROJECT MANAGEMENT / INFORMATION MANAGEMENT

402nd AFSB-South Box 206 (MRAP)
APO, AE 09366
Phone: +1 (967) 497-0874
Email: ryansimmons@gmail.com

LEADERSHIP PROFILE

Project Management
Strategic Business Planning
System Architecture & Design
Systems Integration/Engineering
Resource Management
Analytics
Cross-Functional Team Leadership
Contractor Management
Client Relationship Management
Virtual Team Leadership
Budget Management
Software Development
Active DoD Secret Clearance

❑ **Accomplished, results-driven software and information management professional** with broad expertise harnessing the power of information to meet client needs. Proven track record of accomplishments, leveraging technological solutions that consistently exceed project requirements and expectations.

❑ **Well-developed technical skills and expert project-management abilities** complemented by highly effective communication and consensus-building skills.

❑ **Keen strategic business-planning and assessment abilities enhanced by strong leadership skills.** Talent for creatively applying technology to meet changing business needs and automation requirements.

❑ **Reputation as highly collaborative business partner with ability to understand and interpret client needs.** Strong leader who works effectively with people at all levels and in all functional areas.

PROFESSIONAL EXPERIENCE

SCIENCE APPLICATIONS INTERNATIONAL CORPORATION (SAIC)   2005–Present
SAIC is a leading provider of scientific, engineering, systems integration, and technical services and solutions.

DIRECTOR OF INFORMATION MANAGEMENT, Mina Abdullah, Kuwait (2009–Present)
Provide strategic IT leadership, direction, and support, handling responsibilities equivalent to a CIO of an organization with approximately 1,000 personnel in Kuwait and an additional 1,000 employees at sites across the Middle East. Manage the Information Management Department: IT Services, Information Assurance, and Information Operations/Automation Services. Accountable for coaching and developing 15–20 direct reports and overseeing annual operating budget of approximately $6M.

<u>Key Contributions & Results:</u>
- **Served as primary source for strategy, guidance, recommendations, and solutions,** convincing the MRAP program office to create an Information Management Department for its forward operations in Iraq, Afghanistan, Kuwait, Oman, Bahrain, and Qatar. Consolidated all elements of collecting, validating, storing, securing, transmitting, analyzing, and presenting information utilized to support operations Enduring Freedom and Iraqi Freedom.

- **Created and executed plan, contributing vision and thought leadership to rebuild the communication infrastructure,** information security program, and IT service management from the ground up for the MRAP Sustainment facility in Kuwait.

- **Worked to identify and implement methods to enhance optimization,** including development of an automation strategy for the MRAP program in Kuwait, creating the framework for collecting and managing data for executive, analytical decision making.

- **Delivered substantial cost savings,** championing a comprehensive IT cost-reduction program, including changing communications and technology providers, revamping phone plans, and streamlining documentation services, **resulting in procurement cost savings totaling $750K per year as well as significant labor cost savings.**

- **Successfully transitioned organization from labor-intensive into a state-of-the-art automated technology facility**, including workflow automation tools, digital pen technology, RFID locator/inventory system, handheld-based applications to support bench stock and tool management, and surveillance system with embedded video analytics.

Page 1

Strategy: Emphasize leadership as well as technical skills and contributions to help this candidate move up to a program manager or IT executive role.

RYAN SIMMONS, PMP– PAGE 2

Phone: +1 (967) 497-0874
Email: ryansimmons@gmail.com

SENIOR SYSTEMS INTEGRATION LEAD, Huntington Beach, CA (2005–2009)
Hired as an integration engineer for a massive modeling and simulation program and progressed rapidly, within 18 months, to direct the C4ISR Simulation Suite, assigned to advance modeling and simulation (M&S) efforts. Later, assumed role as System-of-Systems Integration Lead.

Key Contributions & Results:
- **Demonstrated outstanding leadership skills and expert knowledge,** leading a team of ~25 software, systems, and test engineers from SAIC, Boeing, and industry partners in erecting the White Sands Missile Range (WSMR) test center and executing one of the largest military simulation tests ever conducted by the Army.
- **Provided strategic leadership** while directing the system-of-systems integration of the FCS Integrated Mission Test 1, representing more than $100M in development, integration, and testing over a two-year period. Conducted one of the largest-ever Department of Defense solider-in-the-loop simulations.
- **Leveraged expert knowledge of business intelligence and business performance management technology** to create the FCS C4ISR Simulation Suite. Devised entire plan in under a year and delivered to the U.S. Army, while managing a virtual team working on-site with the military and subcontractors around the world.

NORTHROP GRUMMAN ELECTRONIC SYSTEMS, Azusa, CA   2003–2005
World leader in the design, development, and manufacture of advanced electronics for military, civil, and commercial use.

SOFTWARE ENGINEER/SOFTWARE LEAD
Worked closely with team of engineers and marketing to propose, design, and implement solutions for streamlining overall architecture of product suite, while focusing on advancing corporate goals. Provided hands-on leadership and direction during complete development life cycle: requirements, design, coding, unit testing, system integration, documentation, and customer support.

Key Contributions & Results:
- **Independently pitched and won $2M funding approval to implement a COTS-based system** to manage collection, storage, and real-time analysis of high-rate satellite payload telemetry. Major results include:
  - **Dramatically decreased time required to develop new analysis capabilities.**
  - **Saved the company thousands in man-hours** and substantially reduced the risk of each test cycle. Since implementation, system has been replicated and shipped out to other sites for use in testing their payloads.
  - **Revolutionized the test process for Northrop Grumman's Surveillance and Reconnaissance** Systems (SRS) division, which produces satellite payloads for the U.S. Air Force, National Oceanic and Atmosphere Administration (NOAA), and National Aeronautics and Space Administration (NASA).

EDUCATION & TRAINING

MS Candidate—Engineering Management
UNIVERSITY OF SOUTHERN CALIFORNIA, Los Angeles, CA

BS, Computer Science, 2003
HARVEY MUDD COLLEGE, Claremont, CA

Highlights of Continuing Professional Training:
- Project Management Professional (PMP)
- Pursuing Certification as Six Sigma Black Belt (completed training and Six Sigma Projects)
- Red Hat Certified Engineer (RHCE)
- Microsoft Certified Systems Engineer (MCSE)

TECHNICAL SKILLS

System Architecture Tools (Doors, Rational Rose); Programming (C++, C, Java, XML); Windows/UNIX Operating Systems (Mass Deployment, Scripting, Administration); Information Systems and Security Policies (DISA, ARMY CIO/G-6, DIACAP, NISPOM, PII); Collaboration Solutions/Workflow Automation (SharePoint); Modeling and Simulation, Development and Integration; Database Design and Implementation (Oracle 10g, MS SQL Server, MYSQL); Microsoft Office Expert; AIT Technology (RFID)

AFFILIATIONS

- Member, Project Management Institute (PMI)
- Chapter Vice President, Association of the United States Army, Kuwait
- Member, Distributed Simulation Tools and Processes Group, Simulation Interoperability and Standards Organization

RESUME 58: BY BARBARA SAFANI, MA, ACRW, CERW, CPRW, NCRW, ROIS

MATTHEW MOORE

186-15 Union Turnpike ▪ Oakland Gardens, NY 11364 ▪ C: 917-222-6111 ▪ mmoore@gmail.com

GLOBAL SOFTWARE EXECUTIVE

Driving sales and operations excellence for sales, service, and support teams in turnaround and high-growth environments.

- Success transforming and optimizing business processes and driving growth in challenging and competitive business environments, including changing economic and market conditions, product acquisitions and integrations, and product maturity/evolution.

- Expertise in turnaround strategy, operational planning, metrics management, and organizational alignment.

- Strong record of achievement blending multiple sales and services cultures and management systems acquisitions into one unified and more productive team.

- Experience leading teams to larger deal sizes, improved compensation plans and metrics, better lead generation, faster sales cycles, and higher close ratios.

CORE COMPETENCIES

Enterprise-Level Solutions	Strategic Alliance Building	Pricing & Licensing Schemas
Consultative Sales	Client/Contract Negotiations	Sales Compensation Plans
Operations Planning	P&L Management	Talent Management/Development

PROFESSIONAL EXPERIENCE

SCI-TECH CORPORATION, New York, NY, 2008 to 2011

Public software company marketing scientific information management and molecular modeling primarily to life sciences and materials manufacturing organizations.

SENIOR VICE PRESIDENT OF SALES & SERVICES
Led turnaround of sales, consulting services, market development, support, and training. Budget $30M; staff: 200.

BUSINESS DEVELOPMENT

- **BUSINESS TRANSFORMATION...**Transformed a product-oriented point solution firm to an enterprise solution consultative sales organization in just 15 months, 2 years ahead of goal.

- **PRODUCT DEVELOPMENT...**Created the vision for a more strategic consulting services branch of the business. Consulting services now account for a 25% margin (7% growth) from a previous negative margin.

- **SALES ACCELERATION...**Increased renewal rate by 23% with a 4% year-over-year order growth rate despite downturn in the pharmaceutical industry. Attained record sales results in 2010.

- **ACCOUNT PENETRATION...**Built sales solutions that reduced overall software spend for clients by 10% while increasing spending dollars with Accelrys by 20%. Increased multi-year $1M+ transactions by 150%.

- **MARKET EXPANSION...**Accelerated new business by 83% by creating the business plan to branch outside of pharmaceuticals and life sciences to materials manufacturing firms.

LEADERSHIP DEVELOPMENT

- **TALENT MANAGEMENT...**Reversed a historically siloed and fractured team, integrated multiple sales cultures, and strengthened company brand and staff by evaluating management team and recommending training, mentoring, and rightsizing. Realized a 10% reduction in budget, 15% increase in productivity, and 12% jump in deal size per client.

continued

Strategy: Create a resume that is highly "perusable," presenting all facts in concise paragraphs. Further focus the reader's attention by introducing each bullet point with bold keywords.

MATTHEW MOORE

C: 917-222-6111 ▪ mmoore@gmail.com ▪ page 2

- **TALENT RETENTION**…Designed and championed revised compensation plans that focused on pay-for-performance and reduced talent management budget by 10%.

- **SALES TRAINING**…Authored value-based and financial-based sales training curriculum delivered to 100+ sales professionals over a 2-year period.

OPERATIONAL EXCELLENCE

- **CRM IMPROVEMENTS**…Elevated close rate, sales forecasting, and accuracy exponentially by introducing enhanced management systems with automated, streamlined, and turnkey processes for tracking subscription renewal rates, customer satisfaction, close rates, time to sale, and deal size.

INTELI CORPORATION, New York, NY, 1994 to 2008

Public software organization selling business intelligence software and services to billion-dollar-plus firms specializing in the financial services sector. Key player in driving organization from start-up pre-public company to a public company with $150M in revenue. Developed sales and execution strategies for each phase of growth. Consistently given increasing responsibility based on success improving operations and expanding business development, market development, and OEM market leads. Managed budgets between $25M and $42M and teams of 100 to 300 people. **Achieved 6 years of continuous growth.**

SVP—GLOBAL OPERATIONS	SVP—NORTH AMERICAN SALES	VP—NORTH AMERICAN SALES	HEAD OF EASTERN REGION
2003 to 2008	2001 to 2002	1999 to 2001	1994 to 1999

GROWTH METRICS

As SVP—Global Operations, transitioned to enterprise solution model to achieve more strategic and high-volume wins. Met goal to "do more with less" in a challenging economic environment.

- **SALES GROWTH**…Achieved revenue growth from $104M to $140M, a 9% overall growth, and grew licensing sales by 13% from $42M to $53M.

- **PRODUCTIVITY GAINS**…Improved productivity per head by 78% from $700K to $1.25M.

- **EARNINGS**…Attained close to a 7-fold increase in earnings per share from 5 cents to 33 cents.

- **OPERATIONS**…Grew company operating margins: 4.5% to 20.6%; international contribution: 21% to 29%.

- **CHANNEL/ALLIANCE CONTRIBUTIONS**…Forged inaugural partnerships with Dell and developed an account expansion strategy resulting in major wins for the company.

INFRASTRUCTURE DEVELOPMENT

In VP and business head roles, built the company's sales and operations functions from the ground up.

- **BRAND BUILDING**…Transformed company's brand from a general software sales firm to a leading software provider for the financial services sector.

- **STAFF DEVELOPMENT**…Introduced quarterly performance appraisals and career counseling sessions. Promoted 4 direct reports during tenure and close to 40 staff members.

- **SALES TRAINING**…Developed solutions-based sales training, methodologies, and roadmaps to create a winning sales team and ensure company's continued success. Implemented robust accountability measures and set clear expectations for performance.

Held additional software sales manager and sales representative roles at ICF Corporation (1990 to 1994), Banks Corporation (1988 to 1990), The Overland Group (1983 to 1988), and Downstate Systems (1981 to 1983).

EDUCATION

Bachelor of Science in Psychology, Boston College, Boston, MA, 1980

THERESA D. BELLS

SENIOR TECHNOLOGY MANAGEMENT
**Maximizing the Power of Advanced, Innovative Technologies to Drive Business Growth,
Enhance Revenue Generation, Control Operating Costs & Increase Operating Performance**

**Application Development | Software Engineering | Database Architecture | Business Intelligence
—Engineering, Manufacturing, Professional Services & Aviation Industries—**

Solid reputation for delivering forward-thinking technology initiatives that efficiently meet diverse business, operational, and industry needs. Top leadership and strategic planning capabilities that serve well in fast-paced environments experiencing rapid change through internal growth, acquisition, and turnaround. Characterized as talented mentor and coach with ability to nurture excellent working relationships with senior executives, management teams, customers, vendors, and employees. Core competencies and technology expertise include:

**Technology Planning & Direction | IT Policy & Procedure Formulation | New Technology Development
Technology Outsourcing Programs | Process Redesign & Automation | Business & Enterprise Architecture
Business Continuity & Data Recovery | Project & Program Management | Cross-Functional Team Leadership
Organizational Alignment & Modifications**

TECHNOLOGY LEADERSHIP & PERFORMANCE HIGHLIGHTS

Liberty Best Financial, Arlington, VA   2009–present
EXECUTIVE VICE PRESIDENT—Enterprise Applications | Shared Services (2009 to present)

Technology Leadership Challenge: Introduce business intelligence, advance technology for security management and data protection, and lead efforts to shrink software maintenance and new purchases costs.

Position Scope: Direct expansive, cross-functional team of 600+ employees including on-shore/off-shore developers, business intelligence, warehousing and application architects, QA/QC, project management, and operations for nation's largest independent mortgage lender. Administer and manage $72 million budget.

<u>Impact & Results</u>:

- **Expert & Enterprise Systems**: Advised senior management on functionality of enterprise systems technology and led design and development of expert systems for sophisticated data collection, analysis, and reporting.

- **Leadership Development**: Designed leadership/staff development programs and introduced concepts of career pathing for technology professionals throughout the organization.

- **Tactical Planning & Direction**: Provided decisive, proactive operating leadership that was critical in transitioning strategy into tactical plans for long-term technology initiatives.

- **Cost Containment**: Championed Datashield security initiative—involving mortgage, banking, insurance, and servicing business units and 82 employees, and requiring expert management of $8 million project budget.

  —Introduced leading-edge systems security and data protection technologies.

  —Helped company circumvent millions of dollars in regulatory fines and avoid negative publicity during a period of heavy industry scrutiny.

- **Technology Integration**: Spearheaded technology integration of all new system requirements and capacity planning needs following merger of company and Best Banks of America Corporation.

- **Cross-Functional Technology Team**: Recruited and assembled top-performing teams challenged to deliver development and operational support services on Lotus and Exchange message systems serving more than 60,000 employees.

continued

Home: 805-523-0434 • Mobile: 805-279-2830 • Email: tbells@aol.com • LinkedIn: http://www.linkedin.com/in/tbells

Strategy: Make a sharp first impression with a well-designed resume that is also reader-friendly and packed with accomplishments.

THERESA D. BELLS   **PAGE TWO**

Liberty Best Financial, continued...

SENIOR VICE PRESIDENT—Data Resource Management (2008 to 2009)

- **Data Center Operations**: Transformed data center operations and centralized data system for entire company through implementation of emerging hardware, software, and warehousing technologies.

- **Business Intelligence**: Chaired and assembled business intelligence committee that established a technology roadmap, centralized key ETL and reporting environments, and standardized technology tools.

Besthomes.com, Richmond, VA   2005–2008
VICE PRESIDENT—Software & Database Engineering

Technology Leadership Challenge: Assume CIO-level responsibilities and lead company's launch into emerging technologies to support rapid business growth and expansion.

Position Scope: Managed quality control, database engineering, software engineering, and technical project management, 110 employees in all. Evaluated business needs and integrated relevant technology and business processes to increase website response time and decrease software and database costs.

Impact & Results:

- **Technology Enhancement**: Transitioned from multiple databases to one centralized model, modified software usage, and implemented leading-edge database software.

  —Combined efforts eliminated systems duplication, expedited data processing time more than 80%, and significantly cut software purchase/maintenance costs by 40%.

- **Database Design**: Developed and delivered multiple cutting-edge database strategies to collect, process, and load data for company's multiple websites and back-end systems.

- **Strategic Partnerships**: Structured and negotiated offshore consulting partnership to facilitate system maintenance and minor development efforts for company's non-strategic systems.

- **Technology Advisement**: Advised senior management on appropriate enterprise systems, capability planning, and technology solutions involving all merger and acquisition activities.

Paris Publishing, Norfolk, VA   1999–2005
DIRECTOR OF ENTERPRISE DATABASE & APPLICATION ARCHITECTURE

Technology Leadership Challenge: Spearhead the design, development, and delivery of advanced technology solutions for company.

Position Scope: Directed application and systems architecture and initiated state-of-the-art database modeling for company operations. Designed company's first website and pioneered web-based applications and manuals.

Impact & Results:

- **Technology Upgrade**: Replaced obsolete technology with advanced Microsoft-based architectures during company-wide system conversion from VAX.

DIRECTOR OF PROFESSIONAL SERVICES, Apple Best Technologies, Chesapeake, VA   1998–1999

EARLY CAREER: Advanced through series of increasingly challenging technical and managerial roles for companies in diverse industries including communications, aerospace engineering, and manufacturing.

EDUCATION

Bachelor of Science in Information Systems Management—Clark University, Worcester, MA

Home: 805-523-0434 • Mobile: 805-279-2830 • Email: tbells@aol.com • LinkedIn: http://www.linkedin.com/in/tbells

FRANK DeLORA

fdelora@hotmail.com
972-503-3597
Dallas, TX 75230

INFORMATION TECHNOLOGY EXECUTIVE

CTO · CIO · VP OF IT

Success-driven IT professional with a record of accomplishment driving increases in productivity, profitability, and customer satisfaction in wide-ranging business environments. Collaborative leader with entrepreneurial can-do attitude and a highly effective management style that promotes a shared vision and positive working relationships. Intellectually aggressive in identifying core problems and setting strategic direction. Thrive on new complicated assignments through passion and demonstrated expertise in:

Core Qualifications

• Business Process Automation & Improvement	• Cross-Functional Collaboration / Leadership
• Datacenter Design & Construction	• Integrating Technology & Business Solutions
• Network Design / Implementation	• Outsourcing / Contract Negotiations
• Startups / Consolidations / Divestitures	• Strategic Planning / Tactical Execution
• Team Recruitment / Development / Deployment	• Client Relations / Solutions Development

Executive Performance

FastComm, Dallas, TX   2005–Present
Wireless infrastructure company operating in under served broadband region.

Chief Technology Officer
Founded, designed, and launched company with two partners.

Technology & Business Solutions

- Enabled delivery of broadband data access to more than 4 million people in regional market through design and construction of wireless datacenter.

- Delivered key infrastructure business solution that positively influenced billions of dollars in untapped regional economic potential.

Cross-Functional Collaboration

- Provided more than 60% coverage for targeted region by identifying critical site location and negotiating 20-year land lease.

Strategic Planning

- Implemented strategic five-year plan to achieve profitability for $100M/year operation from startup.

Contract Negotiations

- Negotiated premium rate 23% below fair market value for bandwidth contract.

- Supported business expansion by negotiating $500K in employment contracts to obtain 100% of required staffing.

Strategy: Use functional headings to break up an otherwise long list of bullet points and call attention to diverse areas of accomplishment that demonstrate strong technical and business skills.

FRANK DeLORA   fdelora@hotmail.com   **Page 2 of 2**

Innovation Technologies, Grand Prairie, TX   1979–2005
Provided information technology consulting to more than 200 clients.

CTO—Technical Advisor
Designed and built computer systems and guided businesses in the use of technology.

Technology & Business Solutions

- Enhanced product development speed and manufacturing change by melding CNC machines, CAD system, and company network into one functional unit.
- Overcame critical limitation in data storage capabilities especially geared to small computer systems by creating multi-processor software system.
- Achieved 100% independence of IT services with minimal disruption or downtime for manufacturing division post-sale from parent company.
- Enabled business office of major Christian school system to operate for seven years at very low cost by providing pro-bono IT services.
- Eliminated downtime for mid-size manufacturing firm by designing and constructing computer center.
- Led turnaround of stalled business project, achieving completion under extreme time deadline.

Cross-Functional Collaboration

- Cut IT expenses 62% by collaborating with multiple internal departments to consolidate computing functions onto one system.
- Increased search speed 60X to 90X by conceiving and pioneering data access solution.
- Facilitated correction of product failures by introducing CAD to reluctant manufacturing client.

Business Process Automation

- Contributed to 5X growth for mail order business, with negligible staff increase, by developing and implementing customized accounting package.
- Automated repetitive processes to create labor savings and business efficiencies.
- Resolved major inefficiencies in resource usage through in-depth research of office workflows.

Network Design

- Designed and implemented network system for financial services company, enabling rapid and efficient handling of investments, trading, and client accounts.
- Minimized system duplication and waste more than 80% for manufacturing company through design and implementation of unified computer network.

Strategic Planning

- Reduced IT spending for client to 67% of industry norm, representing less than 1% of sales, for 14 consecutive years.
- Cofounded and led local Computer Business Association for five years.

EDUCATION / AFFILIATIONS

B.A., *Accounting*, SOUTHERN METHODIST UNIVERSITY, Dallas, TX
A.A., *Accounting*, BROOKHAVEN COMMUNITY COLLEGE, Dallas, TX

Local Area Network Dealers Association, Founding Member
Novell Users Group, Dallas, TX, Founding Member

BARCLAY M. JONES

1015 Walker Road, Baltimore, MD 21202

Home (410) 682-6490　　　　barclayjones@verizon.net　　　　Mobile (410) 591-2810

Information Technology Executive

Strategically focused technology leader with outstanding record of planning and delivering high-quality systems and services aligned with organizational objectives. Deeply involved in business strategy, quality initiatives, and alignment of activities that drive growth, improve performance, and increase profitability. Extremely capable in leading global teams and leveraging technology to support corporate goals and drive revenue.

Strategic Planning	Project Management	IT Strategy
Cost Analysis	System Development	eCommerce
Software Development	BMC Remedy	ITIL Methodology

Experience and Achievements

PRICEWATERHOUSECOOPERS LLP　　　　　　　　　　　　　　　　　2000–Present
Global leader in assurance, tax, and advisory services with 160,000 employees and more than $25B in revenue.

Global Vice President of IT Service Quality, Baltimore, MD (2009–Present)

Direct staff of 150 IT professionals in multinational locations charged with tracking key indicators, measuring organizational performance, and delivering communications support across organization of more than 4,000 IT professionals. Achieved success and recognition on multiple projects working within annual budget of $4M.

✓ Created and maintain dashboard for CIO and executive audience to provide consolidated and comprehensive views of organizational performance, customer feedback, client satisfaction, information security threats, and other key operating metrics.

✓ Sponsor Catalog of Services representing $1B in annual technology investments. Project includes service definitions, key performance indicators, service levels, and pricing that supports more than 5,000 applications used throughout the organization.

✓ Lead projects to develop and execute communication strategies for the global IT organization, including an online collaboration environment and content management for all internal publications, databases, documents, and newsletters.

✓ Develop communication strategies that enable the organization to prioritize initiatives, keep teams informed of project activities, manage IT investments, and establish consistent service levels.

Director of Business Services, Baltimore, MD (2006–2009)

Utilizing ITIL methodology, led process-driven IT services department, located across 31 countries, with an operating budget of $5M and P&L responsibility for more than $80M.

✓ Spearheaded preparation of the annual business plan and a $225M budget highlighted with introduction of a Budget Book to enhance transparency of the process and to provide CFOs a higher-level knowledge of the connection between IT investment and business value received.

✓ Locked in savings of more than $3M annually by establishing more efficient and cost-effective processes for managing deployment and repair of PC equipment through a centralized depot. Served 20,000 users across 50,000 transactions per year.

✓ Deployed implementation of BMC Remedy to 5,000 users in 140 countries. Project identified, tracked, and managed more than 50,000 new incidents per month.

Continued

Strategy: Showcase a progressive career with one of the world's leading financial advisory firms and highlight a series of sophisticated technology projects that spanned the global operation.

BARCLAY M. JONES – Page 2

Home (410) 682-6490   barclayjones@verizon.net   Mobile (410) 591-2810

PRICEWATERHOUSECOOPERS LLP, continued

Director of Tax Technology Services, Charlotte, NC (2002–2006)

Managed 100-person, U.S.-based tax and IT group that created technology strategies, identified investment opportunities, developed infrastructure systems, and implemented enterprise-wide software applications. Managed $50M budget with full P&L responsibility. Member of the PricewaterhouseCoopers Technology Architecture Team that recommended international standards for application architectures and networks.

✓ Authored and published PricewaterhouseCoopers' first set of standards for Local Area Network technologies and oversaw the design and installation at 60 offices throughout the organization.

✓ Recommended and led a $40M investment in developing a tax document management system that stored more than 5TB of data and enabled scanning, storing, and sharing of documents. Platform resulted in profitability exceeding $1B and was recognized as the first virtual tax practice in the industry.

✓ Led eCommerce initiatives and supported online systems for tax consulting, audit, and assurance services, including a complete information security infrastructure for 300 clients that drove revenue of more than $10M annually.

✓ Collaborated with IT leaders in UK, Germany, Australia, and Canada to leverage investments and support common initiatives. Developed common platforms that resulted in 10% reduction in IT investment and increased quality of services to multinational clients.

Development & Infrastructure Manager, Charlotte, NC (2000–2002)

Directed software development, infrastructure engineering, quality assurance, and Tier 0 through Tier 4 support for the U.S. tax practice. Managed staff of 50 and prepared annual budget of more than $5M.

✓ Wrote multiple tax software applications, including a multistate tax apportionment system that resulted in more than $10M of increased revenue.

✓ Led design, implementation, and postdeployment support of the organization's first electronic mail system with total expenditure of less than $100,000.

Education and Certifications

B.S., Computer Information Systems   University of Maryland, 1999

ITIL Service Management Methodologies, V2, V3

Complete 40+ Continuing Professional Education (CPE) credits annually.

Robert E. Wilson

1002 Walker Road, Charlotte, NC 28272

Home: (704) 459-8761   robertwilson@gmail.com   Cell: (704) 459-6249

Infrastructure Enterprise Architect
Director ~ Leader

Maximize technology resources to support strategic business initiatives

Proven record of recovering stalled projects; driving complex systems integration; and developing robust, high-quality infrastructure to support business processes. Talent for developing high-performing teams that deliver successful solutions. Full complement of project and business management skills. Ability to communicate, collaborate, and create synergy at all levels of the organization to move projects forward.

Core Competencies

• Strategic Planning	• IT Strategy	• Cost Reduction
• Joint Ventures	• IT Infrastructure	• Risk Management
• Restructuring	• Ecommerce	• Workforce Planning
• Change Management	• Cost/Benefit Analysis	• Regulatory Compliance

PROFESSIONAL EXPERIENCE

SALLIE MAE, Charlotte, North Carolina   1996–Present

Nation's leading organization for saving, planning, and paying for higher education. Manages more than $184M in educational loans through colleges, universities, and state and federal agencies. With the student lending program recently taken over by the US government, Sallie Mae is restructuring and implementing multiple cost-reduction initiatives.

Director of Enterprise Architecture (2009–Present)

- ✓ Lead team of 7 in architecturally crafting business and technical change initiatives to convert legacy loan-servicing system to a commercial, vendor-supported software application. On target to deliver **savings of more than $50M** over next 3 years.

- ✓ Establish direction on service levels, negotiate with vendors and business sponsors, integrate with internal and web-based customer systems, and coordinate with application development team to establish direction for overall system design and implementation.

- ✓ Champion innovative and successful interface design using an ontological-based approach to configure interfaces and provide common language for use within the disparate application systems and by users.

- ✓ **Launched SOA governance team** to manage cultural changes and user resistance to long-entrenched processes and mindsets. Developed best practices, trained application development teams, and ensured technical compliance.

Senior Technical Architect (2005–2009)

- ✓ Shepherded architectural project for successful implementation of Department of Education's direct-lending contract after government takeover of student loan program. Collaborated with CEO and other executives to establish separate environments for technical and application infrastructures to provide a single view of all existing and new loans serviced by Sallie Mae.

~Page 1~

Strategy: Start with a branding statement and provide ample evidence throughout the resume. Note that the bullet points are crisp and demonstrate strong problem-solving skills.

Senior Technical Architect (2005–2009), continued

✓ Developed architectural framework and data collection methodology for repository of business processes and technologies and spearheaded its use to establish an opportunity for a UK subsidiary. Project provided key information for team of new executives and identified more than **$50M in cost savings opportunities** over a 3-year period.

Technical Architect (2000–2005)

✓ Led architectural review of loan origination process, designed data warehouse, and created platform used for integration of systems when Sallie Mae acquired USA Group.

✓ Assumed architecture responsibilities late in the troubled development cycle of Open Net File Management. Turned the project around for a successful implementation.

Business Technology Advisor (1996–2000)

✓ Served as lead architect on a $30M, 5-year effort to develop a new loan origination and guarantee servicing platform. Project required application design patterns, frameworks, and a method to provide web access and resulted in Sallie Mae becoming a reference customer for IBM.

✓ Led research, development, and implementation of a large, web-enabled mainframe application, using an object-oriented approach to encapsulate existing 3270 program methodology.

PLATFORMS ~ SYSTEMS ~ TECHNOLOGY

• SOA	• WSM	• Oracle	• DB2	• IDMS
• Eagle II	• REST	• SOAP	• Java	• COBOL
• CICS	• FEAF	• TOGAF	• ESB	• WSDL
• SQL Server	• ExportSS	• XML Schema	• UDDI	• WE-Security

PERSONAL PROFILE

Education: University of Virginia, Charlottesville, VA   **B.S., Computer Science**

Publications: *Encapsulating the 3270 as Program Methodology*
CICS Transaction 390 Magazine 2000, Vol. 2, Issue 7.

Presentations: *Encapsulating the 3270 as Program Methodology*
Presented at Computer Collaborators, CA World 2000, Washington, DC.

~Page 2~

Robert E. Wilson
Home: (704) 459-8761   robertwilson@gmail.com   Cell: (704) 459-6249

Emily A. Liu

6062 S Arapahoe Circle
Mobile: (303) 453-0087

Greenwood Village, CO 80015
Email: emily.a.liu@q.com

Vice President of Engineering

Medical Devices • Telecom • Consumer Electronics • Digital-Audio Processing

Award-winning R&D Engineer, Inventor, and Engineering Manager with 20+ years of experience advancing the state-of-the-art in digital design. Versatile and creative developer of extremely profitable products in diverse markets. Fluent English and Mandarin. Active secret clearance.

- **Technical Expertise**: Ultra low-power circuitry, CMOS, bipolar IC design, digital signal processing, and embedded software. Diverse applications include wireless telecom, medical devices, consumer electronics, audio, and hearing aids.
- **Business Savvy**: Licensing and business-development expertise. Deep experience in the business side of entrepreneurial startups and emerging technologies.
- **Creativity**: More than 20 inventions—inventor or co-inventor on 15 commercialized patents. Recognized expert in signal processing, hearing aid technologies, and speech recognition.

Technical Proposals	Digital, RF, and Analog Design	System Analysis and Design
Program Management	Business Process Improvement	FDA and FTC Compliance
Audio Signal Processing	Strategic Product Planning	Technology Evaluation

Professional Experience

MICROMED DEVICES, INC., Denver, CO   **2009–2011**

Class II medical-device company that develops innovative insulin-pump technologies for type-1 diabetes.

Vice President, Research & Development

Managed $6M budget and 18 scientists and engineers. Led all technical development of M2 products, including design, verification and validation (V&V), testing, and product transition from R&D to manufacturing. Improved compliance processes, quality controls, and teamwork.

- Turned around troubled design of first product—within one month—by pinpointing root causes of unresolved mechanical and electrical problems.
- Defined and implemented V&V protocols and testing. Collaborated closely with manufacturing. Set up comprehensive practice audits and prepared documentation that led to 510(k) application.

MED-RF, INC., LaJolla, CA   **2007–2009**

Formerly Medtronic Development LLC. Outsources development-and-research services for medical-device companies.

Promoted to Vice President of Product Development (2008–2009)

Program Manager and Consultant (2007–2008)

Led team of electrical, mechanical, and software engineers that supported Fortune 100 clients by providing complex technical proposals, project plans, budgets and financial forecasts, product-design processes, and design execution. Produced 16 successful and extremely complex proposals for clients.

- Led major redesign of *Port Identifier System* that led to a large new contract. New design incorporated a 3-D antenna array, which enabled accurate 3-D detectability at 5.98 MHz—vastly superior to the original design, and easier to manufacture.
- Designed a piezoelectric pump and fluidic module—implantable, RF, and inductively powered—for an anti-obesity product marketed by Johnson & Johnson.

Page 1

Strategy: Lead with an expansive summary that incorporates a branding statement as its first sentence. Follow with a concise presentation of strong engineering achievements.

Emily A. Liu   *Mobile: (303) 453-0087*   *Email: emily.a.liu@q.com*   *Page 2*

DIGITAL OPTICS CORPORATION, Beaverton, OR   2002–2007

Developed FDA class III (implantable) ophthalmic products for patients with retinal degenerative diseases.

Promoted to Vice President of Research & Development (2004–2007)
Director of Product Development (2002–2004)

Transformed a proof-of-concept prototype into a highly successful product. Met tight deadlines and coordinated cross-functional engineering teams—dispersed throughout the U.S. and Canada—including biomedical engineers, physicists, contract manufacturers, and animal-research scientists.

- Completed development of initial product—the *Artificial Silicon Retina Device*—a semiconductor-based, neural-stimulation device implanted in sub-retinal space of the eye.

- Implemented design-control process and key FDA QSR requirements. Established manufacturing facility, including class 1000 clean rooms, in Oregon.

DIGITAL EAR, INC., Walnut Creek, CA   2000–2002

Leading middle-ear implant hearing device company. Approximately $2 million annual revenue and 24 employees.

Vice President, Research and Development

Directed all engineering and research. Completed design enhancements to the semi-implantable product, developed a totally implantable product, and supported products already deployed.

- Developed an implantable (middle-ear) hearing device incorporating ASICs, DSP, custom microphone, rechargeable battery technology, biocompatible enclosures, and associated hardware and software.

- Designed advanced iterations of the *Floating Mass Transducer*, a micro-electromagnetic component that connects to the ossicular chain of the middle-ear.

SONIC INSTRUMENTS, INC., Pleasanton, CA   1998–2000

Early-stage company that developed advanced hearing instruments based on novel one-size-fits-all technology and software audiometer. Approximately 20 employees.

Vice President, Engineering

Led product design, verification, and transfer to production for hearing aid and audiometer products.

- Developed several new ITC and CIC-type hearing aid products incorporating proprietary shell technology, disposable silicone tips, DSP, and advanced analog electronic modules.

- Strengthened intellectual property (IP) portfolio with 4 new patents and 10 new filings. Successfully negotiated cross-licensing agreements for Sonic's technology.

LIN-E-EAR CORPORATION, Longwood, CO   1987–1998

Worldwide leader in hearing aid products. Approximately $200 million total assets and more than 1000 employees globally.

Promoted to Director of Electronic Systems and Microelectronics (1996–1998)
Promoted to Manager of Electro-Acoustics and Electronic Technologies (1989–1996)
Senior IC Engineer (1987–1989)

Recruited by former colleagues at Hughes Research as senior EE designer for audio signal processing circuits of the new hearing aid development project.

- Designed and patented a programmable signal compressor subsystem for advanced hearing aid IC that incorporated low-power, bipolar, nonlinear circuits including a novel analog multiplier.

- Executed a successful public stock offering (IPO) in 1993, as member of original Hughes Research team that founded Lin-E-Ear Corporation in 1987.

ADDITIONAL EXPERIENCE

HUGHES RESEARCH LABORATORIES, Palo Alto, CA (1982–1987): Member of Technical Staff, Audio Signals Group, Medical Applications Laboratory (1985–1987). Member of Technical Staff, Mobile Baseband Group, Special Terminals Development Laboratory (1982–1985).

EDUCATION

M.S., Electrical Engineering, Stanford University, Palo Alto, CA, 1982

B.S., Electrical Engineering, University of California, Los Angeles, CA, 1981

CHAPTER 11

Resumes for Managers and Executives in Accounting, Corporate Finance, Banking, and Financial/Investment Management

- Accounting Manager/Payroll Administrator
- Division Controller/Chief Financial Officer
- Financial Management Executive
- Senior Tax Executive
- Finance Executive
- Chief Operations Officer/Chief Risk Officer
- Finance and General Management Executive
- Financial Investment Manager
- Financial Services Manager
- Global Business Relationship Manager/Financial Analyst
- Senior Financial Executive/Vice President
- Investment Services Financial Executive/Director
- Financial Risk Manager

DAVID L. PRINCE

P.O. Box 802 ▪ San Diego, CA 92001 ▪ 609.555.4560 ▪ dlprince@hotmail.com

SUMMARY

Accounting Manager / Payroll Administrator combining cross-functional competencies in all phases of accounting, information systems, and staff supervision and management. Proficient in managing and developing financial reports and controls using staffing and technology efficiencies. Ability to contribute as a team player and interface with professionals on all levels. Expertise includes:

- Payroll Administration
- Automated Accounting Information Systems
- Inventory Control & Purchasing
- Financial Reporting

- Quarterly & Year-End Reporting
- Corporate Tax Compliance
- Corporate Accounting
- Job Costing

PROFESSIONAL EXPERIENCE

Platinum Choice, Los Angeles, CA   2006–Present
    CONTROLLER (2009–Present)
    ACCOUNTANT (2008–2009)
    OUTSOURCED ACCOUNTANT (2006–2008)

Plan, manage, and provide leadership for accounting department, including payroll, budgeting, cost accounting, managerial accounting, financial reporting, financial analysis, and purchasing. Scope of responsibility spans both the corporate and divisional levels, including two out-of-state subsidiary business units. Provide financial expertise to outside firms, including banks, auditors, and government authorities.

- Manage $4 million in annual operating budgets allocated for personnel, facilities, and administrative expenses.
- Established improved accounts receivable and collection policies that reduced outstanding receivables by 25% during the first quarter.
- Implemented automated cost accounting systems to analyze profit improvement opportunities.
- Worked in cooperation with management teams to restructure corporate pricing on all major product lines, resulting in a 14% profit improvement.
- Oversaw implementation and development of MRP system, ensuring the integration of all reporting processes.
- Successfully guided the company through annual outside audits.
- Complete timely federal and multi-state sales, payroll, and property tax return filings.

Smith, Jones, & Heath, CPAs, Lake Forest, CA   2003–2006
    ACCOUNTING CONSULTANT

Recruited to provide diverse finance, accounting, payroll, and tax-preparation functions for one of the largest independent Orange County CPA firms.

- Prepared financial statements: payroll; sales and property tax returns; and federal, state, and local income tax returns.
- Streamlined accounting processes to reduce workpaper and document requirements.
- Worked closely with clients in structuring general ledgers and evaluating their software needs.

CONTINUED

Strategy: Align resume with career goals by emphasizing payroll expertise in the Summary section, position descriptions, achievement statements, and Computer Skills section.

DAVID L. PRINCE	609.555.4560	PAGE TWO

PROFESSIONAL EXPERIENCE (CONTINUED)

Taylor Baking Company; Chicago, IL   1993–2002
DIVISIONAL SALES MANAGER (1998–2002)
ROUTE SALES SUPERVISOR (1996–1998)
SALES ROUTE DRIVER (1993–1996)
Total responsibility for all sales and operations in the Northern Illinois and Southern Wisconsin territory.
Hired, trained, and directed the development of approximately 20 employees.

- Managed high-profile territory, generating new business and maximizing existing account sales for more than 400 accounts.
- Sales talent to cultivate relationships, expand customer base, and maximize account sales.
- Managed the route sales force and supervised all inside operational personnel at various locations.

EDUCATION

San Diego State University
BA IN BUSINESS MANAGEMENT (1991)

COMPUTER SKILLS

- Experienced with the following software for payroll preparation: QuickBooks/QuickBooks Pro, Peachtree, PenSoft Payroll, Class, and CFS Payroll Systems.
- Skilled in most accounting software programs, including SYSPRO, Peachtree, QuickBooks, QuickBooks Pro, Accountants ATB, T-value, Depreciation Solutions, Class, WS-2, Preform Plus, ProSystems, and Quicken.
- Proficient in Excel, Word, Access, WordPerfect, and GoldMine.

JULIA JACKSON, CPA, CMA
Email: jjackson@mail.com

204 East 5th Avenue
New York, New York 10011

Mobile: (718) 567-8904
Residence: (914) 764-0967

DIVISIONAL CONTROLLER/CHIEF FINANCIAL OFFICER

Senior accounting professional with 14 years of experience in financial reporting, analysis, forecasting, budgeting, cash management, auditing, and controls for multi-site manufacturing and industrial organizations. Solid interpersonal skills and cross-functional team interactions (Sales, Production, Information Systems, Human Resources) coupled with effective leadership abilities. Core competencies include:

- A/R, A/P & G/L Account Analysis
- Financial Statements & Management Reporting
- Operating & Capital Budget Preparation
- Tax Reporting & Preparation
- Credit Reviews & Approvals
- Job Costing & Variance Analysis
- Banking & Insurance Management

- Accounting Policies/Procedures Development & Establishment
- Inventory Management & Reconciliation
- Staff Training & Development
- HR, Benefits & Risk Management
- Automated Financial System & Business Software (PC & Mainframe)
- Regulatory Compliance

PROFESSIONAL EXPERIENCE

NORTHEAST FORGING INDUSTRIES, INC. — New York, New York   2008 to 2011
A division of Regulation Corporation, with 2 locations and combined annual revenues of $85 million. Company supplies carbon, alloy, and stainless forgings primarily to heavy truck, construction, automotive, aircraft, and oil industries.

DIVISIONAL CONTROLLER
Challenged to hire/train professional staff, strengthen divisional accounting functions, and implement/maintain financial controls. Managed a staff of 4 responsible for A/R, A/P, Payroll/Benefits, and Cost Accounting. Reported directly to site General Managers with dotted line to Corporate Controller.

Key Accountabilities & Accomplishments
- Managed month-end/year-end close and financial statement preparation. Analyzed balance sheets, P&L, cash flows, and budget variances. Assisted operational management to resolve variances.
- Supported corporate and divisional strategic planning efforts through forecasting and operational/capital budget development activities.
- Managed physical inventory ($12 million combined value) and reviewed for obsolescence, movement, and valuation.
- Established and maintained credit/collection policies; reviewed and managed divisional banking and lending relationships. Supervised and audited daily bank account reconciliations for 3 cash accounts.
- Monitored self-funded insurance account and prepared monthly forecasts.
- Traveled monthly to Wisconsin location for staff training and supervision. Developed strong relationships with operational managers.
- Oversaw external audit process and provided all necessary worksheets/data to minimize billable hours.

Page 1 of 2

Strategy: For this recently downsized individual seeking a divisional controller position with a manufacturing corporation, stress hands-on corporate accounting experience over public accounting background.

PROFESSIONAL EXPERIENCE (continued)

CHEYENNE, INCORPORATED—Milwaukee, Wisconsin   2003 to 2007
A $40 million, wholly owned subsidiary of Point Footwear, Incorporated (acquired in 1996). A manufacturer and global distributor of industrial footwear and protective clothing.

CONTROLLER

Recruited to manage a professional staff of 5 responsible for credit management, A/R, A/P, cost accounting, and MIS. Challenged to hire and train staff in key management positions (accounting, credit, MIS) vacated shortly after merger. Additionally, challenged to match reporting/procedures to parent corporation. Position reported to Cheyenne COO with dotted line to corporate CFO (Point Footwear).

- Oversaw financials; performed divisional reporting, analysis, forecasting, and budgeting.
- Tracked operational improvements versus targets; assisted operational management in cost-savings initiatives and working-capital optimization.
- Oversaw MIS department; worked closely with IT staff to integrate parent requirements with existing automated financial systems.

CONLEY, MC DONALD & COMPANY—Milwaukee, Wisconsin   2002 to 2003
Local public accounting firm serving clients statewide.

AUDIT SENIOR

Performed auditing procedures, prepared monthly/quarterly statements and entries, and monitored performance of various clients including banking institutions and non-profits.

PRICEWATERHOUSE—Milwaukee, Wisconsin   2001 to 2002
Big 6 public accounting firm with 50+ offices nationwide.

AUDIT SENIOR

Performed external audits for manufacturing/industrial firms and informed senior managers of performance and findings.

CLIFTON GUNDERSON, LLP—Madison, Wisconsin   1996 to 2001
13th largest public accounting firm in U.S. with offices in 13 states.

AUDIT SUPERVISOR (1999 to 2001)
STAFF ACCOUNTANT/IN CHARGE (1996 to 1999)
Performed public accounting activities for client base of manufacturing and construction firms.

EDUCATION, CERTIFICATIONS & PROFESSIONAL AFFILIATIONS

Accounting Coursework (21 Credits)—Marquette University—Milwaukee, Wisconsin
BS (Finance)—University of Wisconsin—Madison, Wisconsin

Certified Management Accountant, 2003
Certified Public Accountant, 1996

American Institute of Certified Public Accountants (AICPA)
Wisconsin Institute of Certified Public Accountants (WICPA)
Financial Executives Institute (FEI)

ROBERT T. DANILOFF

402–835–8941
rtd@email.com
34223 Wind Mill Drive, Omaha, NE 68046

FINANCIAL MANAGEMENT EXECUTIVE
Expert in cost control, team building, and financial analysis

Results–oriented senior management professional with the reputation of a goal-oriented visionary and effective communicator. Effective in reorganizing, streamlining, and strengthening financial operations to maximize performance and profitability. Respond to operational and financial challenges with confidence, determination, and focus.

Strategic & Business Planning	Information Systems Management
Internal Financial Controls & Budgeting	Cash Management
Turnarounds, Acquisitions & Mergers	Regulatory Compliance

PROFESSIONAL EXPERIENCE

NATIONAL INVESTMENT, LTD., Omaha, Nebraska
(A four-broker dealer holding company with more than $350 million in annual revenues)

Chief Financial Officer — 2009 to 2011
Selected to lead the organization's financial operations post-acquisition. Member of the executive management team reporting to the CEO. Directed financial analysis; internal and regulatory reporting; cash management; G/L, A/P, and A/R; tax reporting; budgeting; forecasting; internal and external auditing; and payroll processing activities that led to long-term improvements in cost savings, profitability, and productivity. Full P&L responsibility for a $60 million operating and $2.5 million finance budget.

- *Reduced monthly reporting processing time by 20 man hours, delivered reports in half the time, and significantly improved reporting accuracy* by centralizing and consolidating G/L closing procedures.

- *Championed key performance metrics* in soundness, profitability, growth, and productivity for broker-dealers, *profitably impacting goal attainment and performance.*

INVESTMENT & HOLDINGS CORP., Arlington, Virginia
($100 million holding company acquired by American National Bank)

Chief Administrative Officer — 2006 to 2009
Selected to turn around numerous leadership challenges and restore operational stability. Managed a $30 million operating budget and a $1.5 million finance budget. Directed a 110–person staff in finance, brokerage operations, technology, and project management.

- Implemented cost controls, reporting requirements, and training to control escalating expense run rates. *Within two months, reduced expenses by 10%, generating a cost savings of $3 million annually.*

- Change-managed failing customer service initiatives. *Deployed new training, hiring practices, incentive programs, and processes, increasing customer satisfaction ratings by 22% and improving employee morale within the first year of implementation.*

- *Negotiated and structured the clearing agreement that achieved a $500,000 savings* over three years and resulted in significantly improved and personalized service.

Continued

Strategy: Turn a responsibility-based resume into an accomplishment-oriented sales document, positioning this individual as a senior-level executive.

ROBERT T. DANILOFF   Page 2   402–835–8941

INVESTMENT & HOLDINGS CORP., continued

Chief Financial Officer — 2004 to 2006
Promoted following acquisition to manage all accounting and finance functions for this newly acquired holding company. Conducted due diligence that precipitated a $9 million acquisition. Oversaw regulatory relations and compliance.

- Pioneered the corporate data warehouse to improve information management. Collaborated with outside consultants to consolidate disparate reporting and tracking processes. *Within first 100 days of implementation, reduced vendor billing cycle times by 30 days, facilitated production of monthly reports to the third business day, and improved revenue-forecasting accuracy from 85% to 95%.*

- Turned around 2.5 years of unprofitability by implementing expense controls and a contract approval and negotiation process. *Reduced monthly operating expenses by $200,000 within 30 days, achieved immediate profitability, and sustained profitability for 38 consecutive months.*

- Established employee training and support programs to turn around low morale, reduce excessive overtime, and improve financial management. Executed mentoring and relationship-building programs, implemented standards and values, and supported training programs. *Reduced overtime by 75% and slashed turnover by more than half.*

FIRST AMERICAN NATIONAL BANK (n/k/a AMSOUTH), Birmingham, Alabama
(Providing financial services to individuals, small and mid-sized businesses, and large corporations)

Hired as a Deposit Operations Manager and fast-tracked through a series of increasingly responsible management positions over a 10-year period. **Developed CSR and Teller Certification Programs** as Branch Operations Manager and **established the organization's first-ever budget processing and controls** as Marketing Retail Program Manager.

Senior Vice President / Strategic Project Director, Nashville, Tennessee — 2003 to 2004
Managed strategic and business planning, directed budgeting activities, and championed nontraditional revenue-generating initiatives. Reported directly to the Vice Chairman.

Brokerage and Trust Division Controller, Nashville, Tennessee — 2001 to 2003
Marketing Retail Program Manager, Nashville, Tennessee — 1999 to 2001

CREDENTIALS / LICENSES

Passed **Certified Public Accountant** exam on first try — 2009
NASD Series 7, 24, 27, and 65

EDUCATION

Bachelor of Science in Accounting
Graduate coursework in Computer Hardware, Marketing, Economics, and Management
University of Tennessee, Knoxville, Tennessee

Continuing education courses in Financial Analysis, Regulatory Financial Operations and Reporting, and Banking

James A. Hastings

1803 Harmon Boulevard
Shaker Heights, OH 44122
216-881-1928
james.hastings@att.net

SENIOR TAX EXECUTIVE
Expert in International and Domestic Taxation Issues

Resourceful and intuitive tax executive respected for expertise on international and domestic taxation. Regularly invited to speak before forums on international taxation, and personally argued private letter ruling before the IRS in Washington, DC, with regard to favorable tax treatment theory formulated on behalf of a multimillion-dollar acquisition. Successfully integrated legal background into a career as a tax expert, providing clients with sound guidance in tax planning and management processes. Regarded as a hands-on manager who is capable of building strong team environments and fosters a sense of pride and integrity among the staff.

Areas of Expertise

- Organizational Restructuring
- Business Development
- Account Management
- Staff Building, Coaching, and Mentoring
- Foreign Tax Credit: source of income, allocation and apportionment, deemed paid credit, and excess limitation/excess credit
- Subpart F: contract manufacturing, and branch rule

- Partnerships and Check-the-Box
- Foreign Currency
- Foreign Taxation: permanent establishment, VAT, GST, withholding taxes, employment taxes, tax treaties, and choice of entity
- Recordkeeping, Reporting, and Disclosure
- Transfer Pricing
- ProFX Tax Preparation Software: BNA
- Planning Software: CCH, BNA, and RIA online and CD Tax Research Tools

CAREER HIGHLIGHTS

JENSEN & PLATTE, LLP — Cleveland, OH
(Major public accounting firm providing broad business advisory and traditional compliance services to middle-market businesses. Employs 1,300 employees at 12 offices throughout Ohio and Michigan.)

PARTNER, June 2008–present
Selected to oversee integration of Cleveland office following firm's acquisition of Clifton Gunderson's Cleveland office. Identified key objectives and goals and oriented both staff and clients on new services while continuing to oversee ongoing projects. **Key Accomplishments:**
- Successfully transitioned staff and clients into new corporate culture.
- Established productivity goals related to chargeable hours, business growth, and service delivery.
- Retained 100% of client base in 16-month period following acquisition.
- Identified new opportunities that melded with new organization and secured new client financial institution and SEC relationships, while increasing personal billings 15%.
- Provided hands-on leadership for successful IT conversions.

GARDNER CLIFTON, LLC — Cleveland, OH
(Among the largest independent public accounting firms in the United States, with 45 offices in 12 states, serving a wide array of publicly and closely held companies.)
MANAGING PARTNER, CLEVELAND / FIRM-WIDE INTERNATIONAL TAX COORDINATOR, 2007–2008
PARTNER / FIRM-WIDE INTERNATIONAL TAX COORDINATOR, 2003–2007
TAX MANAGER / FIRM-WIDE INTERNATIONAL TAX COORDINATOR, 1999–2003
INTERNATIONAL TAX SPECIALIST, 1997–1999
Progressed through organization, culminating in oversight of Cleveland office and firm-wide international tax operations. Accountable for recruitment, hiring, supervision, staff performance and evaluation, fiscal planning, and administration of 15-person regional office. Additionally, provided direct oversight of partners and staff on all matters relating to international tax planning and compliance. Enacted directives on technology and expertise syndication.

Page 1

Strategy: Enliven a complex tax background by incorporating multiple business contributions as well as areas of professional expertise.

James A. Hastings

Résumé - Page Two
james.hastings@att.net

CAREER HIGHLIGHTS

GARDNER CLIFTON, LLC *(continued…)*
Key Accomplishments:

- Forged relationship with major commercial clients, contributing significantly to growth of Cleveland-office revenue from $887,000 to $1,281,000 and personal book of business from $140,000 to over $500,000 within four years.
- Coordinated $50 million leveraged acquisition of U.S.-based multinational group with subsidiaries in Belgium, Denmark, France, the United Kingdom, and Hong Kong.
- Collaborated with institutional lenders, domestic and foreign law firms, and foreign-chartered accountants to carry out above deal. Provided complex structural planning models and solved "deal-busting" EU corporate-directive problems.
- Invited on numerous occasions to speak on U.S. tax matters affecting international business both domestically and abroad.
- As member of international tax committee, traveled extensively overseas, provided multinational tax consulting services, and developed and instituted international tax training programs.

Prior Professional Experience
TAX STAFF, Meaden & Moore, Inc. — Cleveland, OH, 1995–1997
TAX STAFF, Packer Thomas & Co. — Warren, OH, 1993–1995
ATTORNEY-AT-LAW — Cleveland, OH, 1990–1993

EDUCATION

FRANKLIN THOMAS BACKUS SCHOOL OF LAW,
CASE WESTERN UNIVERSITY — Cleveland, OH
JURIS DOCTOR, 1989

UNIVERSITY OF WISCONSIN — Milwaukee, WI
BBA, ACCOUNTING, 1986

PROFESSIONAL DEVELOPMENT

- American Bar Association, **TAX SECTION MEETINGS,** twice annually, since 1998
- Internal Revenue Service Institute on **CURRENT ISSUES IN INTERNATIONAL TAXATION,** George Washington University, Washington, DC, 1997, 1998, 2006
- Florida Bar and Florida CPAs Joint **INTERNATIONAL TAX INSTITUTE,** Miami, FL, 1999, 2000, 2004
- **CITE INTERNATIONAL TAX SEMINARS,** Toronto, ON, and Los Angeles, CA, 2003, 2005
- Harvard University, Tufts University, and MIT Joint Program on **NEGOTIATION FOR SENIOR EXECUTIVES,** Cambridge, MA, 2007

PUBLISHING CREDITS / CONFERENCES / AFFILIATIONS

- "S-Corp Shareholder Salaries: Source Questions," International Taxation, 8 Mar. 2010, p. 1,500
- Ohio Export Launch, State of Ohio, June 2009
- 10th Immigration and Naturalization Law Seminar, Federal Bar Association, December 2006
- American Institute of Certified Public Accountants (AICPA)
- American Bar Association (ABA); 10-year Member Tax Section, Foreign Activities of U.S. Taxpayers Committee
- International Fiscal Association (IFA)
- Ohio Bar
- Ohio Society of Certified Public Accountants
- Board of Directors, Cleveland School of the Arts, 2007–2009
- Board of Directors Cleveland Engineering Society, 2006–2008

MICHAEL D. KARAS

3245 Shadow Trail — Old Hickory, Tennessee 37138

Home (615) 758-4467 — mikekaras@mindspring.com

EQUIPMENT LEASING & FINANCE EXECUTIVE

Top-producing equipment leasing and finance specialist with more than 10 years of experience in originating, negotiating, structuring, and closing profitable deals. Cultivate and maintain strong, established network of contacts with bank officers, lease brokers and dealers, and equipment vendors. Possess expert knowledge of lease financing terms, lease structures, documentation procedures, and current tax and depreciation laws.

An articulate communicator able to convey complex information in meaningful terms. Adapt quickly to new circumstances and environments.

Advanced computer user in both PC and Macintosh environments. Experienced with MS Office (Excel, Word), InfoLease, InfoAnalysis, SuperTrump, LeasePak, Internet navigation and research, and email.

Experience Summary

‣ Manage all facets of leasing operations, including sales and marketing, structuring, documentation, and accounting.

‣ Follow through with a high degree of customer service to ensure repeat business from all sources.

‣ Proactively solicit new business prospects through direct contact, cold calling, networking, and referrals.

‣ Establish and maintain positive relationships with key equipment vendors to ensure profitable disposition of used equipment. Assist in the collection of delinquent accounts.

‣ Provide individual and group sales training to commercial and corporate bank officers, with a focus on how to recognize a qualified prospect.

Career History

VICE PRESIDENT 2005–Present
Volunteer Leasing Corporation / Volunteer Bank — Nashville, Tennessee

‣ Challenged to lead start-up operations for Volunteer Leasing's entry into the East Tennessee market, overseeing sales, documentation, and accounting. Presently manage a five-state territory comprised of MO, KS, KY, TN, and AR. Report to Group Vice President and Sales Manager.
‣ Target middle-market and large-ticket transactions, such as hi-tech, tractor-trailer, manufacturing, and energy management. Currently on track to generate $40 million in lease transactions for 2012.
‣ After Volunteer's merger with Northstar Bank in 2008, was selected as part of team to determine pricing and accounting systems for new, consolidated leasing department.

ASSISTANT VICE PRESIDENT 2003–2005
First National Bank — Knoxville, Tennessee

‣ Established new sales territory in East Tennessee, from Chattanooga to the Tri-Cities area. Reported to Group Vice President of Leasing.
‣ Closed $6 million in sales the first year; increased sales 66% the second year to $10 million.

Continued

Strategy: Use a combination format to avoid overlap of job duties; create an expansive Experience Summary to highlight areas of expertise right up front.

MICHAEL D. KARAS   mikekaras@mindspring.com   Page Two

Career History (continued)

BANK OFFICER.. 2001–2003
National Exchange Bank — Memphis, Tennessee

▸ Collaborated with bank lending officers, lease brokers, and equipment vendors to provide small-ticket leasing services. Sales territory included entire southeastern U.S. except Florida. Reported to First Vice President.

▸ Generated $5 million in annual transactions.

ASSISTANT SALES MANAGER 2000–2001
US Lease Plans, Inc. — Hendersonville, Tennessee

▸ Networked with customers, developed sales leads, and strengthened relationships with other leasing companies and funding sources.

▸ Prepared documentation for equipment lease transactions, including UCC filings, resolutions, master lease documents, and other supporting documentation.

Education

BACHELOR OF ARTS — Marketing — Minor in German — 2000
Vanderbilt University — Nashville, Tennessee

Affiliations

▸ Tennessee Trucking Association
▸ National Association of Equipment Lessors
▸ Equipment Lessors Association

William Hall

H: 212-877-2323 ▪ M: 917-545-7766 ▪ hall@gmail.com
55-01 Vernon Boulevard ▪ Long Island City, NY 11101

Chief Operations Officer/Chief Risk Officer

Executive Profile

- **OPERATIONAL EXCELLENCE** – Excel at creating the vision for and building operational infrastructures that systematize processes, eliminate redundancies, reduce costs, and create corporate accountability.

- **RISK ACCOUNTABILITY** – Skilled at inaugurating initiatives to ensure compliance, mitigate corporate exposure and risk, minimize financial hardship and loss, assess client creditworthiness, and ensure integrity of the company product mix.

- **THOUGHT LEADERSHIP** – Serve as key senior management team member on 20 corporate steering committees that affect every part of the business, including audit and regulatory examinations, technology, security, deal commitments, new products, and trade execution.

Operational Leadership Snapshot

▪ Risk & Control Metrics	▪ Business Continuity Planning	▪ Merger Readiness Assessments
▪ Loss Events Data Collection/Review	▪ Privacy/Records Management	▪ Audit & Regulatory Coordination
▪ Vendor Risk Assessments	▪ Fraud/Information Security	▪ Corporate Governance
▪ Sarbanes Oxley (SOX) Coordination	▪ Market Risk/Credit Exposure	▪ Business/Product Review

Professional Experience

BNP PARIBAS BANK, New York, NY — **1999 to Present**

SVP & SENIOR OPERATIONAL RISK OFFICER	New York, NY	2004 to Present
SVP OF OPERATIONAL RISK MANAGEMENT	Freeport, NY	2002 to 2004
SVP OF BROKERAGE OPERATIONS	Freeport, NY	1999 to 2002

Recruited to create the firm's inaugural operational risk team to track, analyze, and report operational risk and manage $1B in daily risk exposure. Established risk hierarchy, metrics, and reporting for Wachovia Securities and its major business units to trim operational expenses by 40% and save millions of dollars. Grew team to core functional area with $7M budget and staff of 30. Member of and subject matter expert for multiple internal steering committees tasked with supporting the corporate infrastructure and delivering superior ROI to stakeholders. *Key milestones include:*

- **REGULATORY COMPLIANCE** – Managed liability, regulatory, and reputational issues and achieved FINRA, OCC, and Basel II compliance by creating an internal database to track losses and pinpoint breakdowns in the process. Built processes to report $100K+ losses within 48 hours and developed monthly reporting to mitigate risk.

- **CREDIT EXPOSURE** – Partnered with treasury services group to systematize processes around reviewing credits, credit limits, and compliance.

- **LOSS PREVENTION** – Trimmed loss revenue from 3% to .5%, exceeding corporate expectations by 200% and saving millions of dollars versus historical losses. Introduced a novel initiative that tied individual bonuses for top 200 executives in firm to loss prevention performance.

- **BUSINESS/PRODUCT REVIEW** – Launched a product team to consolidate existing sales products, manage integrity of product mix, review new products' underwriting and fee structures, and assess performance of products.

- **TECHNOLOGY PROJECT AUDITS** – Review close to 500 technology projects and service-level agreements with 1,000+ vendors to keep mission-critical projects on track and allocate necessary funding.

LEADERSHIP SOUND BITES

- Recruited to BNP as one of the youngest Senior Vice Presidents in the firm.

- Began career at BNP managing 70% of the operations for BNP Securities despite no previous brokerage experience.

- Voted by peers as #1 functional staff within the business.

- Convinced 95% of staff to relocate from Freeport to New York City following BNP merger.

Continued…

Strategy: Highlight "sound bites" in a shaded box to emphasize leadership achievements that complement and balance the financial and technical accomplishments of this risk and compliance executive.

William Hall

H: 212-877-2323 ▪ M: 917-545-7766 ▪ hall@gmail.com
Page 2

BNP PARIBAS BANK

- **OPERATIONAL QUALITY ASSURANCE** – Key member of executive information security investment committee charged with auditing client reporting and creating QA processes. Currently developing an integrated portal to ensure consistent reporting and achieve regulatory compliance.

- **BUSINESS CONTINUITY/DISASTER RECOVERY** – Consolidated disaster recovery sites and recycled PCs to better use resources with no increase in costs.

- **MERGERS/OPERATIONAL INTEGRATIONS** – Successfully rolled out a risk management tool to track events, milestones, and readiness assessments in conjunction with merger activity.

- **OPERATIONS REENGINEERING** – Created the operational transformation to support straight-through processing for Wachovia Securities; saved $1.2M in year one while increasing capacity in several areas by 500%. Achieved objectives by conducting one-on-one meetings with brokers at 100 branches, tightening processes and redeploying staff without increasing headcount.

ABN-ANRO GROUP, New York, NY   1994 to 1999

PROJECT MANAGER OF OPERATIONAL ANALYSIS, 1997 to 1999

Developed/analyzed sales and operational metrics. Launched IT cost center and installed data platform that monitored the group's telephony and other computer networks for the company's start-up secured credit card business.

- Trimmed $750K off internal maintenance costs by developing a new IVR application that automated customer service tasks and decreased need for service center staff.

- Increased performance by 97% by reengineering the back-office management system.

LEADERSHIP SOUND BITES

- One of the youngest managers in the company's history.

- Recruited and hired staff of 40+ salespeople and 2 managers.

SALES MANAGER, HOME EQUITY GROUP, 1995 to 1997

Managed sales for the company's start-up home equity loans business.

- In just 4 months, designed and rolled out an online loan processing system.

- Implemented a troubleshooting system that automated trend analysis and general reporting features and constructed the group's first contact management system.

- Managed a 24/7 IT center handling 3,000+ calls per day.

OPERATIONAL ANALYST, 1994 to 1995

Managed process improvements, including an automated call system and back-office fulfillment process for the bank's cell phone service.

HALLCO COMPANY, Freeport, NY   1993 to 1994

Started up auto parts distribution company servicing the tri-state area.

Education

B.S., Business Administration, New York University   1991

ESTHER C. VAN DIJK

23 Oxford Avenue • Jersey City, NJ 07306 • Phone: (201) 357-1149 • evandijk@yahoo.com

FINANCE AND GENERAL MANAGEMENT EXECUTIVE

International Business Protocol — Turnarounds — Team-Building

Management Executive with MBA and 17 years of progressively responsible management experience. Expertise in turnaround and M&A management in highly competitive, global markets. Record of quickly integrating and revitalizing companies through:

- Strategic Planning
- Team Building & Leadership
- Company-Wide Action Plans
- Implementing Best Practices
- Finance & Accounting

- Budgeting, Pricing & Cost Control
- Information Technology
- Contract Negotiations
- Human Resources
- Cross-Cultural Communications

PROFESSIONAL EXPERIENCE

Fast-track, 17-year career with Mayne Group — a world leader in the steel industry headquartered in the UK, reporting $9.5 billion in sales and employing 47,000 personnel.

CFO AND ACTING PRESIDENT — Metal Works, Jersey City, NJ   2007 to Present

Recruited as CFO to manage integration of Metal Works — Mayne Group's newly acquired wholly owned subsidiary ($30 million, 120 employees). Shared general-management responsibilities with two other executives after upper-management transition. Restructured and turned around company to profitability through development and implementation of company-wide action plan. Accomplished integration within few months.

Achievements:

- Captured $1.5 million in savings within eight months through key role in instituting aggressive purchasing program.
- Ended union strike immediately after assuming role of president, acting as negotiation leader. Reached cost-effective three-year collective bargaining agreement.
- Selected and implemented integrated company-wide ERP business information system (MAPICS) comprising sales, purchasing, inventory control, and financial and cost accounting support.
- Eliminated 20% of clerical jobs, rendering $175,000 in annual savings.
- Increased major production line productivity 100% by soliciting input from technical industry experts to enhance manufacturing performance.

Other accomplishments include:

Financial Management

- Realized $0.5 million profits in first quarter 2010 after losses of $2 million in 2009.
- Initiated and successfully negotiated refinancing of $15 million in bank loans from outside lenders to internal Mayne loan, resulting in 3% decrease in interest rate (from 8% to 5%).

General Management/Human Resources

- Spearheaded cultural change through input from office and factory employees, instituting employee suggestion system and open-door policy.
- Thwarted lawsuit using mediation skills to reach agreement and settle out of court.
- Developed objectives-based performance measurement system as tool to create strong, cohesive teams, focused on common goals.
- Realized union relationship improvements through diplomatic negotiations.

Page 1 of 2

Strategy: Position this financial executive for a general management role by emphasizing her skills and achievements in both areas.

ESTHER C. VAN DIJK

Page 2 of 2

Phone: (201) 357-1149 • evandijk@yahoo.com

FINANCE CONTROLLER — Lyon Steel Company, Lyon, France   2004 to 2007

Appointed Finance Controller for Lyon Steel Company, a $75 million French global market leader of plated steel for the battery industry, employing 500 employees; 50% subsidiary of Mayne Group at time of hire. Member of management team; supervised staff of 25. Integrated Lyon Steel Company with Mayne Group and benchmarked with sister company in the United States.

Achievements:

- Facilitated 100% acquisition by Mayne Group in 2005.
- Played key role in successful turnaround from losses to profitability within one year by developing and implementing company-wide restructuring program.
- Authored business plan and developed and implemented system of key-performer indicators.
- Eliminated 15% of workforce while maintaining operability, focusing on high performers.

PLANT CONTROLLER — Mayne Group — Various sites, The Netherlands   1995 to 2004

Selected by senior management for prestigious position of Plant Controller in 2002 after proven abilities in increasingly responsible positions. Handled $1.5 billion Flat Products Division after various controlling assignments for 15,000-employee production site (1995 to 1998) and for $500 million Steel Processing & Trading Division (1998 to 2002). Directed 30 employees at largest of five product groups, consisting of three major plants with 2,200 employees.

Key accomplishments in various positions included:

- Facilitated $200 million cost cut by compiling categorized data of cost-reduction options.
- Reduced staff 10% for entire product group by initiating proactive and creative cost-reduction program following thorough financial and functional analysis.
- Handled communication with technical personnel: able to "translate" lingo and reach core issues.
- Joined international team that led $200 million joint venture initiative with an Italian steel manufacturer.
- Interfaced extensively with trade, production, and distribution companies.

EDUCATION, TRAINING, AND AFFILIATION

POST-MASTER'S CONTROLLERS PROGRAM (2001)
(Equivalent of American Ph.D. Program)
VRIJE UNIVERSITEIT — Amsterdam, The Netherlands

MASTER IN BUSINESS ADMINISTRATION (1994)
VRIJE UNIVERSITEIT — Amsterdam, The Netherlands

ASSOCIATION OF PROFESSIONAL CONTROLLERS
The Netherlands — member since 2001

BOARD MEMBER
METAL WORKS

Computer proficiency: SAP ECC 5 ERP; Infor ERP XA; Windows; Microsoft Office: Word, Excel, PowerPoint, Project, Outlook; Internet research.

DIANE CURRY

229 Windemere Road • Duluth, GA 30296
dianecurry@hotmail.com • Mobile: (770) 620-0309

* FINANCIAL INVESTMENT MANAGER *

Highly ethical, performance-focused finance professional seeking to apply strategic planning skills to the financial and investment industries. Eager to learn new skills, take on new challenges, and complete any education/licensing examinations necessary for career growth. Leverage expertise in client relations to advance business development activities in financial products and services. Strong comprehension of financial elements including assets, liabilities, cash flow, risk analysis, budgeting, and investment strategies. **Demonstrated core competencies include:**

⇒ Strategic Investment Planning	⇒ Client Relationship Management	⇒ Risk Management
⇒ Financial Planning & Analysis	⇒ Regulatory & Audit Affairs	⇒ Forecasting
⇒ Financial Modeling	⇒ Financial Reporting	⇒ Account Reconciliation

PERFORMANCE HIGHLIGHTS

- Directed high-level strategic planning to drive business development and expansion initiatives, including recommendations for financial investments.
- Perform financial needs analysis and recommend appropriate products to meet clients' needs.
- Delivered informational sales presentations to potential clients and assists throughout completion of application process while strengthening client relationships.
- Consistently exceeded Wachovia's sales goals, achieving President's Awards by outperforming competition and delivering high levels of customer service.

PROFESSIONAL EXPERIENCE

Lintek Group, Atlanta, GA   2009–Present
A nonprofit organization that provides benefits administration for Social Security recipients across the northern region of Georgia.

FINANCIAL CASE MANAGER
Administer financial management of Social Security benefits for recipients, providing expert assistance in budget planning and development, money management, bill payment, preparation of comprehensive financial reports, and negotiation of debt repayment plans. Personally manage Social Security benefits for 75 clients totaling $630K per year.

- Research and evaluate clients' history and background, manner of thinking, and capabilities, assisting clients by interacting with a wide range of agencies, including HUD, Department of Social Services, hospitals, and physicians.
- Act as liaison between service providers and recipients, discovering and making available every possible resource that will be beneficial to clients' well-being.
- Demonstrate good oral and written communication skills, interpretation capabilities, counseling techniques, problem-solving skills, and appropriate decision-making skills.

Curry Custom Homes, Duluth, GA   2000–2009
Curry Custom Homes provides outstanding value as it works to construct superior homes to meet clients' needs.

VICE PRESIDENT/CO-OWNER
Senior operating executive with full responsibility for strategic planning, sales and marketing, design services, tax and quarterly reporting, AP/AR, budgeting, and financial performance. Dedicated career to the start-up, development, and accelerated growth of the business. Demonstrated outstanding success in relationship building with community partners, organizations, and leaders to position the company as a strong corporate citizen, enhance market awareness, and drive long-term business development efforts.

CONTINUED

Strategy: Make the most of diverse business and financial experiences to help this job seeker transition to a role in financial services.

VICE PRESIDENT/CO-OWNER (Continued)

- Co-authored and executed business plan, built organizational structure, and contributed vision and thought leadership during startup and growth phases.
- Instrumental in growing business from zero to 15 custom homes valued at $6M over a 5-year period.
- Served as primary source for sales and marketing strategy, recommendations and solutions, big-picture perspective, and quantitative market research.
- Worked closely with advertising agency to determine market opportunity, go-to-market strategy, and development priorities targeting consumers.

Wachovia Bank (formerly First Union), Atlanta, GA   1996–2000

Financial services company provides online banking, bill pay, brokerage, loans, financial planning, investing, lending, and insurance services.

FINANCIAL SALES REPRESENTATIVE/CUSTOMER RELATIONS MANAGER

Increased sales by devising high-impact presentations promoting mutual funds and annuities to new and existing clients. Served as relationship manager, assessing client needs, providing financial advice, and determining customers' loan and deposit needs. Leveraged exceptional communications skills to deepen customer relationships. Acted as customers' advocate and secured suitable credit and cross-sell products and services. Demonstrated expertise in sales and credit, negotiating and prospecting, and accounting and finance.

- Created sales plan for each client, paying close attention to details while promoting an array of services, including mutual funds and annuities, credit and lending solutions, and personal banking products.
- Developed and maintained an in-depth knowledge of products and services, as well as knowledge of competitors and competitive products.
- Continually expanded referral network through contact with various internal and external partners.
- Partnered with leadership across multiple markets, utilizing best sales practices to increase production.
- Proactively increased client base through networking, business development activities, and leveraging client referrals.

EDUCATION & LICENSES

Bachelor of Science, Marketing
UNIVERSITY OF GEORGIA, Athens, GA

• • • •

(Previously held)
FINRA Series 6 and 63 Licenses
North Carolina Life and Health Insurance License

COMPUTER SKILLS

QuickBooks Pro; Microsoft Word, PowerPoint, and Excel

RESUME 72: BY MARJORIE SUSSMAN, ACRW, MRW, CPRW

BRAD W. ARMSTRONG

4865 First Street, Sylvania, OH 43560
419-555-5555 • bwa@emailservices.com

FINANCIAL SERVICES: SALES MANAGEMENT & OPERATIONS

Seventeen-year record of revitalization, growth, and profitability within highly competitive consumer-lending markets, building top-performing organizations on a foundation of operational excellence and dynamic sales. **Natural leader** with strong team-building skills and an abundance of positive energy to inspire, empower, and motivate beyond expectations. **Performance-focused executive** with hands-on approach to creating and managing efficient organizations. Highly competitive, utmost integrity, strong work ethic.

Proven Expertise

- **Strategic Planning:** Open-minded and collaborative in developing strategic direction, using creative vision to develop and implement long-term best practices.
- **Sales Management:** Gain competitive market advantage and set award-winning records through the conception, development, and implementation of aggressive sales campaigns.
- **Operations:** Demonstrated ability to streamline operations, reduce costs, boost profits, and lead district-wide initiatives that support strategic business objectives.
- **Personnel Development:** Personally involved in recruiting top talent, advancing individual careers, and molding top-producing sales teams.

Performance Highlights

- **Triggered** $28.7M bottom-line profit as District Manager.
- **Delivered** 40% average annual receivables growth against a 15% target over 7 years.
- **Exceeded** all goals to receive highest 2 annual performance ratings over 14 years.
- **Promoted** 7 people to district management and 32 to branch management.

Unique Value

- Continuous Process Improvement & Implementation
- Team Leadership, Coaching & Mentoring
- Change & Turnaround Management
- Sales & Relationship Building
- Training Seminars, Coaching Workshops & Manager Meetings
- Personal Engagement & Visibility with Teams
- Activity & Efficiency Metrics
- Customer Focus
- Recruitment & Retention of High-Quality Talent

EXPERIENCE

FIRST BANKING SERVICES COMPANY, Cleveland, OH, 1995–Present

Seventeen years of progressive experience with Fortune 50 FBS Company. Consistently a top performer, delivering revenue and profit growth against a backdrop of tumultuous organizational change and a turbulent economy. Boosted resiliency by perfecting sales execution, streamlining workflow, developing strong teams, and empowering individuals with unwavering support to improve bottom-line performance and organizational effectiveness.

▶**DISTRICT MANAGER,** 2002–Present
Promoted to accelerate growth and profitability of the district's mortgage and consumer-lending portfolio. Aggressively recruit and coach high-quality talent and create collaborative environments that encourage team dynamics and individual success. Recognized as first-class District Manager: Manage effectively in a matrix organization, always exceed targets, and continuously identify and implement process improvements for superior sales, customer service, underwriting, and fulfillment.

Sales Leadership

- **Drove operational, marketing, and business development strategies** that resulted in $829M loan volume and more than $28.7M bottom-line profit over a 7-year period.
- **Grew average annual receivables** at a rate of 39.3% against goal of 15% from 2003–2009.
- **Generated 7-year average annual profit growth** of 27.6%, more than double 10% target.
- **Created customer-focused value proposition** that catalyzed 79% upswing in mortgage applications the first month—a methodology adopted division-wide.

AVERAGE ANNUAL GROWTH

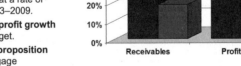

- **Ramped up cross-selling efforts** following business model change that suspended mortgage lending. Remained a leading district—top 10% for auto loan, credit card, and ancillary insurance product sales.
- **One of 4 District Managers** company-wide selected for pilot project transforming branch into virtual call center with sales capability expanded to 3 states. Through superior game-planning and intense team preparation, branch soared to #1 producer of mortgage packages in the first month.

Page 1 of 2

Strategy: Highlight stellar results with an eye-popping chart. Break up lengthy list of accomplishments by dividing it into logical groupings clearly defined by subheadings.

BRAD W. ARMSTRONG   Page 2 of 2   419-555-5555 • bwa@emailservices.com

Operations Leadership

- **Collaborated with senior executives** on developing yearly profit plans, budget forecasts, product enhancements, incentive plans, and business development programs.
- **Introduced expense control initiative,** igniting $153K+ savings—19% below plan and best in region.
- **Cut district operating expenses** $786K by identifying and winning approval to close unprofitable branch.
- **Streamlined workflow** between sales and underwriting to reduce turn time and expedite closings.
- **Prepared and managed** annual regulatory reviews by federal bank examiners and annual external audits, passing all exams and audits with no exceptions.
- **Created first-ever, standardized on-boarding process** to shorten new-hire time to productivity—a program adopted region-wide.
- **Top-Performing District Manager** (profit per loan) region-wide; consistently in top 5 of 101 nationwide, 2010.

Team Leadership

- **Recognized as #1 recruiter division-wide,** building pipeline of talent through year-round recruiting.
- **Overcame challenges of employee turnover,** lackluster performance, and a modest sales incentive package by big-picture mentoring and proactively hiring career-minded individuals aspiring to leadership roles.
- **Traveled constantly** to each branch for onsite coaching of sales associates and mid-managers, yielding high-performance regional results: 5 of top 10 sales performers (of 276); 4 of top 10 producing managers (of 59).
- **Mentored 76-member sales force,** maintaining high retention rate, strong performance, superior customer service, and strict regulatory/corporate compliance.
- **Promoted 7 members** to upper-level management roles and more than 34 to mid-level management roles.

Committee Leadership & Personal Awards

- **Senior Leader of Diversity Council,** increasing diversity 8.86% district-wide, 2008.
- **District Manager Circle of Success Honoree,** 2003–2006, 2008–2009.
- **Q1 Contest Winner,** 2003–2007.

▶**BRANCH MANAGER,** 1997–2002

Champion and driving force behind restructuring efforts that converted 2 struggling offices into key contenders. Planned and managed all day-to-day operations: loan underwriting and credit decisions, cash flow analysis, cash control, collections, loan servicing, marketing, and expense control. Recruited, developed, and retained superior sales force. Steered key initiatives on customer service, receivables gain, corporate profit, and bad debt control.

- **Modified and collected** on delinquent loans to mitigate losses and manage defaults.
- **Developed key B2B relationships** to supply all district branches with leads for short-term and future growth.
- **Identified, graded, priced, and negotiated** bulk purchases of receivables ranging in size from $150K to $1M.

Awards

- **Q1 Contest Winner,** 1999–2002.
- **Sales Coach of the Year,** 1998, 1999, 2001.
- **Star Performer** (highest honor company-wide, overall operations), 2001.

▶**CREDIT MANAGER,** 1995–1997

Achieved performance-based promotion to management role. Quickly established reputation for competitive drive, strong sales, and outstanding leadership. Chosen to train new hires on best practices in first year.

Awards

- **Best Balanced Employee** (sales and business development).
- **Rookie of the Year.**

EDUCATION

BS in Business Administration (Finance Major), Magna cum Laude, OHIO UNIVERSITY, Antioch, OH, 1995

GERALD BERGER

5001 Woodlake Lane
Charlotte, NC 28222

Home: 704-123-1234 Cell: 704-123-4321
gerald.berger@westover.com

GLOBAL BUSINESS / RELATIONSHIP MANAGER

Contract Negotiations • Business Development

A decisive financial analyst skilled at hedging risk, dispersing exposure, and identifying major gaps in profitability forecasts, communication infrastructure, information sharing, and business processes.

Background in corporate and investment banking, commercial property management, and international business practices. Qualifications include:

- "At-risk" business financial analysis
- International currency, letters of credit, and credit agreements
- Software and technology systems evaluation
- Competitive and market analysis, specifically in China
- Bond and stock transfers, debt and equity trusts, and financial accounting (GL)
- MBA, Global Business Management, China concentration, Wake Forest University, 2005

Recognized as a negotiator and persuasive presenter who listens well and breaks down barriers — engendering trust and confidence in a positive and fair outcome.

PROFESSIONAL HIGHLIGHTS

WESTOVER BANK (formerly Universal Union National Bank), Charlotte, NC   2003–present

Capital Markets Portfolio Analyst, AVP (2006–present)
Corporate & Investment Banking Loan Administration

Manage relationships with brokers, client CEOs and COOs, and other financial institutions to track, analyze, and sell loans and collect fees for a portfolio of over 200 companies in forest products, textile, and utility groups. Specialize in "special situation" client base at risk of bankruptcy.

As an internal liaison among Operations, IT, and Customer Relations:
- Consulted with IT designers to fine-tune and streamline the database system that tracks corporate loans and ensures accurate capture of fees. Modeled and tested all contingencies to deliver an error-free system that eliminated duplicate information and paperwork and improved the processing time tenfold.
- Researched and recovered over $150,000 in unpaid fees for utilities department.

Corporate Trust Debt Services Manager, AVP (2003–2006)

Interfaced with bond administrators, upper management, and operations to oversee the accuracy and timeliness of $1 billion per month in bond payments. Managed 19 analysts.

- Promoted to Bank Officer after one year.
- Discovered embezzlement by former Senior Trust Officer, leading to recovery of over $7 million of bearer bonds.
- Evaluated and recommended software/technology infrastructure proposals, working with software vendors and internal analysts. Resulted in a $1+ million software contract.

Continued....

Strategy: Support this candidate's goal of transitioning to international management by emphasizing his recent MBA degree in global business management, noteworthy international experiences in academia, and domestic financial background.

gerald.berger@westover.com   **GERALD BERGER,** page two   Cell: 704-123-4321

APEX MANAGEMENT, Charlotte, NC   1999–2003
Property Manager
Managed a $20 million, 400-unit property, the company's largest. Led a staff of eight employees.
- Consistently exceeded budgeted net operating income.
- Brought delinquent rent to zero within three months on a property that had never achieved zero delinquents for previous five years.
- Selected (out of 77 managers) to test and evaluate new property-management software.

THE CAROLINAS S&L, Daysville, NC   1996–1999
Branch Manager

INTERNATIONAL EXPERIENCE

BABCOCK SCHOOL OF MANAGEMENT, China   June–August 2009
East Asia Management Program Fellow

Unable to ignore the enormous opportunity for global commerce with China — volunteered for this business/academic experience traveling across China from Beijing to Shanghai to Hong Kong.

- Focused on the challenges and risks of entering into a developing market in the face of cultural and economic barriers as well as political and legal constraints.
- Acquired an understanding of Chinese business practices — their need for control, technology, and capital; their appreciation of American technical/financial expertise; and their complex system of bartering and negotiating between government and corporate officials.
- Concluded that it is worthwhile and necessary for American companies to expend the resources to assess and predict the profitability and risks involved in Chinese commerce in order to reap the potential and protect the interests of all concerned.

SOFFLE INTERNATIONAL, Inc., Charlotte, NC   March–June 2009
A leading French construction company ranked in the top ten internationally.

Financial Analyst/Consultant
Analyzed the viability and risks of further expansion into the Chinese market. Evaluated construction material and equipment costs, quality control, credit financing, labor development issues, economy, demand, competition, and political/legal factors.

- Recommended that SI refocus its business model and utilize its 15-year presence in China to function as a consultant to the Chinese construction industry and to other foreign companies seeking to supply the industry. This would leverage SI's ability to find new niches and to develop Chinese alliances, creating competitive advantages for future construction opportunities.

EDUCATION

Master of Business Administration, 2010
Concentration in Global Business Management
WAKE FOREST UNIVERSITY, Babcock Graduate School of Management, Winston-Salem, NC

Bachelor of Arts, 1996
Economics and Business Administration
LENOIR-RYNE COLLEGE, Charlotte, NC

RESUME 74: BY MARTIN BUCKLAND, CPRW, CPBS, JCTC, CEIP, CJST

GERALD BAKERSFIELD

567 Echo Avenue, Toronto, Ontario M5E 2D8
Phone: 416.335.1487   E-mail: gbakersfield@cogeco.ca

Global Financial Perspective

Executive Management • Money Market • Foreign Exchange
Asset Liability Management • Retail Banking

Competent, decisive, and dedicated senior financial executive with an extensive knowledge of the global economy. Considered a leader, mentor, and motivator; recognized for proactively and efficiently directing a team to deliver results during variances in the economy. Visionary, strategic, and conceptual thinker; able to generate new ideas and initiate change. Results driven; work judiciously and methodically to achieve and exceed company-mandated goals. Thrive on a challenge; critically scrutinize and evaluate fiscal statements, liabilities, and responsibilities. Combine sophisticated financial expertise with tactical execution of global bank-wide initiatives to enhance customer service, bank operations, and bottom-line performance. Culturally sensitive; effective communicator and negotiator; develop profitable rapport with all levels. Unique perspective of the Canadian political environment with respect to the Province of Quebec.

PROFESSIONAL EXPERIENCE

Banca Commerciale Italiana of Canada, Toronto, Ontario   1992–2011

Held the following progressively responsible positions:

VICE PRESIDENT—TREASURY   2007–2011

Tasked with proactively contributing to the bank's objectives by efficiency, expediency, and profitability in the Treasury Department through proficient money market and foreign-exchange desk management.

Accomplishments:

• Played an active role with the Project Management team in facilitating a relocation of the trading room. Process involved comprehensive needs and facility assessment, staff recruitment, computer-systems research, tendering, purchasing, and installations. Project completed within budget and strict time schedule.

• Launched a unique Treasury System delivering real-time positions since recognized by and installed by the bank's Italian head office and other foreign units. System permits an error-free capability, increased productivity, and more succinct position keeping.

• Contributed to bank's reaching the $2 billion asset level, a first for the Canadian branch. Managed the asset-liability portfolios including liquidity, FX, and interest-rate risk.

• Met the majority of company-defined profit targets during tenure throughout a fluctuating economy.

• Worked with IT, Risk Management, and a Reuters consultant to upgrade the KONDOR+ system from version 1.8 to 2.0. Process involved regressive testing to ensure stable data transfer.

Responsibilities:

• Played an active and critical role on the 6-member senior management team. Acted as treasury representative and at times reported in person to Board of Directors.

• Traveled to key global financial centers, ensuring and maintaining liquidity and identifying new financial partners.

• Oversaw all money-market and foreign-exchange dealing and corporate dealing desks. Monitored market information, variations, bank traders, Reuters News, Dow Jones, and print, TV, and trade journals.

• Controlled Canadian, U.S. dollar, and Euro cash management. Checked the cash position and manipulated cash flow to maintain profitability.

• Managed the treasury's statutory and OSFI compliance.

• Supervised 10 staff, including Treasury Services, Money Market, and Foreign Exchange Managers. Responsible for all human resource issues, recruitment, scheduling, appraisals, budgeting, and profit-target issues.

• Liaised with Italian Head Office Departments and branches, Credit International, and Securities and Syndications.

• Handled the $5 million defined-benefit plan for the bank's Canadian operations.

CONTINUED

Strategy: Expand on the candidate's sound and diverse international money-market experience in the top section, with accomplishments making up the bulk of the resume.

GERALD BAKERSFIELD PAGE 2

ASSISTANT VICE PRESIDENT—TREASURY 2005–2007

Accomplishments:

- Oversaw the introduction of the KONDOR+ system, which significantly improved accountability, instant market analysis, pricing of products, and maintenance of positions. Recognized by the senior management team as an integral component of productivity and reporting improvements and streamlined operations.
- Actively addressed a critical business-development issue by leading a team tasked with designing and building a new trading room. Completed on time and within strict budget.

Responsibilities:

- Worked judiciously in partnership with Executive Vice President to support the department operations, priorities, objectives, and tactical plans.
- Guided the policy and procedure development to support the regulatory authority requirements.

SENIOR DEPARTMENT MANAGER 1998–2005

- Promotion recognized as the first Canadian management position to be filled by a non-Italian citizen.
- Developed the Y2K Liquidity Contingency Plan in partnership with other departments.
- Selected by senior banking peers to fulfill the Director, Financial Markets Association of Canada (formally FOREX of Canada), position for one year.
- Facilitated the complex centralization of the corporate currency exchange, eliminating the retail responsibilities and permitting better management over the foreign-exchange and money-market clientele.
- Instrumental in raising the Canadian asset level to $1 billion Canadian for the first time.
- Implemented the Bank of Canada zero-reserve environment.

MONEY MARKET TRADER/FX TRADER 1992–1998

- Actively managed the asset and liability gap positions; developed trading relationships to provide access to liquidity.
- Handled customer activity, providing information and booking money-market/FX transactions.

Continental Illinois of Canada, Toronto, Ontario 1989–1992

Held the following two positions:

POSITION KEEPER/TRADER

AUDIT OFFICER

Royal Canadian Mounted Police, Regina, Saskatchewan 1989

CONSTABLE

- Successfully completed initial training. Posted to Maple Ridge, British Columbia.

EDUCATION

Strong proponent of continuing education. Relevant financial courses include:

• Canadian Treasury Functions	• Bank of Montreal, Toronto
• Treasury Functions	• Banca Commerciale Italiana, Milan
• Futures	• Dean Witter (Carr Futures), Toronto
• Asset Liability Management	• Risk Conferences Limited

Sheridan College, Oakville, Ontario 1989

CERTIFICATE—Business Administration, Accounting and Finance Major

COMMUNITY INVOLVEMENT

Participated in the Terry Fox run for 17 of the last 21 years. Raised $15,000 in total, $3,500 in highest year.

ARTHUR SALAZAR

1234 N. Carpenter Lane
Los Angeles, California 90069

(323) 555-1234
artsalazar@email.com

INVESTMENT SERVICES FINANCIAL EXECUTIVE
Financial Planning / Budget Management / Internal Reporting / General Accounting
Project Management / Financial System Technology / Leadership / Relationship & Consensus Building

❑ Highly motivated, results-driven financial professional with 14 years of experience developing, presenting, and implementing value-added recommendations for improvement. Strong analytical, technology, and communication skills with a track record of achievements in financial planning and project management.

❑ Strong leadership and team-building skills with ability to coordinate cross-functional groups to accomplish objectives and meet critical deadlines in a fast-paced, high-growth, dynamic environment. Committed to high ethical standards. Consumer, shareholder, and employee focused.

MBA • Big Four CPA Experience • Bilingual English/Spanish

PROFESSIONAL EXPERIENCE

U.S. INVESTMENTS CORPORATION, Los Angeles, CA • 1998 to Present
Achieved fast-track promotion to positions of increasing responsibility for industry-leading financial services and e-commerce provider with diverse product offerings including discount securities brokerage, mutual funds, electronic brokerage, and bank-like products. Annual revenues grew from $300 million to $2 billion.

Director, Planning and Analysis (2005 to Present)
In charge of corporate financial planning, budget process, and evaluation/implementation of information technology upgrades utilized by 100+ analysts. Direct staff of seven; interface on regular basis with 200+ co-workers at all corporate levels; report directly to Corporate Controller / VP of Finance.
- Lead company's annual operating-plan process, managing continuous process improvements to support high growth cycle and migration to a decentralized planning and budgeting business unit.
- Develop spreadsheet models to support financial targets and strategic allocation of funds to business units. Consolidate budgets into financial statements; deliver high-level presentations.
- Orchestrated new planning process and launched investment-analysis guidelines that support a highly volatile environment.
- Spearheaded acquisition and implementation of new integrated planning, reporting, and analysis tool that generated productivity improvements in finance groups across multiple divisions. Concept was enthusiastically endorsed by user community, and vendor selection was adopted as corporate standard.
- Implemented Windows-based state-of-the-art financial software application, replacing proprietary mainframe budgeting application. Accomplished complex conversion within three-month window.

Manager, Revenue Reporting (2004 to 2005)
Analyzed and prepared periodic reports of customer-segment revenues to support business diversification. Managed revenue-reporting definitions and databases, ensuring company-wide consistency and efficiency. Completed numerous special projects for Controller and CFO encompassing project tracking, contingency planning, and internal billing.
- Coordinated company-wide effort to develop corporate definitions for customer-related data and published first definitions manual. Successfully achieved consensus among cross-functional team of support managers.
- Managed information technology team in developing revenue databases to support common definitions throughout company. Served as springboard for a later data warehousing project.

CONTINUED

Strategy: Capture the reader's attention at first glance with important highlights: executive-level experience, an MBA, and a Big Four CPA background. Use the Professional Experience section to show consistent promotions and quantifiable achievements.

(323) 555-1234   ARTHUR SALAZAR • PAGE TWO   ARTSALAZAR@EMAIL.COM

U.S. INVESTMENTS CORPORATION, continued

Manager, Financial Systems (2002 to 2004)
Orchestrated corporate-wide resource management reporting system used by accounting and cost-center managers for financial reporting and variance analysis.
- Managed monthly data production, distribution, and quality control in addition to user training and customer service. System received widespread praise by users for reliability and flexibility.

Senior Financial Analyst/Accountant (1998 to 2002)
Evaluated accuracy of financial analysis on investment proposals. Analyzed budget variances. Prepared top-down corporate estimates, consistently achieving goal of less than 2% variance in net income. Developed complex variable-compensation and breakeven-analysis models.

PRICE WATERHOUSE, Los Angeles, CA • 1996 to 1998
Auditor
Participated in financial audits across diverse industries including manufacturing, broadcasting, and banking. Prepared corporate tax returns.

EDUCATION

MBA; Concentration in Finance; UNIVERSITY OF CALIFORNIA, Los Angeles, CA; 1996
B.S. Accounting; BOSTON COLLEGE, Chestnut Hill, MA; 1994
CPA; State of California; 1998

SKILLS

Proficient in multiple business applications including Microsoft Office (Word, Excel, PowerPoint), Hyperion Pillar and OLAP (Budgeting & Analysis), PeopleSoft (General Ledger), Windows, Outlook.

LARRY WILLIAMS

215 Crestview Avenue
Asheville, NC 28815
828.354.1258
lwilliams@msn.com

SUMMARY of QUALIFICATIONS

Effective Negotiations
Energy Trading

Market Research &
Analysis

Financial Planning
Price Forecasting
Portfolio Modeling
Cost/Risk Analysis
Budget Preparation

Project Management

Communication Skills
Customer Liaison
Sales Force
Suppliers
Pipeline Companies
Interstate
Intrastate

Problem-Solving

Sales & Marketing
Leadership

Compliance/Accountability

Supply Management

Professional & Personal
References

A goal-oriented, high-energy professional innovative in identifying and implementing strategies in FINANCIAL RISK MANAGEMENT to capture cost improvement opportunities while impacting bottom-line profits. Strong organizational and analytical skills demonstrated by successfully applying business principles in commodity market analysis, risk reporting and strategic development.

PROFESSIONAL EXPERIENCE

CENTRAL SOLUTIONS   Asheville, NC

Central Solutions is the energy retail arm of Central Energy that focuses on large industrial, commercial, institutional and governmental customers that are energy-intensive with a significant level of energy-related costs. Central Energy is a $58 billion, Fortune 20 global energy company headquartered in Asheville, NC.

Financial Commodity Manager	2009 – PRESENT
Supply Management Representative	2007 – 2009

- Analyze supply management customers' electric and gas market price exposure and recommend options to best meet individual customer objectives to mitigate price risk and meet energy budget.

- Assist sales force by participating in presentations to prospective customers, describing supply and risk management.

- Serve as customer representative in facilitating financial transactions (NYMEX, OTC energy swaps and options) designed to mitigate customers' floating energy market price risk.

FAST TRACK ENERGY MARKETING   Lexington, KY

Fast Track Energy Marketing is the energy trading division for Fast Track Energy Corporation—a $4.3 billion, Fortune 500 energy-services holding company headquartered in Lexington, KY.

Facilities Operator	2006 – 2007
Energy Coordinator	2005 – 2006

- Directed the day-to-day marketing operations for natural gas processing and intrastate pipeline distribution systems.

- Managed and evaluated existing imbalances and balancing agreements with four interstate pipelines and transportation customers to ensure accurate records and identify potential marketing opportunities.

- Scheduled natural gas across pipelines into and out of storage facilities.

- Tracked nominations in a gas accounting information system to ensure proper customer invoicing.

EDUCATION

BUTLER UNIVERSITY, Indianapolis, IN
Bachelor of Science Degree, 2005
Major: Business Marketing

Strategy: Create an eye-catching format that, in a matter of seconds, shows skills that are essential in the energy and utilities industry.

CHAPTER **12**

Resumes for Manufacturing, Operations, and Senior/Executive Managers

- Maintenance Director
- Purchasing and Supply-Chain Manager
- Environmental Health and Safety Manager
- Chief Operations Officer (COO)
- Plant/Operations/General Manager
- Senior Manufacturing and Operations Executive
- Communications Executive
- Chief Executive Officer
- Senior Executive
- Senior Management Executive
- President

951 Hancock Street, Belvidere, Illinois 61008
jmarsden@gmail.com ■ 815.555.5555
LinkedIn.com/in/JulesMarsden

Jules Marsden

DIRECTOR OF MAINTENANCE

Quality Assurance ■ People Management ■ Technical Expertise

MANAGEMENT PROFILE

Meticulous technician with 17+ years of deep and rich hands-on experience in aircraft maintenance and team leadership. A valuable partner to senior management. Solid record of providing critical operational expertise to leverage growth and achieve efficiency and profitability. Excellent communication and call-to-action skills.

AREAS OF EXPERTISE

Cost Reduction	Quality Control	System Management
Operating Leadership	Productivity Improvement	Policy Development
Repair & Maintenance	Engine Overhauls	Inspections
Sheet Metal	Corrosion Control	Assembly & Rigging

EXPERIENCE & ACCOMPLISHMENTS

POPLAR GROVE AIRMOTIVE, Poplar Grove, Illinois, 1995 to Present
A leading aircraft maintenance, repair, and overhaul (MRO) facility for rare, vintage, and corporate aircraft in the Midwest

ENGINE SHOP MANAGER | AIRFRAME & POWERPLANT (A&P) MECHANIC, 2006 to Present

Promoted to lead 14 A&P craftsmen in Part 145 Engine Shop. Supervise engine overhauls, inspections, repairs, and troubleshooting. Oversee Engine Shop scheduling and production, quality control (QC), and airworthiness directive (AD) compliance. Developed and implemented equipment maintenance policies.

■ Managed 10 months of continuous shop operation with no downtime:
  □ Developed and implemented a scheduled preventive maintenance program that reduced breakdowns and improved equipment longevity.

■ Maintained an injury-free workplace for 13 consecutive months:
  □ Strengthened safety procedures and training.
  □ Held shop personnel accountable for wearing personal protective equipment.

■ Conducted process audits:
  □ Created flowcharts to illustrate complex processes.
  □ Identified deficiencies between observed processes with the process described in the Repair Station Manual (RSM).

■ Excel in organizing and coaching personnel to work effectively in teams.

■ Brought in $389K of revenue in 9 months.

continued

Strategy: Clearly demonstrate in-depth expertise in the field of aircraft maintenance. Highlight impressive performance and safety records.

jmarsden@gmail.com
815.555.5555

Jules Marsden

Page 2

INSPECTOR (IA) | A&P MECHANIC, 2004 to 2006

Handpicked to inspect Continental and Lycoming engines and approve them for return to service. Devised and implemented well-defined SOPs and processes. Wrote procedural manuals for A&P education and reference.

- Improved recording process of test data from newly overhauled engines.

- Inspected completed work to certify that work was performed in accordance with AC 43.13-1B.

- Maintained repair logs, documenting all preventive and corrective maintenance.

- Ensured that all inspecting, measuring, and testing equipment was calibrated and traceable.

- Qualified and observed non-certificated persons performing maintenance and alterations.

LINE A&P MECHANIC, 1995 to 2004

Hired to perform 100-hour, annual, and progressive inspections on various types of aircraft with inventory totaling $1.7M. Excelled in discovering hidden problems through careful attention to detail and process. Challenged to improve efficiency and performance by optimization of existing procedures.

- Reduced costs and improved productivity by overhauling maintenance-inspection schedules:
  - Created database to plan and track flight school's aircraft inspections.
  - Developed bar-coded shop tool inventory controls.
- Extended flight school's average engine life 140% beyond TBO with FAA approval.

EDUCATION & TECHNICAL TRAINING

- Bachelor of Science, Engineering, 1994, Bradley University, Peoria, Illinois

- Aviation Maintenance Technology, 1995, National Aviation Academy, Bedford, Massachusetts

- Private Pilot Training, 1997, Poplar Grove Airmotive, Poplar Grove, Illinois

- Inspection Authorization Course, 2005, American Airman Ground School, Ronkonkoma, New York

RICHARD K. TOBER

1010 Schreier Road • Rossford, OH 43460
Residence: 419-667-4518 • Mobile: 419-667-6224 • E-Mail: rktober@netzero.net

SENIOR INTERNATIONAL SUPPLY-CHAIN MANAGEMENT / PURCHASING EXECUTIVE
Transportation & Logistics • Production Planning • Packaging

Performance-driven Six Sigma Black Belt Senior Executive offering 15 years of comprehensive achievements within Supply-Chain Management, Purchasing, and Production Planning. Leveraged business acumen across diverse cultures and economies. Developed performance-based, low-cost solutions through aggressive negotiation with new and existing suppliers and use of outsourcing.

Solid history utilizing out-of-the-box approaches, adapting to new business environments, and negotiating win-win agreements. Recognized for ability to incorporate innovative management techniques that result in enhanced business practices, increased productivity, and profits. Forged strong business relationships focused on teamwork, service level, and cost containment. Fluent in German, Spanish, and Mandarin.

AREAS OF EXPERTISE

- **Strategic Supplier Development**
- **Change Management**
- **Planning & Development**
- **Operations Management**
- **Creative Problem Solving**

- **Inventory Management**
- **Cost Optimization and Control**
- **Import / Export Operations**
- **International Operations**
- **SAP Implementation**
- **Supplier Consolidation**

- **Quality Assurance**
- **Leadership / Team Building**
- **Supply-Chain Analysis**
- **Relationship Management**
- **Project Management**

MBA, Finance • George Washington University, Washington, DC
BS, Industrial Engineering • Clemson University, Clemson, SC

CAREER BACKGROUND

MOSER CHEMICAL, Toledo, OH
Leading international science and technology company with a presence in more than 150 countries. Provides innovative chemical, plastic, and agricultural products and services to essential consumer markets.

MANAGER, DOMESTIC / INTERNATIONAL SUPPLY CHAIN (2007–2011)
Chlorinated Organic Business Unit ($650 million in sales / $65 million Supply Chain Budget)

Introduced supply-chain initiatives by restructuring business-wide domestic and international operations and spearheading contract negotiations. Oversaw 30 direct reports in managerial roles throughout the world; reported to division Vice President.

Career Highlights:

- Delivered $18 million in cost savings over three-year period primarily through use of intercompany supply-chain teams involving strategic suppliers and strategic customers.
- Achieved benchmark pricing for drumming-related activities, resulting in outsourcing of all activity in North America and shutdown of two packaging lines in Europe and Germany.
- Developed cross-cultural relations with international team members; supervised seven-person planning team with members from the US, Germany, Hong Kong, and Brazil. Team integrated operations of 10 plants at five sites on three continents, with production of more than 2 billion pounds per year.
- Installed and commissioned a keg-packaging line that centralized the filling of 15-gallon stainless-steel returnable containers and included a container-tracking system.

Page 1 of 2

Strategy: Highlight transferable supply-chain management and purchasing skills and showcase the candidate's ability to lead international cross-functional teams.

RICHARD K. TOBER
Residence: 419-667-4518 • Mobile: 419-667-6224 • E-Mail: rktober@netzero.net

GLOBAL BUSINESS PLANNER AND PROJECT MANAGER FOR CHEMICALS (2003–2007)

Career Highlights:

- Led international teams in the establishment and implementation of business planning and monthly forecasting policies and procedures, enabling an across-the-board inventory reduction of 65% and releasing $25 million in working capital.
- Conducted an in-depth worldwide supply-chain study analyzing all work processes between product manufacturer and delivery to customer. Study served as basis to reengineer and streamline supply chain and identified low-hanging opportunities for additional cost savings.
- Pioneered use of domestic contract terminals for primary storage, achieving lowest terminal costs within Moser and release of capital money associated with terminal projects.
- Increased domestic process capability of distribution system to meet increasing quality requirements for products, reducing product contamination defects from one per hundred orders to less than one per thousand orders.
- Established worldwide supply-chain teams with all strategic suppliers, strategic service providers, and strategic customers both domestically and internationally.
- Achieved largest single-lane-rail rate reduction in Moser's history by developing a water-compelled alternative, saving Moser over $1 million per year and customer $2 million per year.
- Won *"Supplier of the Year Award"* on three separate occasions.

BUSINESS OPERATIONS MANAGER FOR CHEMICALS (1996–2003)

Career Highlights:

- Optimized use of raw materials in short supply by identifying intermediate products that could be alternatively purchased and diverting short products into higher value-added opportunities. Purchased up to 70,000 MT per year of intermediate products.
- Maintained supply-demand balances.
- Resolved domestic and international logistics and product-quality problems.

PROFESSIONAL TRAINING & DEVELOPMENT

International Relations • International Finance

Stepping Toward Quality • Improving Vendor Relations • Project Management

Six Sigma • Green Belt / Black Belt Training

Statistical Analysis Techniques • Managing Difficult People • Train the Trainer

Dale Carnegie—"Enhancing Communications"

BARBARA L. STANFORD

2700 Banner Drive NE, Washington DC 20018
Telephone: 202-696-0040 / Email: bstanford@aol.com / Cellular: 202-709-5019

SENIOR MANAGEMENT

Environmental Health & Safety ▸ Facilities Management ▸ Technical Services

Bringing World-Class Performance and Compliance to Manufacturing and Production Operations
Infusing global manufacturing operations with advanced, state-of-the-art engineering solutions that streamline processes, curtail hazardous waste costs, and elevate environmental and safety standards

EXECUTIVE PROFILE

Unwavering success record in devising manufacturing and plant operating strategies that eliminate redundancies; automate processes/systems; increase production output; and deliver productivity, quality, and efficiency gains.

Impressive career history of developing award-winning initiatives and engineering solutions that generated a net total of $34.5 million.

Proven reputation for designing cutting-edge manufacturing facilities and implementing continuous improvement processes that revolutionize environmental safety and health regulation standards.

Notable Career Achievements & Milestones

* Architected environmental, health, and safety programs and policies that became **"benchmark"** and **"world class"** models that were fully adopted throughout the Smart Razors Company.

* Expanded Smart Razors' product portfolio/annual revenues by developing six new products while simultaneously **containing $650,000 in production and operation costs.**

* Engineered and **designed a $2.5 million, environmentally friendly, state-of-the-art manufacturing facility** that became primary prototype for future facility developments at the Smart Razor Company.

* Optimized manufacturing operations to **efficiently generate more than 1 billion products (Paper Buddy)**, a monumental feat for the first time in the division's history.

* Earned **National Safety Council's prestigious Sweepstakes Trophy** for maintaining the best safety records and programs for seven straight years, an unmatched feat in the manufacturing industry.

EXECUTIVE PERFORMANCE HIGHLIGHTS

The Rubber Guys, North America   2007–present
DIRECTOR, Environmental Health & Safety—San Jose, CA (2009 to present)

Hand-picked by North American Operations to oversee the overall compliance of thirteen manufacturing, distribution, and R&D operations in Mexico, Canada, and US. Charged with recruiting, hiring, and training a qualified environmental health and safety (EHS) team. Conducted additional safety and awareness training for up to 5,000 employees.

▸ **Environmental Health & Safety Management:** Decreased occupational injuries 400% by developing and implementing world-class EHS and risk management policies, programs, and practices.

▸ **Cost Reduction & Savings:** Identified $3.5 million reductions in worker compensation costs through business-wide checks-and-balances systems.

▸ **Facilities & Logistics Management:** Delivered $5.8 million in savings by strategically managing the closures of company's California and Wisconsin manufacturing facilities.

CONTINUED

Strategy: Build a strong Executive Profile section that brings impressive and record-setting achievements to the forefront.

BARBARA STANFORD   EMAIL: BSTANFORD@AOL.COM / CELLULAR: 202-709-5019   PAGE TWO

DIVISION MANAGER, Technical Services—San Jose, CA (2007 to 2009)

Retained as a key executive member of transition team following The Rubber Guys' acquisition of the Stationery Product Group, a division of Smart Razors Company. Challenged to execute 100-day operational plan and fully integrate manufacturing operations for Paper Buddy products. Managed environmental health and safety standards for entire operations.

▸ **Asset Management:** Verified more than $120 million in company assets, processes, and equipment transfers to support division's sale to The Rubber Guys.

▸ **Environmental Health & Safety Programs:** Collaborated with Los Alamos Lab to implement state-of-the-art technology that purged hazardous materials from production operations. Efforts resulted in a "Clear Air Award" from California's South Coast Air Quality Management District.

▸ **Manufacturing Engineering:** Realized $4.75 million in annual cost savings by orchestrating relocation strategy to transfer environmentally challenged manufacturing facility to new facility in Mexico.

Smart Razors Company, San Jose, CA   1999–2007
DIVISION MANAGER, Technical Services (2005 to 2007)

Promoted to lead and direct all engineering and facilities management activities for Stationery Products Group. Integrated technology/engineering solutions that produced efficient, cost-effective operating processes. Performed routine audits of company's facilities in China, India, and Mexico.

▸ **Strategic Planning & Direction:** Demonstrated expert technical and administrative leadership role in responding to natural disaster; salvaged materials and restored business to normal operations in only two weeks.

▸ **Operations Reengineering:** Reduced annual hazardous waste 12% and captured $4 million in savings by instituting effective operational standards.

▸ **Manufacturing Technology Integration:** Introduced state-of-the-art air pollution control technologies and innovative engineering solutions that reduced factory air emissions 90% and saved company $250,000.

▸ **Cost Savings & Avoidance:** Shrunk annual utility and energy expenses more than $2 million by renegotiating vendor contracts/purchases and instituting energy conservation policies.

▸ **Customer Relationship Management:** Increased and maintained customer satisfaction rating to more than 98% by establishing customer awareness programs and customer focus strategies.

MANAGER, Chemical, Environmental & Safety Engineering (1999 to 2005)

Tasked with revamping and restructuring manufacturing facility plagued with poor health and environmental safety standards. Assumed directive to streamline operations, eliminate occupational hazards, and decrease levels of manufacturing waste and air emissions.

▸ **Turnaround Management:** Upgraded division's safety and manufacturing standards to highest, best-performing operations in entire company while generating $1.2 million in savings.

▸ **Manufacturing & Operations Reengineering:** Reduced operating costs by $1.4 million and lowered occupational and environmental hazards by incorporating $2.5 million in equipment and process improvements.

EARLY COMPANY EXPERIENCE: Delivered significant contributions to company's revenue growth and production output through **Manager of Engineering & Maintenance** and **Project Engineer** positions. Top position achievements included **triple-digit increases** in process, equipment, and operational efficiencies.

EDUCATION

BS, Chemical Engineering—University of Michigan, Ann Arbor, MI

Joseph E. DiCarlo

44 Sampson Rock Road
Milford, MA 01757
res. 508.555.1212 • cell 508.631.0202
jedicarlo@mindspring.com

EXECUTIVE PROFILE

- Highly accomplished manufacturing executive qualified for COO/Divisional–Operations–General Manager's position with company demanding expertise in all aspects of operations management, P&L, manufacturing, engineering, and new product design/launch.
- Solid track record of successful experience includes optimizing productivity, improving profitability, and successfully turning around declining operations. Innovative and creative problem-solving skills.
- Performance-, process-, and results-driven in commitment to quality and continuous improvement.

PROFESSIONAL EXPERIENCE

BOSTON METAL-TECH, INC. • Revere, MA   2000–Present
Vice President, Operations (2005–Present)
Direct overall operations of one of the nation's largest surface-finishing contractors, with accountability for manufacturing, laboratory, quality, engineering, new product development, production control, tooling, safety (workers' comp/health insurance), and regulatory affairs; company employs up to 900 across 3 shifts in 4 locations. Support a dynamic customer base comprising 650 active accounts globally; strategic accounts include such customers as Boeing, AT&T, L'Oreal, Compaq, and Ford Motor Company.

Select Accomplishments ...

- Increased sales by $3M over 2 years; led research and development team launch of electroplating on liquid-crystal polymer substrates.
- Produced $800K in annual sales through development/installation of plating process to clean and chrome-plate highly polished aluminum writing instrument components.
- Achieved key cost-saving objectives through following initiatives:
  - Realized annual savings of $600K through conversion of premium workers' compensation plan to self-insured program; launched Safety Committee, training programs, and rewards programs. Total consecutive days accident-free: 3,100.
  - Orchestrated development of paint-manufacturing software system that eliminated nonusable product and yielded annual material/labor savings of $125K–$180K.
  - Led research/development of electroplating treatment process: Saved $95K annually.
  - Implemented just-in-time delivery and renegotiated terms/prices with suppliers; result: 11%–15% reduction in chemical-procurement costs.
- Recipient, MCE Perfect Compliance (4 years); Environmental Achievement Award.

As **Director of Engineering** (2000–2005), key accomplishments included the following:
- Identified key projects in area of regulatory compliance and established comprehensive, proactive program; Boston Metal-Tech falls under purview of many regulatory agencies.
- Reengineered alternative fuel boiler; result: $400K annual savings via recycling of energy and reduction in heating oil; avoided hazardous-waste shipping/exposure to liability.
- Engineered and launched thermal-oxidizer program for VOC destruction/energy recapture.
- Collaborated with MIS to automate 80% of regulatory-reporting process; result: Reduced quarterly hours from 500 to 50 and improved accuracy while assuring regulatory compliance.

Continued

Strategy: Diminish description of job duties to allow a strong focus on measurable achievements across multiple areas of operations.

Joseph E. DiCarlo   cell 508.631.0202 • jedicarlo@mindspring.com   Page Two

ADAPTIVE TECHNOLOGIES, INC. • Billerica, MA   1996–2000
Manufacturing Engineering Manager
Directed Manufacturing and Industrial Engineering Groups for contract manufacturer (consignment and turnkey PC board and computer-systems assembly and testing); developed and managed Documentation Control Department. Managed 3 engineers and 4 associate engineers; coordinated technical support instrumental in assisting sales force with marketing of services. Provided labor and material costing for all production-quote estimates.

Select Accomplishments ...

- Designed and executed layout of 65,000-sq.-ft. manufacturing facility.
- Improved operational productivity by 18% through launch of team development programs; ergonomic workstation improvements increased efficiency 5%–20%.
- Streamlined manufacturing support operations by standardizing all processes, systems, and procedures; result: 98% on-time delivery of product.
- As a result of key value-engineering initiatives, reduced labor and material costs by 16% for product-handling changes, saved $50K annually from development of wave solder zero-defects program, and produced $30K annual savings through implementation of semi- and automatic component-performing equipment.

COMPUTER EQUIPMENT CORPORATION • Waltham, MA   1990–1996
Manufacturing Engineer, Special Systems Division
Implemented process equipment and assembly/test procedures for mechanical, PCB, cable, and systems configuration. Managed introduction of new electro-mechanical/PCB products and process equipment into manufacturing. Directed and trained process engineers in industrial engineering, product costing, and facilities layout.

Select Accomplishments ...

- Managed project team for renovation and layout of 30,000-sq.-ft. manufacturing and office facility; implementation resulted in annual savings of $180K.
- Key projects implemented included automatic costing system, bar coding, and new Electro Static Discharge (ESD) Control Program.
- Developed X-Bar and Control Limit Charts for manufacturing operations.

EDUCATION

MASSACHUSETTS INSTITUTE OF TECHNOLOGY • Cambridge, MA
- **Bachelor of Science, Industrial Engineering** (1990 Honors Graduate)
- Alpha Pi Mu Industrial Engineering and Tau Beta Pi Engineering Honor Societies

CONTINUING EDUCATION … Successfully completed numerous professional management, environmental, compliance, OSHA, and Haz-Mat training courses throughout career.

AFFILIATIONS / CIVIC

AMERICAN MANUFACTURING ASSOCIATION
- **Board of Directors** (2006–Present); **Vice President** (2004–2005)

MASSACHUSETTS COUNCIL OF MANUFACTURERS — **Vice President** (2009–2010)
MILFORD PARKS & RECREATION DEPARTMENT — **Soccer Coach** (2008–Present)

WILLIAM T. PARKERSON

35 Sunderland Drive
Cedar Grove, NJ 07009

E-mail: parkersonw@compuserve.com

Home: (732) 599-6694
Cell: (732) 599-4481

PLANT / OPERATIONS / GENERAL MANAGEMENT EXECUTIVE

Multisite manufacturing plant/general management career building and leading high-growth, transition, and start-up operations in domestic and international environments with annual revenues of up to $680M.

Expertise: Organizational Development • Productivity & Cost Reduction Improvements • Supply Chain Management • Acquisitions & Divestitures • IPOs • Plant Rationalizations • Safety Performance • Customer Relations • Change Agent

CORE COMPETENCIES

Manufacturing Leadership—Strong P&L track record with functional management experience in all disciplines of manufacturing operations • Developing and managing operating budgets • Spearheading restructuring and rationalization of plants and contracted distribution facilities • Initiating lean manufacturing processes, utilizing SMED principles • Establishing performance metrics and supply-chain management teams.

Continuous Improvement & Training—Designing and instituting leadership enhancement training program for all key plant management • Instituting Total Quality System (TQS) process in domestic plants to promote the business culture of continuous improvement • Leading ISO 9001 certification process.

New Product Development—Initiating plant-based "New Product Development Think Tank" that developed 130 new products for marketing review, resulting in the successful launch of 5 new products in 2000.

Engineering Management—Overseeing corporate machine design and development teams • Developing 3-year operating plan • Directing the design, fabrication, and installation of several proprietary machines • Creating project cost-tracking systems and introducing ROI accountability.

PROFESSIONAL EXPERIENCE

BEACON INDUSTRIES, INC., Maspeth, NY (2002–Present)
Record of continuous promotion to executive-level position in manufacturing and operations management despite periods of transition/acquisition at a $680M Fortune 500 international manufacturing company.

Vice President of Manufacturing (2005–Present)

Senior Operating Executive responsible for the performance of 7 manufacturing/distribution facilities for company that experienced rapid growth from 4 plants generating $350M in annual revenues to 14 manufacturing facilities with revenues of $680M. Charged with driving the organization to becoming a low-cost producer. Established performance indicators, operating goals, realignment initiatives, productivity improvements, and cost-reduction programs that consistently improved product output, product quality, and customer satisfaction.

Achievements:

- Selected to lead corporate team in developing and driving forward cost-reduction initiatives that will result in $21M savings in 3 years through capital infusion, process automation, and additional rationalizations.

- Saved $13M annually by reducing fixed spending 11% and variable overhead spending 18% through effective utilization of operating resources and cost improvement initiatives.

- Cut workers' compensation costs 40% ($750,000 annually) by implementing effective health and safety plans, employee training, management accountability, and equipment safeguarding. Led company to achieve recognition as "Best in Industry" regarding OSHA frequency and Loss Workday Incident rates.

- Reduced waste generation 31%, saving $1M in material usage by optimizing manufacturing processes as well as instituting controls and accountability.

- Enhanced customer satisfaction 3% during past year (measured by order fill and on-time delivery percentage) through supply-chain management initiatives, inventory control, and flexible manufacturing practices.

- Trimmed manufacturing- and shipping-related credits to customers from 1.04% to .5% of total sales in 2007, representing annual $1.8M reduction.

Continued

Strategy: Bring out core competencies with a detailed introduction; then support these areas of strength with significant achievements listed with the chronological work history.

WILLIAM T. PARKERSON – (732) 599-6694 – Page 2

- Decreased total inventories 43% from 2005 base through combination of supply-chain management, purchasing, master scheduling, and global utilization initiatives.

- Rationalized 3 manufacturing plants and 6 distribution facilities, saving $6M over 3 years.

General Manager, Northeast (2002–2005)

Assumed full P&L responsibility for 2 manufacturing facilities and a $20M annual operating budget. Directly supervised facility managers and indirectly 250 employees in a multiline, multicultural manufacturing environment. Planned and realigned organizational structure and operations to position company for high growth as a result of acquiring a major account, 2 new product lines, and 800 additional SKUs.

Achievements:

- Reduced operating costs by $4.5M through consolidation of 2 distribution locations without adverse impact on customer service.

- Accomplished the start-up of 2 new manufacturing operations, which encompassed a plant closing and the integration of acquired equipment into existing production lines for 2 new product lines; achieved without interruption to customer service, 2 months ahead of target, and $400,000 below budget.

- Increased operating performance by 15% while reducing labor costs by $540,000.

- Reduced frequency and severity of accidents by 50% in 3 years, contributing to a workers' compensation and cost-avoidance reduction of $1M.

- Decreased operating waste by 2% for an annual cost savings of $800,000 in 2 manufacturing facilities.

- Negotiated turnkey contracts for 2 distribution warehouses to meet expanded volume requirements.

- Maintained general management and administrative cost (GMA) at a flat rate as sales grew by 25% annually over 3 years.

ROMELARD CORPORATION, Detroit, MI (1988–2002)
Division Manufacturing Director (1998–2002)

Fast-track advancement in engineering, manufacturing, and operations management to division-level position. Retained by new corporate owners and promoted in 1998 based on consistent contributions to revenue growth, profit improvements, and cost reductions. Scope of responsibility encompassed P&L for 3 manufacturing facilities and a distribution center with 500 employees in production, quality, distribution, inventory control, and maintenance.

Achievements:

- Delivered strong and sustainable operating gains: Increased customer fill rate by 18%; improved operating performance by 20%; reduced operating waste by 15%; reduced inventory by $6M.

- Justified, sourced, and directed the installation of $10M in automated plant equipment.

- Implemented and managed a centralized master schedule for all manufacturing facilities.

- Reduced annual workers' compensation costs by $600,000.

- Created Customer Satisfaction Initiative program to identify areas of concern; implemented recommendations, significantly improving customer satisfaction.

Prior Positions: Manufacturing Manager (1996–1998); Plant Manager (1995–1996); Engineering Manager (1993–1995); Plant Industrial Engineer (1988–1993).

EDUCATION & PROFESSIONAL DEVELOPMENT

Bachelor of Science in Manufacturing Engineering
Syracuse University, Syracuse, NY

Continuing professional development programs in
Executive Management, Leadership, and Finance

JEFFREY K. HUNTINGDALE

70 Lookdown Arrow Street • Wichita, Kansas 67226 • (306) 698-2563 • huntjk@slscom.com

SENIOR MANUFACTURING & OPERATIONS EXECUTIVE
Start-Up, Turnaround, and High-Growth Manufacturing Operations

QUALIFICATIONS SUMMARY

High performance, results-driven Senior Executive with a career demonstrating visionary leadership, expertise, and distinguished performance in business startup, turnaround, and operational management of multi-site, national, and international manufacturing operations. A catalyst for change, combining tactical execution of strategic initiatives with strong leadership of cross-functional staff and development of key alliances to capture and enhance overall quality, productivity, business, and bottom-line financial performance.

CORE COMPETENCIES

- Strategic Planning & Execution
- Analysis & Problem Resolution
- Team Performance Optimization
- Process Analysis & Reengineering
- Productivity & Performance Improvement
- Vendor Selection & Negotiations
- Quality Control Leadership
- Supply Chain Management
- Cost Reductions & Profit Growth
- Purchasing & Materials Management

EMPLOYMENT HISTORY

SMITHVILLE, INC., WICHITA, KANSAS   2003 to Present
Rapid promotion through increasingly responsible positions, implementing manufacturing-improvement strategies to capture cost reductions and deliver strong revenue gains.
Chief Executive Officer (2006 to Present)   **Vice President—Operations** (2004 to 2006)

Senior operating executive with full responsibility for strategic planning, development, and operational management within this motor-vehicle parts-manufacturing company. Scope of accountabilities encompasses management of all manufacturing processes; quality assurance; purchasing; warehouse safety and government compliance; and shipping/receiving. Establish and build strategic alliances with vendors, outsourced processors, and key customers to reduce expenses and drive profitability. Responsible for staff recruitment, training, and support and cross-functional team leadership and development. Identify and implement continuous-improvement measures including lean manufacturing, TQM, and cycle-time reduction.

☑ Entrepreneurial drive and vision demonstrated through set-up and development of successful international motor-vehicle fabrication subsidiary, Smithville Motors.

☑ Accelerated annual sales from $8 million to $150 million; grew Wichita premises threefold; optimized staffing levels through development of successful local/international manufacturing subsidiaries, aggressive turnaround leadership, process redesign and optimization, and implementation of strategic staffing initiatives.

☑ Captured 65% reduction in overhead through consolidation of departments.

☑ Optimized productivity 45% through development and implementation of weekly performance-monitoring and reporting methodologies.

Continued…

Strategy: Bring out the candidate's most relevant experience, beginning with core competencies and highlighted by strong achievements throughout his career.

JEFFREY K. HUNTINGDALE   huntjk@slscom.com   Page 2

- ☑ Secured net savings in excess of $120,000 per year through material waste/cost reduction.
- ☑ Decreased accidents almost 90% through introduction of formal Safety Program.
- ☑ Authored and received state funding grants totaling $66,000 for employee training.
- ☑ Pioneered creation and implementation of quality-assurance system as per standards approved by major commercial automotive-industry companies.

Quality Assurance Manager (2003 to 2004)
Diverse role, developing and implementing sound quality-assurance procedures, with accountabilities spanning Material Manager, Shipping-Receiving Supervisor, and Compliance Officer functions.

MORSEN PTE, KHAN YUNIS, ISRAEL   1998 to 2003
Recruited to spearhead all facets of motor-vehicle manufacturing company start-up, with fast-track promotion to VP role.
Vice President (1999 to 2003) ***Director of Planning & Development*** (1998 to 1999)
Planned, developed, and implemented start-up initiatives including building, infrastructure, equipment, and staffing; researched, assessed, and wrote project feasibility studies. Interfaced with key organizations, consulates, and embassies. Created and executed manufacturing quality assurance. Developed marketing materials to promote company on both national and international levels. Oversaw all administrative and manufacturing operational functions; recruited, supervised, and supported 60 cross-departmental personnel.

- ☑ Secured $10 million in funding through development of alliances with key organizations.
- ☑ Orchestrated start-up and core operational strategies; developed solid foundations that facilitated company growth.
- ☑ Pioneered benchmarking manufacturing methodologies.

EDUCATION

MBA — Wichita State University   1998

Bachelor of Science, Electrical Engineering (BSEE) — Wichita State University   1996

PROFESSIONAL MEMBERSHIPS

Wichita Area Chamber of Commerce

Jillian Berger, APR, SPHR

4732 Southern Avenue | Chattanooga, TN 37450 | 423.332.0980 | jillianb@hotmail.com

Award-Winning Communications Executive

More than 10 years of experience at a global Fortune 100 company, delivering an optimal blend of strategic and technical savvy to propel an organization's internal and external communications to improve market position. Exceptionally skilled in uniting multiple cultures to understand and embrace a corporate vision, increasing employee engagement and collaboration.

Areas of Expertise

• Media Relations	• Writing/Editing	• Strategic Planning
• Branding	• Web Content Management	• Change Management
• Public Relations	• Presentations	• Coaching/Mentoring
• Internal Communications	• Team Leadership/Motivation	• Fluent in Japanese

Professional Experience

Komatsu Limited, Tokyo, Japan   1999–Present
World's second largest manufacturer of construction and mining equipment, diesel and natural gas engines, and industrial gas turbines. Sales $32B+ in 2010; 93,000+ employees worldwide.

U.S. Organizational Effectiveness Executive, Chattanooga, TN (2008–Present)
Communications Manager, Asia Pacific Region, Beijing, China (2006–2008)
HR Communications Manager, Corporate Public Affairs, Tokyo, Japan (2005–2006)
Senior Communications Representative, Corporate Public Affairs, Tokyo, Japan (2004–2005)
Communications Representative, Corporate Public Affairs, Tokyo, Japan (2003–2004)
Senior Communications Specialist, Komatsu Financial Products Division, Chattanooga, TN (1999–2003)

Rapidly promoted through a series of progressively responsible positions. Initially hired to launch employee communications program; subsequently sought after to develop and implement global HR systems and corporate communication strategies at all levels including emerging markets. Currently working at the intersection of corporate communications and employee engagement.

Organizational Effectiveness

✓ Developed and implemented strategy for providing organizational effectiveness and engagement-related services to 32 Komatsu dealers, suppliers, and customers located in 14 countries on six continents representing more than 33,000 employees.
   • Customer satisfaction rating of 94%; 100% believe program is heading in right direction.
   • Projected profit to date is up 40% from 2010.
✓ Consulted on global employee accountability assessment project, conducted in conjunction with development of new enterprise business strategy.
✓ Collaborated with key regional leaders to develop an ethics and compliance strategy for AP region.

Global Communications

✓ Developed and implemented an employee communications strategy for AP region encompassing operations in more than 12 countries.
✓ Increased overall communications effectiveness by 7% in one year; surveys indicated that 90% of AP employees had clear understanding of business strategy.
✓ Developed and launched *Front and Center,* an award-winning internal communications network that included multiple touch points; program highlighted in December 2008 issue of *Strategic Employee Publications*.
✓ Conceptualized, planned, and delivered conferences in China and India to help Komatsu communicators better understand corporation's strategic and tactical approach to communications.
   • Attendees subsequently established communication vehicles, including websites, branding strategies, and print materials.
   • Brought corporate public affairs staff to conferences so they could convey emerging-market stories to employees in the U.S.

Page One

Strategy: Stack all the job titles from a 13-year career with the same company and then group accomplishments under functional headings. This allows placement of the most relevant achievements towards the top even if they are not the most recent.

Jillian Berger, APR, SPHR   jillianb@hotmail.com   **Page Two**

Komatsu Limited, *continued*

Leadership
- ✓ Managed three-person communications team in China and Singapore and collaborated with team of 20+ communicators located throughout AP region to implement a regional communications strategy that included clear roles and responsibilities, well-documented processes, and effective distribution outlets.
- ✓ Supervised team of 16 to provide HR communications to 100,000+ employees worldwide, resulting in 94% of company's HR managers and professionals expressing that team provided a value-added service.
- ✓ Developed new team of professional communicators that provided support to Human Services Division, resulting in 90% of employees regularly accessing main internal communications channel within one year.

Change Management
- ✓ Delivered major contributions to development and implementation of integrated communications process in support of "Komatsu Future Vision"—company's enterprise business strategy.
- ✓ Drove communication and change management strategies for global launch of HR management system and shared services business model; developed website content, PowerPoint presentations, video broadcasts, employee newsletter, employee meetings, and executive staff updates.

Awards and Recognition
- ✓ Silver Anvil Award—Internal Communications, Public Relations Society of America for rollout of major healthcare benefits changes
- ✓ Award of Merit—Newsletter, International Association of Business Communicators, Chattanooga Chapter
- ✓ Best of Class—Public Relations Campaign, DeRose/Hinkhouse Memorial Communications Awards

EARLY CAREER EXPERIENCE
Corporate Communications Specialist, Feature Reporter, Staff Writer
- ✓ Led design team that produced corporate newsmagazine 10 times a year for 60,000 customers globally.
- ✓ Edited daily employee newsletter for company's 2,000+ employees.
- ✓ Covered news beats including city government, police, health, education, and religion.

Education

GEORGIA STATE UNIVERSITY, Atlanta
Master of Arts in Corporate Communication

UNIVERSITY OF TENNESSEE, Knoxville
Bachelor of Arts in Journalism

Certifications & Affiliations

KOMATSU LIMITED   2010
Change Master Certification

SOCIETY FOR HUMAN RESOURCE MANAGEMENT   2006
Senior Professional in Human Resources (SPHR)

PUBLIC RELATIONS SOCIETY OF AMERICA   1998
Accredited in Public Relations (APR)
Former president of Chattanooga chapter

Anthony A. Simukonis

400 Front Street • Rye, NY 10580 • Cell: 914.219.0487 • Email: tonsimukonis@simukonis.com

Chief Executive Officer

Aerospace • Semiconductor Capital Equipment • Automotive
Lean Manufacturing • Finance • Sales Growth • Business Restructuring • Cost Reduction

Accomplished CEO with exceptionally strong background in finance and operation. Able to confidently take charge of any type of business. Known for strong relationship-building and business-development skills, and particularly expert at building trusted relationships among customers, employees, and labor unions.

- **Business Turnarounds**: Took charge of 4 troubled business units, reversed a downward spiral in each case, jump-started cash flow, and established positive growth that led to successful sale, integration, or ongoing positive growth.
- **Lean Manufacturing**: Successfully implemented Lean for 7 major production sites. Acquired deep knowledge of Lean theory via close collaborations with Shingijutsu, the top consultancy for Lean and Toyota Production System.
- **International**: Developed new business opportunities and recruited key partners throughout East Asia and India.
- **Elite Leadership Program**: Handpicked for an elite, 6-person leadership-training program and management team that restructured Boeing Corp. (profiled in *Industry 2.0*, a best-selling business book).

PROFESSIONAL EXPERIENCE

GENERAL ROBO MEXICO INC, Various Locations   **2009–2011**
Unit of General Robo (NYSE: ROBO). Produces electro-optic equipment and services for semiconductor manufacturing. Approx. $38M total sales.
Corporate Vice President and Managing Director

Drove the simultaneous turnaround of 3 troubled divisions based in Mexico, Korea, and Taiwan. Successfully executed turnaround plans—all within 21 months—that set the stage for a threefold increase in Robo's stock price).

Robotic Systems Inspection Division (SID), $9M Sales, Nogales, Mexico

- **Business Challenges**: SID was bankrupt and losing $12M per year. SID had been #1 in its niche, but top customers—including Intel—had lost all confidence in SID's technical competitiveness.
- **Actions and Results**: Drove cost reduction and major product improvements to accomplish "Mission Impossible #1" for Robo: Improved product accuracy from 13 to 3 microns—within 16 months—while maintaining benchmark speed. Also achieved lowest total-cost-of-ownership (TCO) in the industry.
  - Wowed customers with improved product. Restored confidence and rebuilt credibility in marketplace. SID achieved its first-ever profitable year (2010). Product was competitive and customers were pleased.
  - Increased addressable market from $26M to $53M; reduced year-over-year overhead expense by $1.6M; and improved gross margin from 48% to 61%.
  - Integrated SID into US operations (Concord, MA) according to plan.

IC Packaging Division (ICPD), $9M Sales, Singapore

- **Business Challenges**: ICPD was bankrupt and losing money.
- **Actions and Results**: Brought the company back from the dead. Restored severely damaged customer confidence; built a new team (reassignments and new hiring); and fixed technical deficiencies.
  - Reduced unit cost by 25%, resulting in gross margin increase from 34% to 50%; first 13% achieved in 6 months, balance achieved in 20 months. Expanded addressable market from 28% to 70%.
  - Directed by corporate HQ to close ICPD—despite protests from top customers—to accommodate financial consultants who advised Robo to streamline its corporate portfolio as preparation for sale.

Flat Panel Display Division (FPDD), $20M Sales, Taiwan

- **Business Challenges**: The division was unprofitable and bleeding cash, so Robo needed an exit strategy.
- **Actions and Results**: Accomplished "Mission Impossible #2" for Robo: Collected $13M in accounts receivable—badly needed cash—that corporate HQ had deemed "uncollectable."
  - Cut annual overhead by $2.5M; closed satellite offices; and reduced travel and material expenses. Improved product quality by refocusing FPDD staff on problem resolution and customer support.
  - Played a leading role during divestiture by persuading Toshiba on the merits of buying FPDD.

continued

Strategy: Use the Challenge, Action, and Results format (see page 25) to portray this individual as "the solution" to multiple business problems.

Anthony Simukonis ....Cell: 914.219.0487......................Email: tonsimukonis@simukonis.com ....Page 2

SIX SIGMA METROLOGY LLC, Princeton, NJ   2005–2008
Global manufacturer of laser-based metrology equipment used by semiconductor companies. Approximately $20M annual sales.

President and CEO

Recruited by Ancora Management—a $200M private equity fund—to lead SSM during post-bankruptcy operations. Restored trust credibility with customers. Refocused team and obtained credit from suppliers; increased sales; and created new products.

- **Business Challenges**: At one time Six Sigma Metrology had been #1 in its niche but the company was losing $12M annually due to poor quality, late delivery, and product obsolescence. Top customers had blackballed the company.
- **Actions and Results**: Established software development capability in India. Consolidated component design and system engineering. Refocused product development and introduced Lean best practices.
    - Grew sales 6% CAGR in 12-months and 51% in 24 months. Doubled available cash flow within 12 months; cut operating expenses $2.6M in 1 year; and increased inventory turns 400%.
    - Transitioned field service, applications support, and after-market operations into a profit center that supported 2,200+ machine tools at 160 worldwide sites. Cut installation time from 16 weeks to 9 days.
    - Reestablished status among leading industry players such as IBM, Intel, and Toshiba. Improved on-time delivery to 90%; and cut manufacturing floor space by 63%.
    - Sold Six Sigma Metrology to a competitor, General Precision Robotics (NASDAQ: GPR).

XTM CORP / AERO TECHNOLOGIES DIVISION, Coca Beach, FL   2003–2004
Produces gears, gearboxes, rotor heads, and complex rotating assemblies for aircraft.

Vice President Operations

- **Business Challenges**: A hostile union had intimidated weak management, and went on strike for 9 months in 2002. Delivery and quality were poor. Bell Aerospace—90% of Aero revenue—was looking for alternative suppliers.
- **Actions and Results**: Implemented lean manufacturing (Toyota Production System). Installed new leadership for shop floor and engineering. Achieved AS9100 quality-management registration within 10 months.
    - Restored pre-strike production levels with half the headcount. Restored Bell as a sole-source customer.
    - Improved inventory turns from 1.8 to 4.0. Reduced customer returns 62% and improved PO cycle times 78%. Increased sales per employee 160%. Decreased major quality audit findings from 27 to 0.
    - Reestablished trust with the union, which touted XTM/Aero as a success story at its national meeting.

NATIONAL STEEL CORPORATION   1999–2002
Manufacturer of super-alloy castings for the aerospace market. Approximately $1.6B annual sales and 9,000 employees.

Promoted to General Manager (2000–2002) | Business Unit Manager (1999–2000)

Took charge of manufacturing, P&L, sales, marketing, finance, and HR for a $100M factory with 250 employees.

- Improved return-on-capital 173% and profit 183%. Collaborated with Time Based Management (TBM), a top manufacturing consultancy and partner of Shingijutsu, Japan, the world's #1 consultancy for Lean Manufacturing.
- Improved sales per employee 24%, on-time delivery 57%, and inventory turns 64%. Cut setup time 54%.

GENERAL ELECTRIC CORP / GE AVIATION, Various Locations   1981–1999
GE Aviation manufactures aircraft engines, space propulsion systems, and industrial gas turbines. Approximately $10B annual sales.

Promoted to General Manager, Turbofan Repair Operations (1996–1999)

Grew a manufacturing business ($43M sales, 250 people) and delivered extremely high quality products on schedule. Acquired deep expertise in Lean Manufacturing via practical implementation and close collaboration with Shingijutsu.

Promoted to Manager of Planning and Business Development (1990–1996)

Negotiated and implemented 3 manufacturing joint ventures—"home runs" in Taiwan, Ukraine, and US—as key member of a 3-person corporate development team reporting to GE's Executive VP. Led M&A due-diligence reviews.

GE Senior Executive Leadership Program (1988–1990)

Handpicked by GE President for an extremely competitive, 2-year Executive Leadership Program. Member of team that cut unit production costs by 24% and consolidated manufacturing floor space from 14M sq. ft. to 2M sq. ft.

Progressed Through Numerous GE Accounting, Financial Analyst, and CFO Positions (1981–1988)

EDUCATION

B.S., Industrial Engineering, Georgia Institute of Technology, Atlanta, GA, 1981

Anil Kapoor

(847) 347-5263 • anilkap@comcast.net • 3 N. Webster Avenue, Lincolnwood, IL 60712

SENIOR EXECUTIVE PROFILE
Start-Up, Turnaround & High-Growth Organizations
Domestic & Overseas Markets

Delivering double- and triple-digit growth by attaining strategic goals, developing win-win business partnerships, and providing skillful, proactive leadership.

Innovative and hands-on leader with an unbroken track record of success:

- TriFlex, Inc.: **Reversed a 65% sales loss and achieved profitability in 2 years.**

- Premier Materials: **Grew sales by 468%.**

- DuPont: **Increased sales from $22M to $63M.**

- P&L Management
- Sales
- Market Development
- Competitive Positioning
- Product Development
- Productivity Improvement
- Negotiations
- Team Leadership

PROFESSIONAL EXPERIENCE

TriFlex, Inc., Chicago, IL
Chief Executive Officer, 2008–Present

Recruited by Chairman to transform a design/technology venture into a manufacturing and marketing operation serving the medical and consumer products markets. ***Brought company into the black from a $770K loss on $1.2M in sales. Also, increased gross margins to more than 50% by implementing cost and efficiency improvements.***

Sales, Marketing & Business Growth:
- Increased sales by 150% to $3M.
- Expanded customer base by more than 300% and developed significant new business in China, Taiwan, and England.
- Entered new markets by developing and patenting new products.
- Negotiated higher credit line and mezzanine financing.

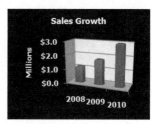

Financial & Operational Improvements:
- Boosted equipment utilization by 100%.
- Reduced plant floor space by 25%.
- Negotiated an 11% price reduction on primary raw material.
- Recruited rep agencies to extend marketing reach without significantly adding to overhead.

Strategic Planning & Positioning:
- Developed and implemented strategic goals to achieve turnaround.
- Conducted market research to determine direction of new product development and product promotion.
- Targeted—and won—multibillion-dollar companies as new customers.

Corporate Branding: Overhauled company brand, including promotional materials and website.

Premier Materials, Whiting, IN
Executive Vice President & General Manager—Automotive Products Division (2000–2007)
Vice President—Automotive Products Division (1995–2000)
Sales Manager—Premier Materials (1992–1995)

Promoted to start up and head new Automotive Products Division for $145M supplier of foam-in-place laminates. Grew it to rank #2 in industry.

—Page 1 of 2—

Strategy: Consolidate an extensive executive career into two tightly written pages highlighted by impressive performance graphs on each page.

Sales & Marketing:
- Grew sales from $31M to $145M in 10 years.
- Increased market share of primary product from 17% to 43%.
- Promoted entry into new markets by developing new products.

Strategic Initiatives:
- Elevated the division from Tier 3 to Tier 2 supplier status by developing additional expertise in supply chain and quality management (ISO 9002/QS 9000).
- Improved efficiency of just-in-time (JIT) deliveries, lowered overhead costs, and eliminated duplicate assets by creating "buyer-supplier parks."

Joint Ventures & Partnerships:
- Initiated and negotiated long-term sales agreements with 3 of the industry's 4 Tier 1 suppliers.
- Developed strategic partnerships and purchasing agreements with major suppliers to expand product line, facilitate entry into new markets, and reduce costs.

DuPont, Richmond, VA
Sales and Marketing Manager—DuPont Auto Products (1987–1992)
Hired to run Automotive Fabrics business unit, which was operating at a loss, and brought it to profitability in first year. *Directed national and international sales and marketing activities.*

Sales & Marketing:
- Brought company from a $500K loss to a $4M profit in 4 years.
- Grew sales by almost 200% in 5 years.
- Increased market share of primary product from 21% to 44%.
- Entered new market to achieve average sales increase of almost 12% in each of 5 years.

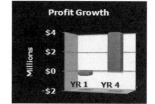

Joint Ventures & Partnerships: Negotiated a technology sharing/marketing agreement with a major Japanese supplier.

Product Development: Developed new product line in 1988 that grew to nearly 40% of total sales by 1992.

Operational Efficiency: Reduced manufacturing costs by strategic outsourcing of specific manufacturing services to 1 supplier and by purchasing new equipment.

EDUCATION

Master of Business Administration (MBA)   TULANE UNIVERSITY
Bachelor of Science (BS)   AMERICAN UNIVERSITY

PATENTS: Two patents awarded; 4 patents pending.

Anil Kapoor   —**Page 2 of 2**—   anilkap@comcast.net

PHILLIP S. KRAEMER

100-A Frederick Road
Baltimore, Maryland 21043

pskraemer@earthlink.net

Home: 443-820-7773
Cell: 443-820-7774

SENIOR MANAGEMENT EXECUTIVE—CEO

Expertise in Driving Growth, Revenues, Competitive Position, Profitability & Value

EXECUTIVE PROFILE

**Consummate Management Executive—True Visionary & Entrepreneur
Startup, Growth, Turnaround & Performance Improvement Expert
Corporate Development Strategist—Deal-Maker**

High-powered executive with a results-charged career in the startup, growth, and profitable leadership of dynamic enterprises doing business in domestic and international markets. Offer high-caliber management qualifications, acute marketing instincts, experience-backed judgment, and excellent timing. Strong orientations in technology and finance. Expert in identifying opportunities or creating them from a seed concept. Accustomed to and effective in high-profile executive roles, making high-stakes decisions and overcoming complex business challenges. Talented leader with an interactive, motivational, decisive management style. Assertive, competitive, intuitive, and innovative—an achiever of exceptional rather than expected results.

CAREER HIGHLIGHTS

- Led profitable private and public companies—from startup through growth into multibillion-dollar businesses spanning diverse industries—with operations and market reach in domestic and international arenas. Achieved 35+% margins and triple-digit ROI.

- Managed cross-border operations and staffs spanning 20+ countries—Japan, China, South America, Europe, Middle East, and former Soviet countries—establishing strong business relationships and political contacts in 6 major countries. Built, mentored, and led teams of talented managers and provided indirect management to cross-functional, multinational workforces in excess of 1,750 employees.

- Structured, negotiated, and consummated high-dollar corporate transactions, financings, and deals—M&A, IPO, JV, convertible preferred stock, equity and debt financings, equipment financings, divestitures—ranging in value from $2 million to $2+ billion. Led all post-acquisition business transition and integration initiatives.

- Secured multiple contract wins with Fortune 50 and Fortune 100 corporations.

PROFESSIONAL EXPERIENCE

SAFFRON SYSTEMS, Baltimore, MD

2002 to Present

PRESIDENT & CEO

Top-ranking executive for an IT startup that has grown from $0 to $2+ billion in annual revenue and operations in 26 countries. Hold full P&L accountability for every aspect of operations—vision, strategic planning and direction, finance, business development, sales and marketing, technology R&D, product/service launch, technical services, customer relations, and key-account management. Built and continue to lead a core management team of 53 (including 22 Country Managers) and provide indirect oversight to a multinational workforce of 1,750+ employees. Authorities and accountabilities include:

LEADERSHIP ACHIEVEMENTS
- Raised $650+ million in funds; acquired $400 million through personal and professional relationships.
- Authored and executed the business plan and succeeded in growing the company from startup to a multinational global technology enterprise and recognized industry leader.

BUSINESS DEVELOPMENT SUCCESSES
- Led the capture team in a strategic alliance to win $1+ billion contract over 5 years with $3+ billion in projected residual revenue over subsequent 3 years—Saffron's share represented 40% of total contract value.
- Captured major share in all competitively important vertical markets—positioning company as #1 or #2 in the market.

continued

Strategy: Use subheadings to steer readers through the core functional areas of the candidate's experience and multiple achievements without compromising readability.

PHILLIP S. KRAEMER   pskraemer@earthlink.net   Page Two

SAFFRON SYSTEMS—PRESIDENT & CEO—*Continued*

KEY ACCOUNTS & RELATIONSHIPS
- Established a global base of business of 7,000+ corporate, institutional, military, and government accounts—AOL Time Warner, Sony, Sears, Walmart, Ford Motors, Toyota, Harvard Medical School, University of Maryland Medical Center, US Navy, US Army, GSA, and numerous others.
- Personally developed, solidified, and managed strategic relationships with the C-level executives of Microsoft, Apple, Cisco, IBM, EDS, DoD, and others.

TECHNOLOGY INNOVATIONS & PROJECTS
- Chief Architect for total systems design. Continue to provide technical and managerial oversight to major projects and products—including new software releases.
- Overhauled the concept, content, and graphic design of the corporate website—managed the installation of high-end e-commerce/CRM features that improved customer accessibility, service levels, and satisfaction.

CORPORATE DISTINCTIONS
- Distinguished by *Fortune* magazine—"Top 25 Technology Companies," April 2010.
- Recognized in *Baltimore Magazine*—"Top 10 Fastest-Growing Companies in Maryland," 2003 (#1), 2005 (#2), 2007 (#2), 2008 (#1), and 2010 (#2).

RESTIN-10, Hunt Valley, MD   1990 to 2002

PRESIDENT & CEO

Acquired a troubled, privately owned specialty design and manufacturing company and grew it into a dynamic, publicly traded, multisite operation with sales and distribution in domestic and international markets. Provided P&L oversight to all aspects of operations—headquarters, 3 US manufacturing plants, 2 off-shore facilities, 3 warehouse operations, and 12+ sales offices. Mentored and provided leadership to the Executive Committee, directed the activities of other cross-functional senior managers, sat on the Board of Directors, managed investor relations, and served as spokesperson to the media.

CORPORATE DEVELOPMENT & LEADERSHIP SUCCESSES
- Led the company through successful IPO (1997) and continued to grow the company by as much as 40% year-over-year until its sale to foreign investors in 1998. Delivered triple-digit ROI to stakeholders.
- Energized a stagnant organization suffering from serious customer service, productivity, and quality issues. Introduced lean manufacturing methodologies, mapped core business processes, and improved employee morale.
- Won buy-in and commitment from the key department heads for the dramatic change in vision and leadership.

OPERATIONAL PERFORMANCE RESULTS
- Conceived and executed an aggressive turnaround and restructure that focused on financial discipline, performance excellence, and culture change.
- Converted $8+ million <u>loss</u> on $22 million in sales (YE 1990) to $39 million <u>profit</u> on $109 million in sales (YE 1999).
- Acquired ISO 9000 Certification.

BUSINESS DEVELOPMENT ACHIEVEMENTS
- Grew annual sales revenue from $22 million to $109+ million, restructured the sales organization and distribution channels, penetrated international markets, and captured 65+% market share in key vertical sectors.
- Led the conceptualization, development, and rollout of 26 new products (commercialized 3 new products within 10 months of assuming leadership), halting a 3-year period without product innovation (1987 to 1991).

EDUCATION

Harvard MBA
Six Sigma Black Belt

PROFESSIONAL & CIVIC AFFILIATIONS

President, Inner Harbor Business Association, Baltimore, Maryland
Chairman, Policy and Ethics Committee, Association of Approved GSA Suppliers
Chairman, Scholarship Committee, Harvard Business School Alumni Association
Certified Trainer, Six Sigma
Member, Board of Directors, Boy Scouts of America
Eagle Scout, Boy Scouts of America

Paul C. Carter

104 Devonshire Rd.
Grosse Pointe Park, MI 48230

paulcarter@mcast.net

Home: 313-822-5259
Cellular: 313-505-4040

PRESIDENT / CHIEF EXECUTIVE OFFICER
Industrial Manufacturing Environments

Entrepreneurial-oriented executive presenting a formidable record leading global business development, manufacturing, and strategic planning teams within manufacturing environments. Recognized for skill at turning around poorly performing divisions, guiding successful start-ups and/or joint ventures, and establishing strategic alliances. Accustomed to interacting and working closely with C-level executives across industry and cultural lines.

Areas of Expertise

- Strategic / Tactical Planning
- Start-Up / Turnaround
- Business Planning
- P&L Management
- Mergers and Acquisitions / Joint Ventures
- Due Diligence / Negotiations
- Operations / General Management

- Organizational Design
- Continuous Improvement Practices
- Computer-Integrated Manufacturing
- Quality Control / Assurance
- Facilities / Plant Design
- Staff Development and Supervision
- Sales and Marketing

CAREER HIGHLIGHTS

THOMPSON-GENERAL AUTOMOTIVE — Dearborn, MI
(Global manufacturer of primarily body-sealing systems, NVH control systems, and fluid-handling systems, with sales in excess of $1.6 billion.)
DIRECTOR, STRATEGIC PLANNING, 2009–2011
DIRECTOR, BUSINESS DEVELOPMENT, 2008–2009

Selected to stay on as director of strategic planning following merger of General Products Company and Thompson Tire & Rubber. Oversaw mergers and acquisitions, strategic planning, and new ventures. Additionally involved in planning, communications, and competitive intelligence. Worked closely with CEO on M&A, made board-level presentations, and held P&L oversight for new ventures.

Key Accomplishments:

- Actively involved in all aspects of sale of General to Thompson, which delivered premium to shareholders of 80% of trailing stock price.
- Cut business-development costs 40% for FY2010 by prioritizing and delaying or canceling projects.
- Successfully managed divestiture of Holt Industries, a plastics business selling product primarily to the appliance industry.
- Generated proceeds well in excess of book value, despite continuing losses, following divestiture of plastics facility in Winnsboro, SC.
- Conducted strategic evaluation of European company for NFS Control Systems Division, which subsequently led to an alliance vs. joint venture or acquisition.
- Guided shift of two emerging ventures from technology to market development, greatly increasing credible sales prospects while significantly reducing overall spending.
- Established corporate strategy, which resulted in the creation of four SBUs. Process entailed completing a strategic-planning process, developing performance targets linking strategy and operating plans, and performing portfolio-valuation process for each unit.
- Greatly improved profitability of poorly performing plastics SBU during temporary assignment as VP/General Manager in 2009. Attained cost savings of 10% and achieved annualized sales of $85 million during six-month turnaround period.

Page 1 of 3

Strategy: Create an accomplishment-rich resume that is laden with automotive industry buzzwords for this senior executive who wants to remain in that industry.

Paul C. Carter

104 Devonshire Rd.	Résumé–Page 2 of 3	Home: 313-822-5259
Grosse Pointe Park, MI 48230	paulcarter@mcast.net	Cellular: 313-505-4040

CAREER HIGHLIGHTS, continued

TELDYN *(Unit of Global Intertech)* — Minneapolis, MN
(Leader in compact fluid power components and systems, serving marine, automotive, recreational vehicles, medical, and general industry markets. Acquired by Parker Jamison in 2008.)
PRESIDENT, 2004–2008

Fully accountable for P&L of $42 million standalone unit, with complete oversight of marketing, sales engineering, product development, finance, human resources, manufacturing, and employee base of 300.

Key Accomplishments:

- Grew the company from $24 million to over $40 million within three years by developing key accounts, expanding sales to several European customers, and securing limited number of government contracts.

- Implemented quality operating system, product-development and strategic-planning processes, and new accounting and MRP systems to facilitate and support growth of company.

- Won large contract for outboard-motor hydraulic trim systems from Mercer Marine, resulting in becoming the sole supplier to Mercer. Laid foundation for long-term relationship through the establishment of pricing structure and integration of technical efforts.

- Achieved significant operational improvements by reorganizing manufacturing operations, hiring key operational personnel, and implementing continuous-improvement practices (5S, statistical methods, process mapping, one-piece flow).

- Increased sales and regained business by creating compensation program that rewarded sales force on individual performance to forecast, rather than on total company sales.

- Integrated U.S. operations of a company acquired by Teldyn's parent company.

HURON AUTOMOTIVE COMPONENTS — Benton Harbor, MI
(Start-up Michigan Motor/Cogwell International joint venture company to develop, market, and manufacture interior features for the automotive industry.)
PRESIDENT, 2001–2004

Accountable for P&L, organization design, 10-year strategic plan, 5-year business plan, and implementation of world-class business practices (including self-directed work teams).

Key Accomplishments:

- Directed formation of start-up venture, including preliminary identification of joint-venture partner and negotiation of final agreement.

- Developed organizational plan and oversaw recruitment of 150 management, technical, and production associates.

- Negotiated modern labor agreement with UAW.

MICHIGAN MOTOR COMPANY — Dearborn and Saline, MI
(Global automotive company.)
SUPERVISOR, ADVANCED MANUFACTURING PLANNING, PLASTIC, AND TRIMS PRODUCTS, 1999–2001

Charged with developing manufacturing strategy for $3.5 billion division, with 13 sites throughout North America and Europe. Devised methods to improve manufacturing efficiencies, created facilities plans for European expansion, and identified initiatives to support growth of newly formed division.

Key Accomplishments:

- Implemented cross-divisional manufacturing cycle-time reduction program.

- Developed plan for initial manufacturing facility in Europe, which involved site selection, plant design, and organizational design.

Paul C. Carter

104 Devonshire Rd. Grosse Pointe Park, MI 48230

Résumé–Page 3 of 3 paulcarter@mcast.net

Home: 313-822-5259 Cellular: 313-505-4040

CAREER HIGHLIGHTS, continued

MICHIGAN MOTOR COMPANY *(continued...)*
Key Accomplishments (continued):

- Led team redesign of 1.6-million-square-foot instrument-panel manufacturing facility.

- Developed divisional Computer Integrated Manufacturing strategy and led implementation of organization to develop key applications.

SUPERVISOR, ADVANCED MANUFACTURING ENGINEERING, 1998–1999
PROCESS DEVELOPMENT ENGINEER, 1992–1998

Led advanced group focused on initiatives to streamline instrument-panel manufacturing via flow-through manufacturing and improved product design at $350 million plant. Fully involved in process design, project management, and software development for automated systems.

Key Accomplishments:

- Developed and implemented automated manufacturing cells and factory-floor automation.

- Reduced lead time from 13 days to 1 by integrating entire manufacturing process.

- Completed broad array of process-development activities, including computer simulation, robotic assembly applications development, design for manufacturability studies, and product-design feasibility activities.

Prior professional experience:

CARTER & CARTER ENTERPRISES, INC. — Houston, TX
(Printing and graphic arts organization.)
PRESIDENT, 1990–1992

NATIONAL SUPPLY COMPANY (division of Armco Steel) — Houston, TX
(Major supplier of oilfield equipment, worldwide.)
ASSOCIATE PRODUCT ENGINEER, 1989–1990

FEDERAL MOGUL CORPORATION — Southfield, MI
(Large manufacturer of industrial products for transportation industry.)
MANUFACTURING ENGINEER, 1988–1989

EDUCATION

MICHIGAN STATE UNIVERSITY — East Lansing, MI
MBA, GENERAL MANAGEMENT, June 2000
BS, MECHANICAL ENGINEERING, June 1988

PROFESSIONAL DEVELOPMENT
- AMA, Management Course for Presidents
- AMA, Mergers & Acquisitions
- Goldratt Institute, Theory of Constraints
- Numerous in-house classes at Ford

CHAPTER 13

Resumes for Consultants and Consulting Industry Executives

- Healthcare/Pharmaceutical Industry Consultant
- Strategic Business Consultant—International
- Professional Services Consultant
- Information Technology Consultant

Brenda J. Miller

Philadelphia, PA · bmiller@verizon.net
LinkedIn: http://www.linkedin.com/in/bmiller · 814.555.5556 (cell) · 814.555.5555 (home)

PRINCIPAL · PRACTICE LEADER · CONSULTANT
HEALTHCARE & PHARMACEUTICAL INDUSTRIES

Consistently create world-class multi-functional teams and lead them to outstanding results. Provide business development and execution best practices learned from having served industry leaders and The White House. Significant P&L responsibility. Extensive experience working with C-Level and Executive groups. Possess invaluable relationships with the nation's elite business leaders and industry experts. Harvard Master's degree.

Career signature: *translating ambiguity into opportunity.*

Select Achievements
➤ Grew Web-based healthcare startup to $5 million and operational profitability in 24 months (DrugStore.net).
➤ Chosen as the commencement speaker for the 2007 graduating class of Penn State University.
➤ Led a team of 40 union employees to production records for General Motors.

AREAS OF EXPERTISE

Strategic Leadership	**Solutions Creation**	**Innovation and Growth**
Business Process Improvement	**Organizational Development**	**Relationship Building**

EXECUTIVE PROFILE

T4 CONSULTING, INC., State College, PA, and Columbus, OH   2005 – Present
Principal and Practice Leader
Advise senior executives in the development of key B2B strategic relationships to drive growth. Primary focus is on Fortune 100 Healthcare and Pharmaceutical companies.
▪ Managed clients, which included J&J, Novartis, and Adams Therapeutics.
▪ Worked with Legal, Finance, Marketing, Sales, Customer Service, and other key groups.
▪ Expanded billings a record-best 36% in 14 months.
▪ Launched the Healthcare/Pharmaceutical consulting practice from startup; led business development, demonstrating resourcefulness in use of limited resources to generate initial new sale channels and client projects.
▪ Led team that helped leadership of a $27 billion pharmaceutical company re-brand its 40-member global trade team; assisted leadership of a $2.4 billion vaccines manufacturer quickly and effectively expand its sales team from 37 to 120.

DRUGSTORE.NET, Alexandria, VA   2000 – 2005
Founding President and CEO
Worked with the Board of the National Association of Chain Drug Stores (NACDS) and launched this startup business with the premise to enhance supply chain relationships between pharmaceutical manufacturers and retail chain pharmacies.
▪ Hired, trained, and developed staff. Created and integrated administrative and operational SOPs. Encouraged a work environment of open communications and continual improvement.
▪ Grew business from $0 to $5 million and achieved operational profitability in 24 months.
▪ Established key customers among largest accounts, e.g. AstraZeneca, Eli Lilly, GlaxoSmithKline, 3M, CVS, Rite Aid, Costco, Winn-Dixie, and Cardinal Health.

EMPORIUM.COM, Columbus, OH   1999 – 2000
Chief Marketing Officer and Senior Vice President
Expanded sales for this pioneer e-commerce site: Emporium had a peak of 350 physical locations in the U.S. in the 1990s and was sold to Stiller Drug of Minneapolis in 2001 to compete with Walgreens and CVS Corp.
▪ Recruited and mentored a multifunctional staff of 25, which included Public Relations, Marketing, and Merchandising.
▪ Negotiated key national contracts with CNN.com and Warner.com.
▪ Surpassed marketing ROI of 560%.
▪ Managed more than 17,000 SKUs of Rx and OTC products in online model.
▪ Achieved 2nd quarter revenue expansion of 129%.

continued

Strategy: Emphasize specific industry expertise by highlighting key consulting projects and major accounts as well as prior corporate experience.

Brenda J. Miller – continued

bmiller@verizon.net • 814.555.5556

RESPIRITORY.COM, Columbus, OH   1996 – 1999
Founder
Built the market presence for this specialty healthcare products e-commerce business.
- Established strategic alliances with leading pharmaceutical manufacturers and non-profit organizations.
- Overcame the challenges inherent to being "new" within an established market.

WARING & TRADE RESOURCES, Houston, TX   1991 – 1996
Director, Retail Energy Services
Established C-level relationships with major commercial real estate firms.
- Provided leadership in negotiations; closed approximately 78% of the firm's contracts.
- Exercised resourcefulness and creativity, e.g. there were no initial real estate relationships for this startup—used available resources to create a new commercial real estate–driven sales channel.

THE WHITE HOUSE, Washington, DC   1989 – 1991
Chief of Staff to President Bush's Economic & Domestic Policy Advisor
Managed a staff of 18 within the Office of Policy Development (OPD).
- Performed key liaison role for White House functions, e.g. speech writing, public liaison, Office of Management and Budget (OMB), and legislative affairs.
- Served as liaison to cabinet agencies: NASA and external groups. Met with C-level officers from F500 firms to discuss policy elements.
- Created and implemented numerous operational best practices.

SUMMARY OF PREVIOUS EXPERIENCE

ERNST & YOUNG, Washington, DC (1987 – 1988)
Senior Management Consultant
Designed a landmark QA/QC program implemented by the EPA as a best practice.

STATE GAS COMPANY, Boston, MA (1986 – 1987)
Management Consultant to VP of Marketing and Sales
Streamlined sales process and compressed sales cycle. Worked while full-time graduate student.

GENERAL MOTORS CORPORATION, Rochester, NY (1985)
Production Manager
Led team of 40 union employees and achieved record production growth of 20%.

EDUCATION

HARVARD UNIVERSITY, Cambridge, MA
Master in Public Policy — Concentration in Business and Government
Selected coursework also completed at MIT Sloan School of Management and Harvard Business School.

THE PENNSYLVANIA STATE UNIVERSITY, University Park, PA
Bachelor of Science, Industrial Engineering
Member of Tau Beta Pi and Alpha Pi Mu engineering honor societies.
Commencement speaker for the 2007 graduating class of Penn State University.

BOARDS

COLLEGE OF INFORMATION SCIENCES AND TECHNOLOGY ADVISORY BOARD MEMBER EMERITUS,
Harvard University

SERVICE ENTERPRISE ENGINEERING ADVISORY BOARD,
The Pennsylvania State University's Department of Industrial Engineering

EDWIN BARNES

40 Howe Street, Wellesley, MA 02181
617-555-2345 • ed.barnes@gmail.com

STRATEGIC BUSINESS CONSULTANT

Asian/Global Partnerships • Innovative Outsourcing Models • Professional Services

Visionary, strategist, and consummate relationship-builder who envisions, defines, plans, and executes effective strategies and operations to drive business performance improvements and manage the human side of change.

Innovator in launching employee services, outsourcing relationships, and global partnerships—transformational ventures that elevate performance to record levels. Change leader and senior executive with Sanya and ATS; strategic business consultant to U.S. and international entities tapping emerging global opportunities.

Highlights

- **Linchpin** for connecting U.S./multinational companies with beneficial business partners and relationships in Asia.
- **Catalyst** for innovative outsourcing solution and expansion of business model to full-scale professional services firm.
- **Driving force** behind evolution of pioneering employee services programs at Sanya into award-winning models and recognized contributors to company performance.

PROFESSIONAL EXPERIENCE

BARNES CONSULTING GROUP, Boston, MA   2008–Present

In demand as consultant to U.S., European, and Asian companies seeking multinational partnerships, business strategy advising, HR outsourcing assistance, and expert guidance to evaluate and execute beneficial business strategies that are heavily relationship-based. Engagements include:

- **Global Business Conceptualization and Launch:** Recruited by Hong Kong investment company to guide strategy for a new business concept. Transformed vague idea into viable business model and written business plan; identified and cultivated potential partners in U.S., China, Malaysia, and Thailand. Business is currently in pre-launch stage and projects expansion to 10 Southeast Asia countries to capture multimillion-dollar opportunities in the emerging outsource EAP field.

- **China Resource Development:** Identified and initiated outreach to people, resources, and potential equity partners in China for a professional services firm. Facilitated dialogue and coached owner on Asian business culture.

- **Business Model Refinement:** Assisted Sanya in post-outsourcing strategic planning to maximize business benefits of new model while ensuring service/satisfaction of internal customers.

AFFILIATED TECHNICAL SERVICES (ATS), Waltham, MA   2006–2008
VP Global Employee Consultation Systems

Executed outsourcing strategy and managed transition of Sanya Human Resources services to outsource partner; remained in leadership role to build and manage company's new practice in Global HR Solutions. Led global operations/P&L of 50 professionals who spoke 13 languages and provided services to 65 countries throughout Europe, Middle East, Africa, Asia, and the U.S.

- **Business Development:** Personally communicated service concepts and delivered sales presentations to key target accounts. In first year, landed contracts with Boeing, Travelers, Lufthansa, IBM, and other global corporations.

- **Business Model Development:** Expanded and enhanced service capabilities by initiating relationships with high-quality vendors; set the stage for fruitful long-term relationships.

- **Client Relationship Management:** Served as principal liaison to the $85M Global Sanya Account.

SANYA, INC., Boston, MA   1987–2006
VP Global Employee Consultation Systems, 1998–2006

Conceptualized, designed, and implemented innovative global service to meet the needs of a dynamic and turbulent workforce. Global Employee Consultation Systems comprised EAP, Workplace Violence, Mental Healthcare Benefits Cost Control, Drug Testing, and Change Management programs/services that were employed for major initiatives across the enterprise (e.g., M&A, divestitures, risk mitigation, performance improvement). Managed $10M P&L, becoming the only HR services organization in Sanya to operate as a business unit.

Strategy: Highlight key consulting projects and the many innovative programs led by this individual throughout a lengthy career in human resources and consulting.

EDWIN BARNES   617-555-2345 • ed.barnes@gmail.com

SANYA, continued

- **New Employee Relations Services Model:** Invented, piloted, and gained executive support for "Integrated Model for Employee Relations Service Delivery," a systemic problem-solving process that successfully identified and resolved workplace problems prior to escalation.

- **Global Expansion:** Built a global platform that influenced international business leaders to adopt and finance strategy; successfully expanded from North America to worldwide acceptance.
  — Became first multinational to recruit local national staff to provide employee services at Sanya sites worldwide.
  — Persuaded country-based businesses and HR leaders to fully finance the operation in each country.

- **Recognition:** Repeatedly recognized for superior quality and financial results, earning national awards and international emulation:
  — C. Everett Koop Quality Award, for reducing health risks, medical costs, and need for services (2006).
  — Welcoa Platinum Award, "the pinnacle of results-oriented worksite wellness programming" (2005).
  — Korean Ministry of Labor adapted the Sanya Model as the basis of government policy requiring EAP in Korean companies.

Director Employee Assistance Programs, 1992–1999

Transformed disparate employee assistance programs into a cohesive global operation that delivered measurable performance improvements through a systemic management-consultation process. Departing from traditional approach, aligned EAP strategy and initiatives with business performance. Recruited, hired, and developed a top-notch team of global professionals. Developed strong network of best-in-class vendors for service delivery.

- **Pioneering Program Launch:** Spearheaded "Drug-Free Workforce Initiative," making Sanya the second multinational company to implement universal random drug testing. Earned Sanya "Six Sigma Quality Award," the first time HR received this prestigious recognition.

- **Long-Term Strategy:** Identified need for systemic strategy to address mental health and chemical dependency issues. Created problem-solving consultation model and engaged management in innovative consultation approach. Reduced mental healthcare costs to half the national average.

- **Culturally Sensitive Program Development:** Identified need for global workplace violence policy; researched the issue globally (U.S., EMEA, Latin America, Asia); developed white paper for senior executives; led initiative to create corporate strategy/policy that was accepted and applied at all Sanya businesses worldwide.

- **Strategy Transformation:** Changed the way the corporation provided support to employees. Identified stress as a major performance factor and conducted research, analysis, strategy development, and executive presentations that influenced Chairman/CEO to launch Premier Employer Initiative supporting a wide range of workplace resources.

- **Business Partnerships:** Developed powerful internal partnerships, easily attracting multi-functional executive and staff support for EAP strategy because of its focus on performance. Expanded influence to change management and other initiatives involving the human side of change.

Manager Employee Assistance Programs, 1987–1992

Recruited to develop the employee assistance concept for the corporation. Pioneered a unique performance-based and management-consultation approach that maximized productivity by resolving organization- and employee-based performance problems.

PRIOR PROFESSIONAL EXPERIENCE: Acquired a systemic approach to mental health, productivity, and employee assistance challenges through public- and private-sector experience.

EDUCATION

M.A., Boston University, Boston, MA
B.S., Tufts University, Medford, MA

SYLVANA CORTEZ

1170 Richmond Trail, Orlando, FL 32812
321.555.8719 ♦ sylvana.cortez@mac.com

PROFESSIONAL SERVICES CONSULTANT / PROGRAM MANAGER

Solving problems and delivering solutions for start-up to Fortune 100 companies.

♦ **Hands-on Management Experience:** Senior operating executive of $35M business; driving force behind organizational and operational structures that professionalized the business and enabled profitable growth.

♦ **Big 5 and Professional Services Consulting Background:** Project Manager with Ernst & Young and Senior Program Manager with X-Tech; software implementation leader for key clients Intel, Apple, and Verizon.

♦ **High-Tech Startup Success:** Ground-floor employee at Med-Tech and X-Tech; wearer of many "hats" and key player in every facet of launching and growing a technology-based company.

♦ **Marketing, Sales, and Business Development Focus:** Creative thinker with success launching complementary service lines, capturing client endorsements/new business, and delivering double-digit sales growth.

♦ **People, Process, and Operational Expertise:** Recognized expert in recruiting right-fit employees, building sound operating structures, and creating order amid the chaos of fast-changing business environments.

PROFESSIONAL EXPERIENCE

GTC HOMES, INC., Orlando, FL   2005 to Present
Vice President / COO / Marketing Manager

Structured and led young company to succeed during both exploding and contracting economies. Joined 4-year-old custom home builder and transformed "seat-of-the-pants" management style into organizational processes, policies, and procedures that created firm foundation for profitable growth.

Created the company's first organizational chart, rewrote all existing job descriptions, and authored a comprehensive employee manual documenting job performance expectations, benefits, and rules of conduct. Implemented 401(k) program, automatic check deposit, personal leave request, drug testing, and employee review systems. Weeded out underperformers and recruited talent consistent with new culture. Managed $1.5M operating budget.

Growth & Profitability

♦ Accelerated company growth—from **$500K** to **$35M** revenues, 5 employees to 40.

♦ Expanded product line from single-family homes to spec homes, multifamily projects, and land development.

♦ Delivered **20%** year-over-year sales growth through effective management of 16 sales brokers, 4 marketing companies, and 3 print companies.

♦ Conceived idea and launched complementary service line—poised to capture new business in a radically shifted real estate market. Wrote business plan and promoted service by networking through professional groups; building relationships with major firms; and creating website, multimedia advertising campaigns, and marketing collateral.

Operations & Program Management

♦ Managed **100+** projects at a time—established goals and timelines, created sales and marketing strategies for each, acquired permits/licensing, and juggled the company's resources to meet competing needs.

♦ Created a collaborative culture of cross-functional teamwork that was instrumental in meeting aggressive deadlines on multiple projects.

X-TECH, San Jose, CA / Orlando, FL   2003 to 2005
Senior Program Manager—Professional Services

Recruited for key role developing and leading software implementation/project management division for fast-emerging company—a Web-based, cutting-edge software startup with clients that included Intel, e-Trade, Apple, and numerous Florida tourist attractions. As one of first 40 employees and first program managers, instrumental in building market credibility to drive growth, establish company as a leading CRM provider, and position for IPO.

Growth & Profitability

♦ Helped create the firm's foundation for defining, selling, and installing protocols for professional services.

♦ Contributed to company's fast success—revenue growth *every quarter* and IPO in second year.

♦ Page 1 of 2 ♦

Strategy: Help this consultant transition back into a larger professional services arena after a five-year hiatus during which she helped manage her husband's construction business. Include highlights from *both* experiences in her summary.

SYLVANA CORTEZ   321.555.8719 ♦ sylvana.cortez@mac.com

X-TECH, continued

Program Management

♦ Ran the *first* pilot project for installation of version 1.0 of the software—a "test case" with Intel that resulted in large follow-on contracts for other departments.

♦ Led project team in *first* international project, a successful software installation for Apple.

♦ Achieved nearly **100%** adoption through on-site training, persuasion, and demonstration of software benefits to end users within client companies.

♦ Chosen by VP to interview and recommend every person hired for the Professional Services organization.

ERNST & YOUNG, San Francisco, CA   2001 to 2003
Project Manager / Consultant

Member of consulting teams engaged by Fortune 100 and Fortune 500 companies to provide expertise in setting up and managing project management offices, developing new systems and processes, solving problems, and designing new pricing models. Highest ranked consultant among peers in the office.

Program Management

♦ Led major technology conversion program for Verizon.

♦ Recognized for ability to "add structure to chaos" in orchestrating multifaceted consulting projects involving complex client operations and numerous team members.

MED-TECH, San Jose, CA   1998 to 2001
Sales / Marketing

Involved in every stage of growing a start-up business to multimillion-dollar revenues and 200+ employees. Hired directly out of college as one of first 11 employees of medical device company. Within 2 years, rose to management level with direct oversight of $300K budget and 12 staff.

Operational, Marketing & Inside/Outside Sales Leadership

♦ In fast-paced, high-energy environment, continuously took on new roles and higher-level functions to meet the needs of a growing business.

♦ Launched new products through trade shows, infomercials, and marketing campaigns. Wrote inside sales script. Started up a call center. Hired and trained staff and trained end users in technology products.

EDUCATION

MBA, University of San Francisco   2002

♦ Completed a notable internship experience—a total operational restructuring of a public service organization to improve efficiency and drive out cost. Worked with team to develop cost-saving improvements that generated nearly **$10M** annual savings.

BA in Business *(Summa cum Laude, Phi Beta Kappa),* University of California at Berkeley   1998

DANA WOZNIAK

7425 45th Avenue SW ■ Seattle, WA 98137
206-555-1255 ■ dana.wozniak@verizon.com

INFORMATION TECHNOLOGY CONSULTANT
PROJECT MANAGEMENT ■ STRATEGIC PLANNING ■ NEGOTIATION

Moving organizations forward with technical expertise, personal insight, and an in-depth understanding of what will and won't work in forming optimal strategy and execution plans.

Expert in custom business applications development and implementation with extensive experience in data-intensive, high-transaction, fast-growth industries. Drive results through expert technical qualifications, exceptional team-building skills, and talent for overcoming technical, organizational, and interpersonal obstacles. Personally credited with rescuing projects, reenergizing project teams, and salvaging relationships with clients to pave the way for ongoing and future strategic partnerships, income revenue, and bottom-line growth.

PERFORMANCE MILESTONES

Project Turnaround Leader:
- **Rescued $4.2M project** and client relationships to meet all deliverables *plus* gain $1.5M in add-on revenue.
- **Revitalized technology upgrade** for 1,800 workstations across 12 sites to achieve project deliverables, restore client relationships, and initiate a strategic partnership for future engagements.
- **Salvaged $3.5M network-monitoring infrastructure** supporting $300M revenue stream.

Contract Negotiator:
- **Directed 4-way auction support system** involving 4 major telecommunications providers. Won all targeted licenses within $4B budget and returned $250M to the corporation.
- **Negotiated $3.5M** data center outsourcing contract that included significant discounts and annual options.
- **Slashed a software development contract 47%** to $18M to save the project.
- **Reduced a vendor bid by $22M**, exceeding corporate goals and strengthening competitive advantage.

Astute Strategist:
- **Launched Program Management Office** for both Trader Joe's and Verizon.
- **Reduced software defects 20%** by instituting standard testing processes and root-cause analysis.
- **Captured $1M annual savings** by restructuring staff, increasing reuse of shared data by 50%, and streamlining future software development projects in a standard information architecture implementation.
- **Increased productivity 400%** by instituting suite of solutions for customer care, ordering, and billing.

PROFESSIONAL HIGHLIGHTS

NORTHWEST CONSULTING ASSOCIATES, INC.

IT CONSULTANT / BUSINESS STRATEGIST, 1999–Present

Repeatedly recruited for complex, long-term engagements for major clients that include Trader Joe's, Verizon, and Starbucks. Provide expertise in IT-related business matters, including comprehensive programs with multimillion-dollar capital budgets, process design/improvements, and contract negotiations. Manage multi-disciplinary teams combining client and vendor staff; deliver regular status reports to senior management. Bring attitude of ownership to each assignment, consistently meeting or exceeding all milestones and objectives—deliverables, quality, time, margins.

Project Highlights:

Trader Joe's

✓ **CORPORATE PROGRAM OFFICE ESTABLISHMENT & MANAGEMENT:** Instituted steering committee, standardized processes and procedures, developed resource planning model, and trained staff. Progressed from track record of zero to 80% on-target delivery of all projects.

✓ **SUPPLY CHAIN MANAGEMENT:** Discovered significant flaws in existing processes and achieved C-level buy-in to build electronic ordering, receiving, and perpetual inventory systems for a $315K monthly savings.

Continued

Strategy: Call out specific projects and highlight well-known client names to establish the credibility and expertise of this IT consultant.

DANA WOZNIAK   206-555-1255 ■ dana.wozniak@verizon.com

Trader Joe's, continued
- ✓ **INTERNAL DATA CENTER OUTSOURCING:** Led IT team to determine functionalities and managed complete project lifecycle from RFI/RFP development through contract negotiations and migration to hosted facility.
- ✓ **SARBANES OXLEY:** Successfully met SOX requirements, including remediation efforts, system stabilization, and operational cost reductions stemming from data center migration.

Verizon
- ✓ **DEDICATED WEB HOSTING:** Developed system to support data center hosting business, including a sales cycle module for "quote to cash" applications. Repackaged project numerous times to avert cancellation and negotiated with vendor to reduce contract from original $34M to $12M. Efforts proved viability of the business unit and saved it from sale.
- ✓ **SHARED BUSINESS SERVICES:** Established program office, project plans, schedules and milestones, risk mitigation, communications, and change control procedures. Negotiated $14M savings on software contract.
- ✓ **ORDERING BUSINESS SERVICES INFRASTRUCTURE:** Instituted standard QC processes and checkpoint milestones to minimize production errors by 20% and improve on-time deliveries by 80%.

Starbucks
- ✓ **PROJECT MANAGEMENT/SYSTEMS METHODOLOGY STANDARDIZATION:** Generated $150K savings by standardizing in-house project management/systems methodology lifecycle rather than purchasing off the shelf. Alleviated internal conflicts with the application of the method company-wide.

High-Profile Logistics
- ✓ **$1M DESKTOP UPGRADE:** Assessed the viability of and reinvigorated stalled technology upgrade while rebuilding deteriorated relationships between client and consulting team.

VERIZON WIRELESS

DIRECTOR OF SYSTEMS DEVELOPMENT, 1997–1999

Implemented full suite of applications to support customer care, order entry, order fulfillment, rating, billing, and inventory management functions. Established data-driven environment, including corporate data model and shared databases for 30+ applications. Managed design and implementation of major client-server computing platform for more than 300 workstations and 22 servers/host processors.

- ✓ **Administered $18.2M budget** and managed 75-member staff.
- ✓ **Completed project $3M under budget** and ahead of schedule.

DIRECTOR, INFORMATION SYSTEMS—PERSONAL COMMUNICATIONS, 1995–1997
DIRECTOR, TECHNICAL SUPPORT—VERIZON MOBILE, 1991–1995
MANAGER, STRATEGIC PLANNING, 1989–1991

- ✓ **Established 10-year Strategic Information System plan** that streamlined processes, decreased redundancies, and delivered $20M annual savings.

EDUCATION

Bachelor of Science, **UNIVERISTY OF WASHINGTON,** Seattle, WA

Ongoing professional development: *Strategic IS Planning, Structured Systems Analysis & Design, Logical Data Modeling, Relational Database Design, Project Management, TQM, SPICE/CMM Assessment Training*

PART III

Cover Letters for Managers and Executives

CHAPTER 14

Writing a Winning Cover Letter

Now that your resume is written, you may think that you're all set to launch your job search. If it were only that easy! Just as critical to the effectiveness and success of your job search campaign is your cover letter. Let's begin our discussion of this vital element in your job search with a concise definition:

> **Cover Letter:** A document that accompanies your resume and is used to highlight your specific skills, qualifications, competencies, achievements, and more that relate directly to the position for which you are applying.

That's right…the best cover letters are letters that are targeted to specific positions (for example, CEO, COO, CFO, CIO, Vice President of Sales, Director of International Marketing, Executive Vice President of Operations, General Manager of Manufacturing). Targeted letters allow you to selectively include information about your past management experience, leadership credentials, training and education, affiliations, professional activities, and other qualifications that directly support your candidacy for a particular position. In essence, you're taking everything about your career, laying it out on the table (so to speak), and then selecting only the information that is most important to your current job objective.

The following example shows a wonderfully written cover letter that is targeted to this candidate's specific objective—a position as Chief Information Officer with a Fortune 500 company.

MARCUS R. WINSTON

4201 Oakhill Terrace
Vineland, New Jersey 08361

mwinston888@aol.com

Home: 856-789-5874
Cell: 856-869-7491

June 15, 2012

John R. Anderson, CEO
Kenilworth Transportation Worldwide
1000 Kenilworth Boulevard
Dallas, TX 77893

RE: Chief Information Officer (CIO) Opportunity

Dear Mr. Anderson:

Leading information technology strategy and worldwide infrastructure development to support aggressive growth plans for Fortune 500 corporations is my expertise. In each of my positions, I have consistently leveraged technology, people, and processes to improve profits. Highlights include:

- As **General Manager—North America Outsourcing Service Delivery** for the $6 billion X-Tech Corporation, I built innovative, award-winning business strategies and infrastructure systems and exceeded the annual margin plan by $4.8 million in 2008, $2.9 million in 2009, $4.8 million in 2010, and $4.1 million in 2011.

- As **Executive Vice President** for AAA Finance, a subsidiary of a $6 billion Fortune 500 insurance company, I developed infrastructure and corporate strategy to support the company's aggressive plan for rapid growth through domestic and international acquisitions.

- As **Area Manager—Information Technology** for a Big 5 consulting firm, I managed relocation of the data center within 7 months and developed a global disaster-recovery program.

- As **Managing Director—Information Resources** for a financial services company, I led the consolidation of 2 data centers, internalized outsourced services, and eliminated $1.3 million in expenses.

- As **Vice President—Information Processing Services** for a worldwide provider of financial services, I led innovative improvements in data center operations, network operations, systems software, hardware planning and acquisition, contingency planning, and change control that reduced expenses and delivered efficiencies.

In addition to these accomplishments, I earned my Executive MBA from Harvard University and have completed extensive leadership training at both the University of Chicago and University of Virginia. I would welcome the opportunity to interview for the CIO opportunity with Kenilworth and will follow up with your office next week to schedule a time to meet.

Sincerely,

Marcus Winston

Enclosure

A targeted cover letter (submitted by Beverly Harvey, CPRW, JCTC, CCM, CCMC, MRW, CPBS, CLTMC, CJSS, COIS).

All too often, job search candidates write general cover letters that can be used to apply for any type of management or executive position with virtually any type of organization. In essence, these letters simply summarize information that is already included on the resume and tend not to be nearly as effective as cover letters that are customized to fit a specific position. Because general cover letters are written without a specific position in mind, they do not highlight information that would be essential in a particular situation. As such, we strongly urge that you stay away from general letters and devote the time that is necessary to develop targeted cover letters that will sell you into your next position.

Another real advantage to targeted cover letters is that the recipient will notice that you have taken the time to write an individual letter to him or her; and, of course, that leaves a great impression. When you are able to integrate specific information into your letter about the company to which you are applying, it clearly demonstrates your interest in the position and the organization, before you've ever had the opportunity to speak with anyone there. Just think how impressed a prospective employer will be when he or she realizes that you've spent the time and energy necessary to research and get to know his or her organization. This good impression, in and of itself, will give you a distinct advantage over the competition.

Six Steps to Writing Better Cover Letters

To help guide you in writing and designing your own winning cover letters, we've created a step-by-step process and structure that will help you to quickly and easily write letters that will get you and your resume noticed, not passed over.

1. Identify Your Key Selling Points
2. Preplan
3. Write the Opening Paragraph
4. Write the Body
5. Write the Closing
6. Polish, Proofread, and Finalize

In order to provide you with an action plan to write your cover letters with ease and confidence, we explore each of these steps in detail in the following sections. Our most detailed discussion is "Step 1: Identify Your Key Selling Points," which is the foundation for your cover letter.

STEP 1: IDENTIFY YOUR KEY SELLING POINTS

What management qualifications, experiences, achievements, and skills do you bring to a company? It's time to evaluate and quantify what it is that makes you unique, valuable, and interesting to potential employers.

Know Your Objective

The best place to start is by clearly identifying *who* you are and *what* your job objective is. Are you a senior operating executive, midlevel sales management executive, production and engineering manager, or high-level corporate finance executive? You must be able to clearly and accurately define who you are in an instant—because an instant is all that you have to capture your reader's attention, encouraging him or her not only to read your cover letter in full, but also to read your resume and contact you for a personal interview.

Summarize Your Experience

Just as important, you must be able to clearly identify why an organization would be interested in interviewing and possibly hiring you. Is it because of the industries in which you've been employed? The management and executive positions you've held? The promotions you've earned? Your accomplishments? Your leadership performance? Your communication and interpersonal skills? Your specific experience and qualifications within a particular industry or profession? Your educational credentials or the universities you attended? Your foreign language skills and international experience? Why would someone be interested in you?

Sell Your Achievements

Your achievements are what set you apart from others with a similar background. They answer the reader's all-important question, "What can you do for me?," because they tell precisely what you have done for someone else. Cover letters and resumes without achievements are simply dry compilations of position titles and responsibilities. They don't sell your unique attributes, and they don't compel readers to pick up the phone and invite you in for an interview.

In thinking about your achievements, ask yourself how you've benefited the organizations where you've worked. In general terms, you can help an organization by

- Making money (revenues, profits, earnings, ROI/ROA/ROE increases, new customers)

- Saving money (cost reductions, streamlining, automating)

- Creating new things (courses, programs, techniques, methodologies, systems, processes, and more)

- Improving existing things (reengineering, redesigning, developing new processes, consolidating)

- Improving staff, departmental, and/or organizational performance (productivity, efficiency, quality, delivery, and customer service)

- Winning honors, awards, and commendations

In writing your achievements, think about the two key pieces of information you want to convey about each of your successes: what you did and how it benefited the organization. The combination of both of these components is what will make your achievements—and, in turn, you—shine.

Who you are, *what* you have achieved, and *why* an organization would want to hire you are critical questions you must ask yourself before you ever begin to write a cover letter. The answers to those questions will directly impact what you write in your cover letter and how you present that information. You must determine what you have to offer that relates to that organization's specific needs, what will be of interest to its hiring manager, and what will entice him or her to read your resume and offer you the opportunity for an interview. That information then becomes the foundation for every cover letter that you write.

STEP 2: PREPLAN

Before you begin writing a single word of your cover letter, you must determine the appropriate strategy for that particular letter. You're not ready to write until you can clearly answer the following questions:

- **Why am I writing this letter?** Am I writing in response to a print or online advertisement, sending a cold-call letter to a company, contacting someone in my network, writing to an organization at the recommendation of someone else, or writing a follow-up letter to a company to which I already sent a resume? The answer to this question will significantly impact the content of your cover letter—the introduction in particular.

- **Have I researched the organization and/or the position?** There will be instances where you know, or can find, information about an organization you are writing to, the services and products it offers, the positions that are open, the types of candidates it hires, the hiring requirements, and so much more. Do your research! The more you know about a company and the position, the more on-target you can write your letters, relating your experience to the company's identified needs. If you know the company is experiencing phenomenal cost overrides, showcase your success in reducing operating costs and improving bottom-line profitability. If the company is plagued with manpower instability, highlight your performance in recruiting and retaining top-quality personnel. Your goal is to find common ground between you and the company and then leverage that to your advantage.

- **Do I have a contact name? Have I double-checked the correct spelling of the name and the person's job title? Do I have the full mailing address or e-mail address?** The fact is that if you write to the Human Resources department of a company, you'll never know quite where your letter and resume have landed. However, if you write to a particular individual (we recommend a senior-level manager or executive) in a particular department with particular contact information, you not only know who has your resume and cover letter, you also know whom to follow up with. This is critical for job search success in today's competitive market!

STEP 3: WRITE THE OPENING PARAGRAPH

The opening paragraph of your cover letter is your hook—your sales pitch—that tells your reader *who* you are and *why* you are of value to that specific organization. It should entice the recipient to read your letter in its entirety and then take the time to closely review your resume. Because the opening paragraph is so critical, it is often the section that takes the longest to write.

> **TIP:** If you're having trouble writing the opening paragraph of your cover letter, leave it for the time being and move on to the body of the letter. Once you've written the rest, the opening paragraph will usually flow much more smoothly and quickly.

There are three questions you must address in the opening paragraph of your cover letter:

1. Who are you?

2. Why are you writing?

3. What message are you communicating?

Your answers to these questions will almost always dictate the type of opening you select. Review the introductory paragraphs for the sample cover letters in Chapter 15 to help you get started developing your own introduction.

STEP 4: WRITE THE BODY

Now you're ready to tackle the real task at hand: writing the body of your cover letter—the key qualifications, leadership performance, accomplishments, successes, and whatever other information you choose to highlight that will entice the reader to closely review your resume and offer you the opportunity for a personal interview.

In order to sell yourself (or any product) as "the answer," you must highlight the attractive *features* and *benefits* of that product. Put yourself in the shoes of the buyer and ask yourself these questions:

• What will catch my attention?

• What's interesting about this candidate?

• What's innovative or unique about this candidate?

• Why is this candidate different from (or better than) other competitive candidates?

• Do I understand the value I'll get from this candidate?

• Do I need this candidate?

• Do I want this candidate?

Regardless of whether you're conscious of it, every time you buy something, you ask yourself these questions and others. It's the typical process that everyone goes through when deciding whether to make a purchase. Keep this process in mind as you begin to write your cover letters. You must clearly communicate the answers to these questions in order to get people to want to "buy" *you*.

> **TIP:** Don't write your cover letter to say, "Here I am, give me a job." Instead, write it to say, "Here I am; this is why I am so valuable; give me a chance to solve your problems." Focusing on the value and benefits you have to offer is a good way to capture the reader's attention. Remember, the employer's most compelling question is "What can you do for me?" not "What do you want?"

Your challenge, then, is to convey your value in a short and concise document—your cover letter. Unfortunately, there are no rules to guide you in determining what to include in each specific cover letter that you write. It is entirely a judgment call based on the specific situation at hand—the position, the organization, and the required qualifications and experience. What you include in your letter is not necessarily based on what you consider to be your most significant responsibilities and achievements from throughout your career, but rather what is *most relevant to the hiring company and its needs.*

Achievements, accomplishments, contributions, and successes are the cornerstone of any effective cover letter. You want to demonstrate that you have the right skills, qualifications, and experience for a particular job. However, you do not want your letter to be a mere listing of job responsibilities. First of all, you've addressed a great deal of that information in the resume that you'll be sending along with your cover letter. You do *not* want your letter to simply reiterate what's in your resume. The challenge is to write a cover letter that complements the resume and brings the most notable information to the forefront.

Depending on the format of your letter, you can convey this information in a paragraph format, a bullet-point format, or a combination of both. Use whichever you feel is most appropriate to convey the particular information. If you decide to use full paragraphs, make sure that they are fairly short to promote readability. Edit and tighten your copy so that every word and phrase conveys information that relates to the employer's needs and your most relevant qualifications.

STEP 5: WRITE THE CLOSING

Now that you've written your introductory paragraph and the body of your cover letter, all you have left to write is the closing paragraph. This paragraph is generally the easiest section of your letter to write. To get started, ask yourself these two simple questions:

- What style of closing paragraph do I want to use?

- Is there any specific personal or salary information I want to include that was requested in the advertisement to which I am responding?

When it comes to choosing a style, closing paragraphs are easy. There are basically only two styles—passive and assertive—and the distinction between the two styles is evident:

- **Passive:** A passive letter ends with a statement such as "I look forward to hearing from you." With this sentence, you are taking a passive approach, waiting for the hiring company or recruiter to contact you. This is not our recommended strategy.

- **Assertive:** An assertive letter ends with a statement such as "I look forward to interviewing with you and will follow up next week to schedule a convenient appointment." In this sentence, you are asserting yourself, telling the recipient that you will follow up, and asking for the interview!

We strongly recommend that you end your cover letters with an assertive closing paragraph. Remember, the objective of your cover letter is to get an interview, so *ask for it!* Furthermore, we also advise that you outline an agenda that communicates you will be expecting the employer's call and, if you don't hear from him, you will follow up. This puts you in the driver's seat and in control of your job search. It also demonstrates to a prospective employer that once you've initiated something, you follow it through to completion. This is a valuable trait for any professional.

Inevitably, there will be instances in your job search when you will not be able to follow up:

- If you are responding to a blind posting, you won't know who to call.

- If you are responding to an advertisement that states "No Phone Calls," don't call.

- If you are sending out 1,000 e-mails to recruiters across the nation, don't waste your time calling them. If they're interested or have an opportunity for which you are suited, they'll call you.

- If you know that you'll never get the individual you want to speak with on the phone, don't waste your time or money.

The closing paragraph of your cover letter is also the preferred placement for any personal or salary information you will include. There are generally only two times you will want to include this type of information:

- **When it has been asked for in an advertisement.** Common requests include such things as salary history (what you have made in the past and are currently earning if you are employed), salary requirements (what your current salary objectives are), citizenship status, or geographic preference.

- **When you are writing "cold-call" letters to recruiters.** When contacting recruiters, we recommend that you at least minimally address your salary requirements (a range is fine) and any geographic preferences in the closing paragraph of your cover letter.

STEP 6: POLISH, PROOFREAD, AND FINALIZE

The process we recommend for writing your cover letters suggests that you first craft the opening, then the middle, and then the closing of each letter. Although the step-by-step process makes the task fairly quick and easy, you will probably find that your letters need final polishing, wordsmithing, and tweaking to ensure that each section flows into the next and that you have a cohesive whole.

Take the time to proofread your letter thoroughly and carefully. Read it for sense and flow; then read it again to check for spelling errors, punctuation mistakes, and grammatical inconsistencies. We cannot emphasize this point enough. The people who receive your cover letter and resume *do* judge your professionalism based on the quality and accuracy of these documents. In fact, in a survey of hiring authorities we conducted for a prior book, *90 percent of respondents* mentioned quality and appearance factors (such as typos, misspellings, and a generally poor appearance) as reasons for *immediately discarding a resume.* Don't take a chance that your carefully written letter and resume will end up in the trash before your qualifications are even considered.

Here are a few things to look out for during the polishing phase:

- **Spelling:** Use your computer's spell-checker, but don't rely on it totally. The spell-checker won't flag an "it's" that should be "its" or a "there" that should be "their." Make triple-certain you've correctly spelled all names: people, organizations, technologies, and so on.

- **Grammar and punctuation:** If you're not confident about your grammar and punctuation skills, purchase an all-purpose reference guide and use it as often as you need to. Don't let your cover letter be discarded because of basic grammar and punctuation errors.

- **Interesting language:** As much as possible, avoid clichés and outdated language (such as "Enclosed please find my resume"). It's difficult to find new ways to express familiar sentiments (such as "I would appreciate the opportunity for an interview"), and it's certainly not necessary to come up with unique language for every phrase. But make sure that your cover letter doesn't sound like a cookie-cutter, one-size-fits-all letter that could have been written by any job seeker.

Our Four Best Cover Letter Tips

Here's our most important cover letter advice, gleaned from our experience writing thousands of cover letters over the years.

DON'T REINVENT THE WHEEL

Much of our discussion has focused on the fact that your cover letters should be written individually based on the specific situation. And that is quite true. The more focused your letters, the greater the impact and the more likely you are to get a response and opportunity to interview. However, you *do not* have to reinvent the wheel with each and every cover letter you write. If you're a sales manager writing in response to advertisements for other sales positions, you can often use the same letter with just a few minor editorial changes to match each opportunity.

SELL IT TO ME; DON'T TELL IT TO ME

Just like resume writing, cover letter writing is sales—pure and simple. You have a commodity to sell—yourself—and your challenge is to write a marketing communication that is powerful and pushes your readers to action. (You want them to call you for an interview!) Therefore, it is essential that when writing your letters you "sell" your achievements and don't just "tell" your responsibilities.

For example, if you are a purchasing manager, you could "tell" your reader that you're responsible for purchasing all raw materials for a major cereal products manufacturer. Great! Or you could "sell" the fact that you've reduced raw materials costs by 22 percent on $25 million in annual purchasing volume. Which letter would capture your interest?

OVERCOME WRITER'S BLOCK

If writing is part of your daily work responsibilities, the process of writing a cover letter might not be too arduous. However, if you do not have to write on a regular basis, cover letters can be an especially formidable task. You can sit and look at that blank piece of paper or computer screen for hours, frustrated and wondering whether the whole world has such a hard time writing cover letters. That's why it is so important to follow the step-by-step process we described at the beginning of this chapter. It is guaranteed to make cover letter writing faster, easier, and much less painful!

If you're still having trouble, consider this simple thought: **You do not have to start at the beginning.** Getting started is often the most difficult part of writing a cover letter. Even after writing thousands and thousands of cover letters, we'll sit stumped, unable to come up with just the "right" opening paragraph. Rather than wasting time and brain power and getting frustrated, we'll just leave it alone and move on to another section in the letter that we feel more confident writing. You'll find that once you get going, new ideas will pop into your head and the more difficult sections will come much more easily and confidently.

ANSWER THE EMPLOYER'S MOST IMPORTANT QUESTION: "WHAT CAN YOU DO FOR ME?"

A powerful cover letter can help you get what you want: a new, perhaps more advanced, and more satisfying position. Understanding what you want to do, the kind of organization you'd like to work for, and the environment in which you'll be most productive is certainly important. Yet you must remember that employers aren't really interested in you. They're interested in *what you can do for them.* If you do not keep this thought in the forefront of your mind when writing your cover letters, you're likely to produce a self-centered-sounding "here I am" letter that probably won't do much to advance your job search.

When writing your cover letters, consider the employer's needs and make sure that you communicate that you can add value, solve problems, and deliver benefits for that employer. You can do this through a strong focus on accomplishments ("Ah, she did that for Acme Technology Partners, LLC; she can do the same for me.") and through careful attention to the wording and tone of your letter so that you appear to be more interested in contributing to the organization than satisfying your own personal needs.

Then review the Cover Letter Checklist at the end of this chapter to be sure that your letters meet all of our requirements for style, appropriateness, quality of text, quality of presentation, and effectiveness. Follow our rules and your letters will open doors, generate interviews, and help you land your next great professional opportunity.

Cover Letter Checklist

Before mailing or e-mailing each cover letter you prepare, complete the following checklist to be sure that you have met all the rules for cover letter writing. If you cannot answer "yes" to *all* of the questions, go back and edit your letter as necessary before mailing it. The only questions for which a "no" answer is acceptable are questions #5 and #6, which relate specifically to the organization to which you are writing. As we have stated previously, in some instances you will be able to find this information, but in other cases (for example, a blind posting) you will not.

		YES	NO
1.	Do I convey who I am and what I offer in the first two sentences of my cover letter?	❑	❑
2.	Is my cover letter format unique, and does my letter stand out?	❑	❑
3.	Have I highlighted my most relevant qualifications?	❑	❑
4.	Have I highlighted my most relevant achievements?	❑	❑
5.	Have I included information I know about the company or the specific position for which I am applying?	❑	❑
6.	Have I highlighted why I want to work for this company?	❑	❑
7.	Is my letter neat, clean, and well-presented without being overdesigned?	❑	❑
8.	Is my letter error-free?	❑	❑
9.	Is my cover letter short and succinct, no longer than one page?	❑	❑
10.	Are my paragraphs short, preferably no longer than three or four lines?	❑	❑
11.	Do I ask for an interview in the letter?	❑	❑

CHAPTER 15

Sample Cover Letters

What follows are six more sample cover letters for your review. Look at them closely. Select opening paragraphs, closing paragraphs, formats, and styles that you like, and then model your own cover letters accordingly. You'll find that by using these sample letters for hints, your letter-writing process will be much easier and faster. To see even more samples and get more help with writing your cover letters, see our book *Cover Letter Magic* (JIST Publishing).

JAMES SWENSON
813-268-0138 ■ jswenson@email.com

2445 Ivy Lane ■ Tampa, FL 33602

August 22, 2012

Dennis Montgomery
Tarzana Modeling Technologies, Inc.
22 Main Street, Suite 1200
Tampa, FL 33614

Dear Mr. Montgomery:

Over the past 20 years, I have provided visionary leadership as an Assistant Controller, Controller, Vice President of Finance, and, most recently, Chief Financial Officer. This progression through the ranks of financial management has honed my business acumen, resulting in a proven track record of results. This is the value and strength that I bring to the position of **Chief Financial Officer** with Tarzana.

Controlling costs and reducing expenses are critical to an organization's profitability and viability. My attached resume is replete with accomplishments—quantified results that went right to the bottom line. Highlights of those accomplishments include the following:

- Directing the **flawless relocation** of corporate offices from Omaha, Nebraska, to Tampa, Florida, and **negotiating a $200,000 tax credit incentive** from the Greater Tampa Economic Development Council.

- **Automating product tracking** through the use of bar-coding technology, **reducing error rates and expediting delivery.**

- **Slashing rising benefits costs** by creating a cost-sharing health insurance plan and bringing short-term disability coverage in-house, **generating a 60% savings** in STD premiums.

I also have reversed inadequate cash flow during a severe revenue slump, resolved tax exemption issues, transformed an underperforming management team, and halted overspending—thereby **winning greater profitability, expanding product offerings, and increasing market penetration.**

If your organization could benefit from the decisive and action-driven leadership of a **Chief Financial Executive** with broad-based international and financial management experience, I would welcome the opportunity to speak with you in more detail. I'll follow up next week to schedule an interview.

Sincerely,

James Swenson

Enclosure

This powerful cover letter clearly communicates the track record of promotion and the key accomplishments this executive candidate brings to the advertised position, while using bold print to draw special attention to keywords, phrases, and numbers (by Cindy Kraft, CPBS, COIS, CCM, CCMC, CPRW, JCTC).

RYAN SAUNDERS

265 Tremont Street ■ Staten Island, NY 10310 ■ Cell: 646-849-2603 ■ rjsaunders@aol.com

August 15, 2012

Jonathan Milan, VP-Staffing Solutions
PLR Recruiters, Inc.
2250 Broadway, Suite 302
New York, NY 10025

Dear Mr. Milan:

After successfully managing construction and restoration initiatives for the **Turner National Golf Course** and **Turner Corporate Plaza,** I am now seeking new challenges with another enterprising organization in need of someone with exceptional build/design, supervisory, and budgeting skills.

Credited with significantly impacting bottom-line profitability, I excel at maintaining a tight schedule and paying particular attention to sequencing during all construction projects. A partial listing of my key contributions to the Turner organization is detailed below.

- **Grew construction contract 500%** from 4-building renovation project to renovation of 7 turn-of-the-century estate buildings, 5 ground-up buildings, a 6-lane competition swimming pool, 4 tennis courts, a water treatment plant, and another 18-hole golf course.

- **Met all construction deadlines 100% of the time** by proactively maintaining close communications with owner, architect, superintendent, and subcontractors.

- **Leveraged knowledge acquired through LEED Professional Certification** to engineer a ground-up water treatment plant that exceeded environmental standards for water safety.

- **Reduced construction budgets by millions of dollars** without sacrificing quality by recommending cost-efficient design changes and closely monitoring subcontractors.

- **Decreased time spent waiting for building permits exponentially** by fostering authentic relationships with building departments and town boards, and adhering to their standards.

- **Halved costs associated with Turner Corporate Plaza restoration project** by delivering project 3 months ahead of schedule.

Over my 15-year career, I have been privileged to partner with numerous high-end architectural firms, including **Davis & Smith, Ian Porter Associates, Gallard & Previ,** and **P. Smith Design,** and I've received international recognition for my work in *Architectural Digest, Casa Vogue,* and *Arbitare and Interiors.* My previous experience as president of my own architectural construction company has shaped my work ethic and contributed to my ability to maintain the owner's perspective with every budgetary decision.

I know that I can add similar value to another construction industry leader and would welcome the opportunity to discuss my qualifications in more detail. My salary requirements are $150,000 to $200,000 annually. Thank you for your consideration and I look forward to hearing from you.

Sincerely,

Ryan Saunders

Enclosure

This writer used a comprehensive approach for writing this recruiter-targeted cover letter to be certain to communicate the depth and wealth of his experience. Notice how salary requirements are stated as a range rather than a specific figure (by Barbara Safani, MA, ACRW, CERW, CPRW, NCRW, ROIS).

MARILYN R. FORRESTER

1616 Caroline Drive, Orlando, FL 32730
C: 407.755.9878 – H: 407.212.9517 – mforrester@yahoo.com

August 9, 2012

Diane L. Weston
President & CEO
Dynamic Markets, Inc.
1000 Liberty Street
Philadelphia, PA 19089

Dear Ms. Weston:

Are you in need of a **Chief Marketing Executive/Senior Marketing Executive** to define marketing strategies and drive implementation and execution?

As **Vice President/Marketing Director** for Peabody National Brands, I have partnered with world-class organizations and Fortune 1000 corporations to develop and lead breakthrough marketing strategies, drive implementation, and increase revenue and market share through advanced CRM implementations. Highlights include:

- **Luxury Cruises:** Led marketing strategy development and partnered with executives regarding the prioritization, refinement, and introduction of new products and services, including a new sub-brand of small cruise ships and a new generation of ocean liners. Drove strategy implementation to transform product-centric approach to targeted online/offline CRM programs.

- **OEM Enterprise Web Management—LG Electronics—ICM North America:** Coordinated strategy development and implementation for e-commerce channel migration, created innovative lead-generation and branding programs, and orchestrated several successful new product launches.

- **American Express Travel–Related Services Company:** Managed programs for cardmember acquisition/retention, Service Establishment Marketing, and Cardmember Financial Services Divisions.

While secure in my current position, I am confidentially investigating greater challenges. If you have a need for a Marketing Executive, I would welcome the opportunity to speak with you and will follow up next week to schedule a personal interview. Thank you.

Sincerely,

Marilyn R. Forrester

Enclosure

This letter writer used a "heavy pitch" to showcase the qualifications of this senior marketing executive and positioned the diversity of her industry experience as an asset in her job search (by Beverly Harvey, CPRW, JCTC, CCM, CCMC, MRW, CPBS, CLTMC, CJSS, COIS).

Re: CUSTOMER SERVICE MANAGER

Under my leadership, the customer service department of Tech-Line was transformed from a business liability to a competitive advantage for the company. We cut hold times by 75% and consistently performed at 95% of the world-class standard of 24-hour problem resolution.

As detailed in the enclosed resume, my background includes more than 8 years of management experience complemented by a strong technical background in applications development. In all of my positions, I have developed solid collaborative relationships with business and technical departments of the company, and I have consistently demonstrated a customer-centric approach that is also sensitive to bottom-line priorities.

I can be a valuable addition to your team and look forward to a personal meeting to discuss how I can deliver results for your company.

Sincerely,

Rafael Lewis
============================
513-739-1265 * raflewis@hotmail.com
294 Aster Lane, Cincinnati, OH 45208

Written as an e-mail message, this short but powerful cover letter begins with some impressive statistics that are sure to interest the reader (by Louise Kursmark).

STEVEN JAMISON
3300 Murrow Drive ▪ Hartford, CT 95580

Email: sjamison@aol.com
Home: 860.624.9976 ▪ Mobile: 860.624.9944

August 15, 2012

Margaret Lawson
Chairman of the Board
TTT Textiles, Ltd.
PO Box 1009
Chicago, IL 60690-1009

Dear Ms. Lawson:

Since you are searching for a CEO who can effectively turn around and lead your company's future growth, you will find below a few examples that demonstrate my leadership capabilities and results:

Crisis, Start-Up + Turnaround Management = Profitability & Competitive Edge

► Challenged to create a viable entity out of a spin-off of 5 underperforming businesses from a major NYSE manufacturing company, my team consolidated 7 independent manufacturing locations into 5 and turned the company into a robust $70 million organization. The results: double-digit sales growth and debt reduction of 32%+ in just 3 years. Previously, I led a team that orchestrated a successful turnaround of a consumer-products manufacturing company, increasing revenue by $35 million and EBITDA by $5.2 million in just 4 years.

Strategic Alliances + Negotiations = Profitability & Competitive Edge

► Negotiated a synergistic partnership with a global competitive manufacturer to shelter a $25 million product line threatened by two major competitors and 50% of corporate earnings. Guided sales and marketing teams to play a direct role in negotiating new and existing partnership agreements, yielding $10 million in annualized business. Consummated a $75 million contract over 5 years for aircraft products.

Performance Management + Quality Improvements = Profitability & Competitive Edge

► Reduced labor and material costs on a product line with deteriorating margins that increased earnings by $2 million through the introduction of Lean Manufacturing principles and quality initiatives. Implemented High-Performance Work Teams and Flow Manufacturing Principles, resulting in 3% annual savings through continuous improvement and cost reductions.

I have enclosed my resume along with an overview of key leadership initiatives that illustrate my results in areas similar to the challenges your company is facing. After you've had a chance to review the materials, I would welcome a personal interview for the CEO opportunity and look forward to what I anticipate will be the first of many positive communications. Thank you.

Sincerely,

Steven Jamison

Enclosure

This writer used a unique format to focus the reader's attention on this CEO's ability to generate profits and win a competitive lead and highlighted notable achievements within the core leadership functions required by this specific opportunity (by Louise Garver, CMP, IJCTC, CPRW, CEIP, MCDP, CJSS, CCMC).

Charles Barnett

charles.barnett@gmail.com | 203-555-5555
79 Fresh Brook Terrace, Guilford, CT 06513

August 22, 2012

Isabel Rodriguez
Executive Recruiters International
2294 Haley Boulevard
Denver, CO 80294

Dear Ms. Rodriguez:

Re: CEO—Industrial Products Company

For your client seeking a high-energy CEO to drive profitable growth in both emerging and mature markets, I offer a powerful blend of experience and accomplishments:

- **Extensive start-up credentials in Asia.** In building Gambon Asia-Pacific from the ground up to more than $100M in revenue, I launched 5 new ventures in several Asian nations and also orchestrated several acquisitions and a joint venture in India.

- **Cost-control and downsizing leadership.** Immediately following my success in Asia, I was asked to turn around Gambon's North American division, which had never been profitable and was losing more than $2M annually. Through consolidation, staff reductions, and a refocus on profitable practices, within a year I led the division to its first-ever positive income results.

- **Cross-cultural expertise that delivers global wins.** Having spent my career around the world, from Mexico and the U.S. to Europe and Asia, I have the knowledge, credibility, and passion to bring together people of diverse cultures to leverage our combined strengths. The result is a significant competitive advantage as we pursue global opportunities—such as a recent competitive bid with GE worldwide that we captured and then grew 1,000%.

In brief, I am a global leader who thrives on steep challenges. I have an extremely high energy level, ability to adapt to any culture, and willingness to travel extensively. Having built Gambon Asia-Pacific into a dominant market leader and led the U.S. operation to profitability, I am now seeking a new challenge—a CEO role with a company anywhere in the world that would benefit from my ability to transform its mission and goals into profitable reality.

May we schedule a time to discuss your recently posted CEO opportunity? I am confident I have the global experience, proven skill sets, and leadership qualities your client is seeking.

Sincerely,

Charles Barnett

enclosure: resume

The meatiest section of this cover letter to a recruiter includes the bullet points, which recap significant experience and career successes for this international CEO (by Louise Kursmark).

Resume Preparation Questionnaire

A resume is only as good as the information that it showcases. To write a great resume, you must take the time to document your complete career history, whether 2 years or 22 years. This raw data is the foundation for everything that you will write. The more raw data, the better, so be as comprehensive as possible when collecting and documenting your experience.

Keeping a running log of your career successes (for example, project highlights, revenue and profit results, productivity and efficiency improvements, customer satisfaction scores) and then updating your resume every six months is a great way to be prepared at a moment's notice when a great career opportunity presents itself.

Use the following Resume Preparation Questionnaire as a guide when assembling all of your career information—your raw data for writing a powerful and well-positioned resume.

RESUME PREPARATION QUESTIONNAIRE

Contact Information

Name:		
Address:		
City:	State:	ZIP:
Home Phone:	Mobile Phone:	
E-mail:	URL (Web portfolio):	
Willing to relocate? YES NO	Willing to travel? YES NO	
Current Salary:	Expected Salary:	

Career Objectives

Answer the following questions as completely and accurately as possible. Not all questions may apply to you. If they do not apply, mark them N/A. Use additional sheets if necessary.

(continued)

(continued)

Position/Career Objective: List your top three job title choices in order of preference:

1. _____

2. _____

3. _____

Is this a career change for you? YES   NO

Long-Range Career Goals:

_____

_____

_____

What are some terms (or keywords) that are specific to your industry and profession?

_____

_____

_____

What skills do you possess that you want to highlight?

_____

_____

_____

Education

List all degrees, certificates, and diplomas you've received; the dates you received them; the school or college; and the location of the school or college. Begin with the most recent and work backward.

College/University: _____ City/State: _____

Major: _____ Degree: _____ Year: _____ GPA: _____

Honors: _____

College/University: _____ City/State: _____

Major: _____ Degree: _____ Year: _____ GPA: _____

Honors: _____

High School: _____ City/State: _____ Year: _____

Relevant Courses/Seminars/Workshops

Include names, dates, places, and sponsoring organizations.

Certifications and Licenses

Certifications:

Professional Licenses:

Military

Include branch of service, locations, position, rank achieved, years of service, honorable discharge, key accomplishments, special recognition, awards, and so on.

Professional Organizations/Affiliations

Include offices held.

Publications/Presentations

Include titles, names of publications, locations of public speaking engagements, and dates.

(continued)

(continued)

_____

_____

_____

_____

Computer Skills

Include hardware, software, operating systems, networks, programming languages, and so on.

_____

_____

_____

_____

_____

Foreign Languages

List level of fluency—verbal/written.

_____

_____

Hobbies

Note that you will want to include on your resume only hobbies that are out of the ordinary and might make a great conversation topic.

_____

Community Activities

List names of organizations, years involved, positions held.

_____

_____

_____

Work Experience

As you consider each position, ask yourself, *"How is this organization better off now than when it hired me?"* Here are some questions to get your thoughts flowing.

- Did you increase sales? If so, by what percentage or amount?

- Did you generate new business, bring in new clients, or forge affiliations?

- Did you save your organization money? If so, how much and how?

- Did you design or institute any new system or process? If so, what were the results?

- Did you meet an impossible deadline through extra effort? What difference did this make to your organization, your team members, and your customers?

- Did you bring in a major project under budget? How did you make this happen? How were the dollars you saved used?

- Did you suggest or help launch a new product or program? If so, did you take the lead or provide support? How successful was the effort?

- Did you take on new responsibilities that weren't part of your routine responsibilities? If so, did you ask for the new projects or were they assigned to you?

- Did you introduce any new or more effective techniques for increasing productivity?

- Did you improve communication? If so, with whom and what was the outcome?

- How did your organization benefit from your performance?

Begin with your present employer. If you're not currently working, you *might* want to start with your volunteer experience—treating it just like a paid position—if it relates to your current career objective. List different positions at the same organization as separate jobs (at least at this point in the information-collection process).

Name of employer:

City/State:	Dates of employment:

Your title or position:

Who do you report to (title)?	Number of people you supervise:

Their titles or functions:

Briefly describe the size of the organization (volume produced; revenues; number of employees; local, national, or international; and so on).

(continued)

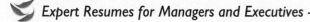

(continued)

What does the organization do, make, or sell?

_____

Where does it rank in its industry in terms of competitors?

_____

Briefly describe your duties, responsibilities, and level of authority. Use numbers (size) and percentages, quantify budgets, state with whom you interacted, and so on.

_____

_____

_____

_____

Why were you hired (or promoted or selected)? What was going on at the organization? Was there a particular challenge or problem you were brought on to solve? Did you have specific performance measurements? (If so, describe them as specifically as possible.) Where was your organization headed? Why did it need you?

_____

_____

_____

_____

_____

_____

_____

_____

Describe four to six accomplishments, successes, project highlights, contributions, or other achievements in this position. Give plenty of details, facts, and figures.

_____

_____

_____

_____

_____

_____

_____

Previous Employment

You will, most likely, need to make multiple copies of this section so that you have one copy for each position.

Name of organization:

City/State: Dates of employment:

Your title or position:

Who did you report to (title)? Number of people you supervised:

Their titles or functions:

Briefly describe the size of the organization (volume produced; revenues; number of employees; local, national, or international; and so on).

What did the organization do, make, or sell?

Where did it rank in its industry in terms of competitors?

Briefly describe your duties, responsibilities, and level of authority. Use numbers (size) and percentages, quantify budgets, state with whom you interacted, and so on.

Why were you hired (or promoted or selected)? What was going on at the organization? Was there a particular challenge or problem you were brought on to solve? Did you have specific performance measurements? (If so, describe them as specifically as possible.) Where was your organization headed? Why did it need you?

(continued)

(continued)

_____

_____

_____

_____

_____

_____

_____

_____

_____

_____

_____

Describe four to six accomplishments, successes, project highlights, contributions, or other achievements in this position. Give plenty of details, facts, and figures.

_____

_____

_____

_____

_____

_____

_____

_____

_____

_____

Appendix B

Resume Verbs: Write with Power and Clarity

Here are nearly 400 of our favorite verbs for writing resumes, cover letters, thank-you letters, LinkedIn profiles, career biographies, achievement profiles, and a host of other online and offline career marketing communications. Use these verbs wisely, and remember the following tips:

- Write with verbs and stay away from phrases such as "Responsible for" and "Duties included." Verbs communicate action and results, and that's precisely what you want to accomplish when writing your resume.

- Each verb communicates a different message. For example, "manage," "coordinate," and "facilitate" seem to say the same thing; upon closer examination, however, that's not the case. Each verb has a unique meaning and very few verbs are interchangeable.

- Don't use verbs that overstate your level of responsibility for a particular company, organization, project, product, and so on. If you have to defend what you wrote, you've lost the opportunity.

- Not all verbs will be appropriate for you, your industry, or your profession. Don't use a verb just because you like it. Rather, use a verb that communicates precisely the right message.

NOTE: In descriptions and bullets for your current job, you will use verbs in the present tense, as shown here. For previous jobs, the verbs should be converted to past tense.

Accelerate	Achieve	Adjudicate	Align
Accentuate	Acquire	Advance	Alter
Accommodate	Adapt	Advise	Analyze
Accomplish	Address	Advocate	Anchor

(continued)

(continued)

Apply	Close	Crystallize	Edit
Appoint	Coach	Curtail	Educate
Appreciate	Collaborate	Cut	Effect
Arbitrate	Collect	Decipher	Effectuate
Architect	Command	Decrease	Elect
Arrange	Commercialize	Define	Elevate
Articulate	Commoditize	Delegate	Eliminate
Ascertain	Communicate	Deliver	Emphasize
Assemble	Compare	Demonstrate	Empower
Assess	Compel	Deploy	Enact
Assist	Compile	Derive	Encourage
Augment	Complete	Design	Endeavor
Authenticate	Compute	Detail	Endorse
Author	Conceive	Detect	Endure
Authorize	Conceptualize	Determine	Energize
Balance	Conclude	Develop	Enforce
Believe	Conduct	Devise	Engineer
Bestow	Conserve	Differentiate	Enhance
Brainstorm	Consolidate	Direct	Enlist
Brief	Construct	Discern	Enliven
Budget	Consult	Discover	Ensure
Build	Continue	Dispense	Entrench
Calculate	Contract	Display	Equalize
Capitalize	Control	Distinguish	Establish
Capture	Convert	Distribute	Estimate
Catalog	Convey	Diversify	Evaluate
Catapult	Coordinate	Divert	Examine
Centralize	Correct	Document	Exceed
Champion	Corroborate	Dominate	Execute
Change	Counsel	Double	Exhibit
Chart	Craft	Draft	Exhort
Clarify	Create	Drive	Expand
Classify	Critique	Earn	Expedite

Experiment	Influence	Master	Oversee
Explode	Inform	Mastermind	Participate
Explore	Initiate	Maximize	Partner
Export	Innovate	Measure	Perceive
Extricate	Inspect	Mediate	Perfect
Facilitate	Inspire	Mentor	Perform
Finalize	Install	Merge	Persuade
Finance	Institute	Minimize	Pilot
Forge	Instruct	Model	Pinpoint
Form	Integrate	Moderate	Pioneer
Formalize	Intensify	Modify	Plan
Formulate	Interpret	Monetize	Position
Foster	Interview	Monitor	Predict
Found	Introduce	Motivate	Prepare
Gain	Invent	Navigate	Prescribe
Generate	Inventory	Negotiate	Present
Govern	Investigate	Network	Preside
Graduate	Judge	Nominate	Process
Guide	Justify	Normalize	Procure
Halt	Launch	Obfuscate	Produce
Handle	Lead	Observe	Program
Head	Lecture	Obtain	Progress
Hire	Leverage	Offer	Project
Honor	License	Officiate	Project manage
Hypothesize	Listen	Operate	
Identify	Locate	Optimize	Proliferate
Illustrate	Lower	Orchestrate	Promote
Imagine	Maintain	Organize	Propel
Implement	Manage	Orient	Propose
Import	Manipulate	Originate	Prospect
Improve	Manufacture	Outsource	Prove
Improvise	Map	Overcome	Provide
Increase	Market	Overhaul	Publicize

(continued)

(continued)

Purchase	Render	Shepherd	Systematize
Purify	Renegotiate	Simplify	Tabulate
Qualify	Renew	Slash	Target
Quantify	Renovate	Solidify	Teach
Query	Reorganize	Solve	Terminate
Question	Report	Spark	Test
Raise	Reposition	Speak	Thwart
Rate	Represent	Spearhead	Train
Ratify	Research	Specify	Transcribe
Realign	Resolve	Standardize	Transfer
Rebuild	Respond	Steer	Transform
Recapture	Restore	Stimulate	Transition
Receive	Restructure	Strategize	Translate
Recognize	Retain	Streamline	Trim
Recommend	Retrieve	Strengthen	Troubleshoot
Reconcile	Reuse	Structure	Unify
Record	Review	Study	Unite
Recruit	Revise	Substantiate	Update
Recycle	Revitalize	Succeed	Upgrade
Redesign	Sanctify	Suggest	Use
Reduce	Satisfy	Summarize	Utilize
Reengineer	Schedule	Supervise	Verbalize
Regain	Secure	Supplement	Verify
Regulate	Select	Supply	Win
Rehabilitate	Sell	Support	Work
Reinforce	Separate	Surpass	Write
Rejuvenate	Serve	Synergize	
Remedy	Service	Synthesize	

INDEX OF CONTRIBUTORS

The sample resumes and cover letters in this book were written by professional resume and cover letter writers. If you need help with your resume and job search correspondence, you can use the following list to locate a career professional. Many, if not all, of these resume professionals work with clients long-distance as well as in their local areas.

You will notice that most of the writers have one or more credentials listed after their names. In fact, some have half a dozen or more! The careers industry offers extensive opportunities for ongoing training, and most career professionals take advantage of these opportunities to build their skills and keep their knowledge current. If you are curious about what any one of these credentials means, we suggest that you contact the resume writer directly. He or she will be glad to discuss certifications and other qualifications as well as information about services that can help you in your career transition.

Carol Altomare, MRW, ACRW, CPRW, CCMC, CJSS
World Class Résumés
PO Box 483
Three Bridges, NJ 08887-0483
Phone: (908) 237-1883
E-mail:
  caa@worldclassresumes.com
www.worldclassresumes.com

Mark Bartz, MRW
Medical Sales Mentor
Tampa, FL
Phone: (863) 248-6105
E-mail: mentor@
  medicalsalesmentor.com
http://medicalsalesmentor.com

Janet L. Beckstrom, MRW, ACRW, CPRW
Word Crafter
1717 Montclair Ave.
Flint, MI 48503
Phone: (810) 232-9257
E-mail: janet@wordcrafter.com
www.wordcrafter.com

Marian Bernard, CPS, CPRW, JCTC, CEIP
The Regency Group
6 Morning Crescent
Aurora, Ontario,
Canada L4G 2E3
Toll-free phone: (866) 448-4672
E-mail: marian@resumeexpert.ca
www.resumeexpert.ca

Debi Bogard
San Diego, CA

Rima Bogardus
Garner, NC

Arnold G. Boldt, CPRW, JCTC
Arnold-Smith Associates
Rochester, NY
Phone: (585) 383-0350
E-mail: arnie@resumesos.com
www.resumesos.com

Carolyn Braden, CPRW
Hendersonville, TN

Martin Buckland, CPRW, CPBS, JCTC, CEIP, CJST
An American Resume
110 Wall St. 11th Floor
New York, NY 10005-3817
Toll-free: (866) 424-1431
Phone: (646) 201-9648
E-mail: martin@anamericanresume.com
www.anamericanresume.com

Donald Burns, ACRW, CPRW, CJSS
Update Your Resume
95-22 63rd Rd. PMB-125
Rego Park, NY 11374
Phone: (917) 519-0487
E-mail: dburns1@donaldburns.com
www.update-your-resume.com

Freddie Cheek, MS Ed, CCM, CPRW, CARW, CWDP
Cheek & Associates
Amherst, NY
Phone: (716) 835-6945
E-mail: fscheek@cheekandassociates.com
www.cheekandassociates.com

Annemarie Cross, CPRW, CRW, CEIP, CECC, CCM, CWPP, CERW
Advanced Employment Concepts
P.O. Box 91, Hallam, Victoria
3803 Australia
E-mail: enquiry@aresumewriter.com.au
www.aresumewriter.com.au

Jean Cummings, M.A.T., CPBS, CPRW, CEIP
President, A Resume for Today
123 Minot Rd.
Concord, MA 01742
Toll-free: (800) 324-1699
Phone: (978) 371-9266
Fax: (978) 964-0529
E-mail: jc@yesresumes.com
www.aresumefortoday.com

Norine T. Dagliano, NCRW, CPRW, CFRW/CC
Phone: (301) 766-2032
E-mail: norine@ekminspirations.com
www.ekminspirations.com

Michael S. Davis, ACRW, CPRW
Davis Résumé Service, LLC
940 Ashcreek Dr.
Dayton OH 45458
Phone: (937) 438-5037
E-mail: msdavis49@hotmail.com

Julianne S. Franke, ACRW, MRW, CPRW, CCMC
Breakthrough Connections
258 Shire Way
Laurenceville, GA 30044
Phone: (770)381-0876
Fax: (770) 381-0877
E-mail: jfrankel@bellsouth.net
www.breakthroughconnections.com

Judy Friedler, ACRW, NCRW, JCTC
CareerPro International
Phone: (877) 889-0094
E-mail: info@rezcoach.com
www.rezcoach.com

Roberta Gamza, JCTC, CEIP, CJST, CONCS
Career Ink
Louisville, CO
Phone: (303) 955-3065
E-mail: roberta@careerink.com
www.careerink.com

Louise Garver, CMP, IJCTC, CPRW, CEIP, MCDP, CJSS, CCMC
Career Directions, LLC
Broad Brook, CT
Phone: (860) 623-9476
E-mail: louise@careerdirectionsllc.com
www.careerdirectionsllc.com

Susan Guarneri, CERW, CPRW, MRWLA, CPBS, MPBS, COIS, NCCC
Susan Guarneri Associates
Three Lakes, WI
Phone: (715) 546-4449
E-mail: susan@resume-magic.com
www.resume-magic.com

Michele J. Haffner, CPRW, CCMC, JCTC
Advanced Résumé Services
1314 W. Paradise Ct.
Glendale, WI 53209
Toll Free: (888) 586-2258
Phone: (414) 247-1677
Fax: (414) 434-1913
E-mail: michele@resumeservices.com
www.resumeservices.com

Alice Hanson
Career Coach
Edmonds Community College
Lynnwood, WA
E-mail: alice.hanson@email.edcc.edu

Beverly Harvey, CPRW, JCTC, CCM, CCMC, MRW, CPBS, CLTMC, CJSS, COIS
HarveyCareers, LLC
Pierson, FL
Phone: (386) 749-3111
E-mail: beverly@harveycareers.com
www.harveycareers.com

Jennifer Hay, ACRW, CRS+IT, CPRW
IT Resume Service
Seattle, WA
Phone: (425) 442-3706
E-mail: jhay@itresumeservice.com
www.itresumeservice.com

Gayle Howard, MRW, CERW, CPBS, JLRC, CWPP, CRS-IT
Top Margin Career Marketing Group
Melbourne, Australia
Phone: 613-9020-5601
E-mail: getinterviews@topmargin.com
www.topmargin.com

Deborah S. James, CCMC, CPRW
President, Leading Edge Resumes and
    Career Services
1010 Schreier Rd.
Rossford, OH 43460
Phone: (419) 666-4518
Fax: (419) 791-3567
E-mail:
    djames@leadingedgeresumes.com
www.leadingedgeresumes.com

Michelle Kennedy, CPRW
Port Washington, NY

Lesa E. Kerlin, MPA, CPRW
LEK Consultants
1703 Meadow View Dr.
Kirkville, MO 63501
Phone: (660) 626-4748
E-mail: lesa@lekconsultants
www.lekconsultants.com

Bill Kinser, MRW, CCM, CPRW, JCTC, CEIP
To The Point Resumes
Fairfax, VA
Phone: (703) 825-3476
E-mail: bkinser@tothepointresumes.com
www.tothepointresumes.com

Wanda Kiser, MBA, CPRW, ACRW, CPCC, CEIP
Advantage Career Services, Inc.
3525 Piedmont Rd.
Building 7 –Suite 300
Atlanta, GA 30305
Phone: (877) 314-8872
Fax: (877) 314-8873
E-mail: resumeinfo@
    advantagecareerservices.net
www.advantagecareerservices.net

Myriam-Rose Kohn, CPRW, IJCTC, CEIP, CCM, CCMC, CPBS, CJSS, CONCS
JEDA Enterprises
Valencia, CA
Phone: (661) 253-0801
E-mail:
 myriam-rose@jedaenterprises.com
www.jedaenterprises.com

Joanne Kowlowitz

Cindy Kraft, the CFO-Coach CPBS, COIS, CCM, CCMC, CPRW, JCTC
Executive Essentials
Tampa, FL
Phone: (813) 655-0658
E-mail: Cindy@CFO-Coach.com
www.cfo-coach.com

Ric Lanham, CCM, CECC, CRW, CCRP, CCTC

Rolande L. LaPointe

Lorie Lebert, CPRW, IJCTC, CCMC, ACRW
The Loriel Group – CoachingROI / ResumeROI
Phone: (800) 870-9059
E-mail: lorie@domyresume.com
www.resumeroi.com

Diana C. LeGere
Petersburg, VA

John Leggatt
Careers Upstairs
1400 W. Washington St. #104-130
Sequim, WA 98382
Phone: (818) 888-3626
Fax: (888) 398-0870
E-mail: experts@careersupstairs.com
http://careersupstairs.com

Lisa LeVerrier
West Palm Beach, FL

Abby Locke, ACRW, MRW, CJSS, NCRW, CPBS
Premier Writing Solutions
6219 140th Place SW
Edmonds, WA 98026
Phone: (425) 608-7200
Fax: (866) 350-4220
E-mail: alocke@premierwriting.com
www.premierwriting.com

Denise Lupardo
Lake Forest, CA

Peter S. Marx

Jan Melnik, MA, MRW, CCM, CPRW
Absolute Advantage
Durham, CT
Phone: (860) 349-0256
E-mail: compspjan@aol.com
www.janmelnik.com

Patrick Moore, ACRW
Resume Specialties
3512 Nolina Ct. NW
Albuquerque, NM 87120
Phone: (503) 321-1988
E-mail:
 patrickmoore@resumespecialties.com
http://resumespecialties.com

Doug Morrison, MRW, CPRW
Career Power
5200 Park Rd., Ste. 227
Charlotte, NC 28209
Phone: (704) 527-5556
E-mail: doug@careerpowerresume.com
www.careerpowerresume.com

Kris Niklawski, ACRW
Resume Select
3317 144th Ct.
Cumming, IA 50061
Phone: (515) 240-2950
E-mail:kniklawski@gmail.com

Loretta Peters, MRW, RPBS, ROIS, RMBS
Enterprising Careers, LLC
DBA Competitive Edge Branding
2389 Main St.
Glastonbury, CT 06033
Phone: (860) 463-1165
Fax: (860) 659-1625
E-mail: lpeters@enterprisingcareers.com
www.enterprisingcareers.com

Sharon Pierce-Williams, M.Ed., CPRW
President, The Resume.Doc
609 Lincolnshire Ln.
Findlay, OH 45840
Phone: (419) 422-0228
Fax: (419) 425-1185
E-mail: sharon@theresumedoc.com
www.theresumedoc.com

Anita Radosevich, CPRW, IJCTC, CEIP
President, Career Ladders
9381 E. Stockton Blvd., Suite 118A
Elk Grove, CA 95624
Phone: (916) 714-6661
Fax: (916) 714-7401
E-mail: careerladdersinc@gmail.com
www.career-ladders.com

Jennifer Rydell, CPRW, NCRW, CCM

Barbara Safani, MA, ACRW, CERW, CPRW, NCRW, ROIS
Career Solvers, Inc.
675 3rd Ave. Fifth Floor
New York, NY 10017
Toll-free: (866) 333-1800
E-mail: info@careersolvers.com
www.careersolvers.com

Debbie Sherrie

Kelley Smith, CPRW
Houston, TX

Reya Stevens, MA, ACRW, MRW
Standout Résumés
Boston, MA
Phone: (978) 897-1547
E-mail: reya@standoutresumes.com
http://standoutresumes.com

Billie Sucher, MS, CTMS, CTSB, JCTC, CCM
Billie Sucher & Associates
7177 Hickman Rd. Suite 10
Urbandale, IA 50322
Phone: (515) 276-0061
Fax: (515) 334-8076
www.billiesucher.com

Marjorie Sussman, ACRW, MRW, CPRW
Dover Productions
Edgewater, NJ
Phone: (201) 941-8237
E-mail: marjorie1130@gmail.com
www.visualcv.com/marjoriesussman

Ilona Vanderwoude, ACRW, MRW, CCMC, CJST, CEIP, CPRW
CareerBranches
P.O. Box 330
Riverdale, NY 10471
Phone: (718) 971-6356
Fax: (646) 349-2218
E-mail: ilona@careerbranches.com
www.careerbranches.com

Vivian VanLier, CPRW, JCTC, CEIP, CCMC, CPBS
Advantage Resume & Career Services
Los Angeles (Valley Glen), CA
Phone: 818-994-6655
E-mail:
    vivianvanlier@careercoach4u.com
www.cuttingedgeresumes.com

Jitka Vesela, M.Ed., ACRW, CPBS, CEIC
1400 W. Washington St. #104-130
Sequim, WA 98382
Phone: (818) 888-3626
Fax: (888) 398-0870
E-mail: experts@careersupstairs.com
http://careersupstairs.com

Mary Ann Wilson, ACRW, CRP
First Impressions
7010 Leestone St.
Springfield, VA 22151
Phone: (703) 941-9150
E-mail: maranwil@aol.com

INDEX